On 31 July, 1988 King Hussain of Jordan renounced all administrative and legal ties with the Israeli-occupied West Bank of the River Jordan. This initiated a new turning point in the Middle East peace process: what had been the Arab–Israeli conflict became the Palestinian–Israeli conflict. On the face of it, this move was a grand gesture to the Palestinians. But, as Madiha Madfai convincingly demonstrates, behind this action lay a history of anger, anguish and frustration with the Middle East peace process.

Dr Madfai presents, for the first time, a comprehensive analysis of the events culminating in the Jordanian decision to break off ties with the West Bank. She focuses on Jordan's role in the USA's peacemaking efforts during the Carter, Reagan and Bush administrations and examines their objectives, the policies passed and their short- and long-term consequences. The author also explores the collaboration and discord between the USA and Israel and assesses the effects this relationship had on stability in the Middle East. Finally, Dr Madfai explains why the American quest for peace had been unsuccessful and suggests positive steps forward.

This book is based on substantial original sources including material from the archives of the Ministry of Foreign Affairs in Amman and from the archives of the Crown Prince Hassan and interviews with the key Jordanian and American decision-makers. It makes a major contribution to our understanding of international politics and the Middle East and will be widely read by students and specialists of Middle Eastern studies and international relations.

Cambridge Middle East Library: 28

JORDAN, THE UNITED STATES AND THE MIDDLE EAST PEACE PROCESS, 1974-1991

Cambridge Middle East Library: 28

Editorial Board

ROGER OWEN (Chair)

The *Cambridge Middle East Library* aims to bring together outstanding scholarly work on the history, politics, sociology and economics of the Middle East and North Africa in the nineteenth and twentieth centuries. While primarily focussing on monographs based on original research, the series will also incorporate broader surveys and in-depth treatments.

A list of books in this series will be found at the end of this volume

JORDAN, THE UNITED STATES AND THE MIDDLE EAST PEACE PROCESS, 1974–1991

MADIHA RASHID AL MADFAI

CAMBRIDGE
UNIVERSITY PRESS

Published by the Press Syndicate of the University of Cambridge
The Pitt Building, Trumpington Street, Cambridge CB2 1RP
40 West 20th Street, New York NY 10011-4211, USA
10 Stamford Road, Oakleigh, Victoria 3166, Australia

© Cambridge University Press 1993

First published 1993

Printed in Great Britain at the University Press, Cambridge

A catalogue record for this book is available from the British Library

Library of Congress cataloguing in publication data
Al Madfai, Madiha Rashid.
Jordan / Madiha Rashid Al Madfai.
    p.   cm. – (Cambridge Middle East library: 28)
Includes bibliographical references and index.
ISBN 0–521–41523–3 (hardback)
    1. United States – Foreign relations – Jordan.   2. Jordan – Foreign relations – United
States.   1. Title.   11. Series.
E183.8.J6A4   1992
327.7305695 – dc20   91–43477   CIP

ISBN 0 521 41523 3 hardback

To my family, Nadim, Khaldoon and Maysoon
Nasser without whose patience and understanding
this work could not have been accomplished.

Contents

Foreword

In most accounts of the diplomacy of the Arab–Israeli conflict, Jordan has been neglected, ignored, or taken for granted. Perhaps this is the fate of small states, especially those with moderate and reasonable leaders. Politicians understandably pay more attention to big powers with big voices. But scholars have also neglected Jordan. Few serious books exist on either Jordan's internal or foreign policies. This is unfortunate in light of the important role Jordan has played in recent Middle East history.

Jordan deserves attention in its own right. Among Arab states of the Middle East, it has achieved an impressive level of social and economic development without the benefit of rich natural resources. Located in a turbulent part of the world, it has managed to survive as an independent state. Compared to many in the region, Jordan has provided its citizens with a degree of stability, security and well-being.

Jordan is worth studying for another reason. In many ways it provides a microcosm in which one can see most of the currents that affect the wider Middle East. Jordan feels the effects of Arab nationalism, Palestinianism, and Islamism. It is a policy based on a traditional formula for legitimacy, but contains a modern, Westernized sector of impressive dimensions. Jordan's neighbours – Israel, Syria, Iraq and Saudi Arabia – each confront it with special challenges. Each is more powerful and each puts pressure on its Hashemite neighbour. But Jordan has survived and even prospered in this dangerous environment. And while maintaining a particularly close association with the West over the years – especially with Britain and the United States – King Hussain has also developed good relations with the Soviet Union. All of this has required a great deal of dexterity.

Jordan's success in the conduct of its foreign policy is measured by its survival and comparatively high level of development. Its biggest setback, however, was the loss of the West Bank and east Jerusalem in the June 1967 war, which has cast a shadow over all its achievements during the past twenty years. King Hussain has personally felt responsible for recovering these territories and has been involved, to one degree or another, in each of the so-called peace initiatives of the past two decades – UN Resolution 242, the

Rogers Plan, the Geneva Conference of 1973, the attempt in 1977 to reconvene Geneva, the Reagan plan of 1982, and the Shultz initiative of 1988. Only the Camp David negotiations in 1978–9 left Jordan on the sidelines, but even then it was a concerned, if doubtful, observer of the process that led to Egyptian–Israeli peace and put forward a formula for Palestinian autonomy on the West Bank.

Jordan has had the advantage of continuity in the conduct of its foreign policy. Although foreign ministers have come and gone, the ultimate responsibility has always been with King Hussain. He has dealt with every American president since Eisenhower. He is the senior statesman in the Arab world today. He knows the players and the issues, as well as the problems and constraints, better than most of his contemporaries.

The author of this study, Madiha Madfai, a Jordanian herself, has decided to focus her attention on one major aspect of Jordan's foreign policy – its relations with the United States concerning the peace process. The story is one of frustration, disappointment and, eventually, disillusionment. From 1967 to 1974, Jordan felt that it had some kind of American commitment to bring about the return of most, if not all, of the West Bank to Jordanian control. The King's files are full of presidential commitments to that effect.

The American interpretation of UN Resolution 242 was not far from that of Jordan at least in the early years, although the Americans always insisted that negotiations must take place. In their view, 242 was not a 'self-implementing' resolution. But when the Americans spoke of future borders that did not reflect the 'weight of conquest', or when they talked of 'minor' adjustments in the 1967 lines on a mutual basis, King Hussain had reason to be satisfied. The problem, however, was that these reassuring words did not lead to any concrete results for Jordan.

With the passage of time, Jordan's prospects for recovering the West Bank began to dim. First there was the clear hardening of the Israeli position. Right after the 1967 war, Israelis spoke as if most of the territory seized in the war would be returned in exchange for peace. Soon, however, the Allon Plan became the basis for Israeli policy. It envisaged permanent Israeli control over substantial parts of the West Bank – at least one-quarter of the total – as well as Israeli annexation of east Jerusalem.

In addition, Jordan's claim to negotiate for the West Bank was increasingly in doubt as Palestinians asserted their own distinctive identity and allied behind the Palestine Liberation Organization (PLO) as their spokesman. The complexities of inter-Arab politics made it difficult for Jordan to compete with the PLO, and in late 1974, the Arab League, meeting in Rabat, recognized the PLO as the sole legitimate representative of the Palestinians. King Hussain, having nothing to show for his efforts over the preceding years, had no choice but to go along with the new Arab consensus.

The Carter years were difficult ones for the King. Initially, he was encouraged by the American commitment to a comprehensive peace settlement. At the same time, he was dismayed to see the defeat of the Israeli Labour Party, whose leaders were familiar to him, and its replacement in power by the Likud bloc led by the fiery Menachem Begin. The ideology of Likud, rooted in revisionist Zionism, held that both the East and the West Banks of the Jordan River were part of Eretz Israel, and many in Likud were fond of saying that the Palestinians already had their state – on the East Bank. This was also the time when Egypt's determination to break ranks with the Arab consensus in order to settle its own conflict with Israel left the Arab world feeling resentful and vulnerable.

The election of Ronald Reagan brought new uncertainties for Jordan. The new President and his Secretary of State were enthusiastically pro-Israeli. They were also fervently anti-Soviet and were inclined to look at regional issues through a Cold War prism. It was not until September 1982, when President Reagan launched his Plan for the Middle East, that Jordan had any reason to believe that the United States was committed to an even-handed outcome.

Jordan was, in fact, absolutely crucial to the Reagan Plan. King Hussain, but not Menachem Begin, had even been given an advance copy of the President's speech. He was clearly expected to pick up the challenge and offer to negotiate with Israel on the basis of the Plan. Begin's firm and convincing rejection of it was beside the point, according to US officials. His reaction was expected. Only if an Arab party came forward with an offer to negotiate could the political climate inside Israel be changed. In brief, Jordan was expected to make the first move, trusting to US influence and the Israeli electorate to bring about a commensurate Israeli response in due course. The King was dubious, especially in light of the US performance in Lebanon, but he was also tempted. Reassurances were requested and given. But in the end King Hussain felt the need for strong Arab support, especially from the PLO. This was not forthcoming and, in April 1983, he pulled back from active involvement with the Reagan initiative.

Jordan's next round in the peace process did not occur until after relations with Egypt and the PLO had been patched up, the Israeli Labour Party had regained control of the Prime Minister's office (albeit in an awkward coalition with Likud), and the American presidential elections had returned Ronald Reagan for another term. The year 1985 looked to be a promising moment in the search for peace, at least compared with other times in the past. Only Syria was strongly opposed to the joint Jordanian–PLO effort to court the Americans.

I personally see 1985 as one of the 'lost opportunities' in the search for Arab–Israeli peace. Much of the story is told in this book. Much of the blame for the lack of movement, I believe, lies in Washington, although others also played significant parts in the failure. King Hussain concluded from this effort that the PLO was a liability in the search for peace, and by year's end he was planning to break with the PLO and turn towards Syria.

This switch of partners may have been advisable for reasons of inter-Arab politics, but Syria was not an easy partner to bring into the peace process. Efforts were made, however, to forge an agreement on holding an international conference on the Arab–Israeli conflict, and Jordan was even prepared to get rather far out on a limb in exploring modalities with the Americans and Israelis. But, as in the past, the efforts crumbled in 1987 and the reasons were familiar ones: Israeli inflexibility, inter-Arab divisions, and American hesitation.

Against this background, the initiative of Secretary of State Shultz, which was launched in March 1988, and which focused heavily on Jordan, seemed doomed to failure. After months of inconclusive discussions with the Americans, King Hussain finally said no. The form of his rejection was particularly striking. It was in a speech on 31 July 1988 that the King renounced Jordan's claims to the West Bank and announced the severance of all administrative and legal ties. Subsequent decisions reinforced this point as salaries to West Bank officials were cut. Henceforth, the King said, the Palestinians would have to fend for themselves. They have chosen the PLO as their representative. Let the PLO recover their occupied lands.

Americans and Israelis were taken by surprise by the King's speech, as were many in the Arab world. Had they been able to read this book they would have understood the frustrations, the disappointments, the sense of limited room for manoeuvre that colours Jordanian foreign-policy calculations. By helping to explain why the so-called Jordanian option never really existed in the past, and most certainly does not exist today, this book serves an important purpose. It also helps to fill a large gap in our understanding of the contemporary Middle East. For these reasons it is particularly welcome.

WILLIAM B. QUANDT
Brookings Institution
Washington DC
25 August 1988

Acknowledgements

This work could not have been completed without the first-hand information supplied by key Jordanian decision-makers and the archives of the Ministry of Foreign Affairs in Amman. Hence, my deepest appreciation goes first and foremost to King Hussain of Jordan whose green light initiated the whole process of research.

I also acknowledge my great indebtedness to Prince Hassan of Jordan whose invaluable insight, intellectual command and thorough grasp of world and Middle Eastern affairs, have enriched this work.

My deep appreciation goes also to Mr Zeid Rifai, former Prime Minister of Jordan; Field Marshal Sharif Zeid Ben Shaker, Prime Minister and former Commander-in-Chief of the Jordanian Armed Forces; his assistant in the General Command Headquarters, General Tayseer Za'rour; Mr Adnan Abu Odeh, former Minister of Court; Mr Marwan Al Qassem, former Minister of Foreign Affairs; Taher Al Masri, former Prime Minister of Jordan; Dr Hanna Odeh, former Minister of Finance; Mrs Leila Sharaf, former Information Minister, and Mr Ali Ghandour, a veteran politician and former Chairman of the Royal Jordanian Airlines.

I am particularly grateful to former Prime Minister Mudar Badran, who lived through many of the harsh days experienced by Jordan. A two-and-a-half-hour interview gave me a great deal of information on some of the major lines of recent foreign-policy undertakings by Jordan and the United States.

My thanks go also to the staff of the Ministry of Foreign Affairs, particularly to Nabeeh Shuqum and Ibrahim Nagaway, for all their assistance during my research in Amman. They go, as well, to Jordan's University in Amman, particularly to Dr Amad and his staff in the reference library.

In the United States, I remain grateful to the Brookings Institution, particularly to its President and Trustee, Bruce MacLaury; its Director of Foreign Policy Studies, John Steinbrunner; and Senior Fellow William Quandt for offering me a fellowship during the summer of 1988. As a MacArthur Scholar, I was able to consult several primary and secondary sources and conduct many interviews with past and present American politicians who participated in shaping the recent history of the Middle East. My very special thanks are reserved for William Quandt whose vast knowledge and familiarity with Middle Eastern politics and personalities led to highly constructive and mutually beneficial discussions about US policy in the Middle East and regional politics. I thank him for reviewing the manuscript and suggesting several ideas, particularly in relation to peace moves and the Carter era during which he was a National Security Council (NSC) Staff Member who participated in the historic meetings between President Carter, President Sadat and Prime Minister Menachim Begin at Camp David. I reserve also special thanks for Harold Saunders, former Assistant Secretary of State for Near Eastern Affairs and former NSC Staff Member, a visiting fellow at the Brookings Institution, whose insight, experience and knowledge of Middle Eastern Affairs were extremely beneficial. I am grateful also to Research Assistant, Susanne Lane, and all the staff members and assistants who made working in the Brookings Institution pleasant and fruitful.

My deep appreciation goes also to all those whom I interviewed in Washington. Among them are – in alphabetical order: Alfred Atherton, former Ambassador to Egypt and former Assistant Secretary of State for Near Eastern Affairs; Zbigniew Brzezinski, former National Security Affairs Adviser (1977–81); Les Janka, former Deputy Assistant Secretary of State, International Security Affairs, Department of Defence; William Kirby, former Deputy Assistant Secretary of State; Robert Neumann, former Ambassador to Afghanistan, Morocco, Saudi Arabia and adviser to President George Bush; Jack O'Connell, head of a public relations firm representing Jordan; Robert Oakley, former NSC Staff – Middle East Affairs, former Ambassador to Somalia and Zaire, and Ambassador to Pakistan; Peter Rodman, President Reagan's Deputy Adviser for National Security Affairs and former staff aid to Henry Kissinger; Nicholas Veliotes, former Ambassador to Jordan and Egypt, former Assistant Secretary of State for Near Eastern Affairs; and Richard Viets, former Ambassador to Jordan. Also, many thanks to Dr Barakat, Director of Jordan's Information Bureau in Washington, and Dr Lutfi of the Jordanian Embassy in Washington for supplying me with some Jordanian documents. I am particularly grateful to Dr Munir Nasser, Managing Director of Intermedia Inc., Washington DC, for his correspondence and contact with publishers in the United States.

Back in London, throughout the process of research, writing and deliberation, I have enjoyed the advice of Mr Philip Windsor of the London School of Economics and Political Science without whose patience, acumen, wit, professionalism and grasp of strategic studies and Middle East Affairs, this work could not have been accomplished. I have also deep appreciation and respect in my heart for Professor Albert Hourani of Oxford University who read the final manuscript and made some important comments. My thanks are also due to Dr Abbas Kalidar, former lecturer in Middle Eastern Studies in London University (SOAS), for reading parts of the manuscript and giving valuable advice. I am grateful to my editor, Margaret Cornell, for her careful editing and her valuable comments on the text, and to all who gave a hand in revising the manuscript, particularly Paul Harper and Spiros Economides. I also wish to thank Patsy de Souza who undertook the laborious task of typing the final draft.

However, I remain solely responsible for the facts and interpretations found in this study, which, as it stands, is a product of my academic work and reflects only my own views, not those of the Jordanian government.

Prologue

In a nation-wide address on 31 July 1988, King Hussain of Jordan announced that he was severing all Jordan's administrative and legal ties with the Israeli-occupied West Bank of the River Jordan.

We respect the wish of the Palestinian Liberation Organization (PLO), the sole legitimate representative of the Palestinian people, to secede from us in an independent Palestinian state . . . The independent Palestinian state will be established on the occupied land after its liberation . . . Liberating the occupied Palestinian land could be enhanced by dismantling the legal and administrative links.

Thus, King Hussain initiated a new turning point in the strategy of the Middle East peace process with a new banner and a new slogan – the Arab–Israeli conflict became the Palestinian–Israeli conflict and the so-called Jordanian option became the Palestinian option to be steered by the chairman of the Palestine Liberation Organization (PLO) or his appointees face to face with an increasingly intransigent Israel on a highly charged diplomatic field. Having branded the PLO as a terrorist organization, and having imprisoned and deported thousands of local Palestinian activists, Israel has justified the promotion of its own idea that it has no one of any political weight in or outside the occupied territories to talk to. And, by denying all freedom of political expression among the Palestinian residents of the West Bank and Gaza, it has made sure that the PLO has the monopoly in expressing the political will of the Palestinians.

On the face of it, relinquishing administrative and legal responsibility for the West Bank was a grand gesture to the Palestinians. But behind it lay a history of anger, anguish and frustration with the so-called Middle East peace process at the helm of which the US has stood since the time of Kissinger's shuttle diplomacy following the 1973 war. Within this context – and as seen then in the Arab world – the more tension grew between Washington and Moscow, the more committed to Israel the US became. Thus, Israel gradually moved away from the role of client to that of partner and, occasionally, competitor, at a time when the US was seeking to protect its own hegemony in the region. The answers to the questions of who was using whom, who was controlling whom, and for what purpose, became blurred. While a latent competition between a pax Americana and a pax Israelica was evident, Arab popular resentment was aimed at both countries, sometimes more intensely against the US. This feeling was based on the premise that Israel was considered a straightforward enemy, while the US backed Israel most of the time unequivocally and in the same breath announced its friendship with many other actors in the region, failing to use its effective leverage on both, if need be, for an equitable solution to the Arab–Israeli conflict.

Hence, in the regional context, Israel has ultimately been left with two options: either to create an imperial Israel which will impose its will on its neighbours by force; or to be an ordinary state which will integrate itself into the region through negotiation and compromise. To choose the first option would mean that the more force it used, the greater popular Arab rejection would become, and the greater the desire for a compromise, on the official level, in the so-called Arab moderate camp. On the other hand, Israel's vast arsenal of American weapons and its strategic alliance with the US have triggered greater security concerns for all Arabs alike. Thus, the region has fallen into a vicious circle, the outcome of which is the radicalism and extremism evident on both sides of the Arab–Israeli conflict. Failing to make an acceptable response to cautious but positive Arab calls for peace, Israel has continued to remain far removed from any global consensus on the pre-requisites for a lasting political solution. So did the US until George Bush and James Baker appeared on the scene (see Postscript).

The instability has been aggravated by the extra-territoriality of the two principal protagonists – Israel and the PLO. In his classic study of Israel's foreign policy, Michael Brecher deals with this issue in relation to Israel.[1]

The presence of externally based foreign-policy interest groups is widespread in an age of 'penetrated political systems': no state is totally immune from group pressures stemming from beyond its territorial boundaries. [However,] Israel is a self-conscious Jewish state; that is its raîson d'être, and Israel is the only Jewish state insolubly linked to world Jewry in the minds of her leaders and of most Jews and of most non-Jews in the European and American world as well.

Among these diaspora Jews, the 6 million or so in North America stand pre-eminent. Not only are they nearly double the Jewish population of Israel, but they have provided Israel's basic means of political, financial and economic support, and have continued to manipulate the US political system to Israel's advantage. The outcome has been felt continuously in the evolution of the Arab political system; Israel's extra-territoriality has brought the global system more concretely into the region's affairs; possible lines of demarcation between regional and global politics have become more blurred.[2]

On the other hand, by virtue of its impact on the international politics of the Middle East, its elaborate linkages, internationally and with the Palestinian people and the Arab World, and its internal dynamics, the PLO, though not a state, is a major Arab actor.[3] But its geographic dispersion, the lack of a well-defined territorial status and the extra-territoriality of the bulk of the Palestinian leadership and people have resulted in the absence of a 'well-defined reference point of political-cum-territorial definitions'.[4] Especially when they take the form of revolutionary movements aspiring to alter the territorial status of a region, non-state actors are confronted with problems of 'control, legitimacy, factionalism, visibility, durability and manoeuvrability'.[5] And as they become more prominent and draw more international support, they run the risk of being portrayed by their adversaries as 'mavericks threatening international legitimacy'.[6]

Within this context, Israel has used all possible means to ensure the disappearance from the Middle East political scene of a viable Palestinian movement – a policy in which the US has acquiesced. Jordan, which has an organic link with the Palestinian people, has patiently withstood pressure to play the role outlined in Israel and the United States while remaining prominent in the strategy of peacemaking in both capitals.

The US continued until 31 July 1988, to insist on a Palestinian role for Jordan. Both the Carter and Reagan Administrations assumed that Jordan could eventually be forced or persuaded to become a primary negotiator for the Palestinians. To deal with Jordan appealed more to the US than to deal with the PLO – taking into consideration US domestic politics against the background of Kissinger's commitment to Israel in 1975 not to deal with the PLO except under certain conditions. But Jordan was never prepared to play the US–Israeli game because Israel would never accept full withdrawal from occupied Arab territory or Palestinian self-determination and the US, under Carter and Reagan, never spelt out a convincing strategy for peace in the Middle East.

Thus, Jordan eventually came to the conclusion that there was no point in continuing the peace process with worn-out slogans that led nowhere. As Professor Harkabi of the Hebrew University, former Israeli Head of Military Intelligence, put it: 'Everyone seemed to take Jordan for granted and the King apparently decided it was time to use shock treatment to teach them a lesson'.[7] On 31 July, King Hussain pronounced the Jordanian option dead, thus initiating a long period of reassessment, particularly in the United States and Israel.

The Israeli government shrugged off the importance of Hussain's move. 'Nobody likes to admit that events have proven their prophecies wrong', Professor Harkabi commented,[8] – a comment which must be read against the background of the deep division in Israeli domestic politics due to the brutal

3

military operations undertaken to quell the Palestinian uprising (*Intifada*) in the West Bank and Gaza which has raged since 9 December 1987. The US brushed aside suggestions that the King's action would further complicate the US peace moves being pursued by Secretary of State George Shultz. 'The American administration is constantly surprised when things happen that it does not want to happen. The Jordanian option never existed except in the imagination of the US and Israeli governments. King Hussain pronounced the end of an illusion which should never have existed', Ambassador Neumann commented.[9]

But Jordan remains interested in peace. Its borders with Israel are longer than those of any other Arab state. As King Hussain has often put it, Jordan has contributed to the peace process until it reached the stage of a consensus to convene an international conference on the Middle East, the purpose of such a conference being to achieve a just and comprehensive peace in the Middle East following the settlement of the Palestinian problem in all its aspects.

This book will attempt to give the background to these developments, culminating in the Jordanian decision to break off ties with the West Bank. It will focus on the perceived Jordanian role in US peacemaking efforts during the Carter and Reagan Administrations, and will present a comprehensive analysis of envisaged objectives, policies undertaken and their short- and long-term consequences. It will focus on the collaboration and discord between a superpower and its ally, and their long-term effect on the stability of the Middle East. Major political steps will be analyzed with the basic aim of examining why the American quest for peace has so far proved fruitless and what must be done to make it succeed. Since the conclusion of this manuscript, some major events have taken place in the Middle East's peace process under President George Bush leading to the eventual convening of a peace conference engineered by Secretary of State, James Baker. A postscript added just before publication will attempt to sum these up.

1 Introduction

The independent Sovereign state of Jordan: some historical considerations

After the First World War Palestine passed from the Ottoman yoke straight into Britain's sphere of influence. So it remained, until 29 September 1922 when the Mandate, allocated to Britain by resolution of the League of Nations on 16 September, was confirmed by the Council of the League. Two Articles of the Mandate are relevant to this study.

Article 2 specified that the national home of the Jewish People was to be established in Palestine and that the Mandatory was under obligation to safeguard the civil and religious rights of all the inhabitants of Palestine irrespective of race or religion. To the Jews this meant their right of return to 'Eretz Israel' or 'Biblical Israel', after their dispersal by the Romans in 135 AD. To the Arabs – Christians and Moslems – it meant an alien intrusion into what they regarded as their homeland for the past thirteen centuries. As divine promises have no standing in international law, the Jews' biblical rights were regarded by the Arabs as a fanciful 'allegation' to further political ends.

Article 25 of the Mandate stressed that 'In the territories lying between the Jordan and the eastern boundary of Palestine, as ultimately determined, the Mandatory shall be entitled with the consent of the League of Nations to postpone or withhold applications of such provisions of this Mandate as he may consider suitable to those conditions, provided that no action shall be taken which is inconsistent with the provisions of Articles 15, 16 and 18 [relating to religious freedom and the open door economy]'.

Just before the Mandate came into force, the British government obtained approval from the Council of the League that certain Articles of the Mandate relating to the establishment of the Jewish National Home were not to apply to Trans-Jordan.[1] And the resolution taken by the Council of the League on 16 September 1922 indicated that,[2]

In application of the Mandate to Trans-Jordan, the action which in Palestine is taken by the administration of the latter country will be taken by the administration of

Trans-Jordan under the general supervision of the Mandatory . . . His Majesty's Government accept full responsibility as Mandatory for Trans-Jordan and undertake that such provision as may be made for the administration of that country in accordance with Article 25 of the Mandate, shall be in no way inconsistent with those provisions of the Mandate which are not by this resolution declared inapplicable.

This became the legal basis for Britain's position in Trans-Jordan. The British representative at the Eleventh Session of the Permanent Mandate Commission declared that Trans-Jordan 'is not a part of Palestine, but is a part of the area administered by the British Government as Mandatory under the authority of the Palestine Mandate'.[3] On 25 April 1923, Sir Herbert Samuel, the first British High Commissioner for Palestine, accompanied by the new Chief Secretary of the Palestine government, Sir Gilbert Clayton, declared in Amman that[4]

subject to the approval of the League of Nations, His Majesty's Government would recognize the existence of an independent government in Trans-Jordan under the rule of his Highness the Amir Abdulla, provided that such a government was constitutional, and placed His Britannic Majesty's Government in a position to fulfil its international obligations in respect of the territory by means of an agreement between the two governments.

Both the British and Amir Abdulla marked the statement as the declaration of Trans-Jordan's independence and, on 25 May 1923, the Amir made a proclamation to that effect.

Over twenty years later, on 22 March 1946, Britain concluded a Treaty of Alliance with Trans-Jordan as a sovereign state and, on 25 May, Amir Abdulla officially became the King of 'the Hashemite Kingdom of Trans-Jordan'. Some two months before the end of the Mandate over Palestine, on 15 March 1948, a second Treaty of Alliance was signed. Thus, at the time of the termination of the Mandate and the subsequent fighting in Palestine, the Hashemite Kingdom of Trans-Jordan was secured as a sovereign state bound to Britain by a Treaty of Alliance which provided for joint defence arrangements guaranteeing the area against attack.

Following the withdrawal of British forces on 14–15 May 1948, the establishment of the state of Israel was declared and Trans-Jordanian troops entered what was later to become known as the West Bank. The Armistice Agreement of 3 April 1949, concluded at Rhodes under United Nations' auspices, terminated hostilities between Israel and the Hashemite Kingdom of Trans-Jordan. While leaving Israel in effective control of areas beyond the lines drawn in the UN Partition Plan of November 1947, it left the Hashemite Kingdom of Trans-Jordan in *de facto* control of the Old City of Jerusalem – East Jerusalem – and its environs, and of the West Bank of the River Jordan. But Article 11(2) of the armistice stipulated that 'No provision of this agreement shall in any way prejudice the rights and positions of either party thereto in the ultimate peaceful settlement of the Palestinian Question, the provisions of this agreement being dictated exclusively by military considerations.'[5]

The Jordanian Constitution was officially published on 1 February 1947 and came into effect two months later. The first elections were held on 2 October 1947 and the new bicameral parliament was opened on 11 November. In December 1948, meetings were held, the first in Jericho and the second in Nablus, of West Bank notables during which resolutions were adopted for the unification of both banks of the River Jordan. Elections were then held to choose representatives of the West Bank as members of the Jordanian Assembly; it was at this time that the name 'Jordan' began to be used for the enlarged kingdom, rather than Trans-Jordan. On 24 April 1950 both Houses of Parliament met in joint session to adopt the following resolution:[6]

In the expression of the people's faith in the efforts spent by His Majesty Abdulla toward attainment of natural aspirations and basing itself on the right of self-determination and on the existing *de facto* position between Jordan and Palestine and their geographic unity and their common interests and living space, Parliament which represents both sides of the Jordan resolves this day and declares:

First, its support for complete unity between the two sides of the Jordan and their union into one state which is the Hashemite Kingdom of Jordan at whose head reigns King Abdulla Ibn Al Hussain on a basis of constitutional representative government and equality of the rights and duties of all citizens.

Second, its re-affirmation of its intent to preserve full Arab rights in Palestine, to defend those rights by all lawful means in the exercise of its natural rights but without prejudicing the final settlement of Palestine's just case within the sphere of national aspirations, inter-Arab co-operation and international justice.

The first clause established the new official name of the country; the second became the basis for Jordan's policy towards the Palestinians.

Three days later, the British Government announced its formal recognition of the union and the applicability of the provisions of the 1948 Treaty of Alliance. There was one important exception, however; the UK recognized only the *de facto* authority of Jordan over East Jerusalem.[7] Pakistan was the only other state to accord *de jure* recognition to the union and in this case it included East Jerusalem. At the regional level, the Arab League adopted a resolution on 13 June 1950 declaring 'the Arab part of Palestine annexed by Jordan as a trust in its hands until the Palestinian case is fully solved in the interests of its inhabitants'.[8] Jordan remained in effective control of the West Bank, East Jerusalem and its northern, eastern and southern environs from the time of the 1949 armistice until the Six Day War of June 1967 when the whole area fell under Israeli military control.

An Arab framework for diplomacy

Once Jordan became independent, it found itself with a new role but one limited within the framework of the Arab world. Divided into a collection of states of unequal size and economic power but of equal dedication to the pragmatic pursuit of their interests within the framework of Pan-Arab concerns and Moslem Arab collective culture, the Arab world conducts its foreign policy hampered by a serious drawback. 'There is a continuous latent tension within its ranks, between the norms of Pan-Arabism versus Pan-Islam and the interests of each state, between role-conception and role-performance, and particularly between Pan-Arab belief systems and state behaviours based on *raison d'état*'.[9]

The common denominators of the Arab world are identity (Arab), religion (Moslem*), language (Arabic), culture and tradition (Arabic–Islamic) and historical experience (foreign domination). All these factors, when combined, have encouraged regional trans-state interaction, professional associations and the proliferation of a dense network of functional linkages between the urban centres, and in resolving minor border or political disputes. But the only formal association, the Arab League, renders itself useless, through its unanimity rule, in achieving Arab unity or in pursuing the coalition-building strategies which are necessary for constructing a more coherent political order.

The Arab sub-system also shares basic political, social and economic concerns. But the political identity of the area is torn between national interests, nationalist ideologies and religious faith particularly in areas such as Lebanon. Legitimacy based on the moral authority of government has proved inadequate in the absence of comprehensive political structures to accommodate the expectations of diverse interests within intra- and inter-state relations. The outcome is a peculiar deterioration of the regional political performance on the international plane.

When a consensual foreign-policy direction was eventually hammered out during the Arab Summit Conference held under the auspices of the Arab League at Fez in 1982, the failure to implement it brought home the realization that foreign-policy objectives with regard to what is seen as the core of the regional problems – the Arab–Israeli conflict – were beyond Arab capabilities. External constraints, predominantly in the form of Israeli–American strategic co-operation and apparent unity of purpose, have led the Arab sub-system to be permanently involved in political turmoil and instability. Thus, King Hussain bitterly declared:

---

* Christian minorities exist in Egypt, Sudan, Syria, Iraq, Lebanon, Jordan and among the Palestinians.

8

The Arab world has rarely been driven by as many difficulties, dissentions and disputes as it is today . . . The underlying causes of instability become increasingly complex and intractable by the day . . . The Arab world is rich with problems and lacking in effective international support for comprehensive and just solutions.[10]

The sources of this instability are not all externally induced. Besides the historical political legacy, natural attributes have contributed to the poor political performance today. The Arab awakening in the latter half of the nineteenth century – while still under Ottoman rule – was eventually threatened by the arbitrary division of the area into spheres of influence after the First World War, and political practice began to concentrate on how to achieve independence and how to adopt 'Western democracy', within the context of Islam, as a social system. But the Arabs' basically patriarchal social structure within which vertical relations demanded extended loyalty to the family, the tribe and the ruler and their age-old semi-feudal value systems and beliefs, with power concentrated in the hands of landowners and traditional tribal chiefs, led to patrilineal and patrilocal tendencies and a pyramid-shaped social-class structure. These natural phenomena, when coupled with insecurity, the covert and overt intervention of foreign powers and the conflict of superpower interests, have become almost insuperable obstacles to political unity. In exasperation, Crown Prince Hassan of Jordan has often said that the Arabs are new practitioners of the complex game of international statecraft, meaning that political developments in the Arab world are not achieving what Karl Deutsch terms the correct ratio of 'loads to capability'.[11] There are no common regional institutions yet to absorb, let alone solve, differences in the political system. The sub-national dimension of the Arab Ummah, described by the Prince as 'centrifugal forces with social and political grievances',[12] further threatens Arab societies with fragmentation. There is still no proper mechanism to deal not only with conflict management but also with the accommodation of ethnic rivalries and political representation on a non-sectarian basis. In the continued absence of peace and security vast human and capital resources are diverted to building up defence forces, particularly against Israel, instead of harnessing efforts to social, economic, cultural and political development.

Goals and constraints of Jordan's foreign policy

A veteran diplomat, with thirty-nine years or so of experience on the throne, King Hussain is among the first to recognize the lack of room for manoeuvre. Addressing the European Parliament on 15 December 1983, he said:

Jordan, King, Government and People have tried their utmost to contribute to the success of several peace initiatives with Israel. We have followed every avenue, exploited every opportunity and bent backwards to accommodate friend and foe alike to see a just and lasting peace prevail in our troubled region.

In the context of the Middle East, that was not enough. Jordan and the Arab world have no power compared with Israel, backed by the US. Hence, the deadlock continues.

Foreign policies are shaped by domestic conditions, by the values and perceptions of policy-makers and by the global and regional environments in which they exist.[13] Jordan is no exception. The link between its domestic and foreign policy is direct. Thus, the Palestinian question, along with the Israeli–American–Palestinian triangle, becomes the corner-stone of Jordan's foreign policy. But, since the Palestinian question remains unsolved, it directly threatens its national security. As Susan Strange put it in general terms: 'Defence is more important than economic growth, political ideology or the legal principle *pacta sunt servanda*.'[14] In the case of Jordan, defence and security become not only inextricably intertwined with the conventional norms of foreign policy, but also the dominant factors.

Jordan's foreign-policy goals might be put in the following order: first defence of national independence against all perceived threats; second, mobilization of external and internal resources for that defence; and third, the utilization of whatever resources remain for economic and social develop-ment. On an equally important and parallel level is the goal of fulfilling political objectives related to domestic politics. And this requires first, the achievement of domestic and regional stability through a just and honourable peace with Israel; second, an earnest endeavour to eliminate other sources of conflict in the region; and third, a parallel endeavour to improve relations with, and among, Arab states, and to organize political, social and economic co-ordination for their collective benefit on both the regional and the international plane.

In furthering these goals the conduct of Jordan's foreign policy is faced with serious problems.[15] First, the age-old aid versus independence problem. In other words, how much of a trade-off can be allowed between the need for foreign and Arab aid and the maintenance of national independence and independent decision-making. Second, the organic relationship between national resources and foreign-policy objectives. In other words, how political aims can be furthered within the context of military and economic capabilities. And third, the balance between security and development. In other words, to what extent either can be sacrificed for the sake of the other without affecting the general performance of the state.

Jordan's concern about security and defence is to a large extent the result of its geographic location which postulates a sort of geographic determinism. Located in the heart of the Middle East and the Arab world, it covers an area of approximately 37,300 square miles (about 35,100 square miles on the East

Introduction

Bank and 2,165 square miles on the West Bank now legally abandoned by
Jordan to the Palestinian Liberation Organization). It is bordered by Syria to
the north, Iraq and Saudi Arabia to the east, Saudi Arabia and the Gulf of
Aqaba to the south – the Gulf being the only sea outlet, giving access to the
Red Sea – and the uneasy long frontier with Israel to the west. Thus it
perceives itself as a predominantly 'encircled' country, which maximizes its
national security problems. As a result, its Arab policy is characterized by
compromise, moderation and mediation. But its contiguity with Israel
arouses extreme anxiety, summarized by King Hussain as follows:

Israel wants to solve the Palestinian problem through one of three policy options: first,
the Jordanian option involving Israel's annexation of the greater and less populated
part of the occupied Palestinian territory and the return to Jordan of the remaining and
more densely populated segment. Second, annexing the entire territories and granting
autonomy to the Palestinian inhabitants without sovereignty over their land on the
ground that they are a large foreign community living on Israeli territory. This entails
an attempt to separate the Palestinians from their lands as a prelude to their
evacuation. And third, the annexation of territory and the eviction of the inhabitants to
Jordan through military force.[16]

These three solutions make Jordan their prime target. A small country, with
long borders unprotected by natural frontiers, it continues to face a large gap
between goals and capabilities.

When interviewed in Amman in 1985, Prince Hassan explained that the
basic constraint on Jordan's foreign policy was the unavailability of avenues
to further legitimate political goals. While the American 'route' has been
absent since Camp David, Jordan had continued to stay on 'the indivisible
line of détente' due to its propinquity to the European Community. It had
continued to maintain a constructive dialogue with the Soviet Union because
of the latter's influence in the region. A second constraint was the
unavailability of resources to meet the needs of the population. Jordan hosted
a great and growing percentage of Palestinian refugees, because of Israeli
policies in the West Bank and Gaza and also the return of considerable
numbers from the Gulf area since the time of the oil glut and the slowing
down of development programmes. Jordan did not have enough resources to
secure stability and improve its standard of living. A third constraint was its
sponsorship of ideas and programmes that promoted comprehensive economic development concepts in the Arab world. It was part of Jordan's role to
promote the concept of complementarity among the components of the Arab
sub-system and to establish an economic strategy that bound the oil-
producing states with the labour-intensive states of the Arab world. The
Arab Summit Conference at Amman in 1980 adopted a joint Arab economic
strategy, but this was disrupted by the first Gulf War.

Tired of years of conflict and stalemate, and aware of the costs of continuing war, King Hussain is determined to achieve a peaceful settlement with Israel, although not at any price. Expectations rose temporarily following the adoption of an activist foreign policy from January 1984 to February 1986. Since this ended in deadlock, Jordan has continued to exist on the horns of a dilemma. Unable to resort to military means in its foreign policy, and unable to break the diplomatic stalemate without the US exerting its leverage over Israel, it remained trapped by its military vulnerability on the one hand, and socio-political and economic constraints on the other. George Bush and James Baker, however, seemed to offer King Hussain a new glimpse of hope. His country became once more the most valued participant in their proposed peace conference held eventually in Madrid on 30 October 1991 (see postcript).

Jordan's strategy for peace

The framework for Jordan's diplomatic strategy for peace is based on the following factors: Security Council Resolution 242 of 22 November 1967 and 338 of 22 October 1973; the 1974 Rabat Summit Resolution; and the 1982 Fez Peace Plan. The ultimate aim is to secure Israeli withdrawal from all the occupied territories including East Jerusalem and to restore the national rights of the Palestinian people in return for a permanent, just and comprehensive peace in the region.

Since Camp David King Hussain has continually called for an international conference to include the five permanent members of the Security Council and the parties to the conflict with the aim of securing a comprehensive and lasting settlement to the Arab–Israeli conflict, but without success. Following the outbreak of the *Intifada* in the West Bank and Gaza on 9 December 1987 the Shultz initiative of 4 March 1988 also came to a halt, stone-walled by Prime Minister Shamir and emasculated by the apparent US reluctance to exert real pressure on Israel – at a time when world opinion was almost unanimous in its criticism of methods being used to quell the Palestinian uprising. The future of the Baker initiative does not seem brighter either.

Two questions arise in this context. What were the basic reasons for the rise and fall of the various Middle East peace initiatives? And what can be learnt for the future? The story recounted in the following chapters will attempt to provide the answer.

2 Kissinger's legacy and imprint on the Middle East

As a result of the June 1967 war, Israeli armed forces gained control of the Palestinian-populated territories of the West Bank and Gaza Strip, the Egyptian Sinai Peninsula and the Syrian Golan Heights. Pending legitimate endorsement of their status, these territories were subjected to what is technically termed 'belligerent occupation' i.e., were subject to international law, in particular to the Hague regulations of 1907 and the Fourth Geneva Convention of 12 August 1949 which specify that the basic duty of the occupying power is to preserve the existing situation.[1]

As a result of the 6 October 1973 war, what became known as 'Kissinger's shuttle diplomacy' began, launched on 21 December in the ceremonial opening of a Middle East peace conference in Geneva, co-sponsored by Dr Kissinger on behalf of the US government and Mr Gromyko on behalf of the Soviet government. Invitations to participate were accepted by Egypt, Jordan and Israel, but declined by Syria, which established its position in a statement published on 22 December:

There will not be a search for peace, a just and permanent peace, due to Israel's endeavours to divert the Geneva Conference to a field of manoeuvres concentrating on side issues in order to block the main goal for which the conference is convened.[2]

In fact, the Syrian position was already clear to Kissinger, when he visited Syria in connection with the invitation to the conference – the first visit by an American Secretary of State for eighteen years. Israel had objected to three paragraphs in the invitation. The first related to Palestinian participation: Israel suggested 'other participants' instead; the second concerned the joint Arab delegation: Israel wanted bilateral committees on a geographical basis; the third involved the date of the conference, originally fixed for 18 December; Israel suggested 21 December; it took place on 21 December. The reason for the delay was understood in the Arab world at a later date. According to the then Jordanian Prime Minister and Foreign Minister, Zeid Rifai, the undeclared aim was to have the opening session as close as possible to Christmas as a pretext for adjourning early.[3] The conference was never re-convened.

In Damascus, President Assad's unswerving courtesy led almost immediately to his agreement on all the proposed amendments to the invitations: 'other' rather than 'Palestinian participants'; 'geographical committees' instead of a 'joint Arab delegation'; 21 instead of 18 December as the date. But as he was leaving, Kissinger casually said to Abdul Halim Khaddam, the then Syrian Foreign Minister, 'See you in Geneva'; and Assad calmly interrupted: 'Geneva! What Geneva?'. The surprised Kissinger was then told that Syria refused the invitiation, that Assad would not participate and that if he had accepted the amendments, it was only because they did not concern him. And as he later told Mr Rifai:

I told Dr Kissinger I couldn't care less how you amend the invitation. You want geographic committees . . . you want Palestinian participation . . . other participants . . . 21st . . . 18th . . . change it the way you like; I accept all the changes because I refuse the whole invitation.

At the opening of the Geneva Conference the parties attending established their positions as follows.[4] The host, the UN Secretary General Dr Kurt Waldheim, stressed the importance of the implementation of Resolution 242 through negotiations for a just and durable peace under UN auspices, starting with the disengagement and separation of Egyptian and Israeli forces on the Suez Canal front. Gromyko saw the practical task of the conference as the working out of a specific and realistic programme for the implementation of the resolution in all its parts:

The Soviet Union is not hostile towards the State of Israel; it is Israel's policy of annexation that has given rise to general, including Soviet, condemnation . . . the contention that Israel is being denied the right to exist has been advanced as almost the main argument in the support of the occupation of other people's territory: this right of Israel was recognised by the very fact of the formation of that state on the decision of the United Nations . . . this right, however, cannot be unilateral. It is unthinkable without respect for the sovereign rights of other states and peoples . . . the legitimate rights of the Arab people of Palestine must be safeguarded . . . the problem of Palestine cannot be considered and settled without the participation of representatives of the Arab people of Palestine.

Kissinger indicated that the separation of forces was the essential first step, prior to the implementation of Resolution 242 in all its parts.

I cannot promise success, but I can promise dedication . . . Peace must bring a new relationship among the nations of the Middle East; it must include concrete measures that make war less likely.

Zeid Rifai, on behalf of Jordan, insisted on complete Israeli withdrawal from all occupied territories including East Jerusalem. Stressing that Syria's absence did not prejudice its right to demand withdrawal from all Syrian territories, he declared:

Questions of withdrawal, boundaries, Palestinian rights, refugees, obligations of peace and the status of Jerusalem are all common concerns and collective responsibility. My delegation, therefore, is not prepared to conclude any partial settlement on matters which we feel are of joint interest with our Arab brothers at this conference.

He clarified this in a later interview in 1987:

When we accepted the invitation to the conference, we did so on the basis of the implementation of UN Resolution 242 and the establishment of a comprehensive peace in the Middle East based on the settlement of the Palestinian Question.

What followed in Geneva, however, was a different story. Following the suggestion of an Egyptian–Israeli committee, Rifai proposed a similar Jordanian–Israeli one. But the proposal was not heeded, the explanation offered then being that it was necessary to move step by step. But another version came out in April 1987 during Rifai's visit to Washington when he met members of the National Security Council, including Peter Rodman, a staff member, who had accompanied Kissinger to the 1973 Conference. Rifai stressed the need for an international conference to establish a comprehensive peace in the Middle East, and expressed amazement at the hesitant American stand on peace-making in recent years, particularly against the background of the 1973 Conference which was basically an American idea, following the adoption of UN Resolution 338. Rodman explained that there was a basic difference: the 1973 Conference had had a ceiling – a disengagement agreement between Israel and Egypt, to which Jordan was not privy and which only the US, Egypt and Israel had agreed to.[5]

Jordan's invitation had made no mention of 'ceilings' or disengagement agreements. In the discussions on the wording of the invitation reference was always to a comprehensive settlement based on the implementation of UN Resolution 242. Nevertheless, Rodman's explanation indirectly supported Jordan's argument for the need for an international conference. For, if the US needed an international conference in 1973 to give that 'prior agreement' legality, then the need existed in 1987 for an international conference to give any negotiations or settlement with Israel the same sort of legality. Rodman stated that if a conference were to be convened, agreement should take place in advance as in 1973.

There was no indication of any prior agreement in the speeches of the Egyptian and Israeli foreign ministers at the 1973 Conference. Egypt's Foreign Minister, Ismail Fahmi, expressed the hope that the Israeli government had realized that Israel's security did not lie in retaining conquered territories or in maintaining military supremacy, and that it would be best to learn to live at peace with its neighbours:

Egypt's determination to work for peace equals its determination to see that all its land, all Arab lands are liberated and that the Palestinians enjoy the right to their territory and to live at peace.

But Abba Eban, the Israeli Foreign Minister, countered that there could not be a return to the former armistice line of 1966–7, that Jerusalem was 'Israel's capital now, united forever', and that Egypt and Israel should pledge themselves at the conference to observe the existing ceasefire line on a basis of reciprocity. In the context of relations with Egypt he pointed out that: 'Israel's aim at this conference is a peace treaty defining the terms of our co-existence in future years'. Both countries therefore agreed on 22 December to establish a joint Egyptian–Israeli military working group to discuss the disengagement of forces.

With the positions of all parties concerned thus firmly established, intensive deliberations continued during the following months, on the make-up of the Arab delegation at the expected resumption of the Geneva Conference, the representation of the Palestinians and its rejection by Israel, and the PLO's refusal to attend a peace conference on the basis of Resolution 242. They all became redundant, however, as the Geneva Conference for a comprehensive peace never resumed. Kissinger had other designs in mind.

Designs: setting the scene

Kissinger's grand design began to take shape during the course of the 1973 war. Zeid Rifai is convinced that Kissinger even indirectly co-ordinated the war with Sadat of Egypt.[6] He bases his conviction on the following argument: Kissinger had always told Jordan and Sadat that US Middle East policy was initiated only on the basis of crisis management, and that in the absence of a crisis there would be no US policy. Rifai clearly remembered him saying, as a National Security adviser, before he became Secretary of State:

I'll only become involved in the Middle East problem if there is a crisis . . . I'll only become involved if I can succeed . . . And if I get involved I will succeed.

Kissinger did eventually become involved and it was left to Sadat, who often spoke of an 'activating war', to create the crisis. According to Rifai, Sadat must have calculated that crossing the Suez Canal, and penetrating the well-fortified Israeli Bar Lev Line, would provide the crisis which would open the door for American intervention to produce a ceasefire and negotiations.

In Rifai's view this logic of events explained what happened during the war. Why was Sadat's military plan different from the joint Syrian–Egyptian plan? He was not supposed to stop after crossing the Canal, but to advance to the Sinai Passes. That was why Syria became engaged in such a ferocious battle; when the Eygptians ceased their advance, Israel turned its attention to the Syrian front. The Egyptian front was more dangerous. Rifai explained:

Kissinger's involvement had tremendously benefited himself and Israel. His nick-name was 'Super K' and he believed it. His main concern was to achieve personal success more than true peace in the Middle East or a long-term strategic gain for the US in the area. As far as Israel was concerned, I still maintain that there are three prominent figures in the history of Zionism: Herzl who initiated the idea; Ben Gurion who established the state; and Kissinger who reinforced its foundations. When Kissinger protested at this I elaborated: 'You were not ready to put pressure on Israel . . . You were reluctant to take any risk of failure . . . You supported Israel's goal of neutralizing Egypt.' Moreover, I frequently told Kissinger that the Arabs couldn't fight without Egypt and couldn't make peace without Syria. He not only believed me, he has also adopted my statement ever since.

Although it is difficult to prove the extent of the co-ordination, if any, between Sadat and Kissinger before the 1973 war, it is not difficult to see that the initial Arab successes during the first week of the fighting undermined all the calculations underpinning America's Middle East policy in the previous few years. The Arabs were not deterred from war by the fact that Israel was kept militarily stronger than the combined forces of the Arab countries; Israel did not win quickly and easily as was the case in the 1967 war; the Soviet Union, despite détente, did not stay out of the conflict; friendly Arab countries used the 'oil weapon' against the US and particular European countries; Western Europe did not show complete solidarity with its major ally; and the two superpowers came close to open confrontation, when the US nuclear alert took place on 25 October 1973.

With the pre-war conceptions thus turning out to be invalid, Kissinger embarked on a special strategy, which, according to his own account,[7] aimed at: preventing a victory of Soviet arms in the hands of Soviet clients (the Arabs) over a traditional friend (Israel) supplied with American arms; demonstrating the futility of Soviet policies, thus making the Arabs abandon their reliance on the Soviet Union and seek co-operation with the US; preventing the humiliation of the Arabs and outright Israeli victory by slowing down diplomacy without appearing obstructionist, speeding up military operations without seeming to intervene, then forcing a ceasefire and initiating talks. In other words, he conceived a limited military success for the Arabs that would save their face and yet persuade them of the futility of their military option. Total Arab defeat, he calculated, would cause leftist coups in the Arab world and Soviet intervention as the champion of the Arab cause. When he started a huge air-lift of war material to Israel on 12 October, he stated: 'I wanted a demonstrative counter to the Soviet air-lift'.[8] Thus, at the end of the October war, the Egyptian Third Army was cut off in Sinai, and the US moved into a pivotal position to prove that it was the only power that could achieve progress.

Kissinger also wanted to defuse the oil weapon. 'I warned that the oil embargo would hamper not spur our efforts.' And he wanted to de-emphasize the Soviet role in the peace process.[9]

Détente did not prevent us from seeking to reduce the Soviet role. But fairness compels the recognition that Moscow never launched an overall campaign against us; and we took pains not to humiliate the Soviets overtly.

Thus, he continued to exclude the Russians while at the same time publicly minimizing their exclusion and privately reassuring them of US intentions to keep them informed. He claimed that he organized the Geneva conference as a symbol of American commitment to overall peace, as a means of keeping in touch with the Russians during the delicate phase while the cease-fire hung in the balance, and as a fall-back position if alternative routes failed.[10] But, in assembling a multilateral conference, he also claimed that his real purpose was to use it as the framework for an essentially bilateral diplomacy, and to reduce the joint auspices to a minimum while at the same time making the Soviets believe that America's sole role would not be sustained and that their time would come to participate fully in the peace conference. 'One of the arts of diplomacy', he boasted, 'is to clothe a rejection in the form of acceptance.'

Achievements

Choosing a step-by-step approach, Kissinger managed, in the course of the two years following the October war, to bring about the following. First, on 8 November 1973, a six-point agreement settled the question of supplying the beleaguered Egyptian army, and the exchange of prisoners of war, and subsumed the problem of demarcation of ceasefire lines under the broader question of disengagement of forces which the two parties agreed to negotiate. Second, on 18 January 1974 the Egyptian–Israeli disengagement agreement was signed, involving the first limited Israeli withdrawal from Egypt's occupied territories. His strategy was to make clear that if the Arabs wanted further US involvement in efforts at a peace settlement, they must first lift the oil restrictions they had imposed, rather than waiting until there was progress on the settlement front. The Arabs did lift the restrictions, on the understanding that the Syrian front would be dealt with immediately. The price the US had to pay was military and economic aid to Israel amounting to $2.6 billion out of which $1.8 billion was a military grant. Egypt was also awarded a substantial economic aid package totalling around $1.5m.[11]

Third, on 31 May 1974, a Syrian–Israeli disengagement agreement was signed. As an inducement to Israel, the US agreed to supply it with arms on a long-term basis, and to support any future military action by Israel against a possible guerrilla offensive originating from Syrian territory. Before signing the agreement, Mrs Meir, the then Israeli Prime Minister, told the Knesset (on 30 May): 'Raids would be answered by all means available with the political support of the US. I make this statement public with the knowledge of the US.'[12] Fourth, on 4 September 1975, the second Sinai agreement was signed. Israel agreed to evacuate the Sinai Passes and hand back the Sinai oil-fields to Egypt. Egypt committed itself not to resort to force, to leave the evacuated territories demilitarized and under United Nations control, to observe reciprocal limitations of armaments and military presence beyond the UN buffer zones and to allow Israel to use the Suez Canal. The US committed itself to supervising an electronic warning system in the Passes and to continuing aircraft and satellite reconnaissance to ascertain compliance with the accord. An important concession was at the same time made to Israel in the form of a Memorandum of Understanding which amounted to a virtual US–Israel alliance in all but name. Israel was to have its requirements for arms, economic assistance and energy met on a long-term basis, and the US gave a long-standing commitment to its security, plus a pledge not to recognize or negotiate with the PLO as long as it refused to accept Resolutions 242 and 338, and to veto any initiative in the Security Council which would harm Israel. Egypt was to receive economic assistance to the tune of $750m.[13]

The Jordanian Front

On 19 January 1974, Jordan presented Kissinger with a withdrawal scheme, requiring Israeli forces to pull back from the Jordan River to a line on the Western edge of the Jordan Valley at a distance of approximately ten kilometres, with the intermediate strip to be a demilitarized zone. Jordan's idea was to test, first, Kissinger's sincerity in seeking a solution to the occupied West Bank, starting with a disengagement agreement on the Jordanian front similar to those concluded with Egypt and being negotiated with Syria; and second, how serious Kissinger and the Israelis were in implementing Resolution 242 in full and on all fronts as stressed by Kissinger in his speech at the Geneva Conference in December 1973.

All Kissinger did was to pass the proposal to Israel and carry back its response indicating adamant opposition to pulling back along the River but showing some interest in evacuating the Jericho enclave and giving access to Jordan through a corridor across the River Jordan.[14] 'As a disengagement agreement we accept', Prime Minister Rifai stressed. Kissinger replied: 'The offer is not a disengagement agreement: it is a final peace treaty.'[15]

The implementation of a final settlement along the lines of what looked in

Jordan like the first step of the previously rejected Israeli Allon Plan appeared to envisage:

(i)   The River Jordan as the eastern boundary of Israel.

(ii)   A 10–15 km belt from the occupied West Bank, running parallel to the River Jordan, to be incorporated into Israel.

(iii)   The heavily Arab populated hilly areas of occupied Nablus and Galilee to be handed back to Jordan provided that 'they were connected by three transit corridors, the first to enable connection between the two Arab pockets, the second to connect them with the Israeli town of Haifa and the third to connect them with Jordan.

(iv)   Gaza to be incorporated into Israel, provided that the Palestinian refugees were removed to the West Bank.

(v)   Jerusalem to remain united as the capital of Israel.

(vi)   Internal autonomy for the Arabs, linked to Israel through a defence treaty.

(vii)   Granting of special rights for access to holy Islamic shrines.

(viii) Most of the Golan Heights to be under Israeli sovereignty.[16]

At a closed session of the Jordanian parliament, King Hussain rejected the Israeli approach. Kissinger did not pursue the issue further. Jordan therefore drew two conclusions;[17] first, that Israel would not implement Resolution 242 on all fronts – it would not abandon the Jordan Valley, nor the cease-fire lines, but only the population, to be administered by Jordan, while keeping the land for itself. Second, Kissinger was not after a comprehensive solution, nor the implementation of 242 on the Jordanian front. Only on the Egyptian front was there a chance for him to achieve personal success, because the Sinai, as he put it, 'was not strategically important to Israel nor overlaid with historical memories'.[18] As former Prime Minister Rifai commented:

No matter how many times we continued to raise the issue with Kissinger every time he passed by Amman, which he frequently did, his answer always showed a complete lack of interest. His main concern was Sinai II. Even the Syrian disengagement was put forward with the aim of completely concentrating attention on the Eygptian front. The second disengagement agreement with Egypt paved the way for Camp David.[19]

Mr Rifai further explained how, after the completion of the disengagement agreement on the Eygptian front, Jordan began pressing Kissinger for a further withdrawal on the Syrian front as a preparatory step for the Jordanian front. It even suggested a unilateral Israeli withdrawal from land under the supervision of the international emergency forces, in order to create an atmosphere conducive to peace. Kissinger did not respond. His negative attitude may have sprung from his conviction that the case was complex, and that if he got involved he would not succeed unless he put pressure on Israel which he was unwilling to do. Former Prime Minister Rifai concluded:

The only way for Kissinger to rid himself of Jordanian demands was to knock us out, once and for all. Kissinger plotted against the Arab nation. And Sadat took part in the plot. The rest of the Arabs fell into the trap.

This was a reference to the events which led to what became known as 'the Rabat Decision'.

The road to Rabat: its implications and aftermath

On 28 October 1974, the seventh Arab summit conference held in Rabat designated the PLO as the sole legitimate representative of the Palestinian people and reaffirmed their right to establish an independent Palestinian national authority in any Palestinian territory that was to be liberated.

The implication of the decision, as Jordan saw it, was elaborated at a later date by King Hussain and a few key Jordanian decision-makers, but curiously the elaboration appeared only in the Arab press. Addressing the seventeenth session of the Palestinian National Council held in Amman in November 1984 King Hussain put Jordan's version:

With the entry of the US replacing the UN as a third party in the peace process after the 1973 war, Jordan was excluded from the peace process. It was suggested that the PLO should replace Jordan in regard to the West Bank, since Israel was arguing that Jordan had no right to claim the West Bank because it had been an occupying power. According to Israel's argument, Jordan had acquired no territorial sovereignty by the time of the 1967 war. Therefore, there was no opposing belligerent to support a belligerent occupation. Following this logic, Israel claimed that it had neither annexed nor subjected the West Bank to belligerent occupation, hence the reference to 'administered territories'. When in Rabat the political burden was transferred to the PLO, Israel, which had been regarding Jordan as an occupying power, suddenly announced its refusal to talk to the PLO and demanded to talk to Jordan.

The features of the plot became apparent. After paralysing Jordan's role, the moves to paralyse the PLO's role began. This was confirmed a few months after the Rabat resolution, when the former US Secretary of State, Dr Kissinger, promised Israel that the US would not talk to the PLO. This was in response to one of Israel's conditions for signing the second disengagement agreement with Egypt. By these stands, Israel aimed to create an atmosphere of confusion and to paralyse any political moves that had any connection with the Palestinian factor in the Middle East crisis. Israel wanted to gain time which it used in order to establish more settlements and change the status of Jerusalem. So, it turned out that the endorsement of the Rabat Resolution was doing Israel a favour because it enabled it to say that Jordan had ceded its right to claim the West Bank and that the PLO was not qualified to talk on behalf of the Palestinians. There no longer existed an Arab government which could defend directly the Palestinian interests.

Former Prime Minister, Mudar Badran commented in a later interview that 'If a disengagement agreement on the Jordanian front had been fulfilled with

the help of Dr Kissinger, the Rabat Decision might not have taken place'.[20]
He explained:

What was more important for us was the land. Once we got it back, we would have
sorted it out with the Palestinians, whose duty would have been to carry the political
struggle further by getting what was allotted to them in the Partition Plan.

This comment reflected Jordanian suspicions that Kissinger might have
played a role in preparing the ground for the 'Rabat Decision'. They were
spelled out by Mr Rifai,[21] who revealed that the 'Rabat Decision' was not the
first along these lines. The same decision had been taken at the previous
meetings of the Arab summit conference in Algiers and the Non-Aligned
Movement in Kuala Lumpur. But because Jordan persisted in its reserva-
tions and refused to abide by it, the decision was not then binding.

Rifai warned Kissinger that the same resolution was going to surface again
at Rabat and that Jordan would abide by it this time: first, because there
appeared to be no possibility of reaching a solution to the Arab–Israeli
problem as a whole; second, because there appeared to be no American
readiness to play a role in dealing with the core problem; and third, because of
Israel's refusal to withdraw, as Resolution 242 specified. Nevertheless he
made a last-minute appeal to Kissinger:

If you are serious about a settlement, a disengagement agreement on the Jordanian
front must take place before Rabat. We must break the deadlock. We must break the
psychological barrier, i.e. the existence of an East Bank and a West Bank with a river
between. The completion of a disengagement agreement and an Israeli withdrawal
from parts of the West Bank will definitely change the atmosphere at the Rabat
Conference.

To Rifai's surprise, Kissinger assured him that the decision on the PLO
would not be adopted; influential Arab countries had been contacted, and
guarantees had been given to that effect. 'It will not be Jordan; it will be the
major Arab countries, notably Sadat, who will take a firm stand.'

At a preparatory meeting of Arab foreign ministers three days before the
summit during which Jordan tried to block the decision or at least prevent its
adoption as a recommendation to the summit itself, Ismail Fahmi, the
Egyptian Foreign Minister, became the outspoken defender of the decision.
Another member of the Eygptian team told Rifai privately that 'Fahmi was
adopting this stand without any instructions from Cairo', and assured the
Jordanian team that the whole situation would change once President Sadat
had arrived. The decision was not adopted by the foreign ministers and the
whole issue was passed to the summit.

Here it remained a divisive issue. With deadlock setting in, a seven-man
committee comprising Egypt, Syria, Saudi Arabia, Algeria, Morocco, Jordan
and the PLO was formed. King Hussain explained the situation again, but

Sadat vigorously defended the idea of PLO representation, continually stressing that he was living for the day when he would see a Palestinian flag hoisted over Palestinian land.

Doubts grew among most of the participants about the possibility of establishing a Palestinian national authority on the land of Palestine once Jordan had regained the West Bank. According to the former Jordanian Information Minister and minister of court, Adnan Abu Odeh, the PLO also showed its displeasure at the idea of extending the disengagement process to include the unresolved state of war between Jordan and Israel on the basis that Jordan had taken no part in the 1973 war and was therefore not entitled to a disengagement of forces. As he put it:

Israel used the argument, so did the Arabs at Rabat. The PLO in particular did not want Israel to release lands so as to be incorporated into Jordan. It wanted any released land to be a site for a future Palestinian state under its own leadership.[22]

Jordan warned that the decision would create insurmountable problems and would entail one of the most massive separations of families and peoples in modern times.[23] Its argument was supported only by Iraq.[24] But it was overruled, and the PLO became, and has remained, the sole legitimate representative of the Palestinian people. King Hussain had no option but to go along with the Rabat Decision.

On a visit to Amman soon afterwards Kissinger was briefed on the decision by Prime Minister Rifai, who well remembered his response. 'I am sorry; *we* miscalculated our manipulative capabilities.'[25] Later when confronted with this quotation Kissinger countered: 'Mr Rifai has misunderstood me. I told him, *you* miscalculated our manipulative capabilities!'[26]

During a visit to the US in November 1983, Adnan Abu Odeh, then Information Minister, challenged Kissinger on his manipulation of Sadat with regard to the decision. Kissinger's reaction was predictable. While fiercely denying the allegation, he said, 'I did not insinuate or suggest anything. It was the Egyptians who were very enthusiastic.' But why? Abu Odeh explained:

After the disengagement of forces on the Egyptian front, Sadat must have had enough of the Palestinian problem. He must have been privately disenchanted with the idea of a comprehensive solution. A comprehensive solution, dealing with the complicated core Palestinian issue, meant the diminishing of a life-time chance to return the Sinai to Egyptian sovereignty and end the state of war with Israel. He was desperate not to tie Egyptian territorial claims to those of Jordan or Syria. But Egypt had been morally committed to a comprehensive solution since Jordan and Egypt under Nasser entered the war against Israel in 1967. Jordan's army was then under Egyptian command. During the war, Jordan lost the West Bank to Israel, and after the war, both Jordan and Egypt accepted Resolution 242. Egypt, Jordan and later on Syria, all became committed to a comprehensive solution. To get out of this tight corner, President

Sadat may have thought that if the responsibility for the occupied West Bank were to be transferred to the PLO, then his withdrawal from commitment to the PLO would become easier than if Jordan were responsible. At this juncture, Kissinger appeared on the scene to give Sadat's thinking a gentle push, and in a very subtle way, by explaining how impossible it was to solve the Palestinian problem due to the existence of two sides claiming the West Bank, Jordan and the PLO, and by insinuating that if Jordan abdicated its role, it would become easier to find a solution. President Sadat must have been convinced. He became the outspoken champion of the PLO at Rabat and he played a big role in persuading Saudi Arabia, Syria and the rest to fall in line.[27]

Were the Arab Heads of State at Rabat abandoning their primary commitment to the Palestinians by placing direct responsibility for the problem onto the PLO, and resigning themselves to a secondary role? Were they seeking a way to appease the PLO, having recognized the futility of efforts to secure the implementation of Resolution 242 because of Israel's stance, backed as it was by Kissinger? King Hussain certainly believed so: 'That is what we resisted as much as we could and regarded it as a relinquishment of a sacred duty.'[28] Some political observers in the West believed that 'the Jordanian–PLO rivalry and the Arab leaders' exasperation at the PLO's pressure and the whole Palestinian question, combined with lack of progress on the Jordanian front, freed Israel from negotiating at all, while placing the whole onus of future progress on the PLO.'[29] But Robert Neumann, then US Ambassador to Morocco, noted the moderate tone of the participants at Rabat. King Hassan II of Morocco, along with the General Secretary of the Arab League, explicitly denounced the three 'nos' – no peace, no negotiations, and no recognition of Israel – of the Khartoum Conference in 1967. His statement that Khartoum was dead was not contradicted by any Arab delegation, including that of the PLO either at that time or since. Yet the media and Dr Kissinger focused instead on the conference's decision concerning the PLO, a decision seen by some other Western commentators as not so much a move towards radicalism on the part of the Arab governments, but rather as an attempt to bring the internally divided Palestinian movement under their more effective control.[30]

The Rabat decision was endorsed by the UN General Assembly at its 30th and 31st sessions. Ever since, Jordan has refused to negotiate on its own on behalf of the Palestinians. 'Even if the Palestinian National Council and the whole Arab world pleaded with Jordan to negotiate alone, we would not do so. It is a historical responsibility. It is a Palestinian responsibility over a Palestinian land . . . Rabat is on', said the former Chief of the Royal Courts, former Foreign Minister Marwan al Qassem in 1983.[31] Officially, however, Jordan continued, until 31 July 1988, when it severed legal ties with the West Bank, to observe the following lines of foreign policy:[32]

(i) According to the Jordanian Constitution and municipal laws, the West Bank could not be alienated from the Hashemite Kingdom of Jordan.

(ii)   The Rabat Decision was a political decision. The Jordanian Constitution did not contradict the decision nor the concept of Palestinian self-determination because their practical implementation could take place only after regaining the occupied lands.

(iii) The Rabat political decision did not affect the Jordanian citizenship granted to all Palestinians living in Jordan and the West Bank. Therefore, all Palestinians bearing Jordanian nationality wherever they lived fell under the jurisdiction of Jordan.

(iv)   As Jordan citizens, they had a duty of allegiance to the King of Jordan. In return, they had rights of citizenship.

(v)   Jordanian laws were still implemented in the West Bank after Rabat. Jordan, therefore, had territorial as well as personal jurisdiction over the West Bank

(vi)   All those holding Jordanian citizenship had to observe Jordanian law. Therefore, any dealings with the enemy – Israel – such as enrolment in the so-called Village Leagues, would be regarded as offering assistance to the enemy, and any one doing so could be charged with high treason.

After the Rabat decision, the US continued to act on the principle that the West Bank and Gaza were occupied territories to which Resolution 242 and the Fourth Geneva Convention of 1949 applied. As far as Jerusalem was concerned, the US considered it occupied land to which the Geneva Convention also applied. The US had affirmed this position in Ambassador Yost's statement to the UN Security Council on 1 July 1969, and it was also reaffirmed at Camp David, in line with numerous General Assembly and Security Council resolutions that regarded Israel's annexation of Jerusalem as illegal, and hence null and void.

Taking all these points into consideration, Jordan's concern with the inhabitants of the West Bank continued to be derived from its long history of association with the Palestinian people. Under international law, the Fourth Geneva Convention, and Security Council Resolution 242, the inhabitants of the West Bank remained, until 31 July 1988, Jordanian citizens up to the time when they were able to exercise their right of self-determination.

The view from Washington

Israeli withdrawal from the 'Jericho enclave' was an American idea, thought to be useful on the grounds of withdrawal from the populated areas first. In one respect, the idea was consistent with the Allon Plan. It satisfied Israeli apprehensions concerning the River Jordan as a security barrier. But there was one big difference: the Allon Plan was meant to be a final arrangement. The American team surrounding Kissinger understood withdrawal from the Jericho enclave to be an interim step. Once Israel became used to the idea of withdrawal it was hoped it would be followed by other steps.

Israel asked Jordan for a declaration of 'non-belligerency' in return for the withdrawal, which Jordan refused. Although Washington regarded the Israeli price as too high for an interim step it could not put pressure on Israel because of fear of the reaction of a narrowly based new Israeli government and of the reaction of the US Jewish community, and also because of the unsettled political situation in the US due to the Watergate scandal and the ensuing Nixon resignation. Moreover, the Arab world was very unsettled before the Rabat summit conference, and there was serious disagreement between the US and Jordan over the elaboration of an agreement, with the US focusing on the populated centres while leaving Israel on the river, and Jordan anxious for a straight pull-back. Other distractions were the Cyprus issue and Vietnam. Thus the focus turned on Egypt and Syria and the immediate issue became not how to find a comprehensive solution to the Arab–Israeli conflict, but the fulfilment of a disengagement process.

Following the first Egyptian disengagement (18 January 1974) and the Syrian disengagement agreement (31 May 1974) there was an attempt to re-assess the difficulties of going back to the Jordanian front. But the question of a disengagement agreement with Jordan had moved well down on Kissinger's priority list, aided by the attitude of the new President, Gerald Ford who had succeeded Nixon on 9 August 1974. President Ford did not see the issue of whether or not to include Jordan and the Palestinians in peace efforts as a key one.

Meanwhile, Egypt insisted on embarking on negotiations for a Sinai II disengagement agreement before the Jordanian front was considered and before the Arab summit in October. Syria, on the other hand, argued that the Jordanian front was the more important. In an effort to help the process along, King Hussain accepted a compromise during his visit to Washington in August 1974; instead of Israeli withdrawal from 10–12 kilometres along the River Jordan he agreed to accept the 'leopard-spot' scheme of allowing some Israeli security installations to remain in the evacuated areas as a transitory arrangement. But during his visit to Washington a month later Prime Minister Rabin expressed a clear preference for a second Sinai accord, to avoid, as he put it to the Americans, early elections in Israel and a return of the hard-line Likud to power.[33]

The Rabat Decision of October 1974 became a watershed in American thinking. The focus turned to a Sinai II agreement. And the definition of the problem became how to keep some momentum going through the presidential elections of 1976, until a new president could tackle – if necessary – the problem of broadening the peace process.

Jordan's theory of Kissinger's role in the Rabat Decision was not believed in Washington. When it was pointed out that Kissinger was warned beforehand, personally, by Mr Rifai, American officials reacted differently. While it was indicated that Kissinger held many private meetings with leaders of the Arab world it was also stressed that he might not have heeded the warning because, according to Robert Oakley of the National Security Council, he 'did not accept everything Rifai told him and Rifai did not always accept everything Kissinger told him'. Moreover, again in Oakley's words: 'We did not see the Rabat Decision coming. Maybe we should but we didn't.'[34]

According to Oakley there was a consensus in Washington that Jordan had been let down in 1974; that the US did not push hard enough, but that Jordan asked more than Israel could accept and Israel followed a hard line.

One has to have the right combination of events. You have to have the right president of the US and the right approach. Israel is tough on us to handle. I suspect that Kissinger promised implicitly or explicitly things he wasn't sure he could deliver and I also expect Jordan heard more than Kissinger was saying and interpreted much more categoric commitment . . . In fact it was partly accidental, partly by design on Kissinger's side I suspect. Kissinger liked to give people the impression that he had unlimited power. But that was not the case.

Oakley reported that Kissinger was heard saying after the disengagement agreement with Syria: 'Now after this disengagement I can do anything.' The Americans started calling him the magician and the Arabs started believing that he could do anything in the Middle East. But on many occasions he was seen to fail to get what he wanted.

Ambassador Atherton indicated that Kissinger was known to say one thing in different ways which eventually led to its being read in different ways as well. Harold Saunders indicated that he said different things to different people because his mind worked on different levels at the same time; what Kissinger professed as his purpose was not necessarily the deeper underlying purpose. Eventually people saw the results of his working on one level at one point and read another level or set of purposes at another. In other words, Kissinger was complex and devious.

There was also a certain amount of misleading communication from Egypt to Washington as to what Sadat was up to. Kissinger thought he had assurances from him that he would handle the situation in Rabat in Jordan's favour, but he did not. Former Ambassador to Cairo Nicholas Veliotes concluded:

Kissinger's greatest failure was not sufficiently seeing the dangers inherent in not moving quickly with Jordan. Whether that was because Sadat didn't want to be caught up in it, whether Sadat preferred to deal with the PLO more than the King, I don't know. What I do know is that we let Jordan down. And Jordan was counting on us.

Evaluation

There was enough of the Cold War warrior left in both Nixon and Kissinger for them to take real pleasure in demonstrating the limits of Soviet influence in the Middle East.[35] Kissinger succeeded in establishing the US as the key diplomatic broker between Israel and the Arabs. On a short-term basis, the Soviet Union was outmanoeuvred by the US. On a long-term basis, however, Kissinger failed to acknowledge that the then main interest of the Soviet Union in the Middle East derived from its growing aspiration to political parity with its fellow superpower and its wish to maintain a world role. The Arabs' interest in the Soviet Union derived primarily from their quest to offset the Israeli military advantage which the US was helping to maintain. The rough and ready classification of the Arab states into pro-American, and therefore moderate, and pro-Soviet, and therefore radical, contradicted the realities of the Middle East political arena. If the Arabs had to be classified at that period, they fell into only one category: that of opposition to foreign domination and in favour of their own national interests. As Professor Arnold Toynbee put it:

The question is whether the Arabs are going to attain their acceptable objectives with the good will and assistance of the West or whether they are going to attain them in the teeth of Western opposition, thanks to Russian support. The way in which they will win decides whether they join our or the Russian camp.[36]

Where Professor Toynbee could have been wrong was in assuming that the Arabs wanted to join either camp. While showing positive neutrality between the two superpowers, they basically wanted to achieve a long-lasting peace in their area and what they termed a just and honourable settlement with Israel. They differed over how to achieve this, but they all agreed that no such settlement was possible if the Soviet Union was totally excluded.

If Kissinger had wanted a long-lasting peace, he would have seen that there was little prospect of achieving it and certainly no hope of ending the escalating arms race without the co-operation of the Kremlin, at least in ensuring the provision of effective guarantees for an eventual over-all settlement. One could therefore conclude that Kissinger was not aiming at a real and lasting peace in the Middle East, but only a relatively stable but illusory status quo[37] through which the Arabs could be nurtured into a state of dependence on the US, while Israel's supremacy over all the Arab states combined would be guaranteed. In this aim he did succeed to a considerable extent. Most of the so-called moderate Arab states, like Egypt and those of the Gulf, are still held in the grip of this illusion.

Kissinger insisted that step-by-step diplomacy would eventually create a momentum for peace. But his open-ended piecemeal method had no built-in mechanism for further development, as was rightly pointed out by the Brookings Report of 1975.[38] Until recently, when he revived something akin to the 'leopard-spot' arrangement,[39] he had never stated clearly in public the shape of the final settlement he was seeking, particularly in regard to the crucial question of territory. He should have faced the fact that the issues between the Arabs and Israel went beyond the disengagement of forces. The Palestinian problem that had caused five wars in the Middle East since the establishment of the state of Israel was not the issue he was out to solve. When Harold Saunders, then Deputy Assistant Secretary of State for Near Eastern and South Asian Affairs, indicated before a House of Representatives Sub-committee on 12 November 1975 that the Palestinian dimension of the Arab–Israeli conflict was the heart of the problem and that it was necessary to take the legitimate interests of the Palestinian Arabs into account in any peace negotiations, Kissinger dismissed his statement as an academic exercise.[40] The Palestinian problem still awaits a solution today.

The destruction of the sort of Arab co-ordination shown by Syria and Egypt in initiating the 1973 war, and the blunting of the oil weapon which the Arabs used during the war, were the immediate issues that dominated Kissinger's thinking. He succeeded in achieving both. The Arabs know it. OPEC knows it too, as former Prime Minister Badran has said:

The seeds of fragmentation that plague the Arab world were sown by Dr Kissinger at a time when the Arabs were vulnerable. He managed to disarm the Arabs of the effective oil weapon. Within OPEC it is believed that Kissinger was responsible not only for its disarray, but also for what we see in the oil market today: Dr Kissinger galvanized Sadat's imagination to the extent of hypnosis. Sadat started nagging the Arabs to stop brandishing the oil weapon, as Kissinger insisted. Kissinger was working at the same time on King Feisal of Saudi Arabia. He was pleading and threatening. 'We will make the value of your oil useless', he kept warning. Using a carrot and stick policy, he also threatened to stop his mediatory efforts on the Syrian front if King Feisal did not lift the oil embargo. Sadat pleaded with the King to do so. 'Please do not make me return the sword of oil into its sheath before it fulfils its purposes, because if I do so, it will never be drawn effectively again', King Feisal answered. But the military situation orchestrated by Kissinger during the October war and the insistence of Sadat who put his whole trust in his newly acquired friend Henry led to the return of the sword of oil into its own sheath never to be drawn effectively again . . . Both the ineffective oil weapon and the situation of the oil market today are the outcome of Kissinger's designs. And this is well known inside OPEC. As far as Egypt and Syria were concerned, there was no misunderstanding between them until Kissinger interfered. The fragmentation was imposed. It was imported by the hand of Kissinger.[41]

To examine the oil market, the conduct of the 1973 war, or the extent of the discord between Assad of Syria and Sadat of Egypt is not the purpose of this book. Nevertheless, one might comment that the meticulously planned and co-ordinated war launched by Syria and Egypt on 6 October started to go wrong before Kissinger's shuttle diplomacy even began. It may have started as early as the second day of the war when the Egyptian forces stopped advancing. Egypt must have concealed from its partner the limited and essentially political nature of its war aims. It wanted a war limited to breaking the stalemate and activating diplomatic efforts to solve the Middle East conflict. Syria wanted total recovery of territory. Kissinger admitted his role in orchestrating the war from Washington, ensuring that Israel had more than adequate supplies of ammunition. Catching Sadat in the state of mind described by Abu Odeh earlier, he started to work on him, as he later boasted:

> We have emerged as the pivotal factor in the diplomacy. Egypt was beginning to move in our direction thereby creating an incentive for radical Arabs to re-examine the premises of their diplomacy. All this had been achieved while we stood by our friends in Israel.[42]

Kissinger did not promise the international community success at the Geneva Conference; he promised dedication in achieving a new relationship among the Middle Eastern countries which would make war less likely. But, by pledging the US not to negotiate with the PLO except under certain conditions, he set in place the horns of the future American dilemma in the Middle East. Although stateless, militarily defeated by many parties and divided, the umbrella organization of the PLO established itself after the Rabat decision as a powerful pressure group with an international network of representation and political influence. And, as the voice of Palestinian identity, it remains a central actor in the region capable of either blocking or legitimizing any political settlement.

Senator Fulbright summed up Kissinger's achievements as 'No more than a very modest gain at best, purchased at an exceptionally high cost.'[43] If Senator Fulbright was thinking of the financial cost borne by the US, this did not worry Kissinger. 'We must show Israel compassion and maybe even affection, or else we might harass it into emotional and psychic collapse. Israel could scarcely avoid panic and might pre-empt US pressure', he explained. In the same tone Golda Meir carried the point further: 'The sense of abandonment would increase desperation and the capacity for irrational behaviour.'[44] *Davar*, the Israeli newspaper, elaborated further: 'Jerusalem seems to believe that if rational arguments fail, we must threaten with irrational behaviour in order to discourage the world, especially the US, from putting pressure on us.'[45] This rationale still prevails today, backed by the US perception, or misperception, that Israel will be more forthcoming in an atmosphere of security induced by steadfast American aid.

But this substantial American aid has not produced the desired result. At one point Israel led a later Secretary of State, Alexander Haig, to complain to the Jordanian government, 'We created a monster in the area difficult to contain.'[46] It led former Jordanian Foreign Minister, Marwan Al Qassem, to comment, 'Needless to say that throughout history, policies of appeasement of aggressors have never worked. Such policies enhance the aggressor's appetite. Only a forceful and firm stance would put an end to such a course of action'.[47]

PART I Jordan in the Carter Middle East policy

3 Carter picks up the threads

President Carter inherited a foreign policy 'stalemated on the level of power, and excessively cynical on the level of principles'. Spurred by his proclaimed commitment to human rights, he saw no reasonable hope for a settlement of the Middle Eastern question without a homeland for the Palestinians.[1] In frequent speeches he stressed that the type of settlement he envisaged would require an Israeli withdrawal to approximately the pre-1967 borderlines and the setting up of a Palestinian entity. Thus, at Aswan in Egypt, he declared on 4 January 1978 to the whole people of the Middle East,

There must be a resolution of the Palestinian problem in all its aspects. The problem must recognize the legitimate rights of the Palestinian people and enable the Palestinians to participate in the determination of their own future.[2]

The Geneva conference: some working papers

Carter's first initiative was to replace Kissinger's previous step-by-step approach with a comprehensive one. It involved a multilateral peace effort with all the leading protagonists, including the Soviet Union, taking part, in order to deal collectively with the full range of issues on the basis of the implementation of Security Council Resolution 242 as a single package. The venue envisaged was Geneva, where the previous attempt at peace-making had been stalled by Kissinger. Leading up to this the US produced three statements. The major one issued in conjunction with the Soviet Union, which had co-chaired the previous Geneva Conference, was published on 1 October 1977. It stressed the need for the Palestinian people to be represented in the negotiations and the objective of restoring their legitimate rights; the necessity of Israeli withdrawal from territories occupied in the 1967 conflict; the need for a termination of the state of war and the establishment of normal peaceful relations on the basis of mutual recognition of the principles of sovereignty, territorial integrity and political independence by all states in the region, with the establishment of demilitarized zones manned by UN troops or observers and the provision of international guarantees by the two superpowers. A deal could be envisaged in which the

33

US acquiesced in accepting, for the first time, the concept of Palestinian 'legitimate rights' as opposed to 'interests', and the Soviet Union agreed to the concept of 'normal peaceful relations' as the goal of the negotiations, with no reference to the PLO and acceptance of the term 'withdrawal from territories' as opposed to 'all territories'. Both the Arab and the Israeli sides objected to some points. The US therefore declared that approval of the statement was not a pre-condition for attendance at Geneva and that the statement was binding only on the two superpowers.

The Soviet Union, however tried to appease the Arabs by producing its own agenda for the conference, which was strikingly different from the US–Soviet statement. It included a demand for Israeli withdrawal from *all* Arab territories occupied in 1967, for the achievement of the Palestinians' inalienable right to self-determination and to the establishment of their own state, and for PLO participation in the conference. The Americans, on the other hand, tried to appease the Israelis by presenting a joint Israeli–American working paper on 13 October, all of whose items were published. Jordan, however, received an additional explanation clarifying that the question of a Palestinian entity would not be excluded from the discussions at Geneva. The published items depicted the mechanics of the Geneva Conference as follows:

(i)   The Arab parties were to be represented by a unified Arab delegation, which would include Palestinians. After the opening sessions, the conference was to split into working groups.

(ii) The working groups for the negotiation and conclusion of peace treaties were to be as follows: Egypt–Israel; Jordan–Israel; Lebanon–Israel. (Lebanon could join the conference when it so requested.)

(iii) The West Bank and Gaza issues were to be discussed in a working group to consist of Israel, Jordan, Egypt and the Palestinians.

(iv) The problem of Arab and Jewish refugees was to be discussed in accordance with terms to be agreed upon.

(v)   The agreed basis for the negotiations at the conference were UN Security Council Resolutions 242 and 338.[3]

From this statement, it was clear that the word 'Palestinian' had been decided upon rather than 'prominent or non-prominent' members of the PLO, that the Palestinian representatives were to be chosen on a personal basis or from a list put forward by the Arab states, and that the invitation to participate would be issued through the office of the UN Secretary General. Secretary of State Vance assured Jordan during a visit to Amman that not only were the Palestinians to be chosen by the Arabs but also that the Palestinian question was to be discussed in the context of a link with Jordan. He stressed that the focus would be on Palestinian self-determination and not on the PLO, and that Israel would not object to self-determination if it knew in advance that the Palestinians would not opt for the PLO and an independent Palestinian state, but for a relationship with Jordan. He further warned that the Palestinian representatives should be acceptable to Israel and that the PLO should not be mentioned at all so as not to give Israel an excuse to boycott the conference.[4]

Classifed as top secret, the third US document was a draft statement of American principles, which was given to all parties during Vance's trip to the Middle East in August 1977. It envisaged the following:

(i) Comprehensive peace negotiations based on Resolutions 242 and 338 leading to the termination of the state of war and the establishment of normal peaceful relations between Israel and its Arab neighbours.

(ii) Withdrawal as called for by Resolution 242 to be mutually agreed in a way that ensured secure and recognized boundaries.

(iii) The withdrawal, and the establishment of peaceful relations, to be phased in over a period of years in parallel synchronized stages.

(iv) The security of the stages and of the final settlement to be ensured by arrangements agreed by the parties.

(v) A settlement that would include provision for a Palestinian entity and for the means of ensuring Palestinian adherence to the terms of a peace treaty – the Palestinian entity to be demilitarized, with provisions for open economic and social relations with Israel. And a way to be sought to permit self-determination by the Palestinians of their future.[5]

This unpublished statement underlined the American understanding of the extent of Israeli withdrawal, namely, not from all the territories occupied in 1967, which was how the Arabs understood Resolution 242, but rather, as agreed with the Soviet Union in the joint statement, from territories occupied, provided that this withdrawal was mutually agreed by the parties concerned. Also, the legitimate rights of the Palestinians referred to in the superpower joint statement were interpreted by the Americans privately as a Palestinian entity not necessarily federated to Jordan, as Vance stated to the Jordanians, but one that applied an open-door policy towards Israel. According to the Americans, such an entity would not be objected to by Israel. Prior discussions between the Israeli and US parties, particularly between President Carter and Prime Minister Begin in Washington on 19 July 1977, underlined the different interpretations and preferences and the extent of agreement or disagreement between the two parties.[6]

In response to the US statement Jordan's position was as follows. First, that the provision regarding withdrawal must state explicitly that this would be from all the territories occupied in June 1967, and that the new borders would be on the lines of the pre-1967 situation, with minor rectifications only as dictated by practical considerations and on a reciprocal basis. Second, that, during the process of implementation and the negotiations preceding it, no measures must be taken by the occupying power which would have the effect of changing the physical, demographic or cultural character of the occupied areas. Third, a provision must be added concerning Jerusalem; East Jerusalem would return to Arab sovereignty but ways and means could be devised to maintain the unity of Jerusalem, with freedom of access to and worship in all the holy places guaranteed. Fourth, the principle of the right of the Palestinian refugees to repatriation and compensation according to the UN resolutions must be reaffirmed. Fifth, the reference to self-determination must be clarified; Jordan's preference was for a transitional, neutral international regime in the occupied Palestinian territories during which elections to decide the political leadership and the future status of the area would be conducted. And sixth, that there were no Jewish refugees as such; that is, there were no Jewish refugees who had been driven out of the Arab countries. All Jews living in the Arab countries who chose to go to Israel did so of their own free will, and could return whenever they chose. No resolution had ever been issued by the UN referring to the existence of Jewish refugees, although there were abundant resolutions referring to the Palestinians driven out of Palestine as refugees.[7]

Private and bilateral deliberations

The PLO

The Palestinian Liberation Organization rejected the US–Israeli working paper in its entirety on the grounds that Resolution 242 alone was not adequate to solve the Palestinian problem in all its aspects. Its shortcomings, as seen by the PLO, had been rectified when the UN General Assembly issued Resolutions 3236 of 22 November 1974 and 3376 of 10 November 1975, both of which specified the right of the PLO to deal with any issue concerning the Palestinians, and to participate in peace negotiations on an equal footing.

The PLO's thinking had been elaborated in official talks in Amman on 23 February 1977 where the need was stressed for a distinct Palestinian identity until the occupied lands were restored and legitimate Palestinian rights were realized on Palestinian soil. 'The emergence of a distinct Palestinian identity would help the emergence of the Palestinian part of the equation', Khalid Al Fahoum, head of the PLO delegation, indicated. He therefore insisted on the priority of establishing a Palestinian authority on any land liberated, affirming in the process the existence of a Palestinian people, something previously denied by Israel, specifically by Golda Meir. Fahoum argued that

Israel's absorption of Palestinian Arab lands in 1948 had been an occupation, and part of the process of establishing its own state. But its absorption of Arab lands after 1967, including the West Bank and Gaza, was an imperialist process. Therefore, he said, 'We must see to it that Israel's domination of Arab lands in 1967 remains imperialist rather than being transformed into an annexationist one as well.'[8]

As far as the Geneva Conference was concerned, the PLO set out its demands as follows: that it should be invited to the conference from the outset on an equal footing with all other parties, as the sole legitimate representative of the Palestinian people. Its presence under these conditions was seen as vital because, alone among all the Arabs attending, it was the party directly involved in the Arab–Israeli conflict over Palestine.

On 26 July 1977 a message reached the White House from the PLO, indicating that it was prepared to live in peace with Israel and there would be 'no possibility of two meanings'. Yasser Arafat was to make this clear in a public statement, as well as in his private commitment to President Carter. In return, however, the PLO wanted the US to commit itself to an independent Palestinian 'state/unit/entity', which could be linked to Jordan. Carter's reaction was to note on the message: 'If the PLO publicly and privately meets minimum requirement of Kissinger–Israeli commitment, we will begin discussions with them.'

A further development took place in the last week of August when the administration received a second message from the PLO sent on the eve of its Central Committee meeting in Damascus. This implied that Arafat would agree to Resolution 242 if the US would make certain private commitments concerning the role of the PLO in future negotiations. Carter's reaction was to note on the message that the US could not certify that the PLO represented the Palestinian people as Arafat had requested.[9]

Looking at these two statements in retrospect, one has grounds for thinking that Carter had missed a vital opportunity for peace.

Israel

In an attempt to suppress the Palestinian identity affirmed by the PLO, Israel refused to contemplate the presence of any PLO member, prominent or not, at the Geneva Conference.

Secretary of State Vance clarified Israel's position during his talks with a Jordanian delegation in Washington on 24 September 1977. On the one hand, he put forward the Israeli claim that no annexational process was being undertaken on the West Bank and Gaza. On the other, he saw Israel's denial of any foreign domination on the West Bank and Gaza as specifically the denial of Arab domination; what Israel was ready to contemplate was the administration of the two areas in a way that gave the Arabs control only of such everyday affairs as municipal services. Asked what Israel intended, Vance said:

First, negotiation with Jordan; second, negotiation with the leaders of the West Bank and Gaza; third, the administration to be only by Israel. Fourth, only services such as health and education would be permitted to be administered by Jordan or the leaders of the West Bank and Gaza. Fifth, as far as military matters were concerned, there would be a need for military posts at well scattered positions which would not affect the every day life of the population. Sixth, the River Jordan was to be the border between Israel and the Hashemite Kingdom of Jordan.[10]

Vance found these proposals contradictory and he told the Jordanian delegation so.

Israel was also apprehensive about the idea of a joint Arab delegation in Geneva. It contemplated the presence of such a delegation only at the ceremonial opening session, which would immediately break up into individual working groups to discuss bilateral issues, provided that the Palestinians were represented within the Jordanian delegation.[11] Israel wanted the negotiations to take place on a government-to-government basis, according to each specific issue involved. It regarded the Geneva Conference as a continuous process within whose framework negotiations could take place in different forms and, if necessary, in different places, according to the aspect of the problem involved.[12]

Israel's basic fears about a Geneva-type conference, or any form of international conference, were summed up by Professor Stanley Hoffman as follows.[13] First, that when all the Arab opponents of Israel were under the same roof, there would be a premium on intransigence; the toughest would set the norm, as they had at Rabat. Second, the step-by-step approach would only postpone the most difficult problem – that of the PLO – which would be the first to surface at Geneva, thus wrecking the conference or at least putting Israel on the spot straightaway over an issue that was domestically explosive. Third, Geneva would re-introduce the USSR into the equation. One of the great merits of the step-by-step approach in Israeli eyes had been that it kept the 'Soviet devil' out. Fourth, in Geneva, the differences in priorities between the US and Israel – already implicit in the step-by-step process – would become explicit. A US on good terms not only with Israel but with several Arab states as well might put even stronger pressure on Israel to reach a settlement. Following this logic from its first articulation in 1977, Shamir was to tell the UN General Assembly on 2 October 1985:

An international conference was a means of evading direct negotiations. It would be a stage for hostile and extreme propaganda and would not serve the cause of peace. Our aim should be the achievement of a bilaterally negotiated peace between our two countries, Jordan and Israel.[14]

Jordan in the tug of war between Syria and Egypt

For Jordan, the Geneva Conference was the right way to fulfil its political aim of obtaining a just, durable and comprehensive peaceful solution with Israel. It therefore saw the necessity for proper preparations, including a united Arab stand and agreement on the items of the agenda. This was the pre-condition for the implementation of a complete Israeli withdrawal from all the territories occupied since 1967 and the guarantee of Palestinian rights, including the right to a Palestinian state in the West Bank and Gaza, as the price for ending the state of war and the signing of peace agreements with Israel.

Syria went along with Jordan's line of thinking, but Egypt dissented. 'It was not the working paper that defined my going to Geneva. I am committed to two principles; Israeli withdrawal and a Palestinian state. So I go to Geneva, confront everybody, put on the pressure and corner Israel', President Sadat declared confidently.[15] He did not seem anxious about knowing in advance where the Americans stood. Although he may have been keen on a private reassurance from President Carter, he recognized the domestic political problems involved in any prior US announcement that Israel ought to withdraw and a Palestinian state be established. Nevertheless he reiterated to the Arabs that it would cripple their stand to take US impotence for granted. Unlike the Soviet Union, the US appeared to Sadat to hold nearly all the cards. The Arabs therefore had to put their trust in the US alone, because it was only under the US umbrella that Israel could be brought to offer anything in return for peace. At the same time he admitted that the US might be unprepared to put any pressure on the Israelis, and that both of them were insisting on bilateral negotiations in order to extract from the Arabs individually what they could not get from them collectively.

It was to avoid just such an outcome that Syria and Jordan joined forces in insisting that the Arabs must go to Geneva as a joint delegation under the auspices of the Arab League, provided that the delegation included PLO members, or Palestinians from the Palestinian National Council (PNC) or others nominated and accepted by the PLO. Jordan in particular was ready to go to Geneva only in the role of a front-line state which was shouldering the legal responsibility for the West Bank on its own, which because of its geographic position had a stake in the security arrangements of the area, and which had taken part in the previous Geneva Conference on the basis of its acceptance of UN Resolutions 242 and 338 and that part of its territory had been occupied. Nevertheless, in deference to the Rabat Decision of 1974 and UN Resolutions 3236 and 3376, it backed the PLO's participation from the outset as the sole legitimate representative of the Palestinian people. Jordan could not see itself, let alone Egypt, representing the Palestinian refugees in

Syria, Lebanon and elsewhere. It therefore left even the border rectification issue in the hands of the PLO.

Both Syria and Jordan concentrated not only on who would represent the Palestinians from among the Palestinians themselves, but also on ways and means of obtaining a commitment to recognize Palestinian rights at Geneva. To overcome the procedural issues raised by the US, neither country saw any harm in issuing one invitation only, to a single Arab delegation, which would then choose the Palestinian representatives in co-ordination with the PLO. The main problem was seen not in the actual invitation of the PLO, but in its recognition as the sole legitimate representative of the Palestinian people.

One point of contention between Jordan and Syria, on the one hand, and Egypt on the other, went beyond the representation of the PLO. Sadat not only insisted that the PLO's direct involvement at Geneva, as an independent delegation, would wreck the conference, but he also demanded working committees organized along Israeli–American lines, namely on the basis of geography rather than subjects. While Syria and Jordan preferred functional groups, on the grounds that the Middle East problem was indivisible, Sadat seemed reluctant to allow the other Arabs to join in discussion of what he regarded as Egyptian affairs. Jordan and Syria insisted that discussions on withdrawal and borders, on peace guarantees, and on the Palestinian people's future, whether in the West Bank, Gaza or elsewhere, should be held in a collective context, whether in plenary or committee sessions. Only strictly bilateral questions – such as the Yarmouk River and navigation rights – should be discussed in a bilateral context. They believed that discussions on a geographic basis would divide the cause. As the Jordanian Prime Minister put it to President Carter in Washington on 28 July 1977, 'A unified Arab attitude on a unified cause – the Palestinian question – would help the Arabs to present decisions or withdraw from previously held attitudes and positions; hence it would be more beneficial to Israel because it would be faced with a unified Arab commitment to any future outcome.'[16]

As far as relations between the Palestinians and the Jordanians were concerned, the Prime Minister told Cyrus Vance on 24 September that fraternal relations should continue, with the type of relationship to be decided after liberation, on the basis of a referendum among both peoples. Asked by a Soviet delegation visiting Amman on 3 July 1977 if Jordan would mind if the choice was a Palestinian state, the Prime Minister answered, 'If the Palestinians so choose, they will be within their rights. If the choice was a special relationship with Jordan, it is for both peoples to decide. Self-determination is on. It is an international norm.'[17]

Another point of contention between Jordan, Syria and Egypt was revealed later by former Prime Minister Mudar Badran.[18] In 1977, he suggested to King Hussain the idea of an Arab rather than a Jordanian umbrella for the

PLO in Geneva. The King agreed and none of the Arab countries voiced any objections, much to the surprise of Secretary of State Vance. It became clear later, however, that President Sadat was not deeply committed to this idea. He led King Hussain to believe that he would never go it alone or abandon his aim of regaining all occupied Arab lands, and that he would see to it that the Palestinians eventually exercised their right to self-determination. As Badran put it, 'The Geneva tactics were hidden from all of us. Sadat favoured the international umbrella as the means to an essentially bilateral arrangement.' He went on to describe King Hussain's shock when he discovered Sadat's intentions:

King Hussain went to Syria to discuss the joint Arab delegation. Assad gave him an absolutely free hand to speak for Syria to Egypt and Saudi Arabia, on one condition, namely that the King would organize a meeting of the three of them, Sadat, Assad and King Hussain, for the purpose of forcing Sadat to sign an agreement never to go it alone . . . As Prime Minister and Foreign Minister at the time, I accompanied the King to Saudi Arabia, where he asked King Khalid to be the witness. King Khalid agreed but suggested Sadat should not be told in advance about the idea behind the meeting, but only after he arrived in Riyadh. It seemed that King Khalid shared Assad's suspicions about the genuineness of Sadat's intentions . . . Sadat did not join us. So we went along to Egypt. At Sadat's house, King Hussain expressed the wish of Jordan, Syria and Saudi Arabia to organize a joint Arab delegation. Sadat was furious. He nearly jumped out of his chair. 'Me? Going to Geneva under a Ba'thist?' – meaning Assad of Syria – 'I would never be under the command of a Ba'thist in a unified Arab delegation' . . . His undiplomatic language astonished King Hussain. I stayed silent as Sadat began to wipe his face. Under the table, I noticed his legs shaking nervously. Then, at an appropriate moment, I asked him, 'Mr President, you and Assad were comrades in arms. We did not share this honour with you during the October war of 1973. Didn't you know, then, that Assad was a Ba'thist? Or was it all right then for a Ba'thist to share your war aims?'

According to Badran, Sadat could find no answer. 'When I suggested a meeting for the three confrontation states, Syria, Jordan and Egypt, at Aqaba in Jordan to put in order a working agenda, he gave us loads of excuses . . . King Hussain watched in pain. Since then and ever since, we believed that Sadat was up to something. It became clear when he torpedoed Geneva by going to Jerusalem.'

Syria was quicker to evaluate Sadat and the prospects for Geneva. While Sadat saw Syria as intransigent, and interpreted this as an excuse not to attend or even to wreck Geneva, Assad suspected, from the outset, that there was a secret agreement between Israel, Egypt and the US to use the comprehensive approach of Geneva to produce a bilateral arrangement. In any case, he was convinced that President Carter would not be able to resist the Zionist pressure at home and abroad for long, and would not therefore be able to honour the joint Soviet–American statement of 1 October 1977. Thus, for Assad, Geneva was a waste of time and effort, unless the US showed some sign beforehand of readiness to put pressure on Israel. He did not regret his initial rejection of the joint US–Israeli working paper because, as far as the Golan Heights were concerned, he believed that they would be returned only after the Palestinian issue was solved, and not vice versa.[19]

Carter reviews the difficulties

In the official US–Jordanian talks held in Washington on 24 and 28 September 1977, the US saw the outline of the difficulties ahead as follows:

(a) Disagreement between the US and Israel (i) on the status of the West Bank and Gaza, which the US regarded as occupied territories, falling under the jurisdiction of Resolution 242, while Israel regarded them as part of Israel; (ii) on how to discuss the future of the Palestinians. While the US had come round to the Arab point of view on the need to discuss it collectively, Israel insisted on discussing it with Jordan alone. President Carter appreciated the difficulties that could face King Hussain if he embarked on such discussions faced by Israel on the one hand and watched by the Arabs on the other, and he understood the need for Jordanian–Palestinian co-ordination before embarking on any such discussions; (iii) over the idea of a joint Arab delegation. While both sides initially saw the merits of a ceremonial opening session leading to working groups, the US came to believe that there were common issues that had to be discussed collectively. While of the view that Egypt could be persuaded to join an Arab delegation, Vance stated solemnly that the US had to confront Israel; even an invitation to the Arab League, as he put it, would infuriate Israel.

(b) Agreement between the US and Israel on the necessity of discussing border issues bilaterally between Israel and the individual Arab states concerned. The US appreciated the problem that would arise for instance if Sadat offered concessions, and Syria insisted on not giving up an inch of occupied Arab territory on any front. Thus the US appealed to the Arabs for moderation and flexibility.

(c) The major obstacle was representation of the Palestinians without the PLO, particularly in view of Kissinger's pledge to the Israelis not to talk to the PLO except under certain conditions. President Carter declared to the Jordanians on 28 September 1977, 'I find it extremely difficult to change the policies of my predecessors.[20]

The talks may not have reflected the developments that actually took place in Washington. William Quandt of the American team put forward this point of view:

In the course of September 1977, Geneva was to be the umbrella under which Sadat and Begin could move forward at whatever pace they could sustain, pulling in their wake, if possible, Jordan, the Palestinians and perhaps even the Syrians. Insofar as they thought Geneva would be little more than a figleaf for another separate Egyptian–Israeli agreement – Sinai III – they had little reason to go along. Yet if their demands for a virtual veto over Egyptian moves were accepted, no progress could be made in negotiations. To resolve the dilemma, the US tried to resort to some constructive obfuscation, giving each party the impression that its concerns were being met. The Egyptians and Israelis were assured that the actual negotiations would be conducted bilaterally. The Syrians, Jordanians and Palestinians were told that there would be a single Arab delegation and that they would have to work out their own negotiation strategy to prevent bilateral deals at the expense of a comprehensive agreement. The Arabs were told that the PLO could be present within the Arab delegation, provided the actual delegates were not well-known officials. At the same time the Israelis were told that they would have the right to object to any new participants, as agreed at the first session of the Geneva Conference in 1973.[21]

This 'constructive obfuscation' proved counterproductive. Deadlock set in with no substantial change from 28 February 1977 when Waldheim submitted a report, under General Assembly Resolution 31/62 outlining the contradictory positions of the PLO and the Arab states, on the one hand, and Israel, on the other, as well as the difficulties surrounding the agenda and programme. As to the major obstacle – the participation of the PLO and the representation of the interests and rights of the Palestinian people – the report stressed the intractability of the problem 'without certain changes in attitudes on all sides [involving] mutual recognition of the legitimacy of the claims of the different parties, in suitable forms and with adequate guarantees, and an effort on all sides to define more clearly the shape of an ultimate peace settlement in the Middle East'.

Sadat's trip to Jerusalem

There was no air of expectation when, on 9 November 1977, President Sadat addressed the annual opening of the Egyptian Parliament. It was just another routine speech, and it remained that way until close to the end, when he informed his audience that he was ready 'to go to the ends of the earth if this will prevent one soldier, one officer among my sons from being wounded – not being killed – just wounded . . . I am ready to go to their own House, to the Knesset itself to talk to them.'[22]

The words were spoken casually, without emphasis. Few of his audience grasped their momentous import. Yet with these words, Sadat had launched the biggest gamble for peace in modern Arab history. Four days later, at a reception for a French delegation to Tel Aviv, Begin announced his government's official invitation to the President of Egypt to come to Jerusalem to conduct talks about a permanent peace between Israel and

43

Egypt. On 16 November Sadat went to Damascus to persuade his partner in the 1973 war that the visit to Jerusalem was the right course to follow. Assad warned him of the violent Arab reaction he would have to face, and the following day, the Syrian government and the ruling Ba'th party issued a joint statement criticizing the proposed visit as an 'unfortunate initiative that is fatal to the Arab nation'.[23]

Three days later Sadat addressed the Knesset. On 25 December, Begin became the first Israeli Prime Minister to be officially received in an Arab country, when he held two days of talks with Sadat in Ismailia. Begin brought with him what amounted to a separate peace agreement with Egypt, together with a skeleton proposal for limited self-rule in the West Bank and Gaza – a proposal which did not come up to Sadat's expectations. The summit meeting reached an impasse, as did the parallel ministerial negotiations on the Palestinian issue. During the subsequent months, the military and political committees established by the Ismailia summit tried in vain to resolve the differences, and Sadat recalled the Egyptian delegation in protest. Attempts by the US to secure a resumption of the talks were unsuccessful. Deadlock seemed again to have set in.

At the time, Sadat gave no impression of being willing to abandon the Arab cause. In a speech to the Egyptian Parliament on 26 November on his return from Jerusalem he asserted that his visit had not resulted in the relinquishing of any of the Arab world's legal or historical rights and that Egypt had no intention of concluding a separate peace with Israel. Egyptian official radio declared, 'Egypt remains firmly committed to the strategic aims of the Arab world, and the purpose of the visit to Jerusalem was to unmask the true face of Israel which presents itself as a true lover of peace.' And there was a trend of Arab thinking which saw the aim of Sadat's trip as 'to show the Israelis that their extermination complex was out of date, that the Jewish state could no longer exploit the Arab rejection of its existence to annex territories in the name of secure frontiers'.[24] It was believed that Israel would have to respond positively.

From the various official Arab statements issued in response to the visit, three main camps can be clearly detected. First, the governments of Morocco, Oman and Sudan which explicitly supported the initiative and welcomed any such opportunity for peace. Second, those led by Syria, including Libya, South Yemen, Iraq, Algeria and the PLO, which rejected it outright. And third, those which, though opposed to the visit, remained somewhat ambiguous. Thus, the reactions of Jordan, Saudi Arabia, Tunisia and the United Arab Emirates were surprisingly mild – 'wait and see', 'surprise' and the need 'to be very careful in reacting to the visit'. They seemed to be taking a middle position which called for wisdom and patience, in the hope that Sadat would achieve something to which they could eventually subscribe.

These achievements failed to materialize. Begin seemed aware that it had been weakness, and even desperation, which had driven Sadat to Jerusalem. 'For Begin', wrote Uri Avineri, a member of the Knesset, 'the visit was a gift from heaven. It was handed to him on a silver platter. It was Sadat who initiated it and paid the full price for it, endangering his life and his regime, and who gave Israel an invaluable prize: full recognition of her existence and legitimacy. What did Begin pay? Nothing at all.'[25]

The official Jordanian reaction to the line taken by Sadat in his speech to the Knesset was favourable. The Information Minister stated that the speech had eliminated many fears and doubts and that the visit had broken the ice and removed the psychological barrier. But was this enough without a well-planned stategy? King Hussain thought that there must have been such a strategy, and he was determined to find out what it was. Soon after Sadat's return to Cairo, he set off via Damascus, and with Assad's backing, to find out what agreements had been achieved behind the scenes. In the words of his Prime Minister, the King was stunned to find that Sadat had gone to Jerusalem without a single plan in his head, without a diplomatic deal behind the scenes, without something . . . anything, in return. He went off just to break the stalemate and to embarrass Israel.

Was President Sadat being naive, a clown, as Kissinger dubbed him when they first met, or shrewd, a man of vision, imagination and trust, as Kissinger described him later? Was he an egoist or a visionary, a brazen opportunist or the most accomplished of tacticians? At that particular juncture it was not clear. But his determination not to admit failure was unmistakable. Urging the international community to play its part he said, 'The Egyptian initiative is no longer just Egyptian, it has become an historic act which the whole world has acclaimed, and no one can erase it from the history of the world.'[26]

By the 'world' Sadat meant the United States. After watching the deadlock following the Cairo and Ismailia talks of December 1977 and the Jerusalem talks of January 1978 between Egypt and Israel, President Carter must have realized that Sadat's Jerusalem trip was not likely to achieve positive results without a strong American involvement. By then, the Geneva Conference had dwindled to a remote possibility, and by February 1978 the world concept of a comprehensive peace in the Middle East had begun to fade, to be replaced by that of a partial solution between Egypt and Israel with some kind of transitional arrangement for the West Bank and Gaza. To help develop a closer relationship with Sadat, Carter invited him to Camp David on 4 February, but their joint Plan of Action failed to lead to any improvement in the Israeli–Egyptian peacemaking as did the American–Israeli–Egyptian talks in July.[27] Carter then took the decision to invite both Sadat and Begin to Camp David on 5 September 1978.

4 The Camp David accords and Jordan

Camp David: wheeling and dealing

Three determined leaders, Begin, Sadat and Carter, met at Camp David between 5 and 17 September 1978, to shape the Accords (for details see Appendix A).

Begin was determined to achieve a separate peace with Egypt that was in no way connected to a home rule arrangement in the West Bank and Gaza. Sadat was committed to fundamental Egyptian interests and the promotion of some sort of success on the Palestinian question. 'I am committed to my speech delivered in the Knesset. It is the Egyptian plan', he declared before his departure for Washington. But that was not the case. Since February 1978, both Carter and Sadat seemed to be thinking of an Egyptian–Israeli Accord only loosely connected to an attempt to negotiate an agreement on the Palestinian question. It was when Sadat proved reluctant to put forward a clear proposal on the West Bank and Gaza that Carter concluded that his real interest was a bilateral Egyptian–Israeli deal. Linkage, Carter began to think, was not that important and, in any event, it should not obstruct the search for a bilateral agreement.[1]

Carter was committed to a positive political achievement that would do credit to his personal involvement, to advancing US interests, and to Israel as a strategic ally. 'Our number one commitment in the Middle East is to protect the right of Israel to exist, to exist permanently and to exist in peace', he declared early on in his term of office.[2] At Camp David President Carter was subjected to a great deal of pressure and counter-pressure.[3]

Since I had made our nation's commitment to human rights a central tenet of our foreign policy, it was impossible for me to ignore the very serious problems on the West Bank . . . Whenever we explored the question of how to involve the Palestinians, Israel objected very strongly. Yet somehow, the plight of these people had to be addressed if there were ever to be a permanent peace . . . The majority of nations recognized the PLO as the representative of the Palestinian people. In international circles the PLO was making great progress . . . But Kissinger had promised Israel not to recognize or negotiate with the PLO and I had confirmed this commitment and always honoured it.

46

His way out of these contradictions was by furthering the idea of a Palestinian identity tied to Jordan, but Begin rejected discussions on a Palestinian entity. 'Although I reminded him that any settlements established on lands occupied by military force were violations of international law, Begin was building up those enclaves as rapidly as possible to prevent the involvement of the Palestinians and Jordanians alike.'[4]

A way had to be found out of the deadlock. Throughout his memoirs Carter reports the wheeling and dealing:

Hussain agreed that the Palestinians in the West Bank and Gaza area should have self-determination but not the right to claim independence . . . The Arabs could see that any independent Palestinian state might be a focal point of radicalism, but because of the powerful political influence of the PLO in international councils and the threat of terrorist attacks, few had the temerity to depart from their original positions in public statements . . . Sadat, who had also been the linch-pin in the negotiations, believed that an independent Palestinian state, although inevitable, must have limits imposed on its independence . . . His insistence, though, on preserving the integrity of sovereignty in the Sinai made me have maximum flexibility and latitude in the West Bank and Gaza. But as Begin would contemplate only limited self-rule, I agreed to find a 'synonym for self-government' which Sadat thought sounded too much like Begin's self-rule.[5]

At Camp David, therefore, it became increasingly clear, as these excerpts indicate, that the concept of Palestinian self-determination was tailored to fit the desires and requirements of the three negotiators and what were perceived as the desires of the Arab governments. With no Palestinians or Jordanians present to speak for themselves, the Accords: Framework for Peace in the Middle East and Framework for the Conclusion of a Peace Treaty between Egypt and Israel were thus hammered out.

Camp David was later elaborated by Jordan's then Prime Minister who was in close contact with what was going on and particularly with the Egyptians.[6] Before leaving for Washington, Sadat telephoned King Hussain to reaffirm his commitment to the Arab cause, and the leaders agreed to meet in Morocco after the Camp David summit. When Begin refused to contemplate the Egyptian plan, Carter leaned heavily on the weaker party in the negotiations. At one point, Sadat telephoned King Hussain, who was then in London, to announce the failure of his mission and his intention to depart immediately for Morocco. Some confusion followed when a news flash was received in Amman that the Camp David Accords had been signed. Prime Minister Badran desperately tried to get in touch with King Hussain, but the King was on his way to Morocco, as agreed with Sadat. In the event, the King never arrived in Morocco; after receiving the news through the telex service aboard his jet, he diverted his flight to Amman.

What had happened in the interim, between Sadat's telephone call to the King in London and the conclusion of the Accords, was explained to Badran by two of Sadat's associates. Ossama Al Baz, now top adviser to President Mubarak, complained that, while isolated at Camp David, Sadat never consulted his team, and that, while applying tremendous pressure on Sadat, the Americans made contact with the outside world extremely difficult. Every American surrounding Sadat, plus the US media, worked on inflating his ego. In Prime Minister Badran's words, 'Sadat floated in his own steamy world of self-esteem. And he lost touch with the realities in the Middle East.'

In an attempt to avoid political discredit and regional ostracism, Sadat emerged from Camp David with an ambiguous framework for self-rule on the West Bank and Gaza, totally unconnected with the Egyptian–Israeli Peace Treaty. His Foreign Minister, Muhammad Ibrahim Kamil, suspecting his intentions beforehand, had promised Jordan that he would resign if he felt that Sadat was steering away from a comprehensive peace. Resenting what he regarded as Sadat's surrender in the negotiations Kamil did indeed tender his resignation at Camp David.

But, at Camp David, Sadat amused the Americans by the contempt he showed for his Arab colleagues.[7] As the self-appointed Arab spokesman he did not want King Hussein to join the talks either, despite the role assigned to the latter in the Accords; as he put it, 'I refused to allow King Hussein to join us at Camp David because of his style of escalating demands and opportunism.'[8] Both Sadat and Carter seemed to think that King Hussein could eventually be forced to play the role assigned him at Camp David.

Jordan's preliminary reaction

The official statement released on 19 September after a full Cabinet meeting presented Jordan's preliminary attitudes towards the Camp David deliberations as follows:

The Government of Jordan, not being a party to the said conference, would like to re-clarify the principles that would govern Jordan's stand in evaluating the full results of the Camp David Conference and the steps and the positions that might follow:

(1) Jordan, which was referred to in several places in the Camp David documents, is neither legally nor morally bound by any obligations regarding issues which it had not participated in discussing, formulating or agreeing to.

(2) Jordan believes in a just and comprehensive solution dealing with the various aspects of the Palestinian problem and the Arab–Israeli conflict.

(3) Jordan considers separate action by any of the Arab parties – away from collective Arab responsibility, which is progress towards the achievement of a comprehensive settlement that would include restoration of the legitimate rights of the Palestinian people, on Palestinian soil and full Arab rights on all fronts – to be a weakening of the Arab position which diminishes the chances of reaching the desired, just and comprehensive solution.

(4)   Any final and just settlement acceptable to Jordan must include Israel's withdrawal from all occupied Arab territories including the Gaza Strip and the West Bank, and, in particular, the return of Arab sovereignty over Arab Jerusalem, which fell under occupation with the rest of the Arab lands occupied in June 1967.

(5)   Likewise, any just and final settlement should clearly provide for the right of the Palestinian people to self-determination in full freedom and within the framework of a peaceful comprehensive settlement which guarantees security and peace to all parties.[9]

Secretary of State Vance flew to Jordan on 20 September to provide answers to a barrage of questions related to the Accords. Unlike the Allon Plan, he tempted the Jordanians, the Accords dealt with the West Bank and Gaza as one entity.[10] But Jordan's Prime Minister was not impressed. 'Do I have to bring out all the files connected with the Geneva Conference and the comprehensive approach, to remind you of what you said and what the American stand was?' Vance replied that he remembered everything. But he also asked him not to expect the US to be more faithful to the Arabs than Sadat of Egypt . . . 'When one party says I agree, we cannot say no you don't. We cannot be more Arab than the Arabs themselves',[11] he said.

On Vance's departure, King Hussein forwarded fourteen specific questions to the American administration which President Carter answered conscientiously. The course of American diplomacy in the peace process at this time can be seen at its most dramatic and ambiguous in this exchange (see Appendix B).

Analysis

President Carter informed the Jordanians that he would undertake an active role in all the negotiations on the Palestinian question, including the West Bank and Gaza. But he committed himself only to the second accord – between Israel and Egypt.

In the event, distracted by the seizure of the American hostages in Iran, Carter never found it possible to bring decisive influence to bear on the peace negotiations. As William Quandt rightly pointed out later,[12] Carter made a number of mistakes. First, he did not assign his Secretary of State to the task, but rather a special negotiator who, no matter how skilful, was not taken as seriously abroad, nor did he have the same easy access to the Middle East leaders. In the US also, he found it difficult to mobilize the resources of the bureaucracy, and had difficulty relating details of his negotiations to a larger strategic design. Second, the timing went awry. After the Egyptian–Israeli Treaty was signed in March 1979, the US did not move quickly enough to lay the groundwork for the negotiations on Palestinian self-government. Instead

Carter let matters drift. To play the role of diplomatic broker was more complicated in the early 1980s, with the onset of presidential elections. Third, the US did not produce a negotiating text as it had done at Camp David. Experience should have shown the futility of asking Egypt and Israel to trade formal proposals. Fourth, King Hussain understandably 'felt insulted' by what he saw as a clumsy attempt to involve him in Camp David, and he turned down the invitation. And fifth, instead of half-heartedly continuing with the Camp David talks, the Carter Administration should either have made a serious attempt to reach agreement or else suspended the talks and started to consider alternatives. The pre-election period could have been used constructively to prepare the way for a new effort after the elections.

Despite periodic sputterings, the negotiations between Egypt and Israel remained in abeyance, as first the US and then Israel underwent election campaigns. Carter was defeated; Begin was safely re-elected.

President Carter did not clarify to the Jordanians who the Palestinian representatives were supposed to be. If they were to be the inhabitants of the West Bank and Gaza, as the Camp David Accords specified, the controversy surrounding their identity could have been complicated and long-drawn-out. On the one hand, Secretary of State Vance conceded in Amman that they might include PLO members living in the West Bank and Gaza. On the other, President Carter affirmed in his answers to the Jordanian questions that the Israeli settlers in the West Bank and Gaza would have to be included in the Israeli delegation. In other words, the Self-governing Authority would represent the Palestinian Arabs in the West Bank and Gaza, but the Camp David Accords referred only to the 'inhabitants'. Hence, Jordan saw President Carter officially leaving the door open for Israel to insist that the Israeli residents of the ever-expanding web of settlements were also inhabitants, and as such could claim the right to be elected as representatives to discuss self-determination, legal rights and the final status of the West Bank and Gaza.

The Palestinians of the West Bank and Gaza were only a fraction of the Palestinian people. When President Carter and the Accords mentioned 'other Palestinians as mutually agreed' to be included in the Jordanian or Egyptian delegations or both, they left unanswered who they might be. There are Palestinian refugees as a result of the 1948 and 1967 wars with Israel, and there are thousands more banished since by Israel as undesirable. There is also the main PLO body outside the occupied territories, endorsed as the sole legitimate representative of the Palestinian people. Of all these Palestinians, President Carter mentioned to the Jordanians at one point that refugees of the 1967 war could be represented in the Egyptian and Jordanian delegations, provided that Israel agreed. The Jordanians turned down the invitation to associate themselves with Camp David, and the Egyptian delegation was therefore the only party left capable of absorbing the Palestinian representatives, whoever they were to be. Even then, they would have been subjected to further limitations: Egyptian and then Israeli approval had to be obtained and any subject raised by them during negotiations required the prior approval of the Egyptian and Israeli governments/delegations.

One might well conclude that the Palestinian role in discussions about the final status of the West Bank and Gaza would have been symbolic and minor. The so-called representatives could not have represented the Palestinian people as a whole in complete freedom. The Palestinians' future would have tended to be shaped by others, and the outcome could thus have become an imposed solution bearing no relation to the internationally recognized norm of self-determination.

President Carter confirmed to the Jordanians in his answer to question 12 that Resolutions 242 and 338 were the basis of discussions. He particularly indicated that 242 applied to all fronts, including the West Bank and Gaza. The Camp David Accords also endorsed this view. But both Carter and the Accords appeared to contradict these resolutions. While 242 emphasized the inadmissibility of the acquisition of territory by war and the need to work for a comprehensive, just and lasting peace, the Camp David framework, and Carter, substituted the concept of balancing sovereignty with security. Carter and the Accords thus envisaged the withdrawal of the Israeli military government and its civilian administration but not the withdrawal of the Israeli occupation forces from certain parts of the West Bank designated as 'security locations'. Hence, Jordan saw Israel as being allowed by the Americans to retain its military forces on occupied land. The final status of the West Bank and Gaza was to be open to negotiation, with Israel able within the framework to press its claims for sovereignty.

Carter and the Accords also contradicted Resolution 338, on which negotiations were also supposed to be based. This resolution specified that negotiations were to take place between all parties concerned under 'appropriate auspices' – meaning in the Arab world an international conference. Of the four front-line states, only Egypt took part in Camp David. And also, contrary to the previously agreed joint Soviet–American chairmanship of the negotiations, they were conducted under the auspices of the US alone.

Both Carter and the Accords claimed that the negotiations were supposed to lead to a comprehensive, long-lasting peace in the Middle East. Instead, they seemed to eliminate Egypt from the Arab–Israeli conflict thus fragmenting in the process the search for a comprehensive peace settlement announced by Carter at the beginning of his term of office. Israel and Egypt were rewarded for their agreement. The US granted Israel an extra $3 billion (for rebuilding houses in the Negev) while Egypt was given $1.5 billion. Thus, the total of US Foreign Assistance Programmes to Israel went up from $1,842m. in 1978 to $4,844m.[13] in 1979 while Egypt's total increased from $943m. in 1978 to $2,589m. in 1979. Concurrently with the signing of the Treaty, Israel and the US concluded an important Memorandum of Understanding which defined certain American responsibilities if the treaty were to be violated, a further pledge to veto any UN action which would adversely affect Israel, and a guarantee of oil supplies for the next fifteen years.

The Camp David Accords were not compatible with international law, in particular with the Fourth Geneva Convention of 1949. Singling out the Israeli settlements, President Carter confided to Jordan that the settlements had actually been established in violation of international law, particularly Article 49 of the Geneva Convention, which explicitly prohibited Israeli settlement in any part of the occupied territories. He also stated publicly on many occasions that Begin had agreed to a five-year settlement freeze. Secretary of State Cyrus Vance reassured King Hussain that there would be such a freeze and all the Arab capitals were given the same assurance. Three days after his departure from Washington following the signing of the Accords, Begin proceeded to expand the existing settlements and to plan new ones.

The implications of this were noted in Jordan. The expansion of the Israeli population living in these settlements, combined with the enforced expulsion of undesirable Palestinian elements in the name of security and the voluntary departure of other Palestinians to escape what they regarded as an iron-fisted Israeli policy, was seen as leading to a situation in which the remaining Palestinians would become a minority while retaining their Jordanian passports. In other words, they would become foreigners living their day-to-day lives in the West Bank and Gaza while fulfilling their political aspirations in Jordan. By the time self-determination was implemented, whether under the Autonomy or any other plan, a great percentage of the population in the West Bank and Gaza would become Israeli citizens of non-Arab origin, who would then have a say in the issue of self-determination for the inhabitants of the territories.[14]

There was a more subtle legal contradiction between the envisaged autonomy and Article 47 of the Geneva Convention, which prohibited the occupying authorities from introducing fundamental changes in the existing institutions and structure of the occupied territories. This complex point can be overstated, and is emphasized here only to show that Israel's policy after the Accords, e.g. setting up 'civilian administration' and 'Village Leagues' in the West Bank and Gaza, was a serious violation of Article 47. Subsequent events signalled unequivocally the determined opposition of the Palestinian people to such 'civil administration' and the autonomy it purported to achieve, and their rejection of certain imposed representatives through 'Village Leagues', carefully chosen to rubber stamp Israeli plans, in defiance of the principle of self-determination.

According to the Camp David Accords and to President Carter's answer to question 11, only the Palestinians displaced from the West Bank and Gaza in the 1967 war had to be re-admitted, and it was up to the permanent committee to decide who would be allowed to return after taking Israeli security into consideration. How many Israel might refuse for security reasons was left open. The rest of the Palestinian population in the diaspora were treated as refugees whose case must be resolved 'promptly and justly' by Egypt and Israel, together with other interested parties.

The right of the Palestinian refugees – all the Palestinian refugees since the creation of Israel – to return or be compensated had been enshrined in UN Resolution 194 of 11 December 1948, and confirmed by several subsequent resolutions. President Carter informed Jordan of his intention not to respect all these resolutions, but only those suitable for implementation according to 'existing realities'. This left a great deal to be answered.

Leaving Jerusalem outside the scope of the Camp David Accords and making it the subject of future negotiations was resented by the Moslem world and particularly by Jordan, under whose jurisdiction East Jerusalem had fallen since 1948. East Jerusalem was regarded, by the US as well as by Jordan, as an integral part of the occupied West Bank, and hence was supposed to be covered by the Geneva Convention. But, on 27 June 1967, the Israeli Parliament had approved three bills authorizing extension of Israeli jurisdiction and public administration over the old city of Jerusalem – East Jerusalem – and other territory of the former Mandate of Palestine which had been under the control of Jordan since the General Armistice Agreement of 1949. The following day, the Israeli government took action under the new legislation to extend its municipal services and controls over the entire city of Jerusalem.

The State Department released a statement the same day declaring that 'the hasty administrative action taken today cannot be regarded as determining the future of the holy places or the status of Jerusalem in relation to them. The US has never recognized such unilateral action by any of the states in the area as governing the international status of Jerusalem.'[15] This was in accordance with President Johnson's warning on 19 June 1967 prior to the Israeli decision, that 'there must be adequate recognition of the special interests of the three great religions in the holy places of Jerusalem' followed by this statement on 3 July to the UN General Assembly:

The safeguarding of the holy places and freedom of access to them for all should be internationally guaranteed and the status of Jerusalem in relation to them should be decided not unilaterally but in consultation with all concerned. These statements represent the considered and continuing policy of the US government... With regard to the specific measures taken by the government of Israel on 28 June, I wish to make it clear that the US does not accept or recognize these measures as altering the status of Jerusalem. We insist that the measures taken cannot be considered other than interim and provisional, and not prejudicing the final and permanent status of Jerusalem.

Such a view was in line with that of the international community, which frequently stated through General Assembly and Security Council resolutions that all Israeli measures in the City, and its annexation, were illegal, and therefore null and void. The US recognized the claims of neither Israel nor Jordan over the City but, on the basis of the Partition Plan of 1947, supported a special status for Jerusalem as an international city.[16]

Finally, the outcome of Carter's so-called comprehensive approach was no more than a slightly modified version of Begin's Autonomy Plan of 27 December 1977, which defined procedures for the establishment of autonomy for the West Bank and Gaza.[17] Only a slight procedural improvement was made. While under Begin's Autonomy Plan the military governor's office was to remain in existence as the ultimate source of authority, the Accords specified that the military government would have to be withdrawn, but leaving Israeli forces in specified locations for security reasons. The Autonomy Plan also proposed, in general terms, a review of the agreement after five years, whereas the Accords specified a commitment to begin negotiations on a final peace treaty which would also resolve the status of the West Bank and Gaza within three years and was to be concluded within five years. Hence the time dimension was accelerated. All other relevant issues remained subject to negotiation.

Jordan's final reactions

Jordan regarded the Camp David framework as a licence to perpetuate what it termed Israel's colonization of the West Bank and Gaza. It saw autonomy proposed only for the people, not for the land, and Palestinian self-rule as a cosmetic concept which would only be used by Israel to legitimize its occupation and to deny Palestinian rights. In other words, it would enable Israel to claim that its occupation had ended, while in fact it would merely be disguised under the cloak of autonomy.

Although it had not been a party to the Accords, Jordan was mentioned fourteen times in the section relating to West Bank and Gaza autonomy. King Hussein was apparently expected to fit meekly in with the plan. As he put it: 'The Arab people were being asked to acquiesce in or support a totally unacceptable situation and were threatened if they did not with the displeasure of the Congress and American public opinion.'[18] He even accused a high-level US delegation to Saudi Arabia and Jordan on 17–18 March 1979, headed by National Security Adviser Zbigniew Brzezinski, of using arm-twisting tactics. Brzezinski had implied that there could be restrictions on the supply of arms if Jordan did not co-operate, and that delivery would inevitably depend on its attitude towards American efforts in the Middle East. Former Prime Minister Badran revealed that arm-twisting did take place on more than one level. Brzezinski implied that it would be dangerous if Jordan failed to play the role envisaged at Camp David – a threat which was taken to mean a future Israeli attack on Jordan with US blessing. American pressure was also applied in the Gulf states not to help Jordan; one of the Gulf Sheikhs told King Hussain frankly, 'I am under pressure not to pay you.'[19] Former Finance Minister Hanna Odeh has also revealed that Jordan had difficulty in borrowing money from the World Bank following the Accords,[20] as Nasser had encountered in his earlier confrontation with the US and Britain. Former Prime Minister Badran revealed, moreover, that the US withheld both military and economic aid from Jordan (see Appendix C). Following the Camp David Accords, there was a time when Jordan was unable to pay its armed forces their wages.[21]

In spite of these difficulties, US covert and overt threats did not seem to inhibit Jordan. Brzezinski's threat of restrictions on arms sales met with a cool response from King Hussain: 'Then we will have to look around and see what we can do to line up alternative sources for military equipment.'[22] When Brzezinski argued that US and Jordanian interests were threatened by radicals and Communists, he was told that Zionism posed an equal threat. 'In fact, the main threat is Israeli occupation and expansionism, the sense of alienation and discord that creates a climate conducive to outside exploitation of the situation', King Hussain said. And when Brzezinski put forward the overwhelming importance of the Soviet invasion of Afghanistan as a threat to the Middle East, the response was that 'criticizing Soviet intervention would not gain American Moslem support, while Jerusalem remained under Israeli occupation'.[23] Comparing the Soviet action in Afghanistan with Israel's occupation of the West Bank and Gaza, King Hussain commented:

In Afghanistan, where there is a foreign military intervention and an invasion of a country, and a resistance to that invasion, why should that resistance be considered heroic, be considered a legitimate right of a people to resist occupying forces, and why should the Palestinians, after years of occupation still be considered as criminals for trying – in the face of non progress towards the solution to their problem – to resist this occupation by any way, by any means available to them?[24]

During an interview in Washington on 8 July 1988, the writer asked Brzezinski whether the Americans had ever thought of inviting King Hussain to Camp David.

We refrained from inviting the King to avoid complicating the process. I don't think there would have been any Camp David agreement if there had been a larger number of participants . . . Why Hussain and Arafat were not in Camp David is rooted in the experience of 1977 when we discovered it was not possible to put together a common united Arab front. Therefore we had a choice of waiting for the slowest party to move forward, or moving forward with the party that was prepared to move more rapidly because that served our interests.

Brzezinski became aggressive when asked about his arm-twisting tactics. He denied ever intending to threaten Jordan by means of Israel. 'It is conceivable that they read into something that we said more than was intended or something different from what was intended.' But he did not deny that one of his team might have mentioned that it might be more difficult for the US to 'sustain the kind or level of military and economic co-operation with Jordan if Jordan proceeded to be obstructive' in the peace process. 'I am sure we emphasized, however, the fact that non-participation would be damaging to the Arab interest.' When he was reminded that it was the autonomy prescribed at Camp David which the Arabs found damaging to their interests and that it was he who urged Begin in December 1977 not to use the word 'autonomy' because 'autonomy is usually used for a district or region which is part of one's own country with a special status', he adopted a hectoring tone.

No. Autonomy is a very vague term. We in fact researched it under international law and discovered a variety of meanings. Therefore it was perfectly appropriate. But . . . King Hussain is not interested in the Palestinians . . . The Arab leadership is not interested in the Palestinians . . . If King Hussain is, as he professes to be, then he must have missed a real opportunity . . . We are not going to be the protagonists of the Palestinians to a greater extent than the Arabs are prepared to be . . . We are not in the business as political philanthropists for the Arabs . . . I don't accept the notion that the US has any obligation to please the Arabs . . . If the Arab side had an ounce of brain in its head, it would realize that the creation of autonomous institutions over a five-year period on a territory defined by the 1967 lines would make it much more difficult subsequently to have any peace settlement other than the 1967 lines . . . But I am sorry to say that the Arab side was never intelligent enough, politically, to take advantage of it . . . The Arabs would like us to negotiate for them and would like the Russians to fight for them . . . I personally am impatient with Arab criticism because it is criticism of the party that wants someone else to solve the problem for it.

Brzezinski was reminded that it was the tremendous American economic and military assistance to Israel which made the United States morally responsible and its role in peacemaking extremely vital.

Of course we have the pipeline to Israel. That is a fact of life; [But] We have no obligation to resolve the problem for 'you'. If 'you' are serious, you either negotiate seriously or 'you' will fight seriously. The problem is that 'you' are prepared to do neither.

At this point the discussion was deliberately geared towards a more constructive note. Brzezinski was asked why there had been a departure from a comprehensive solution.

There were real difficulties on both sides. Israel was very fearful and obstructionist. And it was almost impossible to create a common Arab front that was willing to participate in a larger conference. It was that that made us more than sympathetic to the notion of finding some alternative solution and Sadat acted as a catalyst in generating that alternative approach.

He insisted that the US was trying to change the status of the Palestinians under occupation through a political process, which, over time, would modify its character from autonomy to something different in the end.

We deliberately preferred not to define, because if we defined that, in the very beginning, then the Israelis and the Arabs could never agree; because the Israelis could never accept statehood for the Palestinians initially, and the Palestinians would never accept anything less than statehood at the end of the process. But certainly to many of us, the notion of the five-year interim agreement involving the creation of autonomous institutions on the territory along 1967 lines would over time create a totally new situation which would permit the Palestinians to have institutions which would in effect express their legitimate political and other rights. That was the basic thought.

If that was the basic concept, nothing worked according to plan. 'We were not for a separate peace. A separate peace would perpetuate the conflict. It is inherently unstable', Brzezinski stated. But he added that once it became clear that a comprehensive solution was not possible a movement towards a wider solution by stages began, with the first stage involving a separate peace between Egypt and Israel. 'At Camp David, we were clearly by then pursuing a stage-by-stage process and no longer a comprehensive solution.'

The first stage involving a separate peace between Egypt and Israel was supposed to be tied to the process of creating autonomous institutions for the Palestinians. But, as Brzezinski put it: 'Israel was not interested in implementing it, Sadat wasn't particularly interested in pushing it – because he wanted in the meantime to get Sinai back – and the other Arabs were not willing to participate . . . so it ended up as it did.' Brzezinski was reminded of the weakness exposed by President Carter when he first met Begin in July 1977. Begin asked the President not to talk any more in public about the homeland or the 1967 lines, and the President acquiesced. 'If President Carter had been more firm . . . maybe the course of events would have been different', Brzezinski admitted.

Thus, under the Camp David provisions, Jordan was to play an important role in determining the final status of the West Bank and Gaza and in co-operation with Israel to maintain security during the transitional period.

But Jordan refused to play such a role, which it regarded as assisting the Israeli occupation authorities in implementing what was seen as 'a barren and empty concept of autonomy'. As King Hussain put it:

The role spelt out for us in our absence was a very humiliating one. To put it mildly, to be the policeman in the occupied territories and to help in the security field. And so we ask: Whose security? Against the people under occupation?[25]

Having received Secretary of State Vance on 19 September 1978, the Jordanian government issued a final statement disavowing any moral or legal commitment to the Accords.

Jordan's acceptance of Resolution 242 meant an implicit recognition of the right of Israel to exist within secure and recognized boundaries. Kissinger claimed that this acceptance had been obtained in 1969 by the promise of Ambassador Goldberg to the UN that the US would work for the return of the West Bank to Jordan, with minor boundary rectifications, and that it would be prepared to use its influence to obtain a role for Jordan in Jerusalem. According to Kissinger, even President Johnson had in effect promised Jordan a return to the 1967 borders with minor rectifications. As he put it, the promise was given 'as a bait for Jordan's acceptance of Resolution 242'.[26] Bait or not, King Hussain had stressed on numerous occasions to the Western and Arab press alike that Jordan had played a leading role in the efforts culminating in the adoption by the Security Council of Resolution 242 and that the US had promised to implement it within six months. It was obviously a promise that the US did not intend to keep.

Later, in 1984, King Hussain further elaborated on the shortcomings of Resolution 242.[27]

We and the US drafted 242 shortly after the destructive 1967 war. The resolution stipulated a simple formula: complete withdrawal in exchange for comprehensive peace and recognition of every one to live in peace in the region. Clearly the factor that the resolution ignored must be incorporated into it at a certain stage. I believe that an international conference in which all sides to the dispute will take part will be the means of solving the problem. I firmly believe that the solution to the problem will be achieved through the participation of the five permanent members of the UN Security Council. Speaking of Security Council Resolution 242, we see the UN Security Council playing the role of guarantor of what might be achieved.

In recognition of the political dimension of the Palestinian question which was ignored by Resolution 242, King Hussain insisted on the PLO's participation on an equal basis in any future international conference. But, in spite of the inadequacy of Resolution 242, he made it clear that he insisted on it as a basis for negotiations because 'It is the only resolution that was passed unanimously by the highest international body that termed the Israeli presence in the Arab territories occupation and stipulated that occupation should be terminated in order to reach a just and peaceful settlement.'

As a presidential candidate, Carter's views were not very different from those of Jordan. 'I think one of the integral parts of an ultimate settlement has got to be the recognition of the Palestinians as a people, as a nation, with a place to live and a right to choose their own leaders.'[28] But as President, he adhered to Kissinger's agreement with Israel – barring negotiations with the PLO – as a matter of choice and policy rather than of law. Kissinger later clarified that the memorandum of understanding with Israel was a statement of policy and that the US remained committed to it as long as the circumstances that gave rise to it continued,[29] but it was not a binding commitment.* Carter's lack of enthusiasm for Palestinian self-determination was also a matter of choice and policy. As an international norm, the principle of self-determination is an American contribution. But at Camp David, Carter reconciled himself to limited autonomy for the Palestinians instead. Having spoken earlier of a Palestinian homeland, he reverted later on to the formula 'entity', accepting as axiomatic the Israeli contention that an independent Palestinian state would inevitably be radical.

In contrast, the Arab world, including Jordan and the PLO, was committed to Palestinian self-determination as a matter of right rather than choice. This implied an independent Palestinian sovereign state free to choose any form of arrangement with Jordan, if it so wished. Confederation was agreed to by all factions of the PLO, including the radicals, at the sixteenth session of the Palestinian National Council – the Palestinian parliament in exile – held in Algiers on 22 February 1985.

Arab reaction

The discord and furore in the Arab world over the Camp David Accords did not occur as a result of the Arabs' objection to the principle of peace with Israel. The fundamental issue was Sadat's unilateral decision to impose his

---

* The 1985 International Security and Development Co-operation Act (P.L.99–83), section 1302, reaffirmed and codified the policy prohibiting negotiations with the PLO. No officer or employee of the US government, and no agent or other individual acting on behalf of the US government, was to negotiate with the PLO or any representatives thereof (except in emergency or humanitarian situations) unless and until the PLO recognized Israel's right to exist, accepted Security Council Resolutions 242 and 338, and renounced the use of terrorism. Although the Reagan administration reaffirmed that policy and welcomed Congressional support for it, the final statement issued on 8 August 1985 reiterated its refusal to accept any Congressional effort to impose legislative restrictions or directions with respect to the conduct of international negotiation, which under Article 11 of the Constitution is a function reserved exclusively to the President. Hence, President Reagan regarded the Act as only a non-binding expression of Congressional views on these issues. This provision was reaffirmed in the Foreign Assistance Appropriations for 1987, P.L.99–591, section 530 and in the Foreign Operations, Export Financing and Related Programs Appropriation Act, 1988. It remained in force until December 1988 (see developments in the last chapter).

own line of thinking upon the Arabs, his bad management of the peace negotiations and the price he paid.

By undertaking to negotiate alone on behalf of the Palestinians and the whole Arab people, Sadat was contradicting the principles of the Arab League, the agreements between Egypt and the Arab states, and the decisions of Arab summits, not to undertake any unilateral negotiations with Israel over occupied Arab lands, except as a result of a decision taken by an extraordinary Arab summit held specifically for this purpose. Moreover, he contradicted the unanimous Arab agreement not to take decisions on behalf of other Arab countries without their precise consent or participation on an equal footing as sovereign independent states. Thus, in submitting the Accords to the Arab countries, he appeared to be forcing a decision on them to negotiate and establish normal relations with a common enemy. In other words, he seemed to be dealing with serious matters concerning other independent Arab parties – Jordan, Syria, Lebanon and the Palestinians – and imposing on them a *de facto* situation, without giving them the right or the opportunity to change or re-draft any paragraph in the Framework he had had a hand in shaping.

Moreover, the Arab states saw many dangers[30] posed for them collectively by Sadat and the Accords. They foresaw that the neutralization of Egypt would result in the diminution of Arab defence capabilities; Egypt's pivotal strength would be lost and the impact of this would be deeply felt. By ridding itself of a two-pronged Arab front, Israel would improve its strategic position and be enabled to concentrate on the West Bank, Gaza, South Lebanon and the Golan Heights with no worries about protecting its hinterland. The Accords and the Israel–Egypt treaty were also seen as enabling Israel not only to gain further economic and military aid from the US, thus shifting the balance of power further in its favour against the remaining Arab states in conflict with Israel, but also to secure its navigation in the Red Sea. The Treaty helped to transform the Red Sea, which was perceived by the Arab world as a vital vein for Israel's penetration and strategic co-operation with the US and other Western countries in the Arab Maghreb, the Horn of Africa and the Indian Ocean, into an Israeli lake.

The Accords and the Treaty also appeared then to increase the danger of the Middle East becoming a potential battle-ground for superpower confrontation. For instance, Sadat's announcement on 27 January 1980 that he had promised the United States facilities to intervene in the Gulf even though the Gulf states did not specifically ask Egypt to do so, made the Arab League very apprehensive. So did his announcement on 23 September 1980 – in a speech delivered in Alexandria – that the US had been granted facilities to defend the Gulf. Sadat was now seen as a strategic partner of the US, in competition with Israel, and eager to offer favours to the Americans in their Middle Eastern policy against the Soviet Union, especially in the wake of the Iranian Revolution and the Soviet invasion of Afghanistan.

The leading role in rallying Arab opposition to the Accords was played by the Iraqi government, whose intensive diplomatic efforts culminated in the convening of an Arab summit in Baghdad from 2 to 5 November 1978, attended by the representatives of 21 of the 22 Arab League members; Egypt was not invited. The conference appealed to the Egyptian government to abrogate the Accords. In the event of its failing to do so, a number of resolutions were adopted to co-ordinate a suitable response, concentrating on the suspension of Egypt's membership of the Arab League and its participation in shared Arab projects, coupled with the removal of the headquarters, offices and branches of the Arab League then stationed in Cairo to other Arab countries. In the same vein, the conference resolved to withhold all assistance, including financial assistance, from the Egyptian government, and to boycott all companies, institutions and individuals in Egypt who dealt directly with Israel.

The resolutions encompassed other considerations, however, notably that the utmost care had to be taken not to harm the Arab people of Egypt, and that the right of the Palestinian people to return to their homeland and the role of the PLO as the sole legitimate representative of the Palestinian people had to be reaffirmed. A 10-year, $3,500m. annual fund for the front-line states and the PLO was established to counter the Egyptian–Israeli rapprochement; over a third of this, $1,250m. annually, was to go to Jordan. It never received the full amount, however. Only Saudi Arabia continued to pay its share, as well as a considerable part of the shares allotted to Libya and Algeria; assistance from Kuwait, Iraq, the United Arab Emirates and Qatar covering their own shares as well as the remaining part of the shares of Libya and Algeria gradually dwindled. By 31 July 1985, the shortfall amounted to $2,263.3m. Moreover, Kuwait decided in 1984–5 to reduce its own share by 40 per cent.[31]

5 An evaluation of the development of American strategy for the 1980s

Every new American administration feels it has a mandate for a new foreign policy. But the new men soon discover that the problems they face are more intractable than they had expected, and the virtues of continuity come to be applauded more than the merits of innovation.[1]

President Carter was no exception. Initially stirred by the moral dimension of the Palestinian problem, he undertook a complete break from Kissinger's approach by propagating the idea of a homeland for the Palestinians and embarking on the Geneva process, which he thought would gradually resolve the Palestinian dimension of the Arab–Israeli conflict within a comprehensive solution of the Middle Eastern problem. When confronted with formidable obstacles, however, he drifted into another process, hoping to achieve at Camp David what he failed to do in Geneva. But the whole exercise proved to be a long shot for which he was not prepared. Faced by what was in effect an Israeli version of a fundamentalist Ayatollah, determined to implement his own autonomy plan for the Palestinians in the occupied territories, he initially protested, 'No self-respecting Arab world would accept your plan. This looks like subterfuge' and at one stage even went so far as to call Begin a psychopath.[2] But he was not willing to stand up to him. Even the issue of linkage between an Egyptian–Israeli settlement and the West Bank/Gaza negotiations, which he had pledged at the outset of Camp David as the single most important question, was not sustained.

President Carter entered Camp David with his mind made up not to back any verbal protest he might make with either action or sanction. 'I do not have any intention to pressure Begin. I do not have any desire to do it, and I couldn't if I wanted to',[3] he told a news conference on 5 March 1978. Vice President Mondale added in early July, emphasizing that he was speaking for the President, 'I pledge to you that my country will not fail to provide Israel with crucial military assistance nor will we use that assistance as a form of pressure', and Secretary of State Vance reiterated that pledge in a testimony before the Senate Foreign Relations Committee on 14 August.[4] All three of them, like many others in the US, were convinced that for strategic, religious, domestic, moral and emotional reasons a special relationship with Israel must be maintained in spite of the cost incurred.

Losing his grip on the negotiations, Carter at one stage appealed to Sadat to help him out of a position described by Brzezinski, who attended the Camp David negotiations, as 'a corner into which he had been boxed by Begin'.[5] Sadat extended a helping hand for which Carter became profoundly grateful.[6]

At Camp David the three leaders, Carter, Begin and Sadat, ended up furthering their own national interests. According to George Washington's dictum that 'no nation is to be trusted farther than it is bound by its own national interests',[7] moral principles usually tend to recede into a secondary role in the formulation of foreign policy. After a period of oscillation between a 'Wilsonian idealistic commitment to a moral solution of the Middle Eastern problem and fascination with Realpolitik',[8] President Carter embarked on the latter course. Putting aside his rhetorical references to human rights – as far as the Palestinians were concerned – he set off to pursue his own national objectives, which were basically to avoid war because of its unpredictable outcome, its after-effects and its dreaded potential for getting out of hand and sparking-off a superpower conflict. Other objectives included the safeguarding of what was perceived in some US circles as a vital strategic ally – Israel; excluding, or at least containing, the Soviet Union in the Middle East and Africa; and protecting Western access to Arab oil, which implied the preservation of the status quo in the Middle East in general and the Gulf area in particular.

Challenged by the crumbling of the Shah's power in Iran during 1978, and the parallel Soviet–Cuban advances in Africa, and later by developments in Afghanistan, Carter suddenly became desperate for a short-term resolution of Arab–Israeli differences in a manner that would entice Egypt into some kind of strategic junior partnership. In other words, Carter substantially revised his strategic agenda for the Middle East, by shifting the main priority away from a political settlement of the Palestinian question towards a military response. Resort to Cold War definitions became expedient. The result was what became known as the Carter Doctrine and the establishment of a Rapid Deployment Force (RDF) as the primary means of preserving the status quo in the region. As Israel was already seen by some hardliner strategists as a crucial part of what was envisaged as an elaborate US base and resupply system ringing the Middle East oil-producing region, pressure on it for what became a side issue – the West Bank and Gaza – became useless.

The Carter Doctrine, embodying the strategy of US policy in the 1980s, suited both Begin and Sadat. Begin saw Camp David as a stepping stone towards regional supremacy, underpinned more formally by the Memorandum of Understanding of March 1979 between the US and Israel. By thus entangling Israeli national interests with the strategic needs of a superpower, Begin saw a unique opportunity to pursue his own historic objectives, namely to secure a separate peace with Egypt, leaving him free on other fronts, in particular to pursue his cherished goal of eliminating the threat of war, while leaving the 'Biblical Lands' to the east open for settlement and integration. On the other hand, tired of unwinnable wars with Israel, and satisfied by acquiring a full partnership with the US, and by the recovery of Sinai, Sadat distanced himself from Arab grievances and concerns. Putting domestic before Pan-Arab issues, he undertook a radical reorientation of Egyptian goals by abandoning the position of dominance within Arab councils which had been the main feature of inter-Arab relations since the Second World War. Relying as he did on American leverage on Israel, he acquiesed in his consequent dependence on the US.

King Hussain was among the first to protest against exposing the Middle East to further superpower rivalry. At a press conference in early 1980, he stated:

Are we talking about allowing the US, which claims to be Israel's staunchest ally, to deploy its power in our area? To uphold what principles and to solve what problems? . . . It is high time that people realized that the lack of an overall settlement is the root cause of instability in this area. Weapons and troop deployments and contingency plans that by-pass such a settlement are bound to be counter-productive and would backfire against the US.[9]

Jordan appeared to believe that if any American security plan for the Middle East were to be effective, it would first have to overcome the sources of local conflict. It also appeared to believe that regional conflicts might have a better chance of settlement or containment through collective Arab co-operation or the operation of a purely regional balance of power, with the possibility that outside powers might see their interests better served, in the long run, by observing rather than intervening. In Jordanian eyes, the intervention of one superpower would inevitably lead, in the political context of the early 1980s, to the intervention of the other, and the interlocking of regional conflicts with superpower competition would maximize the danger for all concerned.

Jordan has always been opposed to foreign alliances and the international-ization of the Arab–Israeli conflict. This opposition stemmed from the belief that internationalization would not only endanger the Arab cause and constitute a threat to the distinctive Arab identity, but would also mean that the principal world powers might at some stage wrest from the Arabs their right to settle their own affairs, so that the problem would become a question of what the superpowers agreed or imposed on the Arabs. 'We in the Arab world reject the idea of a second Yalta',[10] King Hussain has emphasized.

President Carter was not sympathetic to King Hussain's stance; hence the application of US pressure to entice him to play the role envisaged at Camp David and beyond. Although he termed King Hussain 'a slender reed' on which to rest the prospects for peace, Carter recognized his importance as a participant in his unfolding plans. But, he maintained, 'Only increased threats to Jordan's existence, or the alleviation of some of its present concerns, could induce King Hussain to play his vital role.'[11] Nevertheless, Carter continued to put pressure on Hussain, as any let-up would entail requesting concessions from Begin, an option which Carter wished to avoid.

Known locally and regionally as tough and resilient, King Hussain endured the pressure. He did not seem to fear the US or President Carter. 'Our national responsibilities are over and above everything. Our national interests are not for bargain or for sale', former Prime Minister Badran commented.

PART II Jordan in the Reagan Middle East policy

6 The evolution of Reagan's strategy

With every American election, there is a big bias towards one side [Israel]. At the same time, we find it necessary to deal with new friends, who most of the time do not realize what the problem is and its background, and who have to deal with many international problems. Because of this, they cannot give them the required time or interest . . . It can be a bitter experience . . . I have had the honour of serving my country and this region for over thirty years and I have seen this take place many times.[1]

Such was King Hussain's summary of his long working relationship with US Presidents who have dealt, each in his own way and time, with Middle Eastern problems. Ronald Reagan proved to be no exception. As a presidential candidate he started to promote, in what might have been a vote-catching exercise, the view that 'Israel is the only strategic asset in the area that the US can rely on.'[2] But in his first presidential press conference, he expressed what now seemed to be a conviction, that 'Israel's combat-ready and even combat-experienced military is a force in the Middle East that actually is of benefit to us. If there was no Israel with that force, we'd have to supply that with our own. So, this isn't just altruism on our part.'[3] Pressed at one point as to whether he had 'any sympathy for the Palestinians', his answer was a flat 'no',[4] unlike his predecessor at the beginning of his term of office.

Reagan lost no time in asserting another personal conviction, namely, that the Soviet leadership was bent on global domination. Bolstered by his own ingrained Cold War beliefs, he was determined to show, in straightforward 'Realpolitik' terms, the strong tough face of America. His underlying view of the world seemed to be of a vast chessboard with only two principal players: the US and the USSR. Hence, local problems – whether political or economic – were to be regarded as pawns in the game. What was not made clear at the start of his presidency was how he would play what he considered local minor 'pieces' and what would happen if the pawns refused to be moved.

The evolving strategy

Having decided *a priori* that the Middle East's problems were being exploited by Soviet conspiracies, President Reagan's disposition was to seek

69

a military remedy. He seemed in no hurry to formulate his own detailed policy for the Middle East, and left the matter in the hands of his Secretary of State, Alexander Haig, whose similarly aggressive concept of power led him to perceive local issues, such as Palestinian rights and even oil diplomacy, as secondary to the security of the Middle East in general and the Gulf area in particular, in the face of what he saw as the Soviet threat. Thus on 18 March 1981, Haig declared in an address to the House Foreign Relations Committee:[5]

We feel it is fundamentally important to begin to develop a consensus of strategic concerns throughout the region, among Arab and Jew, to be sure that the overriding danger of Soviet inroads into this area are not overlooked.

What Haig meant was clarified by Dr Fred C. Iklé, Under Secretary of Defense for Policy, in a comprehensive statement about the future US policy in the Middle East made to AIPAC, the American–Israeli Public Affairs Committee on 18 May 1981: 'It is the Soviet presence in the Middle East which most concerns us now.' After citing its political presence in Libya, Syria, Iraq, Afghanistan, South Yemen and Ethiopia, he went on:

This geostrategic configuration is one which is aimed at denying the US access to the region. It is one, to accentuate the obvious, which threatens the friends of the US and in particular increases the ultimate danger to the security of Israel.

To confront this situation and effectively develop and deploy countervailing power, he indicated that 'The US must establish a place to stand in the region should it become necessary.' He further outlined the procedure for action, foreseeing the necessity of 'putting flesh and muscle on the skeleton' of the RDF, improving the capability for rapid mobilization, transferring arms to the area with critical links to the larger security structure, and improving military co-operation with countries of strategic importance and strengthening their security assistance, with the lion's share going to Israel and Egypt. Iklé's outline also stressed the importance of supplying Saudi Arabia with AWACS, not only for its defence and the defence of the Gulf, but also for the security of oil supplies. As far as Israel was concerned, advancing its long-term security and ensuring its continued economic stability were paramount. He also stressed the need to find a workable peace between Israel and the Arabs, one that was not dictated by the Soviet Union, nor by 'terrorists'. 'If a consensus for peace would not be possible', he said, 'then, at least, let us work for a modus vivendi.' However, in order to help the peace process, Iklé's outline emphasized the importance of the US presence on the ground and of continuing to build on the Egyptian–Israeli Treaty. The Carter Doctrine and the RDF were to be extended to encompass the security of the Middle East as well as the Gulf area, and the Camp David process was to be maintained.

The strategic consensus, the Arab world and Israel

The strategic consensus elaborated by the new Administration required Arab allies and Israel alike to transcend their regional hostilities and conflicting national interests in order to support the US against the menace of the USSR and its 'proxies' in the region – a threat which was highlighted by the demise of the Shah and the Soviet invasion of Afghanistan. Alexander Haig made his debut in Middle East affairs in April 1981, in an effort to peddle the concept of strategic consensus. While accepting the principle put forward, Israel expressed concern over US efforts to achieve consensus with the Arab states against the threat of Soviet intrusion into the area. Underlying this concern was the belief among Israeli officials that 'Another war with the Arab countries is likely and US regional efforts can contribute to threatening Israel's security'. The US agreed that 'Efforts to modernize the Arab states to deter Soviet expansion can also expand the Arabs' potential capability against Israel.' The CIA even believed that 'This could exacerbate Israel's concern about the Arab threat and could foster Israel's pre-emptive attacks in a future crisis.'[6]

On the other hand, the Arab states were concerned about the US–Israeli strategic co-operation. The strategic consensus was seen to manipulate the Arab Middle East to the advantage of the US and the West in general, and the disadvantage of the USSR, with no account being taken of the Arabs' own national interests. They had foreseen that the reinforcement of the RDF concept would eventually lead to the US banking on Israel as the most powerful and trusted ally and protector of Western interests in the area while endeavouring to enlist the Arab states as junior strategic partners. If Israel accepted the idea of strategic consensus in spite of its apprehensions, it was realized that it did so in order to achieve its own expansion and hegemony at the expense of the Arab states.

The Israeli political commentator Gideon Samit writing in *Ha'aretz* of 24 February 1981 interpreted the plan as that the Israeli defence forces would maintain US equipment, needed as a back-up system for the strategic consensus, in combat-readiness for use in a military operation in the Gulf. He added:

As for Israel, the US equipment will be put at its disposal in times of special emergency as was the case during the air-lift in the 1973 war with the Arabs. Since the equipment will not be owned by Israel, it will not be included in the list of US equipment sold to Israel, and Israel will even be paid for maintenance expenses.

Such articles in the Israeli press inevitably fuelled Arab apprehensions. So when Haig told King Hussain during his April 1981 trip, 'We want to be friends against the Soviet Union', Hussain replied, 'We want to be friends too. But the one who threatens us and wants to occupy Amman is not

Brezhnev. It is Sharon.'[7] In the clearest terms, he pointed out that in the Jordanian view Israel lay at the heart of the matter and that the Palestinian issue was of greater immediate concern to Jordan and the Arab World than Soviet influence or even Soviet reinforcements in Afghanistan. Once the Palestinian crisis was solved, all the countries in the area, including Jordan, would be more ready to listen to American proposals for containing the Soviet Union, and regional stability resulting from a durable and just solution to the Palestinian problem would have an in-built mechanism to deter Soviet influence. It was further pointed out that no Arab would agree to Israeli troops being deployed on Arab soil, regardless of the circumstances, and no security arrangements such as were proposed could be agreed to until there was a comprehensive peace with Israel which would take justice for the Palestinians into consideration.

Israel dismissed the Jordanian arguments as academic. In an effort to downgrade the importance of the Palestinian question and the urgency of solving it – which would require Israel to make compromises – Shamir put it this way:

The Middle East is a mosaic of peoples, languages and cultures. The region is permanently in ferment. Some outsiders, sincerely but out of ignorance, believe that a solution of the Arab-Israeli conflict would lead to regional stability and open a new era of progress. Nothing could be further from the truth.[8]

And the US seemed to agree with him.[9]

To say that Shamir's argument represented only a fraction of the truth is no understatement. Professor Walid Khalidi has explained:

There is a continuous struggle between centripetal and centrifugal forces in the Arab world. The former are grounded in the ideologies of Pan-Arabism and Pan-Islamism and their non-doctrinaire versions which take the form of sentiments, cultural solidarity, inter-personal contacts and enlightened self-interest. The latter stem from the more restrictive perspectives of individual states, ruling elites and leaders and ethnic sectarian and tribal subnational forces. But within the Arab world, six issues dynamically interact: the Palestinian problem; the Arab–Israeli conflict; domestic change and instability; oil prices; inter-Arab relations; relations with the outside world.[10]

Professor Khalidi maintained that it was ludicrous to say that the non-resolution of the Palestinian problem and the resulting perpetuation of the Arab–Israeli conflict were responsible for all the developments in the six fields listed above; but it would be 'sloppy regio-politics' to fail to take their significance into account.

These arguments were of no concern to President Reagan or Alexander Haig. As with Nixon and Kissinger, there was enough of the Cold War warrior in both of them to produce a sense of real pleasure in their short-sighted activities to outmanoeuvre the Soviet Union. Their next step was to expand the rationale for the use of the RDF.

The concept of RDF/CENTCOM, the Arab world and Israel

Contingency planning for the projection of US forces into the Gulf was speeded up with the enunciation of the Carter Doctrine in 1980. Thus, the Rapid Deployment Joint Task Force was formally established on 1 March 1981 under the Reagan Administration, with headquarters at MacDill Air Force Base in Florida. And, on 1 January 1983, it was redesignated as the US Central Command (CENTCOM). Although CENTCOM had no operational forces of its own, it could call upon reserves of some 300,000 personnel drawn from units in all four services.[11] The location of CENTCOM headquarters in Florida, however, tremendously complicated its ability to deploy rapidly. For this reason, considerable emphasis had been placed upon arrangements with friendly states in the vicinity of the Gulf, both to stockpile some supplies, in addition to those at Diego Garcia, and for routine and emergency use of the facilities in the region.

Given its special relationship with the US, Israel was well-suited and eager to play an explicitly crucial part in this system. Oman agreed to permit access for US facilities, which was regarded by the US as a key asset for CENTCOM.[12] The US also obtained transit and exercise agreements with Morocco and facilities in Turkey. But neither Saudi Arabia nor the rest of the Gulf states (and not even Egypt under Mubarak) could overtly play their assigned roles or explicitly offer the US bases without fear of repercussions in the Arab world. Nevertheless their security was tremendously improved with US help. Well-publicized and in-depth joint exercises were held with Egypt and bases were eventually obtained in Somalia.

It became increasingly clear that CENTCOM was the principal weapon envisaged by the US in its resolve to counter or deter any perceived or imagined Soviet thrust into the Gulf area. The Soviet Union was not, however, the only potential external threat. The Arab Middle East in general, including the Gulf area, saw Israel as well as Khomaini's Iran as a far more immediate menace. Hence, they became very wary of the potentially threatening nature of US military activities directed towards the region in any capacity other than as a counter to the Soviet Union. As the Soviets were not seen by the Arabs as a direct threat to the area, it was not difficult to imagine how American use of the RDF/CENTCOM to counter a regional or internal threat could have been considered as an external threat by one or more Arab states.

CENTCOM'S extensive strategic links with Israel, as well as the Arab states, also contained their own paradox for the US. Israel was ready to support US military strategic purposes in the region, but its desperate search for security in terms of Eretz or Greater Israel, at the expense of lands whose inhabitants were also included in the strategic consensus and the RDF/ CENTCOM concept, jeopardized those same purposes. Thus Israel's potential contribution carried with it a military advantage but a political disadvantage. For President Reagan, the military advantage was the more important, as he placed greater emphasis on global strategy than on peripheral concerns.

Jordan vehemently resented these American manoeuvres. In its view American intervention in the social and political fabric of Arab states would only complicate matters further, and thus become harmful and counter-productive. In an interview, in August 1985, former Prime Minister Badran put it this way:

When I discussed the RDF rationale with General Brown, I advised him not to get involved in a rapid or a slow deployment force in the Middle East. 'You can be sure that if you align yourself with any Gulf ruler, or prop up any ruler, you will guarantee that his own people will turn against him. You are not well qualified for an internal Gulf operation.'

He gave General Brown an example:

When South Yemen intruded into North Yemen in the 1970s, it was not the Americans who persuaded South Yemen to end hostilities. It was the Arabs who did so. Even Iraq, which was regarded by the Americans as a radical state, warned radical South Yemen to stop its activities or face the consequences. Jordan was ready to dispatch forces to Yemen too, if South Yemen did not heed the warnings . . . I explained to General Brown that the RDF is a false concept. What was more practical was to build up our defence capabilities, provided that weapons received from whatever source would have no strings attached.

These views were widely held on the popular level in the 1980s. But the US was not sympathetic to them. The RDF/CENTCOM plan, supported by its main proponent, Israel, was to remain in high gear for some time yet.

7 The US, Israel and Jordan; collaboration and discord

Assistance to Israel

Arms supplies are a major factor in US strategy toward the Middle East. 'Security assistance and arms sales improve our forward defense and help our friends to defend themselves', Secretary of Defense Weinberger explained in testimony before the House Foreign Affairs Committee on 9 February 1984. 'These military assistance programs are the overseas counterparts of our defense efforts and represent no less an investment in US national security than the programs for the Department of Defense itself. It is an essential instrument of overall US defense strategy and foreign policy.'

The US commitment to assist Israel in economic and military terms is based upon what is perceived as its value as a strategic asset in the Middle East; and support for Israel is rooted in perceived common cultural, religious and political values. The fact that some Arab countries are also supplied with weaponry in an attempt to improve their capability to meet threats from Iran or elsewhere – but excluding Israel – and to deter what was seen then as Soviet expansionism, poses a problem for the US in that it could also increase the potential Arab threat against Israel. Israel is therefore always provided with more assistance than the Arabs not only to maintain the balance, but also in the hope that by thus providing it with a cushion of security, Israeli pre-emptive attacks on the Arab states can be prevented.

According to the US General Accounting Office (GAO) report released on 24 June 1983, the US has given assistance to Israel since 1948, totalling up to fiscal year 1982 over $24 bn. This included about $16 bn in military loans and grants, about $6 bn in economic assistance loans and grants under the security assistance programmes, and over $2 bn in other non-security assistance programmes including funds for housing guarantees, Export-Import Bank loans and aid for re-settling Jews from the Soviet Union. Aid levels increased significantly after 1973, almost half of the military assistance being in the form of grants; since 1975, economic aid has been on a cash transfer basis, which means that funds are not linked to specific programmes or commodity imports. During fiscal year 1982, Israel was authorized to obtain its grant funds before its loan funds for military purchases; this allowed it to defer, for many years, interest payments of approximately $19m.

For fiscal year 1983, the US Congress approved $1.7 bn Foreign Military Sales assistance with a grant element of $750m.; this was meant to appease Israel for the sale of AWACS and F-15 aircraft to Saudi Arabia. It also received a trade offset arrangement from US firms, when it made FMS purchases; such commitments to purchase specified amounts of Israeli goods or services are common under commercial arms sales but unusual under FMS. Israel also asked for additional concessions such as permission to purchase Israeli goods with FMS credits; normally FMS credits are used for purchases in the US. Israel has also been provided with military technology with export potential. The GAO report confirmed that this would have an adverse impact on the US economy, and could affect the US ability to control the proliferation of such technology.

More recent figures were supplied by Secretary of State Shultz in his statement to the Committee on Foreign Affairs of the US House of Representatives on 19 February 1985. During 1986, the military sales account was to rise to $1.8 bn as opposed to $1.4 bn in 1985, and Shultz indicated that the Administration was recommending a significant increase in FMS on a grant basis. He further added that in October 1984, the US and Israeli governments agreed to establish a joint economic development group to supervise economic development in Israel, and the role of US assistance in support of Israel's adjustment programme and development objectives. He also specified that during Peres's visit in October 1984, the US agreed to promote foreign investment in Israel, particularly in the high technology area. As far as aid in 1987 and 1988 was concerned, Israel got $3 bn for each year, $1,200m. in ESF and $1,800m. in FMS.[1]

According to the uncensored draft GAO report the US government understands that US weaponry sold to Israel has been used for attacks on Arab countries, violating the purpose for which it was provided, and has enabled Israel to occupy Arab lands and, with US financial assistance, to maintain the building of settlements in the occupied territories. It also understands that its silence on the settlements gives the impression of its tacit endorsement of such policies, and that the structure of its military aid package is not related to Israel's compliance with US foreign policy. Nevertheless, the US does not cut off the flow of weapons as the law provides when violations occur: it merely questions such moves. It understands Israeli fears that its enemies are too close, which means an understanding, if not an implicit approval, of Israeli undertakings against Arab allies of the US in the Middle East. The government calculates that any cut in the assistance programme would trigger a crisis in political relations between Israel and the US. It could lead to a perception among the Arabs that US support for Israel was waning;

hence the peace process, as defined by the US and Israel, would be halted. Moreover, it would weaken Israel's military capability, and Israeli economic difficulties could lead to a request for a rescheduling of military debts.

Nevertheless, by providing arms to Israel and certain Arab allies, the US contributes to a spiralling arms transfer process in the Middle East. For instance, the sale of AWACS and F-15s to Saudi Arabia led to an increase in FMS assistance to Israel. The US government acknowledges the impact of its policies on the Middle East arms race. Yet, in his State of the Union address in 1985, President Reagan declared:

Dollar for dollar, our security assistance contributed as much to global security as our own defense budget. Strengthening our friends is one of the most effective ways of protecting our interests and furthering our goals. Foreign assistance is a prudent investment in our future and the world's future.

Assistance to Jordan

'The preservation of Jordan's security, integrity and its unique character remains a matter of the highest importance', President Reagan stated in November 1981.[2] Why? 'It was only because Jordan figured high in almost every peace process envisaged for the area. President Reagan wants to enter the history books, as President Carter did, as a promoter of peace via Jordan's envisaged role in the process', Prince Hassan of Jordan commented.[3] Secretary of State Shultz confirmed the Prince's analysis in his testimony to the House Committee. 'Our economic and military assistance programs are needed to strengthen Jordan's security and economy, both of which are vital to enable Jordan to confront the risks involved in playing a significant role in the peace process.' But the US set limits to its assistance to Jordan. 'Any decision on future sales to Jordan or any other country in the region will be made in the context of my administration's firm commitment to Israel's security', President Reagan declared in February 1982.

The House sub-committee, in the mark-up of the financial year 1986 Foreign Aid Appropriation Bill, passed the so-called 'Smith Amendment' which read as follows:

Section 403: It shall be the policy of the Congress to consider a Jordanian request for major defense articles upon the commencement of direct negotiations between Israel and Jordan, if Israel is willing to enter into such negotiations.

In the joint conference debating the 1986 Bill, it was proposed that the Smith Amendment be modified in the following manner:

(a) Middle East: The Foreign Military Sales Financing authorized by this Act, for Jordan, is provided and increased in recognition of the progress Jordan has made in the search for a just and lasting peace in the Middle

East and to encourage further progress, in recognition of the continuing defence needs of Jordan, and in the expectation that Jordan will enter into direct negotiations with Israel, based on UN resolutions 242 and 338 and the Camp David Accords, in order to resolve the state of war between these two countries.

(b) Certification: it is the view of the Congress that no foreign military sales financing authorized by this act may be used to finance the procurement by Jordan of advanced US aircraft, new air defense weapons systems or other new advanced military weapons systems, and no certification may be made pursuant to Section 36(b) of the Arms Export Control Act with respect to a proposed sale to Jordan of advanced US aircraft, new air defence systems, or other new advanced military weapons systems, unless the President has certified to Congress that Jordan is publicly committed to the recognition of Israel, and to negotiate promptly and directly with Israel under the basic tenets of UN Resolutions 242 and 338 (and the Camp David Accords).[4]

The final version actually deleted the reference to Camp David but stressed that 'Jordan must express its readiness to negotiate promptly and directly with Israel under the basic tenets of UN Resolutions 242 and 338.' The idea was to avoid two situations which might be uncomfortable for Jordan. First, by expressing its 'readiness to negotiate' – and it takes two to negotiate – Jordan would avoid becoming hostage to Israel's reluctance to do so. Secondly, by using the word 'directly', rather than 'direct', Jordan would avoid the translation into Arabic as 'bilateral, face-to-face' negotiations with Israel and stress the meaning as 'immediately' or 'expeditiously' instead. The wording of the final version was totally acceptable to Jordan, and King Hussain seemed to meet the conditions laid down by Congress. But, on 24 October 1985, the Senate banned an arms sale to Jordan worth $1.9 bn pending direct negotiations with Israel. Jordan was given until March 1986 to consider the situation. As Jordan's lobbyist, Denis M. Neill, commented: 'After the King had jumped through hoops, they raised the price and created a higher hoop.'[5]

The general attitude in Washington seemed to be that if assistance, whether economic or military, was granted to Jordan, it would be aimed not at dangers emanating from Israel or Iran, or at radicalism or terrorism, but at Arab states and forces which objected to peace moves dictated by the US and Israel. In order to qualify for American arms, Jordan had first to enter into direct and prompt negotiations with Israel. Whatever it did to placate the US, however, the level of weaponry recognized by the US as necessary for its defence would always be just sufficient to avoid endangering what was envisaged as Israel's security. And, even if Jordan was willing to enter into such direct negotiations with Israel, the initiative would in the last resort be left to Israel. This meant that Israel would not be pressured by the US to enter such negotiations, even if King Hussain abided by the American rules.

From intensive interviews conducted in Jordan in 1985 with both officials and members of the general public, it can be confidently stated that the American approach was regarded by a large section of the Jordanian population as bizarre, insensitive, senseless, and brutal arm-twisting, to say the least. The only restrained diplomatic tone was heard from King Hussain himself, against whom the US pressure was mostly being applied. 'One wouldn't like to use the word blackmail, but it is totally unacceptable', he said. Behind such a pronouncement lay amazement at what he termed 'the peculiar and indefensible American commitment to Israel's security alone, a commitment which seems to equate security with conquest'.[6] In a speech from the throne at the opening of a new session of parliament in November 1985, he declared, 'We wish to reiterate here our unwavering determination to meet our armed forces' need for the most advanced weapons and equipment from all sources available to us regardless of the obstacles placed in our way.' And Prince Hassan affirmed

Jordan is determined not to make the acquisition of its armaments subject to the whims, desires or approval of Israel and its American supporters. This is not a question of injured dignity, but one of principle. Our independent sovereignty and territorial integrity should not be – and we will not allow it to be – secondary to that of Israel.[7]

There is no doubt that the US has often used arms sales and economic assistance as a device for applying political pressure.[8] In deference to Israel, Jordanian requests for arms to enhance its defensive capabilities were almost always denied by the US Congress. At best, a small portion of the request was granted with strings attached. The following events serve as illustrative examples.

In November 1974, during the Ford Administration, Jordan requested the following air defence weapon systems: improved Hawk batteries; Chaparral mobile, light SAM missiles; Vulcan radar-guided AA guns; Redeye portable surface-to-air missiles; and the Florida NADGE sensor and command-and-control systems. This request was based on informal advice from experts in the US Department of Defense and arrangements were made with the Saudis to finance the package. As the negotiations proceeded, other senior US officials decided that such a sale would be a threat to Israel. What was formally offered in April 1975 was withdrawn three months later mainly due to Congressional objections. A compromise was reached in September whereby the 14 Hawks – designed as mobile missiles – were offered on condition that they be placed permanently in an area other than the Jordan

Valley and only around the capital, Amman. The offer was accepted on the understanding that the finance would be totally secured through US military assistance.

In September 1976, negotiations started on the Hawk package, which was slightly expanded to include the following: 14 fixed-site Hawk batteries with 84 launchers and more than 500 missiles; 100 Vulcan radar-guided self-propelled 20mm AA guns; and 300 Redeye missiles. Saudi Arabia offered $540m to finance the sale. The US agreed to give Jordan what it had originally requested apart from the Chaparral mobile SAMs and Florida NADGE air control and warning system which were turned down due to concerns related to Israel's security.

During the Carter Administration, Jordan in 1978 requested the sale of F-16 fighters to replace its old fighters. According to Jordan the request was ignored and no alternative recommendations were made involving any other type of aircraft. The US government went further, threatening to suspend all military assistance in an attempt to force Jordan to join the Camp David peace process and, on 29 March 1979, the House of Representatives approved a military aid bill denying Jordan any funds until it played the role assigned to it by the Camp David Accords. Regarding this as blackmail, Jordan turned in anger to France in June 1979, requesting 36 F-1 Mirage fighters. Concerned that Jordan might apply to Moscow for military assistance, President Carter promised to consider Jordan's request of mid-1978 for 300 M60 A3 tanks. In September 1979, Jordan proceeded reluctantly with its deal because the US intended to delay the delivery of the thermal sights which provided the tanks with night-fighting capabilities, and to insist that Jordan give up an equal number of M48 tanks. Under these circumstances Jordan – while accepting the offer with the attached conditions – turned to Britain in November 1979 for 274 British Chieftain tanks, known in Jordan as Khalid tanks. In response the US Congress approved the dispatch of 810 M60 tanks to Israel in October 1980.[9]

Appendix C shows how the Carter Administration reduced US budgetary support to Jordan from $40m. in 1978 to $20m. in 1980. On 17 June 1980, King Hussain visited Washington for talks with President Carter. While he stressed the need for the military equipment denied him by the US, because of Jordan's vulnerability, he reiterated his stand against the Camp David Accords and emphasized the need to return to an international conference within a UN framework, to conduct peace talks in the presence of the PLO, and to address the question of Palestinian self-determination. Political developments in the Middle East in the next few months convinced the King that, with the door closed by the Carter Administration due to Jordan's refusal to play the role assigned to it by the Camp David Accords, he had to turn to an alternative source, namely, Moscow, to build up his defence capability. These political developments were connected with Syria's stance against Jordan. Syria, an ally of Iran in the Gulf War, mobilized its army in November 1980 along the border with Jordan, which was a staunch ally of Iraq, the official explanation being that Jordan was backing Moslem Brotherhood extremists against Assad's regime. Saudi Arabia temporarily defused the tension which, however, arose again in February 1981, when Syria's pretext was to stop any possible Jordanian deal with the US and Israel over the West Bank.

On 26 May 1981, King Hussain arrived in Moscow to negotiate the purchase of an air-defence system. While publicly endorsing the Soviet Union's proposal for an international conference on the Middle East – a signal to Syria that in no circumstances would he join the Camp David Accords – King Hussain clarified that the Soviet deal had been undertaken because of the vulnerability of his country to air attacks from Syria in particular. It was also a signal to the US that Jordan was not contemplating any aggressive action against Israel. In November 1981, a contract was concluded with the Soviet Union for the purchase of 20 SAM-8 vehicle-mounted surface-to-air missile units and 16 ZSU-244 AA gun units. It was understood that Iraq was to finance the package, which was worth $220m., less than half the $470m. paid for the 'fixed site' American Hawk missiles. However, Iraqi financial constraints due to the Gulf war meant that Jordan eventually had to finance the deal itself.

The details of the Russian deal became public by the end of January 1982. The new American President, Ronald Reagan, was keen to try his hand at cultivating closer ties with moderate Arab countries, such as Jordan and Saudi Arabia, in the hope that they could gradually be seduced into co-operating with the Camp David programme. He was also anxious to stop Russian supplies arriving in Jordan. He therefore sent his Secretary of Defense, Caspar Weinberger, to Amman in February 1982, in the hope of persuading Jordan to cancel the Soviet arms deal. With the failure of this mission, another US delegation, headed by Francis J. West, Assistant Secretary of Defense for International Security Affairs, arrived in Amman in early May, for the same purpose. West received a request for 36 F-16 fighters and Hawk and Stinger missile systems, among other items. The request was turned down almost immediately; the mere announcement by Weinberger in February that he had discussed the possibility of such a sale had touched off a storm of protest in Israel, and led Begin to warn the American President against any future sales to Jordan in a letter dated 15 February. The Reagan Administration recommended that Jordan replace the order for the F-16s with one for the less effective F-5Gs in the hope that Congress and Israel might not object.

In the event not a single item was approved by Congress. Instead the largest arms sale to Israel in four years – 75 F-16 jet fighters – was announced in May 1982, in addition to the sale of 75 F-16s concluded in 1978. Furthermore, as noted earlier, President Reagan proposed arms sales to Israel totalling $1.4 bn in 1982 and $1.7 bn in 1983. The whole US approach to Jordan, compared with the way it dealt with Israel, caused consternation in the Arab world. The announcement of the intended revival of strategic co-operation between Israel and the US, after the Sharon–Haig meeting in Washington in May 1982 and shortly before the Israeli invasion of Lebanon, provoked a similar reaction.

King Hussain returned to Moscow in June 1982 to discuss the possibility of Soviet help in enhancing Jordan's defence system. On 30 June, a deal covering various items, including SAM-8 missiles, was announced; however, the contract was not concluded until 1984. On arrival in Washington on 20 December 1982, King Hussain was faced by yet another demand. This time Washington stipulated that, in order to receive any advanced US weaponry, Jordan would have to enter into peace talks without PLO representation. In response, the King made three points. First, that continued Jewish settlement in the occupied territories was irrefutable evidence of Israel's unwillingness to enter negotiations in good faith, and if the practice continued, it would be absolutely impossible for him to join any talks. The practice did continue, however, and in August 1983 the US vetoed a UN Security Council Resolution requesting the dismantling of the settlements in the occupied territories. Second, that, even if Israel halted the settlements on the West Bank forthwith, he could not negotiate on his own because the Palestinians, represented by the PLO, would have to be a party to any solution. And third that, if he had to go so far as to seek arms from the Soviet Union, it was because of the attitude prevailing in Washington.

In October 1983, a key House sub-committee rejected a request from the Administration to provide Jordan with $225m. to set up what was termed in Washington a mobile Jordanian Strike Force, to help the Gulf states combat potential unrest. However, following the agreement to enhance strategic co-operation between Israel and the US – undertaken during the Shamir/Arens visit to Washington in November 1983 and which he hoped would forestall the Israeli government's objections – President Reagan informed Israel of his intention to revive the request. He assured Israel of his intention to limit Jordan's use of any equipment to the Gulf area; even the C-130 transport planes which were part of the deal would remain the responsibility of the US Air Force.[10] Repetition of the request in January 1984 met with stiff opposition, however, not only from Israel but also from Congress, on the grounds that the deal would present a threat to Israel. The Western media claimed that Washington was training a Jordanian force comprising two brigades of 8,000 soldiers, and that the money requested was for specialized equipment and transport planes needed by what was termed a Jordanian Rapid Deployment Force, an extended arm of the American Rapid Deployment Force. 'It was all fabrication. It was totally untrue. A Jordanian RDF does not exist. It has never existed', Sharif Zeid Ben Shaker, then Commander-in-Chief of the Jordanian armed forces, said when interviewed.[11] 'Furthermore', he added, 'no such training and no distribution of Jordanian forces under the name RDF has ever taken place.'

According to Sharif Zeid, what happened was as follows. An American mission approached Jordan to discuss the possibility of extending help to the Gulf area following the Iranian revolution. Jordan informed the mission that it was already giving such help; more than 1,000 Jordanian experts were helping to train the armies of the Gulf states. Help was also given to Kuwait in the 1960s when it was threatened by Abdul Karim Kassim of Iraq – and to Tunisia in its independence struggle. It was also given in the 1970s to Oman when it was threatened by South Yemen. Sharif Zeid maintained that, whether it received help from the US or not, Jordan would always give help when it was approached by an Arab country, not only because of its obligations under the Arab League Defence Pact, but also because of its conviction that it was part of an Arab world whose stability and security were vital to it. The American mission asked if Jordan wanted any backing from the US. 'It was an American suggestion. We did not ask specifically for anything', Sharif Zeid stated. On this basis, President Reagan approached Congress for a $220m. appropriation to enhance the combat readiness of the Jordanian armed forces.

In turn, King Hussein stressed to the Western media that the Jordanian forces would be used only in self-defence against any threat, whether from Israel or any other source, or at the request of Arab countries, but never at the behest or on behalf of the US or any other outside power.[12]

Appendix C shows how American economic assistance to Jordan decreased during President Reagan's first term of office. Budgetary support, which amounted to $20m. in 1980, vanished completely. Technical assistance grants were halved and then halved again in 1981 and 1982, before being increased in the following two years in an obvious attempt to encourage Jordan to enter the Middle East peace process on American terms. Under Public Law 480, Title I (Loan) vanished completely from 1980, as did Title II (Grant) in 1984. Military aid under FMSC and IMET similarly declined from $29.3m. in 1980 to only $1m. in 1981, ultimately rising to $2.5m. in 1985. General credits were the only form of aid which grew steadily, from $50m. in 1980 to $90m. in 1985.

Jordan lies at the hub of the eastern Arab world. By virtue of this geographical location, it is more directly affected by regional security or instability than any other part of the Arab world. On its western flank it shares an extensive cease-fire line with Israel. Hence it perceives itself as the vulnerable front-line defence of the Arabian Peninsula. Jordan's insistence on securing major defensive weapons systems stems from its view of its national and regional obligations, and of the danger it faces from Israel in particular. It believes that its defence lies ultimately in its own hands. This conclusion has been reached in the 1980s because of the gradual change in American approaches to the region, as Prince Hassan explained:[13]

Compared with the early 1950s – when the US believed that the surest way to curb Communist expansion in the Middle East was by preserving the Arab Islamic identity, character and regional stability – the US is nowadays reverting to different concepts. Regionalism is substituted by bilateralism, foreign policy is substituted by diplomacy. Bilateral relations with states of the region are being established on the basis of purely materialistic self-interest, taking into consideration the political cost incurred in the American domestic political arena.

In replacing regionalism, bilateralism assumed greater importance with the promotion of the strategic consensus rationale, among rival states which share no collective consensual concepts. Even the RDF concept, promoted in the early 1980s, is becoming a concept which will be out of date, with the development of the Star Wars programmes. If the US can eventually develop the capability to defend itself solely from the American continent, its interest in the rest of the world would be left to be guarded by its trusted protectorates. Hence the relationship with Israel is becoming a total relationship. Israel is currently taking advantage of its 'second tier' relationship with the US to promote what are perceived in Washington as US regional interests against the USSR. But by establishing a total strategic relationship with Israel, the US is surpassing all reasonable limits by by-passing not only the region as an entity, but also all bilateral relations with Arab states.

Our relationship with the US had been a special one, in different aspects. Since Camp David and the predominance of the Congress in shaping whatever is left of US foreign policy, our relationship deteriorated to its lowest point. Through the US insistence on ignoring legitimate Palestinian rights – a basic ingredient for the stability of the region – we became very cautious in our dealings with the US.

Our relationship with the US is currently a 'one-tier' relationship. We have economic, political, security and social concerns. When we establish a dialogue with the US, to address these issues, we do so from the point of view that the US ought to promote the identity and continuity of the region for the sake of its stability, vital for the stability of the world . . . But the broadmindedness necessary to enable it to understand that the unsatisfied individual carries with him the seeds of instability is seriously missing. If the stability of the Gulf area is deemed to be the predominant issue, the US ought to understand that the security of the Gulf complements that of the area around it. The US can only defend oil-fields. But the mere attempt to do so would push thousands and thousands of Arab Moslems in the area into the arms of promoters of radicalism, be they rightists or leftists.

From this survey of the relationship expressed in September 1985, one can conclude that Jordan's understanding of regionalism, of the interrelationship between Middle Eastern issues, and of the importance of its existence as a stable moderate state, does not coincide with the views of Washington. This explains why the US abandoned Jordan to fend for itself against the surrounding threats.

The predominant threat was that posed by the expansionist policy of Israeli hawks. First, what were they to do with the Arabs now under Israeli occupation? The domestic political debate pitted those who saw Israel's borders in politico-religious terms against those who viewed them primarily in security and strategic terms. The territorial solution advocated by Likud aimed at the maximization of Israeli control over the occupied territories aided by a grid pattern of Israeli settlements which split up and isolated the Arab areas. Once control was completely established, it was envisaged that the Arab population, or most of it, would prefer to emigrate or would be encouraged or forced to do so. The transfer of Arab lands into Jewish hands implied the transformation of the remaining minority of the Palestinians into a marginal proletariat working at manual and unskilled jobs in Israeli-controlled enterprises. The remaining problem was what to do with the rest who could not be absorbed and who resisted forcible evacuation.

The Labour Party, on the other hand, offered a sociological solution for the occupied territories which could save Israel from upsetting the demographic and ethnic balance, and also preserve the Jewish character of the state. This was to get rid of responsibility for the indigenous Palestinian population along with some of the heavily populated areas of the West Bank via a deal with King Hussain. Initially prepared by Yigal Allon, the Israeli Foreign Minister from 1971 to 1977, the Allon Plan has become a permanent option in Labour thinking. It implied adding the majority of the Palestinians of the West Bank and Gaza to the Palestinian refugees who fled to Jordan as a result of the Arab–Israeli wars. The Israeli army had to remain positioned along the Jordan Valley, where a string of Jewish settlements had already been established. King Hussain had to assume responsibility for the administration and security of the area, crushing any Palestinian activity against Israel from territory under his control. In other words, he was expected to assume the burden of the refugees, to waive all claims on Jerusalem and to provide for the Palestinian national identity, and the Palestinian right to self-determination, in Jordan.

From the political point of view, the Jordanian option removed the necessity of dealing directly with the PLO, by handing over the problem to the Jordanian government. It was convenient for both of Israel's main political groupings, who sought the liquidation of the PLO and prohibited any form of contact with it. Both supported the idea behind the establishment of settlements, although they differed on where and at what pace they could be established. Both basically regarded Jordan, with some variations, as 'the

Palestinian state'. As the Labour leader, Shimon Peres, put it in an interview in 1981:

On the political plane our government, unlike Begin's, will be willing to withdraw from occupied territory on the West Bank and Gaza Strip. These territories would be transferred to the Jordanian–Palestinian State which would include the majority of the existing Palestinian population.[14]

Such pronouncements strengthened Jordan's view that a change in government or governmental structure in Israel could provide no revolutionary change in Israeli policies, because the Arab world was not actually dealing with different political figures or schools of political thought. It was dealing with Zionism as an ideology. Thus the 'Jordanian Option' was envisaged in Jordan as no more than an attempt to force a wedge between Jordan and the PLO, and widen the differences between the Arab states. As it was strongly believed that no people had the right to impose a solution regarding the future of another, the mere idea of a Jordanian Option was seen as an attempt to obscure the right of the Palestinian people to self-determination on their own soil.

Suggestions about a political settlement of the Palestinian problem on Jordanian soil stemmed originally from an implicit, and sometimes explicit, reference to the former British Mandate applying to Palestine as well as to the East Bank of the River Jordan. But the historical facts set out in Chapter 1 proved the situation to be different. The intention behind the assertion that the Mandate also applied to the East Bank was to show that there was still room for a Palestinian State/homeland/entity on the East Bank, since it too 'was part of the Mandate of Palestine'. What was more serious, from Jordan's point of view, was that this argument wrote off the legitimate national rights of a whole people, the Jordanian people. It was tantamount to calling for the destruction of an independent sovereign state, a member of the United Nations. Hence, according to Jordan, the relation of the Mandate to the search for a political solution now could be seen as follows:

(a) Paragraph 2 of the Preamble to the Mandate, relating to the establishment of a Jewish Home in Palestine, clearly stated that nothing should be done which might prejudice the civil and religious rights of existing non-Jewish communities in Palestine. At that time, these so-called non-Jewish communities constituted 92 per cent of the population. The establishment of Israel in 1948 deprived more than a million Palestinian Arabs of their homes and basic rights. If the Mandate provisions were to be applied within the context of a political settlement today, the need to reinstate these rights of the Palestinian Arabs had to be recognized.

(b) The UN Partition Plan, Number 181(11) of 29 November 1947, partitioned Palestine and allocated roughly 56 per cent of Palestine to the Jewish state and 44 per cent to the Arab state. Israel, however, emerged in 1948 occupying 78 per cent of Palestine. Thus, from the legal viewpoint, if there were territories to be reallocated, they had to include the 22 per cent of Palestine Israel additionally occupied by force in 1948.

(c) Security Council Resolution 242 of 22 November 1967 called for Israel's withdrawal from Arab territories occupied in June 1967 and emphatically affirmed the principle of non-acquisition of territory by force. Consequently Israel's withdrawal from the West Bank became a logical pre-requisite for the establishment of a just and long-lasting peace.[15]

The idea that 'Jordan is Palestine' had found no widespread support anywhere outside Israel and some circles in the United States. The thesis reflected a determination by some hardliners to supplant the Palestinians of the West Bank and Gaza, to squeeze them out through economic and military pressure, and to place the burden of Palestinian homelessness and statelessness on Jordan. By absolving itself from responsibility, Israel, or at least the hardliners, aimed to justify and legitimize the occupation, while relieving the international pressure by declaring that a Palestinian or a refugee question no longer existed, because the Palestinians were in their own home, Jordan. The promotion of such ideas was seen by the Arab world as an attack on the legitimacy of Jordan as a sovereign state. And it was seen by Jordan as a declaration of war. As King Hussain put it in 1981:

Such a stance means that Israel considers itself established on its own land and that the solution of the Palestinian cause is a Jordanian issue, outside the territories occupied by Israel. This can take place only through a military operation whose objective is the occupation of Jordan.[16]

Despite its economic limitations, Jordan has received an influx of refugees as a result of the Arab–Israeli wars. But no political observer could ignore the determined opposition Palestinians had voiced to all proposals for resettlement anywhere other than in what they regarded as their homeland, and from which they were forced to flee. Farouk Nasser, a prominent Palestinian millionaire working in Saudi Arabia in the 1970s and early 1980s, told *Time* magazine in 1980:

I tell you why I want to go to Palestine: I was born there. I know the trees. I know the streets. I know everybody. I live like a king. But Palestine belongs to me. Begin after all is a Pole.[17]

After conducting interviews with many Palestinians scattered throughout the world, *Time* magazine concluded:

They speak with many accents but the message is the same, forceful and unrelenting in its demand for a homeland and desire for return. Their political views vary, as do their opinions on the best way to achieve their goal of an independent state. But as a people, they have managed to force a special bond of community rooted in an obsessive longing for the idealized soil of Palestine.

It could be said that a state of mind has developed among the refugees which stigmatized assimilation into other Arab societies as an act of disloyalty. 'It is difficult to imagine a social group with a more homogeneous outlook and definition of the past and the present than the Palestinian people.'[18]

The 16th Palestinian National Council (PNC) held in Algiers on 22 February 1983 stated, however, that future relations with Jordan should be founded on the basis of a confederation between two independent states. The 17th PNC session held in Amman on 22 November 1984 re-emphasized the distinct nature of Palestinian–Jordanian relations, and the need to bolster these relations through a future confederation. In an attempt to clear up any doubts about the nature of this confederation, Yasser Arafat, the Chairman of the PLO, stated:

The struggle is for the liberation of our homeland and the realization of the inalienable Palestinian right to return to our homes and property and our right to establish our independent Palestinian state on our Palestinian soil with Jerusalem as its capital. We announce this clearly so that no person or side will have illusions about any alternative homeland other than Palestine.[19]

Addressing the same session King Hussain put the 'special relationship' in a geopolitical context:

Palestine is the invader's threshold to Jordan, just as Jordan is the gateway of conquest to Palestine. Defending Palestine means defending Jordan. This is the special relationship that has governed and will govern our Jordanian policy.

Permanently exiling the Palestinians to a country they did not regard as their own was seen in the Arab world as a recipe for perpetual instability, not only in Jordan but in the region as a whole. Jordanians in particular wondered: could not an unstable Palestinian–Jordanian state in Jordan, with a disgruntled Palestinian majority in exile, with its greater geographic depth and military power, be more dangerous to Israel than a demilitarized entity/homeland/state on the West Bank and Gaza?[20] Could it not present itself as a more convenient territory for Soviet influence than a settled entity/homeland/state absorbing Palestine nationhood on Palestinian soil?[21] Could it not present itself as a suitable territory for Israeli disruption and interference and thus extend Israel's influence, and also threaten Jordan's oil-rich neighbour Saudi Arabia?[22] Could it not be a pioneering project for disintegrating the social and political fabric of the Arab world?[23] These types of questions suggested the existence of a deeply rooted belief in Jordan that Israel's military power could not and will not make up for its inferiority complex in a sea of Arab states, heavily populated and rich with future prospects, and that this underlies its determination to disrupt them. Hence,

Jordan's determination to strengthen its defences – despite the hardship incurred – with help from whatever source and at whatever price.

The history of mankind is a graveyard of great cultures that came to catastrophic ends because of their incapacity for planned, rational, voluntary reaction to challenge. Jordan had been always determined to face the challenge because it was determined to survive.

8 Two cases of collaboration and discord

The first half of this chapter focuses on the Israeli invasion of Lebanon, because of its destabilizing effects on the region as a whole, and therefore on Jordan. Its demonstration of the intrinsic weakness of US Middle East policy and of the dominance of Israeli influence over that policy make it an important factor in the overall US–Arab relationship. The second half of the chapter deals with the attempt to revive the US initiative with the launching of the Reagan Plan.

1982: The Israeli invasion of Lebanon

June 1982 witnessed a major act of war, as Israel embarked on a large-scale iɴvasion of Lebanon. To achieve peace for Galilee by establishing a 25-mile security zone inside Lebanon was the first declared Israeli aim. But Galilee was already enjoying peace as a result of the July 1981 ceasefire negotiated by Philip Habib, the then US special envoy in the Middle East. It became increasingly clear that the declared original aim was a smoke screen for ulterior motives, as General Eitan, the Chief of Staff of the Israeli army, elaborated in *Ha'aretz* of 9 July:

The Israeli march into Lebanon was a part of the struggle over Eretz Israel. That is the point. This whole battle in Beirut, it is the struggle over Eretz Israel. A war against the enemy that has been fighting over Eretz Israel for a hundred years.

The relationship between the invasion and the need to obtain the submission of the Arab population in the occupied territories was clearly delineated by Defence Minister Sharon: 'The bigger the blow and the more we damage the PLO infrastructure, the more the Arabs in Judea and Samaria [West Bank and Gaza] will be ready to negotiate with us and establish co-existence.'[1] The backbone and spirit of the Palestinians had to be broken in Lebanon so as to put into effect the Israeli version of autonomy in the occupied territories. 'Not only its hands and fingers in the West Bank must be amputated', *Ha'aretz* of 23 May intoned, 'but its head and heart in Beirut must be dealt with.'

90

By smashing the PLO, the symbol of Palestinian identity, Israel hoped to achieve another associated aim, which was expressed in *Ha'aretz* of 25 June, by the Israeli scholar Yehushua Porath:

The government's hope is that the stricken PLO, lacking a logistic and territorial base, will return to its earlier policy of terrorism. It will carry out bombings throughout the world, hijack airplanes and murder many Israelis. In this way the PLO will lose part of the political legitimacy that it has gained, and will mobilize the large majority of the Israeli nation in hatred and disgust against it, undercutting the danger that events will develop among the Palestinians so that they might become a legitimate negotiating partner for future political accommodation.

General Sharon later elaborated on numerous occasions yet another aim: to ensure the installation of an amenable government in Lebanon which, with the help of Israel, would disarm and expel all unwanted forces, such as the Syrian deterrent force, the PLO and the Murabitoun, an indigenous Lebanese militia.[2] This grand design was in line with earlier Zionist dreams, eloquently expressed by Moshe Dayan, that not only should Lebanon ally itself with Israel, but the territory from the Litani River southward should be totally annexed by Israel.

The Litani River strikes a sensitive chord in the Arab world, where it is believed that Israel's aim has always been to obtain access to, or possibly control over, its waters which are the major sweet water source in Lebanon. The Arabs are convinced that water, a scarce commodity in the Middle East, has dominated the strategic thinking of Israel since its creation in 1948. King Hussain warned the Arab leaders, at their first summit meeting in Cairo in 1964, that, 'As Israel needs water, the Arabs will be the victims. After diverting water from the River Jordan, Lebanon will be next.'[3] It had also been noted in Jordan that Israel bargained with Sadat to divert water from the Nile to the Negev but that, after his assassination, the subject was temporarily dropped.

Within this framework, Israel's aim was seen from the outset of the invasion as, first, to accentuate the differences between the religious sect: in Lebanon, in other words, to divide and rule. It was further predicted that, if Israel did not succeed in persuading the Maronite President of Lebanon to co-operate, it would work to obtain a 25-mile security belt in the South of Lebanon which would include the water sources. Jordan went so far as to believe that, despite all the propaganda campaigns conducted by Israel and the US against the Syrian forces in Lebanon, Israel did not in fact want them to leave as they provided a credible pretext for Israel's forces to stay as well as opportunities to export Lebanon's divisions to Syria, which is similarly made up of ethnic minorities.

To justify eliminating the so-called centre of terrorism required an assessment of the actual violence perpetrated by the PLO, in order to establish the proportionality of Israel's response. The figures for Israeli victims of Palestinian 'terror' were given by General Sharon at the beginning of the invasion; in the fifteen years prior to the invasion, he stated that 1,392 Israeli lives had been lost through PLO violence,[4] but Israeli police archives gave the figure as 282. According to *Ha'aretz* of 16 July Sharon's figures included 285 Israeli soldiers who died in combat, 392 Palestinians from the occupied territories, including alleged bombers whose bombs exploded prematurely, and 326 individuals who were killed in various places by Palestinian activists. To justify the vast economic cost and the loss of more than 20,000 lives – after the Sabra and Shatila massacres – on the grounds of self-defence thus lacks credibility. It could indeed be stated that Israel's action was 'overwhelming, pre-meditated and out of all proportion to any initial wrong'.[5]

Interference in Lebanon's affairs had no legal validity, as Israel had no warrant to sit in judgement on whether Syria had violated the terms of the 1976 Arab League Agreement under which it was invited into Lebanon. Whether or not the PLO had also violated the 1969 Agreement concerning its activities in Lebanon was also a matter solely for the legal government of Lebanon, however tenuous its hold. Israel could not interpret agreements to which it was not a party. And the maintenance and enhancement of Lebanon's sovereignty was a matter between Lebanon and the Security Council of the United Nations.[6]

It is an established fact that the US not only had advance knowledge of Israel's plan to invade Lebanon, but also did nothing to stop it, on the basis that the action was, as Alexander Haig proclaimed, 'in response to an international recognized provocation and the response is proportionate to that provocation'.[7] Sharon was reported in the *Washington Post* of 15 June as follows:

I never spoke with the Americans about plans, time-tables, schedules. But for almost one year, that is since last September, I have been discussing with them the possibility that the operation would take place. I discussed it various times with Alexander Haig when he came to the Middle East. I discussed it with Weinberger when I went to Washington last November . . . I discussed it repeatedly with Ambassador Habib . . . When I spoke to them about Lebanon, I kept warning them: don't be caught by surprise if or when we do it . . . or if or when we do it, don't tell us that you are caught by surprise.

The Begin government had been attempting to persuade President Reagan that there could be no sequel to the Egyptian–Israeli peace treaty unless the Palestinian base in Lebanon was eliminated. The Reagan Administration accepted Israel's first aim of destroying the PLO militarily and politically, having agreed that the Palestinian problem should be settled in a manner that would ensure the disappearance from the political scene of a viable

Palestinian movement. Haig's announcement, on 28 January 1981, that international terrorism would be the focus of US policy was in line with Reagan's dictum that terrorism should be dealt with swiftly and unequivocally. Soviet financial aid and training for some elements of the PLO provided the US with enough evidence to show that the PLO embodied Soviet-sponsored terrorism.

On 6 June, the day the invasion began, Reagan received a letter from Begin assuring him that the army would push the PLO back to a distance of 25 miles to the north. But, contrary to this assurance, Israeli forces had reached the outskirts of Beirut by 10 June, and by 14 June had completely encircled it. This rapid advance brought them into direct conflict with Syrian ground forces. When the UN Security Council demanded that Israel withdraw its forces forthwith and unconditionally to the internationally recognized boundaries of Lebanon, Haig quickly proclaimed that 'The resolution is no longer adequate to the needs of the situation.'[8] A resolution sponsored by France proposing that the Palestinian forces and Israel institute a limited withdrawal from Beirut was vetoed by the US on 20 June as an attempt to preserve the PLO as a political and military force.[9]

With the single exception of a full Israeli military conquest of Beirut, the US Administration supported each and every Israeli goal as proclaimed. But unable any longer to ignore the public outrage over the severity of the attacks and the heavy casualties, President Reagan on 4 August called the Israeli assault disproportionate and appealed to Begin to stop unnecessary bloodshed. Begin responded in fury: 'Nobody, nobody is going to bring Israel to her knees. You must have forgotten that Jews kneel only to God.'[10] On the same day the Security Council adopted another resolution censuring Israel for the invasion of West Beirut. The US this time abstained and instead issued a plea to Israel to cease its destruction of West Beirut for as long as it would take Philip Habib to negotiate a Palestinian withdrawal. Begin warned that Habib must hurry, for Israel was losing patience. So Habib hurried, but not enough; Israel resumed its ferocious attacks, compelling him to suspend the negotiations. Reagan then warned Begin, in a telephone conversation, that if the bombing of 12 August was not stopped, Habib would have to suspend his efforts.[11]

Finally the negotiations were completed; the PLO agreed to leave on condition that the US gave written assurances for the safety of all the Palestinian civilians left behind. Habib declared:

The governments of Lebanon and the US will provide appropriate guarantees for the safety of law-abiding Palestinian non-combatants left in Beirut, including the families of those who depart. The US will provide its guarantees on the basis of assurances received from the government of Israel and from the leaders of certain groups with which it has been in contact. My government will do its utmost to ensure that the assurances are scrupulously observed.[12]

To supervise the withdrawal, the Security Council asked for the dispatch of
UN military observers from 1 August but, because of the Israeli rejection of
such a force, the US, although it voted for the resolution, did nothing to
enforce it. Instead, it sent 800 Marines on 25 August – the first US military
presence in Lebanon during the conflict – to join a multinational peace-
keeping force. By 30 August, the Palestinian evacuation had been completed,
and by 11 September, the multinational force withdrew apparently convinced that its 'mission was accomplished'.

The assassination of the newly elected Maronite President, Bashir
Gemayel, on 14 September, just two weeks after the PLO evacuation,
unleashed a dramatic chain of events. The Israeli army pushed into West
Beirut almost immediately, in violation of the agreement just concluded with
Habib. The well-publicized massacres at the Sabra and Shatila refugee
camps destroyed the credibility of the US as the guarantor of the Beirut
Agreement. The multinational force returned and, on 29 September, the US
Marines landed again in Beirut.

Confronted by the political vacuum left in Lebanon by the Israeli invasion,
the Reagan Administration sought first to pick up the pieces by pursuing a
variation of the Israeli plan, namely, to take over as 'guardian' of the new
President, Amin Gemayel, and gradually transform Lebanon into a stable
pro-American state at peace with Israel. The Marines became central to the
administration's hope of exploiting what was confidently seen as another
window of opportunity for US diplomacy and another major setback for the
USSR in the region. While not disavowing the Israeli initiative, the US
prevailed on Israel to pull back its forces from West Beirut, inserting itself
instead politically and militarily into the Lebanese conundrum. This must
have been welcomed by Israel, for US involvement in Lebanon meant the
deflection of world attention, including that of America, from the West Bank
and Gaza.

The first turning point in America's involvement came when George
Shultz, the new Secretary of State, committed his authority and prestige in
acting as midwife for the agreement between Israel and Lebanon of 17 May
1983. This seemed to equate the Israeli presence in Lebanon with that of
Syria, although the latter had taken place with the approval of the Arab
League and in response to an invitation from the then Lebanese government.
But the agreement also treated a trilateral conflict as if it were a bilateral one.
Instead of associating the Syrians with his mediation effort, Shultz ignored
them and backed Israel in a deliberate attempt to 'punish' Syria because of its
fraternization with the Soviet Union. To make matters worse, the terms of
the agreement were presented to Syria as a *fait accompli*.

The agreement, with its secret protocols, represented a blatant infringe-
ment of Lebanese sovereignty. It called for the termination of war and

normalization of relations between Israel and Lebanon, but gave Israel special rights in South Lebanon. In so doing it also threatened Syria's interests in Lebanon, which not only have historical roots, but also stem from security requirements, especially in the region of the Bek'aa Valley. A neutralized Lebanon exposed Syria's western flank to an Israeli thrust; without Syrian fortifications in the Bek'aa, Damascus and the cities in the centre of the country would have been robbed of protection. Israel established a surveillance base on the Barouk mountain high over the Bek'aa. Carefully monitored, Syrian SAMs were well entrenched in the Valley. So Syria viewed the agreement as not only helping to legitimize the Israeli invasion, by giving Israel special rights in South Lebanon, but as constituting a grave danger to its security. The agreement was also viewed as wresting Lebanon from Syria's influence into that of Israel. Moreover, if Lebanon followed Egypt into a separate peace treaty, Syria saw the loss of all chances of leverage on the issues of the Golan Heights and a Palestinian homeland, because a demilitarized Sinai and a neutralized Lebanon would allow Israel to complete its annexation of the West Bank and Gaza. As Syria was pursuing a comprehensive Middle East settlement to include the Golan as well as the Palestinian issue, it refused to retreat from Lebanon until there was a complete Israeli withdrawal and the establishment of Lebanon's authority right up to the Israeli–Lebanese armistice line.

The agreement, which was the high point of US expectations, began to falter with the filing of accusations that it was a sell-out of Arab interests. The Americans admitted that the agreement was in effect a peace treaty between Israel and Lebanon, although it was not so labelled. They also admitted that it was less than perfect. But they argued that the idea behind it was to put an end to attacks on Israel from Lebanon and to secure a partial Israeli withdrawal, backed by a promise to withdraw completely at a later stage.[13] As the Arab states saw no possibility of Israel making such a concession, Jordan and Saudi Arabia suggested to the Americans – without prior arrangement or consultation between them – that the security and political aspects of the agreement should be differentiated.[14] As both governments favoured a comprehensive rather than a partial Israeli withdrawal from occupied lands, they considered that the security aspects between Israel and Lebanon could be dealt with bilaterally, while the political aspects were postponed until further negotiations took place which included all the Arab parties concerned. Shultz went so far as to assure the Jordanians – before the agreement was concluded – that a comprehensive Israeli military withdrawal would take place first, followed by a peace agreement.[15] When the agreement was concluded prior to withdrawal, he confessed that he could get no more concessions from Israel.

The resulting protracted stalemate suggested that US policy had come to a dead end. In deference to Israel, the US kept pressing Gemayel to reject any modification of the agreement, although in its existing form it hindered him from broadening the base of his government. In the end, he renounced it on 16 February 1984, thus marking the end of one of the least successful episodes of US policy towards the Middle East in recent years.[16]

Meanwhile, on the ground, the heavy casualties led Israel to retreat from the Chouf mountains on 4 September 1983 to more secure lines along the Awali River. But it did not first ensure the withdrawal of the Phalange which it brought with it into the Chouf, a well-recognized Druze stronghold. The district thus became a time-bomb of Israeli making. With Israel arming both sides, the ensuing fighting marked the second crucial turning point for the US in Lebanon. American firepower was directed at the Chouf in a bid to save the Maronite Christian Militia and the Lebanese army from defeat by the Druze there and also in the hills above Beirut. American aircraft began provocative flights over Syrian artillery positions.

On 23 October, a truckload of explosives destroyed the Marines' headquarters at Beirut airport, killing 241 Marines. Almost immediately another truckload killed 59 troops from the French unit and, on 4 November, a similar operation killed 60 Israelis and their prisoners. Apparently more determined than ever, President Reagan announced that 'The perpetrators cannot take over that vital and strategic area of the earth.'[17] The perpetrators were indeed local Lebanese Shi'a Moslems. Reagan ordered the Marines to escalate the battle by means of the guns of the American Sixth Fleet lying off Beirut.

He had by now become obsessed with the idea of frightening Syria into a withdrawal from Lebanon by a show of military muscle. 'If Lebanon ends up under the tyranny of forces hostile to the West, not only will our strategic positions in the Eastern Mediterranean be threatened, but also the security of the entire Middle East, including the vast resources of the Arabian Peninsula.'[18] Lebanon, in other words, was now seen as a pawn in the endless East–West power struggle; according to this interpretation, Syria was a Soviet instrument, and the Shi'a and Druze were its surrogates. This perception underlay Reagan's decision to expand the role of the Marines from one of self-defence to one of support for the Lebanese army, and finally to order provocative oversights of Syrian artillery positions and to resort to naval shelling. Thus, step by step, the Marines were entangled in a mission which Israel had already abandoned in despair.

They soon came to be seen as siding with one of the factions in the protracted civil war, particularly since, while they were stationed in Lebanon, the US signed a further strategic co-operation agreement with Israel. They became a target of the forces opposed to the minority-based Gemayel government, and a hostage to the enemies of the US and Israel.

They united in opposition against them the passion of the Iranian revolution, the stubborn nationalism of Syria, and the enmity of the Lebanese Shi'a, who were exasperated beyond endurance by Israel's savage reprisals and heavy-handed occupation. This dogged concentration on Lebanon, to the virtual exclusion of all other aspects of the Arab–Israeli conflict, underscored how drastically the Reagan Administration had lowered its sights, until it was using the Marines as the cutting edge of a strategy aimed solely at shoring up the Gemayel government. Even Amin Gemayel realized the shortcomings of the American approach. 'Please', he appealed, 'continue concentration on the basic peace process. Lebanon was torn apart because of the absence of the peace process. And without a peace process it will take Lebanon a longer time for reconciliation.'[19]

It became increasingly clear, however, that the Marines were entangled in a mission that had nothing to do with peacemaking or indeed any peace process. A limited US military presence was inadequate to cope with the possibility of a major war – against Syria – which would also risk confrontation with the USSR. The few thousand members of the MNF clearly could not sort out the complex and intractable Lebanese problem by force of arms, and the resort to firepower thus became no more than a show of bravado in the face of helplessness. Ultimately President Reagan abruptly withdrew all but a token rearguard of the 1,800 Marines to the naval ships off the Beirut coast in February 1984. The remaining forces joined them in March, and on 30 March with the minimum of publicity, they slipped away from the Lebanese coast, demonstrating the defeat of Reagan's most ambitious foreign-policy undertaking in the Middle East.

It took Israel several more months to learn the limitations of its military power. The Cabinet decided, on 14 January 1985, on a unilateral three-phase withdrawal plan from Lebanon, leaving behind a virulent new enemy; the previously quiescent Shi'a Moslems of South Lebanon, who had been galvanized by religious faith and radicalized by the vicissitudes of foreign occupation, and who would afterwards fight with far more zeal and success than they had ever displayed before. The lesson that not every problem can be resolved by resort to arms was admitted by Defence Minister Rabin, when he told a meeting of the World Council of Synagogues in Jerusalem in February 1984 'Only a political solution could end guerrilla warfare in Lebanon. If there was an illusion that there could be one war in Lebanon which could end terrorism, it has been proven that it was an illusion.'[20]

Distressed by the casualties sustained during the invasion – 650 according to the official figures – Peres declared to the returning soldiers: 'We do not want Lebanese lands or Lebanese waters or Lebanese politics.' Reducing his goals to the minimum, he added, 'But if any one fires at us, nothing will prevent us from responding at once as is appropriate.'[21] Peres's declaration did not match the political developments which followed. Israel established a 'security belt' – as predicted by Jordan at the beginning of the invasion – in Southern Lebanon, manned by its Lebanese proxies. The area was subjected to an iron-fist policy, with escalating reprisals and counter-reprisals and mounting casualties on all sides. The security belt developed into a zone of direct and indirect Israeli control which proved to be much deeper than that which existed under Saad Haddad before the 1982 invasion. That had been a narrow strip between UNIFIL and the frontier. The signs were that the new zone was slicing through the eastern part of the UNIFIL zone to incorporate bridges over the Litani River, the strategic Beaufont Castle on its northern bank and the Hasbaya area in the southern approaches to the Bek'aa Valley.[22] The Jezzine salient remained under the control of Israel's militia surrogates linked to the security zone by a corridor.[23]

It was believed in the Arab world that, through this security zone, Israel maintained a platform for manipulation and political interference which would enable it to reach not only into the geographical and political heart of Lebanon for the foreseeable future, but also beyond Lebanon as well. As former Foreign Minister Marwan Al Qassem put it: 'The security zone is a dangerous precedent. What happens if resistance movements acquire rockets with a one hundred mile range? Would that require widening the security zone to incorporate further Arab lands?'[24] And he concluded: 'The Lebanese crisis brought about by the invasion is but one manifestation of the unresolved problem of Palestine. The way to deal with Lebanon is to resolve the overall crisis, not vice versa. Israel should not be allowed to reap the fruits of her aggression.'

The aftermath

The US retreat from Lebanon had serious repercussions in the wider Middle Eastern arena. The Syrian President enhanced his influence within Lebanon and the Arab world, through his success in blocking US plans. Amin Gemayel, the abandoned Lebanese President who paid the price of accepting US patronage, was eventually forced to acknowledge Syria's reassertion of its role as the dominant external influence in the country.

The overall beneficiary of President Reagan's misguided course of action in Lebanon was the Soviet Union. Reagan's strategic misconception created the very opening for the USSR which US policy was ostensibly desperate to plug. A senior American diplomat in the Middle East was asked why in his opinion the USSR did not challenge the US in Lebanon more vehemently. He answered, 'They waited for it to fall apart for us.' He added in frustration, 'And then they stepped in and picked up the pieces.'[25] The Soviets indeed appeared to be doing just that. The closer Syrian–Soviet military relationship that has since developed was a direct consequence of the massive Syrian aircraft losses at the outset of the invasion. After this uneven battle, Syria was able to press the Soviet Union not only for large-scale resupply of advanced weapons, but also for a promise of direct Soviet support in the event of an Israeli attack, thus reinforcing undertakings given earlier by Gromyko. The Soviet Union supplied Syria with an advanced air-defence system based on SAM5 and SAM6 missiles, as well as with long-range ground-to-ground missiles such as SS21s, and some 6,000 Soviet military technicians were reported to be in Damascus for a time, training the Syrians in the use of these and other systems.

On the other hand, Israel's intervention in Lebanese affairs, through the so-called security belt established in South Lebanon, had led Amal, the main Shi'a political organization in Lebanon, to ask the Soviet Union for arms to combat Israeli military pressure. Syria, with Iran's encouragement, is understood to have played a part in opening a direct channel of communication between Amal and Moscow. Interviewed by *The Observer*,[26] a Shi'a resistance spokesman indicated that turning to the Soviet Union was a choice forced on them by Israel's 'iron fist'. He also revealed details of the structure and strategy of the anti-Israel and increasingly anti-West guerrilla groups, not only Shi'a but Sunni, Christian and Druze and secular groups like the Syrian Social Nationalist Party, then active in Lebanon. All were united in stepping up attacks against the Israeli army, with the aim of sweeping it totally and unconditionally out of Lebanon, and in hatred of the US, which was seen as Israel's main supporter.

Thus, a vicious circle developed, in which American–Israeli collaboration – which provoked the intimacy among the Soviet Union, Syria and others – grew to an unprecedented level after the Lebanese débacle. In response to Syria, its proxies and by extension to the Soviets, the US increased military and economic aid to Israel to an astronomical level. To further buttress the link between the two governments, Defence Ministers Weinberger and Arens agreed in Washington on 19 March 1984, to a five-year renewal of the Memorandum of Understanding between them. This provided for expanding co-operation in research and development between the two defence establishments. It also improved the terms for the sale of Israeli arms to the US armed forces, permitting Israeli firms to compete on an equal footing with their American counterparts.[27] Congress voted to provide Israel with an advance of £2.6 bn from the 1985 budget.[28]

With the militarization and polarization of the highly volatile Middle East region, it became increasingly chimeric to attempt to bring the Arabs and Israel together in a collective security arrangement under American protection, against the common foe of international communism and terrorism. The ever-closer US association with Israel undermined the grand American design of strategic consensus, sharpened Arab apprehensions about unsolved regional conflicts, raised increased doubts about the effectiveness of the American role in the region and heightened the distrust of America's motives and of its intended role as an honest broker in resolving Arab–Israeli differences. Two weeks before his assassination, in January 1984, Professor Malcolm Kerr, the President of the American University at Beirut, lamented:[29]

I have yet to see an American President follow our interests in the Middle East very carefully, and intelligently. There is in the US a shallow conception of the Middle East, a conception that has not come to grips with the strategic, political, economic and human realities.

The unidentified group which claimed to have killed him declared: 'He was a victim of US foreign policy in the Middle East.'

The Reagan peace plan interlude

It took the US the experience of Lebanon to face up to what the Arab world had been stressing all along, that, in the words of George Shultz in his Congressional testimony:

The crisis in Lebanon made painfully clear a central reality in the Middle East: The legitimate needs and problems of the Palestinian people must be addressed and resolved urgently in all their dimensions. Beyond the suffering of the Palestinian people lies a complex of political problems which must be addressed if the Middle East is to know peace.

Shultz also stressed that, although the Palestinian and Lebanese problems were two different issues, they were related to each other. 'We must not let Lebanon distract our attention from the Palestinian problem.' At the same time, he pointed out that the Lebanese situation was linked to the question of Israel's security, and Israel's security was in turn linked to the security of the West. 'No one should dispute the depth and durability of American commitment to the security of Israel. I recognize that democratic Israel shares with us a deep commitment to the security of the West.'

One could conclude that after the enforced departure of Alexander Haig from office and of the PLO from Beirut, and with the memory of the heavy casualties in Lebanon fresh in the memory, a new attitude would begin to take shape in Washington. There was a desperate need to deflect the negative repercussions of the Israeli mission on the US's standing in the Middle East, and regain, or wrest away, the initiative in the region from Israel, in the hope that relations with moderate Arab countries could be improved. The strategic consensus concept could then be resurrected and a firmer defence constructed for the Gulf and the whole of the Middle East against Soviet encroachment. President Reagan therefore unveiled a peace plan for the Arab–Israeli conflict which envisaged peace neither on the basis of the formation of an independent Palestinian state – as propagated by the PLO – nor on that of Israeli sovereignty over, or permanent control of, the West Bank and Gaza – as propagated by the Likud – but on that of a final resolution of the Palestinian problem in association with Jordan, which would be designated as the representative of the Palestinian people in the negotiations. The Reagan Plan also advocated Israeli withdrawal – within the context of Security Council Resolution 242 – from all fronts, with the final borders to be determined by the extent of the true normalization and security arrangements offered in return. President Reagan left the formula for Jerusalem vague, stating merely that it should be 'indivisible'.

Two weeks before the Plan was unveiled, two American ambassadors, Veliotes and Viets, carried the details to Jordan. 'Why not to Israel?' Ambassador Veliotes was asked in an interview in Washington on 13 July 1988. 'Because the aim was to demonstrate, particularly in the aftermath of Lebanon, that this was an American plan. If we were to give it to Begin earlier, no matter what was in the plan, we were going to be vulnerable to the charge that it was really an Israeli plan the Americans were supporting.' 'And what was King Hussein's immediate reaction?' Ambassador Viets was asked, also in an interview in Washington on 5 July 1988. 'Concern as to whether this initiative represented a genuine American effort to resolve the Arab–Israeli issue, an effort in which the full resources of the US government would be brought to bear, an effort in which the US would remain committed to its proposal, an effort which the US would sustain.'

To reassure Jordan President Reagan sent two personal letters to King Hussein during his visit to Washington in December 1982. The first promised, among other things, that if the King would merely offer to enter peace talks with Israel, the US would try to halt the building of Israeli settlements in the West Bank and Gaza and Jordan would not be pressed to join in negotiating transition arrangements until a freeze on new Israeli settlement activity had been achieved; once peace talks had started, the US would put forward an 'American draft' of ideas for a possible agreement; the transitional arrangement for the occupied lands should be effective as soon as negotiated, and it was hoped that talks would then begin immediately on deciding the final status of the territories. The President also offered to reward the King by pressing Congress to allow Jordan to buy a squadron of F-16s. The second letter recorded Reagan's personal commitment to the talks and to UN Resolution 242. It may have been meant to show the doubting Arabs that the President meant business.[30]

Obviously, Reagan promised more than he could deliver, but it was assumed that both letters were written and signed in good faith. The

President must have thought that his personal popularity and standing within the country as a whole would support and sustain the types of commitments he had made. And his administration, which lacked experience in high-level negotiations on complicated international issues, must have thought they could handle Israel as well as Lebanon.

In late December 1982 Congress handed Israel $500m. President Reagan fought the decision publicly on policy and on budgetary grounds. As Ambassador Veliotes put it:

We knew this money was going to be viewed in Israel and everywhere else as payment for Lebanon. We fought and we lost. With it we lost any chance of moving on the Reagan Plan . . . I am not suggesting if the vote had gone the other way we would have succeeded either in getting Israel back to the Lebanese borders on a better time-table or better conditions . . . but at least we would have demonstrated that we were not rewarding the Israelis for what they had done in Lebanon. That was something we did to ourselves. The President was clearly sold out.[31]

But when interviewed in Washington on 12 July 1988 Ambassador Robert Neumann rationalized it all:

American policy in the Middle East is politics and therefore can be carried forward only if the President himself takes an interest in it. Once he does, he puts his political position on the line and then he becomes the victim of political counter-pressures. The presidential leadership is indeed a double-edged sword.

Analysis and reactions

The Reagan Plan was an elaborate extension of the Camp David formula, with its success or failure hinging on Israel's approval and the extent of Jordan's participation, which, in turn, was dependent upon a green light from the PLO. On the surface, the plan seemed to strive for a balance: Israel was denied permanent control, and the Palestinians were denied statehood. But, in adding that the final status of the occupied territories was to be reached through 'the give and take of negotiations', President Reagan in fact gave Israel considerable room for manoeuvre.

It may be recalled that the Camp David Accords also stated that negotiations between Egypt, Israel, Jordan and the local Palestinians should take place to determine the final status of the West Bank and Gaza. As Israel was to participate, there was no possibility of establishing an independent Palestinian state, and that was the very reason why the Camp David framework met with a rebuff from the PLO. Reagan, Shultz and his predecessor, Haig, must have concluded that the military defeat of the PLO – as a result of the Lebanese invasion – would now preclude it from adopting such a position this time. Its departure from Lebanon and the destruction of its territorial base seemed to rule out its having a veto on any decision concerning the Palestinian issue. What was not taken into account, however, was the re-emergence of the militarily defeated PLO outside Lebanon, with its political stature and influence not only intact but actually enhanced by what was popularly regarded among the Arabs as its heroic stand for 80 days in Beirut against the might of Israel. The longest period previously that the combined military machine of the Arab states had withstood Israel was two weeks during the 1973 war.

Reagan's suggestion of a transitional period of autonomy for the inhabitants of the West Bank, leading to their eventual linkage with Jordan, complemented his own interpretation of the Camp David Accords. But, by insisting that the Palestinian identity could be expressed only within the Jordanian context, he was inviting a determined challenge from the Palestinians, not only to defend their separate identity and their right to self-determination, but also to reassert the PLO's role as the organized expression of that identity. President Reagan did not satisfy Israel on this point either, because it claimed that association with Jordan amounted to support for the creation of a Palestinian state, since there would have been nothing to prevent a Palestinian political entity associated with Jordan being handed over to the PLO by King Hussain.

The Reagan Plan acknowledged the 'homelessness' of the Palestinians, 'their just yearning for their identity', and that the problem was 'more than a question of refugees'. But what attracted attention was the reference to the 'legitimate rights' of the Palestinians. Did use of such a tautological phrase imply that some Palestinian rights – such as national rights – were not considered legitimate because they contradicted Israel's national rights, and that therefore the internationally recognized right of peoples to self-determination was not legitimate as far as the Palestinians were concerned? Such a conclusion is supported by the fact that self-determination and national rights were both terms deliberately excluded from the Camp David Accords and the Reagan formula.

At every stage of his initiative President Reagan declared that the US commitment to Israel's security was 'ironclad'. The Arabs argued that, while they were moving towards accepting Israel as an established entity, the latter hung on to their territories on the pretence that this was the best means of achieving security, and threatened more expansionism to the point where security guarantees were in reality needed more by the Arab side, including the Palestinians in particular, than by Israel. They further stressed that it was anachronistic for a modern garrison state equipped with the latest weaponry in the American arsenal to insist on a nineteenth-century military concept of territorial buffer zones for its security.

On the other hand, the Reagan Plan must have annoyed Begin extremely, with its declaration that the US 'will not support [Israel's] annexation or permanent control of the occupied territories'. Washington believed that it was not in Israel's long-term interest to try to rule over the more than one million Palestinians living in the West Bank and Gaza. Nevertheless, withdrawal was not even an option in Begin's eyes, given his claim that 'the biblical land of Israel' was not occupied within the meaning of international law. Therefore, in Begin's view, Resolution 242 was not to be applied either to the West Bank or Gaza.

Israel must also have been annoyed about Jerusalem. The Reagan initiative emphasized that the City should remain undivided, and that its status should be determined by negotiations. The official text of the Camp David framework had made no mention of the City, which Israel declared its permanent and undivided capital. The Reagan Plan did not suggest that it should be taken away from Israel, but it left open the possibility of other solutions, such as internationalization. At least that was how Jordan understood it, in the belief that President Reagan wanted to put off the Jerusalem issue in order to overcome Israel's outright rejection of his plan.[32]

Reagan's demand for a freeze on settlements also contradicted Israel's assertion that it had an inalienable right to establish such settlements, which it regarded as an integral part of its national security. So it did not take Israel long to make up its mind. Within less than twenty-four hours, it rejected Reagan's Plan outright by a unanimous Cabinet decision, on the grounds that the plan represented a serious deviation from the Camp David Accords. Furthermore, Israel expressed its fury in practical terms, by allocating on 5 September 1982 the equivalent of $18.5m. for the construction of three new Jewish settlements in the West Bank, and also approving the building of seven others, including one in the Gaza Strip. This brought the total settlements established or planned from June 1967 to 5 September 1982 to 109, with a Jewish population estimated to be approaching 30,000, within an Arab population of over 1,000,000. As of 1 January 1985, there were 9,000 Jewish families living on the Israeli-occupied West Bank – a total of 42,500 people in 144 Jewish settlements, according to a study produced by the West Bank Data Project, an independent research group headed by a former Jerusalem Deputy Mayor, Meron Benvinisti.[33]

Jordan, on the other hand, saw many positive elements in the Reagan Plan, such as the fact that neither side had to declare its adherence to the Camp David Accords.[34] It even discerned an improvement on the Accords in that the Reagan Plan committed the Americans to Resolution 242 as the basis for peace negotiations, and gave a crystal clear redefinition of the resolution, which had become blurred during the Camp David negotiations, and reinstated the land for peace formula which was its basis. It reiterated that Resolution 242 had to be applied on all fronts including the West Bank and Gaza. And it envisaged a relationship between peace and withdrawal which implied total peace for complete withdrawal.

The Reagan Plan also implied that the West Bank and Gaza were Arab lands, parts of Palestine occupied by Israel. Hence, the federal arrangement was to take place between parts of Palestine and an independent state, Jordan. It put on record President Reagan's rejection of Israel's claims of sovereignty over the West Bank and Gaza. President Carter, in contrast, had from the outset left the whole issue of sovereignty subject to negotiation.

Jordan estimated that, if developed and followed with vigour and resolution, the Reagan Plan would ultimately lead to Israeli withdrawal to the 1967 borders, with only minor rectifications that would not reflect the weight of conquest; in other words, it represented the readoption of the Rogers Plan, which had been approved by Jordan, rejected by Israel and outmanoeuvred by Kissinger's shuttle diplomacy. It also believed that implementation of the Plan would ultimately stem the tide of extremism in both Israel and the Arab world, and contain the politics of fragmentation.

The Reagan Plan offered a practical mechanism for establishing peace in the region, if only because it was the plan of a superpower that had all the means of persuasion at its disposal. It reaffirmed American determination to achieve peace in the region. It also reiterated the rights of the Palestinians. Restoring these rights meant for Jordan relief from occupation, an end to the prospect of the Palestinians' enforced evacuation to Jordan and elsewhere, an end to the absorption of the West Bank and Gaza by Israel, and an end to the threat of Jordan's absorption by Israel. Finally Jordan did not see the Reagan Plan as contradictory to a similar plan put forward by Jordan in 1972. The only difference, in fact, was that the solution was based on an 'association with Jordan' instead of a more specified 'United Kingdom'.

Jordan did, however, pinpoint negative elements in the Plan. It said no to the PLO, no to a Palestinian state, no to demolition of the settlements, and yes only to legitimate Palestinian rights, which implied no to Palestinian national rights; even on the last point the plan was not adequate or comprehensive enough because it failed to establish a link between the issue of Israel's security needs and a clear recognition of Arab legitimate rights in Palestine. Yet as Jordan was keen to put an end to Israel's expansionist tendencies, and to retain the Palestinians' identity on Palestinian land, it felt that the new American plan must be encouraged by the Arabs because if it met with a negative Arab reaction, no American administration would ever have the courage to adopt a similar stand. It was thought that a basis for peace could be established only if American foreign policy treated all sides in the Arab–Israeli conflict on an equal footing. As it was put to President Reagan by King Hassan of Morocco:

In spite of Soviet support for the Arabs and the closeness of attitudes and political postures, the Soviet Union is not effective. If our struggle is with Czechoslovakia, then we'll go to the Soviet Union for a solution. But our struggle is with Israel. In spite of Israel's arrogance and its rebuff of American advice, Israel is not independent. The US has all the means of persuasion if it chooses to use them.[35]

Reaction within the Arab world varied between those, led by Jordan and Egypt, who believed that the plan's positive elements could provide the potential for momentum in the peace process and those, led by Syria, who believed that the plan was not a serious framework for peace. As the then Syrian Foreign Minister, Abd Al Halim Khaddam, explained:[36]

The struggle with Israel went beyond the issue of its occupation of the West Bank, Gaza and the Golan Heights. These parts of the Arab world were occupied during the 1967 war, not in 1948 when Israel was established on Palestinian lands. Hence the basic issue remains – as it was in 1948 – the future of the Palestinian people in exile. It is the essence of the whole problem.

Thus, the principle of land for peace, the framework of the Reagan Plan, was rejected by Syria from the outset. Khaddam listed the following reasons:

(i)　　It gave the impression of the existence of doubts about Arab rights of sovereignty over their lands occupied by Israel.

(ii)　　It set a precedent for future deals. Any further Israeli aggression leading to more acquisition of territory would entail another deal involving further peace conditions for the return of the newly occupied lands. The whole process would never end. Hence the principle of the inadmissibility of the acquisition of territory by force had to be firmly established and not allowed to be related or confused with the peace process.

(iii)　　The end of war with Israel and normalization of relations could not be a condition for peace. There could be peace but not relations with Israel, such as was the case between the US and Cuba.

(iv)　　True peace could not be established between the strong and the weak. Hence it was important that the US should stop feeding Israeli aggression with military hardware and stop raising the alarm whenever the Arabs endeavoured to acquire defensive weapons; there had to be a balance of power.

Within the PLO, opinions appeared to be divided, with the militant Damascus-based factions expressing outright rejection of the plan. The rest of the Arab world, including the mainstream PLO, withheld official comment in view of the imminence of the Fez Arab League summit which was eventually held between 6 and 9 September 1982, and which concluded with the unanimous adoption of the so-called Fez Plan (see chapter 10). Both Plans were inspired by the provisions of Security Resolution 242. The Reagan Plan lacked some principles of the Fez Plan but, given the realities of the international situation, the Fez Plan lacked the mechanism to make effective progress. Thus the Reagan Plan provided the vehicle which could propel the Fez Plan forward, if President Reagan were to follow up his plan with determination. Jordan vigorously proceeded to explore this possibility. It believed that it could be achieved through an agreement between Jordan and the PLO on the establishment of a relationship – yet to be defined – that would govern the future of the Jordanian and Palestinian peoples through joint action based on the Fez Plan, Resolution 242 and the principles of the Reagan initiative. Growing opposition by the mainstream PLO to the Reagan Plan coincided with growing American involvement in Lebanon, and the gradual loss of US credibility, not only because of Lebanon but also because of its restrained handling of Israel despite the latter's outright rejection of the Reagan Plan and its defiance of the freeze on settlement construction. Nevertheless, there was a burst of diplomatic activity. The federation/confederation concept was explored by the PLO and Jordanian officials notably during a meeting between King Hussain and Yasser Arafat on 10–13 October 1982. Further talks were held in Amman on 30 November to set up a joint commission to work out a PLO–Jordanian formula for Palestinian participation in any possible negotiations with the US on a Middle East settlement. Talks between President Reagan and an Arab League delegation took place in Washington on 22 October to evaluate the common and divergent elements of the Reagan and Fez Plans and the rationale behind references to the Camp David Accords in the Reagan Plan. A further official visit to Washington was undertaken by King Hussain on 21–23 December, during which he discussed with President Reagan the obstacles to any future Jordanian participation in the peace negotiations process, namely, the continued settlement activity in the occupied territories, the non-participation of Palestinians including the PLO, and the continuing deterioration of the situation in Lebanon. More talks between Hussain and Arafat were held on 9–10 January. Moreover, a meeting of the PLO Executive Committee took place in South Yemen on 27–30 January 1983, following which a communiqué was issued seeking to reconcile the difference within the organization by condemning any peace plan which failed to recognize the national rights of the Palestinians, and by describing US policy as anti-Palestinian, but without specifically rejecting the Reagan Plan. The rejectionist factions based in Damascus boycotted the three-day meeting.

A meeting of the Palestinian National Council was held in Algiers in mid-February 1983. On 27 February the 16th PNC issued a communiqué rejecting the Reagan Plan because

The Reagan Plan in style and content does not respect the established national rights of the Palestinian people since it denies the right of return and self-determination, and the setting up of the independent Palestinian state and also the PLO – the sole legitimate representative of the Palestinian people – and since it contradicts international legality. Therefore the PNC rejects this plan as a sound basis for the just and lasting solution of the cause of the Palestinians and the Arab–Zionist conflict.[37]

The PNC, the Palestinian Parliament-in-exile which embodies the most comprehensive representation of the Palestinian people inside and outside the occupied territories, agreed there and then to a future confederal arrangement with Jordan. Finally, on 10 April 1983, King Hussain announced his refusal to join the negotiations suggested by President Reagan without a clear mandate from the PLO. He decided to 'leave it to the PLO and the Palestinian people to choose the ways and means for the salvation of themselves and their land and for the realization of their declared aims in the manner they see fit'.[38] He further clarified that

We in Jordan, having refused from the beginning to negotiate on behalf of the Palestinians, will neither act separately nor in lieu of any body in the Middle East peace negotiations. Jordan will work as a member of the Arab League in compliance with its resolutions to support the PLO within our capabilities and with the requirements of our national security . . .

Peace efforts thus seemed to reach a dead end. Frustration started to mount in Jordan. To make matters worse, a House Sub-committee voted on 12 April 1983 an extra $315m. for Israel, while confirming the denial of the sale of advanced weaponry to Jordan until it proceeded to negotiations without the PLO.[39] The US resumed its arms deals with Israel with the sale of Sidewinder missiles.[40] It also allowed Israel to buy American parts for its new Lavi fighter, designated as a replacement of American-supplied Skyhawks and Phantoms.[41]

The aftermath

It is a basic rule of foreign affairs that a great power does not launch major initiatives on difficult problems unless it is serious. 'Don't start something you cannot finish', King Hussain warned President Reagan before the announcement of his plan.[42] It was good advice.

If judged by that standard, President Reagan's initiative was a model for sheer embarrassment. Before it received the coup de grâce from the PLO, it had been fatally weakened by Israel's outright rejection and defiance, and the inept half-hearted diplomacy of the President and his Secretary of State, George Shultz. In short, they were not serious.

The reluctance of the American Administration to act promptly and decisively in its peacemaking undertaking was seen in the Arab world as a major cause of the failure of co-ordination efforts between Jordan and the PLO.[43] When King Hussain eventually said 'No', political observers and American decision-makers reckoned that he and others in the region would pay the price. Few believed the price would be paid in the US, whose credibility among moderate Arabs had then been further damaged as had its ability to temper Israel. One party was bound then to gain influence as a result

– the USSR. It was in fact decisively working its way back into the regional game.

When Begin curtly rejected the Reagan Plan, President Reagan looked for a saviour, as Carter had done with Sadat when he was challenged by Begin at Camp David. But King Hussain refused to oblige without receiving the green light from the PLO. Begin then seemed relieved; as the Israeli journalist Ammon Kapeliouk put it in the *International Herald Tribune* of 5 January 1984:

> The Likud government was mortified by the existence of Arab moderation. More than once, Begin has declared that even if the PLO recognized the right of Israel to exist and accepted 242, Israel would not negotiate with the PLO. More than once Shamir declared that all that Israel wants is that the PLO disappear from the face of the earth.

The reason for this attitude, Kapeliouk explained, 'was Israel's refusal to contemplate the idea of returning territory occupied in 1967'. He further elaborated:

> Movement is what Begin was determined to avoid. He wanted time to complete the construction of Greater Israel, not talks at which he would be asked to make concessions. Hence the rejection of the Reagan Peace Plan and his tactical exploitation of the Lebanese side-show, to shelve until too late any consideration of the disposal of the occupied territories.

The Reagan Administration never grasped what King Hussain and the PLO needed as a minimum condition to proceed, namely, concrete evidence of America's commitment and clout – any sign which would show that Reagan could make his plan work. But no evidence of American determination was forthcoming. In the West Bank, Begin proceeded ever more aggressively with his policy of colonization. The US responded neither with action nor words. Or if they did, they were not audible. Why then should even the most moderate of moderates who understood the urgent need for negotiations put any faith in American credibility, in the hope of getting for himself and for his country something, or even anything, in return? All that President Reagan was able to offer was a series of promises it was certain he could not deliver. Under these circumstances it was difficult to see why King Hussain should opt to stand by the President, breaking ranks with his kinsfolk in the process, when neither Israel nor the US had anything to offer him in return.

Begin succeeded not only in derailing the peace process, but also in forcing a change in Reagan's regional agenda by preoccupying him solely with Lebanon. But if President Reagan failed to shift Begin on the Lebanese question, who would believe that he could succeed on the far tougher issue of the West Bank? The US policy failure in Lebanon severely limited Reagan's ability to influence events in the Middle East, and he knew it. 'If we get out', he stated feebly, 'it also means the end of any ability on our part to bring about an overall peace in the Middle East, and I would have to say it means a pretty disastrous result for us worldwide.'[44] When he eventually did remove the Marines from Lebanon, he no longer had the morale or the stamina to implement what he was on record as having said earlier, 'If we don't succeed in Lebanon, we can try again and again to deal with the Arab–Israeli conflict by reviving the Plan.'[45] Begin had totally destroyed Reagan as an effective force in Lebanon and with him he further weakened US credibility as an honest promoter of peace in the region.

What made matters worse for the President was a secondary but related dilemma: How could the US move decisively in the face of Syria's new power of veto over the peace process, which had manifested itself so forcefully when it aborted the 17 May Agreement between Israel and Lebanon? In any struggle between Syria and a US-backed Israel over Lebanon's future political orientation, Syria seemed to have the upper hand. And Syria was determined to torpedo any peace movement which was not conducted via Damascus.

T.E. Lawrence once predicted that the British would lose their nerve with the Arabs. 'We would', he said in 1928, 'hold on to them with ever-lessening force till the anarchy is too expensive and we let go.' Now the Americans, following the Lebanese debacle, were losing their nerve. And, as the Washington political commentator Claudia Wright observed, 'They were not sure whether to loosen their grip or reinforce it. They were not certain which Arabs to hang on to and which to let go of.'[46]

The only way out seemed to be to drop all the Arabs and bury Reagan's only innovation in the same tomb which contained the remains of the Rogers Plan and the first half of the Camp David Accords. And then follow the dictum: If you can't beat 'em, join 'em. The unprecedented US–Israel strategic relationship[47] that developed as an outcome of Lebanon, offered final proof of Reagan's acquiescence in Israel's rejection of his plan.

9 The US and Jordan: how 'much' became 'too much'

Jordan and Lebanon

The repercussions of the Israeli invasion of Lebanon, and of the US intervention and premature withdrawal, were deeply worrying to Jordan. In its view, peace between Israel and Lebanon should have been addressed after Israeli and Syrian forces had withdrawn from the country, as part of a comprehensive peace between Israel and its neighbours and not before. It also thought that the US Marines and the MNF should have stayed until Syrian and Israeli forces were withdrawn and national reconciliation among the warring domestic factions was under way.

The American failure in Lebanon harmed Jordan, in the sense that the ensuing confrontation between Syria and Israel brought about a radical shift in the balance of power which was of vital consequence for the political middle ground in the region.[1] Their respective desires to dominate the area were seen as leading Israel formally to annex the West Bank, and to leave the territorial integrity of Lebanon permanently compromised. This trial of strength, it was feared, would expose Jordan to mounting pressures from the west as well as the north, accompanied by a further influx of refugees as a result of the social and economic dislocation inflicted on the Palestinians both at home and in exile abroad. Social disruption in Jordan would follow, as American-backed Israelis and Soviet-backed Syrians battled it out for dominance in the region as a whole. Furthermore, it was feared then that superpower support would encourage both Israel and Syria to establish strategic links between the Mediterranean and the Red Sea–Gulf theatres.

Settlements, Jerusalem and Jordan

Up to 1980, the US government had continually maintained the illegality of the Israeli settlements established since the June 1967 war, wherever they were located, including Jerusalem.[2] Security Council Resolution 446 of 27 March 1979 reaffirmed the Fourth Geneva Convention of 1949 as far as the occupied territories were concerned, and deplored Israel's failure to abide by previous UN resolutions. It also called on Israel to desist from taking any action which resulted in changing the legal, geographic and demographic situation in the Arab territories occupied since 1967, including Jerusalem. It is noteworthy that President Carter's Ambassador to the UN voted in favour of the resolution.

Security Council Resolution 465 of 1 March 1980 called on Israel to halt further settlements in the occupied West Bank and Gaza and ordered it to dismantle the existing settlements. The resolution referred to Jerusalem as part of the occupied territories. It reaffirmed the view of the Security Council that none of the measures taken by Israel to change the physical character, demographic composition, institutional structure and status of the Palestinian and other Arab territories occupied since 1967, including Jerusalem, or any part thereof, had legal validity and that Israel's policy and practice of settling parts of its population and new immigrants in those territories constituted a serious obstruction to achieving a comprehensive, just and lasting peace in the Middle East.[3] Again the US Ambassador to the UN voted in favour of the resolution. However, two days later, on 3 March, the White House announced that the US had intended to abstain because of the reference to Jerusalem, but a failure in communications resulted in its voting in favour. This move, which followed objections from Israel, indicated the first change in the American stance on Jerusalem, which had always been one of clear-cut recognition of its status as part of the occupied territories, to which the Fourth Geneva Convention applied. The Department of State, however, concurrently submitted 40 official documents to the House Foreign Affairs Committee demonstrating the consistency of Resolution 465 with prior US positions on the establishment of settlements.[4] The softening of the US position coincided with political developments in the Middle East itself, following the signing of the Camp David Accords and the ensuing new twin-pillar policy – of reliance on Egypt and Israel – for the security of the Gulf.

In April 1980, the US vetoed a UN resolution affirming the right of the Palestinian people to establish an independent Palestinian state, and calling on Israel to withdraw from the occupied territories, including Jerusalem.[5] While it had always opposed the establishment of an independent Palestinian state, it had never before voiced its opposition to Israeli withdrawal from occupied territory and never mentioned implicitly or explicitly that Israel should stay in East Jerusalem. The veto provided the second clue to the changing attitude in Washington.

On 14 May the Israeli Knesset began consideration of the Basic Law which reaffirmed Jerusalem as the capital of Israel. On 30 June – the same day that the Knesset passed the first reading of the Jerusalem Law – the Security Council passed Resolution 476, which deplored Israel's changing of the status of Jerusalem. The US abstained. This was the third noticeable departure from the previous US attitude as expressed in support for UN resolutions 276 and 298, both of which censured Israel for the measures it had taken in Jerusalem and urged their cancellation. When the Basic Law was finally passed by the Knesset and adopted by the government, the Security Council issued Resolution 478, which condemned the act as a violation of international law and hence null and void. It called upon all states which had established diplomatic missions in Jerusalem to withdraw them from the Holy City. The US voted in favour of the resolution. The earlier US abstention when the Basic Law was being discussed by the Knesset, had seemed implicitly to give the green light to Israel. However, after the implementation of the Basic Law, the US joined the international condemnation of the Israeli measures in what seemed like an effort to avoid the embarrassment of contradicting the unanimous international position on Jerusalem. It was a highly sensitive issue for the whole of the Moslem world, but the US seemed to assume that UN resolutions – and other international declarations on their own – had no legislative force and created no legal obligations for member states. World forums provide only a barometer of the international consensus, and no state, including Israel, would heed the international consensus if it believed that it was detrimental to its own national interests.

More obvious changes in US attitudes took place concerning the 'settlements'. Less than one month after assuming the presidency, Reagan declared:[6]

I disagreed when the previous administration referred to them [the settlements] as illegal. They're not illegal . . . I do think perhaps now with this rush to do it and this moving in there the way they are is ill-advised because if we're going to continue with the spirit of Camp David to try and arrive at a peace, maybe this, at this time, is unnecessarily provocative.

This scaling-down of the US attitude towards the establishment of Jewish settlements in occupied lands, from the initial view that they were illegal, to the view that they were an obstacle to peace, and then only an impediment to solving the Palestinian question, caused tempers to rise throughout the Middle East. Prince Hassan noted:

If the erosion of the American position continues the settlements may become, as my brother King Hussain has put it, just an eyesore. It would be tantamount to the USA abdicating completely its role as a mediating superpower if, as Richard Murphy, the Assistant Secretary of State, says, the USA refuses to become an agent to pressurize Israel to withdraw.[7]

One might add, in this context, that if something is initially condemned as illegal, it cannot later be considered legal unless the law itself has changed. There was no change in international law on the settlement question, nor on the Jerusalem question, but there was a new political interpretation put on it by the US.

Other events

Jordan's resentment at the US reinterpretation of previously held principles reached a climax during 1983 and early 1984, following three events of major political significance. The first involved a Bill promoted by Democratic Senator Daniel Moynihan to force the Administration to move the US Embassy in Israel from Tel Aviv to Jerusalem, which gained the support of at least 36 Senators and about 200 Congressmen. If adopted, it would not only have been in defiance of UN resolutions, but would also have incensed the whole Moslem world, for which Jerusalem has deep religious significance. Secretary of State Shultz cautioned that 'Forcing a precipitate transfer of the Embassy would be damaging to the cause of peace.'[8] A former State Department Middle East expert, Harold Saunders, protested to the Senate Foreign Relations Committee that 'The final status of Jerusalem must be negotiated by the parties with interests there, not unilaterally imposed by conquest.' In Cairo, Ambassador Veliotes asked a group of visiting Senators to give him time before the Jerusalem Bill was passed to move himself and his staff out of town before the riots started. Because of the sensitivity of the issue, nearly all nations maintained their diplomatic missions in Tel Aviv. The mere introduction of the Bill obviously caused considerable consternation in Jordan, under whose jurisdiction East Jerusalem had been until the June 1967 war.

The other two events were connected with two personal requests from King Hussain to President Reagan. One was a plea not to veto a UN Security Council resolution drafted by Jordan condemning Israeli settlements in the West Bank as illegal. The US vetoing of the resolution, in August 1983, sent the King 'climbing right through the roof', according to reliable sources in Amman. The other was a plea to the President to use his good offices with Israel to grant travel rights to 160 PNC members living in the West Bank and Gaza to attend a proposed meeting in Amman, under the chairmanship of Yasser Arafat, in November 1984. Again President Reagan failed to oblige. Such a rebuff was seen by some political observers as a loss of face for King Hussain, for in discussions with Arafat at the end of February 1984, the King had assured him that he would use his special relationship with the US to persuade Israel not to repeat the ban on travel abroad which it had imposed during the 1983 PNC session in Algiers. The presence of PNC members from the West Bank would have helped to ensure a working majority for the moderate line advanced by Arafat to counter the more radical elements backed by Syria. In the event, the working majority was in fact established without their presence.

Incensed by these developments, King Hussain travelled to Washington in February 1984 to review events and to extract from the US an assurance that it would stand by Jordan and other Western-orientated Arab states, even in a presidential election year. His failure to get this assurance convinced him that things had gone too far, and he resolved to transform the heated diplomatic exchanges between the US and Jordan into a public debate.

The diplomatic crusade turns public

It was on 15 March 1984 that King Hussain decided to attack the US publicly for the first time, in an interview with *The New York Times*:

I now realize that principles mean nothing to the US. Short-term issues, especially in election years, prevail. I am concerned about the US and its double standards everywhere . . . The saddest point for me is that I have always believed that values and courageous principles were an area that we shared with the US.

The continuing Israeli occupation of the West Bank was at the heart of his concerns:

We see things in the following way: Israel is on our land. It is there by virtue of American military and economic aid that transfers into aid for Israeli settlements . . . Israel is there by virtue of American moral and political support to the point where the US is succumbing to Israeli dictates . . . The US is not free to move, except within the limits of what AIPAC, the Zionists and the State of Israel determine for it.

King Hussain was also defiant towards Congress. Congressional objections to arms sales to Jordan, he stressed, would hinder nothing because other sources were available for the defence of his country. Speaking to Western and Arab journalists and broadcasters in March 1984, he stated, to considerable local and regional applause, that 'If the price of the US missiles was the dignity of my country, then that was too high a price to pay.'[9] Furthermore, 'If this issue was to become a sordid one, in which the dignity of my country was in jeopardy then, thank you very much, we don't need them.' The King was a very angry man. Asked by the present writer if no more could be expected from the US by way of peace efforts, he gave an assurance that this was not the case. 'The door is not closed yet . . . The US could be a major factor, but not as an ally of Israel nor as a mediator, but as a superpower adhering to its principles and respecting its commitments.' Referring to the Soviet role in peacemaking he added:

The US has no right to object to the presence of the Soviet Union at any new peace negotiations, but because the USSR is allied with Syria and the US with Israel, neither superpower is in a position to act as an honest broker in peace talks. Efforts to resolve the conflict will be strengthened only by involving the five permanent members of the UN Security Council.[10]

King Hussain was careful to exclude the US President from his attacks. 'I am not critical of the President of the US who I have said time and again I consider to be a friend and a man of honour and principle.'[11] Rather he regretted the weakening of the office of the presidency. Citing the events of 1956, when President Eisenhower in an election year forced Israel to withdraw from Sinai, the King referred to 'the tragedy of the erosion of the highest authority in the land'.[12] By absolving the President from such criticism he gave the impression that he hoped that President Reagan – once he was free of the Zionist lobby's leverage after the presidential elections – could still play a significant role in the peace process.

It was obvious that the King wanted to demonstrate that, given the conditions prevailing in Washington, Jordan would not agree to be taken for granted any longer. Rather, it would speak up for itself. By transferring the argument from the seats of decision-making in Washington and Amman to the mass media, King Hussain was submitting his case to world and particularly American opinion.

This new approach was well received at home, and throughout the Arab world. Having been regarded by the West as the most pro-Western and the most pragmatic leader in the Arab world, as well as a moderate and exceptionally clever political operator, the King's uncharacteristic outburst sparked widespread comment. The general conclusion was that he had made his point, that the US was mishandling the Middle East, and that its Middle East policy was drifting aimlessly.

King Hussain's remarks incensed Congress, to the point where the Administration decided to cancel the projected sale of 1,613 Stinger missiles to Jordan rather than submit the request to Congress and risk a humiliating defeat. President Reagan was originally in favour of the sale, as a way of enhancing US standing among moderate Arab nations following the setback to US policy in Lebanon. With Washington counting on Jordan eventually to enter into negotiations with Israel, the Stinger sale had assumed even greater importance as an incentive for King Hussain. The King, on the other hand, regarded the sale as a test of the Administration's ability to carry out what it believed was right in the face of Israel's opposition and that of its supporters in Congress. And President Reagan failed the test. He decided that it would be less risky to abandon the appearance of support for the King than to alienate Israel's supporters before the elections. And, astonishingly enough, he told AIPAC about the decision to cancel the Stinger sale before many key administration officials were informed. A State Department spokesman explained that this was because the decision had been preceded by discussions on a possible trade-off.[13] The Administration would cancel the sale of the missiles in return for Congress agreeing to kill the Jerusalem Bill, a stark example of the constraints on US policy in the Middle East. President Reagan had to defend himself in a speech to the Conference of the United Jewish Appeal in March 1984.[14] He explained that, in response to the growth of Syrian power and the rise of the Iranian threat, the US must protect moderate Arabs from radical pressure; since Jordan's security was crucial to the security of the entire region, he saw it as in the strategic interest of both the US and Israel to help meet Jordan's legitimate defence needs. Obviously neither Israel nor its supporters agreed with him.

Abandoning the sale of the Stinger missiles sent the world's arms dealers flocking to Amman. On 27 March 1984, Richard Luce, the British Minister of State at the Foreign Office, held a meeting with the Jordanian Foreign Minister, during which he announced that the British government would send a team to Jordan on 8 April to discuss a Javelin missile deal as a replacement for the Stinger.[15] The French Defence Minister, Charles Hernu, announced in September 1984 that France would sell Jordan Mistral missiles as a replacement.[16] He also acknowledged that France had already provided Jordan with 33 French-built Mirage fighters, that an agreement had been reached for the delivery of 13 additional planes, and that a Franco-Jordanian military commission had been set up to study Jordan's request for French arms. Michael Heseltine, the then British Defence Minister, held further talks with King Hussain in Amman on 22 October 1984 to discuss Jordan's military requirements. These visits culminated in the conclusion of agreements with France and Britain for the supply of defensive weapons. Further details of Jordanian-British co-operation became public in August 1985. Defensive equipment worth £270m. was to be supplied, and finance to be arranged, following two memoranda of understanding with the Jordanian government initiated in August 1985, signed on 19 September during Mrs Thatcher's visit to Jordan.[17]

As far as the Soviet Union was concerned, co-operation with Jordan for the supply of air defence systems had been made public since January 1982. Answering questions at the Royal United Services Institute in London on 6 December 1984, King Hussain declared that he would buy further arms from the Soviet Union because the US was no longer able to supply what he needed for Jordan's legitimate self-defence. On 6 January 1985, the Commander-in-Chief of the Jordanian Army announced that the Soviet Union was supplying Jordan with a new air defence system, including surface-to-air missiles, which was to be ready for installation in early 1985.[18]

Offended and apprehensive, the Reagan Administration wanted to offer Jordan proof that it was not totally abandoning it in its peace efforts in the Middle East. In what appeared to be a tantalising carrot and stick policy, the Administration submitted a request to Congress on 13 June 1985 for a $250m. economic aid package to Jordan to be spread over two years. This, however, ignored Jordan's 'shopping list' of arms which included F-20 and F-16 fighters and the Hawk and Stinger missile systems. In spite of opposition within Congress, the request was granted. Israel had already won $1.5 bn in economic aid.[19]

On 4 February 1986, Secretary of State Shultz asked Congress, in a formal published letter, to postpone indefinitely any further consideration of a presidential idea to sell Jordan advanced military weapons worth $1.9 bn. This was obviously a move intended to pre-empt Congress's rejection, since the feeling was that King Hussain had not made sufficiently forceful or speedy efforts to hold direct bilateral negotiations with Israel; arms deals should therefore be rejected until such talks began. It was recognized that Jordan had been trying to make progress – which had already been rewarded by the $250m. economic assistance. To receive military aid, the King would have to take the final step and negotiate directly with Israel without the PLO's participation.[20]

It had often been explained to the US that Jordan was not seeking to disturb the region's military balance, nor to acquire an offensive capacity, nor to pose a threat to Israel's security. But, if credibly armed, it could at least create a stable deterrent against the uncertain intentions of Israel, and other dangers emanating from the Gulf War. Unheeded, King Hussain, a traditional friend of the US, remained firmly convinced of the need to improve the defensive capability of his country, if necessary by turning towards Europe and, reluctantly, the USSR, which were in any case offering cheaper equipment, with no strings attached.

PART III US, Jordan and Arab approaches to peace

10 The Arab framework for peace

We favour a settlement, but not any settlement, not peace at any price: a settlement that does not resolve the Palestinian problem or the question of the Golan, or Israel's or Jordan's or Lebanon's or Syria's right to exist with reasonable security within a recognized territory, is no settlement at all, for natural forces would be at work to overturn it before it was signed.

This statement by Prince Hassan of Jordan seems to sum up the Arab governments' attitude towards peace in the 1980s.[1] Listing the essentials for a settlement he stated:

Central pre-requisites are: firstly, the Palestinians must be allowed to freely exercise their national right of self-determination, and secondly, Israeli withdrawal from territories occupied in 1967. Security measures (such as arms or force limitations, observers etc. . . .) may be an integral part of any agreement. Issues such as security measures, juridical status, corridors of transit and communication, representation, foreign nationals etc. . . . are important and are proper subjects of negotiations. In some cases, security requirements may dictate minor modifications to specific lines previously disputed. Yet such exchanges must result from negotiations aimed at mutual security and based on the two principles identified, not as a result of force or threat.

The Fahd and Fez Plans

The first Arab peace plan, which became known as the Fahd Plan, was made public in August 1981. It proposed:

Israeli withdrawal from all Arab territories occupied in 1967, including Arab Jerusalem.

The dismantling of Israeli settlements established on Arab lands since 1967.

A guarantee of freedom of worship for all religions in the holy places, and practice of religious rites for all religions in the Holy Shrines.

An affirmation of the right of the Palestinian people to return to their homes, and compensation for those who do not wish to return.

The West Bank and Gaza Strip to have a transitional period under the auspices of the UN, for a period not exceeding a few months.

The establishment of an independent Palestinian state with Arab Jerusalem as its capital.

All states in the region to be able to live in peace.

The UN or some member states of the UN to guarantee implementation of these principles.

Prince Fahd added on 2 November 1981: the Palestinian factor is basic: no peace without the Palestinian people, and no Palestinian state without the PLO.[2]

The details of the Fahd Plan were shaped and spelled out by the PLO Chairman, Yasser Arafat, in co-operation with Prince Fahd of Saudi Arabia. In Arab circles it became known as the 'Palestinian Plan' and thereafter an Arab plan after its adoption by 16 of the 21 Arab states taking part in the first Fez summit of November 1981. But the rejectionists in the Arab camp, led by Syria and some Palestinian elements within the PLO, foiled its full adoption. Realizing that it was not possible to reach a consensus – particularly because of the absence of President Assad of Syria – King Hassan of Morocco adjourned the summit only a few hours after it had opened and the Plan was temporarily withdrawn in spite of objections from Jordan. It was re-presented with minor amendments and adopted at the second Fez summit the following September, 1982, this time with Syrian endorsement.

Why did Syria object to the Fahd Plan and endorse the Fez Plan? Former Prime Minister Badran, explained:[3]

It was because of Saudi diplomacy. Saudi Arabia, the consensus-builder in the Arab world, which did not believe in, or encourage, Arab confrontation, played a big role. After a period of contact, persuasion and gestation, Syria came round and joined hands with the Arab consensus. A thorough look at both plans will indicate that both were identical in substance. Nothing changed in Fez except Syrian acquiescence through Saudi diplomacy.

Syria, however, must have seen an important change. Unlike the Fahd Plan the Fez Plan underlined self-determination and national rights for the Palestinian people, the role of the PLO as the sole legitimate representative of the Palestinian people (Article 4) and the role of the Security Council – as opposed to 'some member states' such as the US – as the guarantor of 'implementation of these principles and peace among all states in the region including the independent Palestine state' – Articles 7 and 8. All these became the corner-stone of peace calls in the region in the 1980s.

Commenting publicly on the Fahd Plan, President Reagan stated:

The Saudis have shown by their own introduction of a peace proposal that they are willing to discuss peace in the Middle East. We couldn't agree with all the points, but it was the first time that they had recognized Israel as a nation and it is a starting point for negotiations.[4]

Asked if there was any part of the eight-point plan that could be incorporated in or added to the Camp David Accords, he replied,

Well, one in particular. I believe that it is implicit in the offering of the plan, recognition of Israel's right to exist as a nation. This is why I have referred to it as a hopeful sign, that there was an official plan whether you agreed with it or not, that indicated the willingness to negotiate which it does imply. The other point in the Plan is that one of the eight points calls for all the states of the region living together in peace. I think we all endorse that.

Following pronouncements from the Begin government that the Plan was 'a Saudi annihilation plan, a model of how to liquidate Israel in stages',[5] nothing more was heard from, and no further action taken by, President Reagan. But something was heard and seen from his Secretary of State, Alexander Haig, who seemed to agree with Begin. Whether or not he was articulating the real but unexpressed thinking within the Administration, cannot be asserted here for certain. But what can be said with confidence is that discussions among US ambassadors to Middle Eastern countries, with the participation of Philip Habib and a small number of academics, took place just prior to the Israeli invasion of Lebanon.[6] In the course of these discussions, it emerged that one view, favoured at the very top of the State Department, though emphatically not by Habib, was that the main task of American diplomacy must be to break what Washington saw as the Syrian stranglehold over decision-making within the PLO. The way to do this was to get the Syrians out of Lebanon, and the only power to carry this out was Israel. The reasoning went that if Israel were to enter Lebanon and deal Syria a humiliating blow in the process, the US would then be able to mediate a simultaneous withdrawal of Syrian and Israeli forces. Although it is quite clear that Habib cautioned strongly against any such calculations, they do appear to have provided the rationale for the conduct of US policy during and after the Israeli invasion.

When the plan went wrong, Shultz stepped in to pick up the pieces. The Reagan Plan emerged eventually on 1 September 1982. Within a week or so, the Arab Fez Plan was also on the table. President Reagan then met the Committee of Seven appointed by the Fez summit headed by King Hassan of Morocco and including the Secretary General of the Arab League.

The Committee's task was to explain the Fez Plan to the five permanent members of the Security Council. King Hassan of Morocco and his team started with the US on 22 October. During his talks with the Committee,[7] President Reagan admitted that he had not expected the Arabs or the Israelis to agree with all the points in his plan, but he had not expected Israel's outright rejection either. 'I reject Israel's negative attitude to my plan', he told the Committee of Seven. He acknowledged that the Fez Plan was a positive plan. As Israel refused to talk to the PLO, he advised the Committee that the PLO should withdraw from the process. And as Israel wanted a clear recognition of its right to exist, he argued that the Arabs must declare this in advance:

True peace starts when another Arab country steps in for talks with Israel. In this case Israel cannot refuse to negotiate . . . You must support King Hussain to step forward without the PLO and with only representatives from the West Bank and Gaza to conduct direct negotiations with Israel.

As far as the Camp David Accords were concerned, President Reagan clarified that he had left them in his plan as a term of reference, because they committed Israel to recognize some form of Palestinian rights and he did not want to lose this commitment. He warned that this was the only way to move towards peace which entailed an end to Israel's occupation, an end to Palestinian suffering and a restoration of Palestinian rights provided that these rights were exercised within a federal relationship with Jordan. President Reagan specifically enquired about the meaning of Article 7 of the Plan specifying that the Security Council should guarantee peace among all states of the region including an independent Palestinian state.

King Hassan explained the Arab view as follows:

The Camp David Accords were designed for a specific time and purpose. But if the Arab countries had regarded them as a suitable means for a solution, they would have referred to them in the Fez Plan in one way or another. The Camp David Accords did not fulfil Arab wishes, either collectively or individually. If King Hussain, brave as he was, had felt that there was a glimpse of hope to restore peace to the region via the Camp David process, he would have expressed his views directly to his fellow Arabs.

We know that the US regards Camp David as a sign of continuity as far as its Middle East policy is concerned. But continuity can also take place in substance and depth rather than just in procedure.

In the presence of Sadat, who signed the Camp David Accords, the PLO was recognized, at the Rabat Summit of 1974, as the sole legitimate representative of the Palestinian people. The Palestinians both in and outside the occupied lands had not waived their support for the PLO. They missed no occasion to show their determination in supporting the PLO as their sole legitimate representative. Hence, the PLO remains the spokesman and the representative of the Palestinian people.

We agree with the US that the Palestinians must be relieved from suffering. But we stress that what we don't have, we cannot give. We don't have the means to give them a future.

The facts that should be taken into consideration are: the determination of the Palestinians on peaceful coexistence with all their neighbours once they get their entity, and the credibility of the guarantees to be given by the Palestinians when they are addressed directly rather than under the auspices of, or via, other parties.

Article 7 of the Fez Plan presents an 'escape route' for the area, from a state of war to a state of peace, as a first step. The second step, involving reciprocal interests and dealings with Israel, may follow if a suitable climate is prepared.

After creating an atmosphere of peace and confidence in the area, we must leave it to each individual sovereign state in the area to decide, in time and for itself, on the extent and ways and means of normalizing relations with Israel.

We are confident because our plan is a just plan. It safeguards all rights within the framework set by the international community.

Our interest in peace is no less than yours, and is, if anything, greater. Therefore, we are ready to build bridges between our two plans, bridges which contain the ingredients of life and continuity.

We know that Israel is arrogant and does not always listen to the US. But no one believes that an Israeli decision is independent from a decision which you make.

We suggest that the only way to eliminate the contradictions is for you to encourage the Jordanian–Palestinian dialogue to reach a positive outcome. An agreement between them on the form of relationship they will have would provide the only bridge which spans our two plans.

It was reported that Secretary of State Shultz was impressed by the Arab explanations. 'This is a historic achievement', he said, and added 'We must move to the next stage.' That 'next stage' did not materalize. Something serious was missing.

It is accepted wisdom that the enduring solution of a conflict such as that between the Arabs and Israel needs determined peacemakers willing to take into consideration the following points as spelled out by Philip Habib in 1985:

Diplomacy, as an alternative to the use of force, needs a base of national strength, clearly defined objectives and public support. Without economic and military strength, diplomacy will falter in a world of confrontation and competing ideologies. Without public support, diplomacy cannot be sustained any more than the use of force.[8]

A thorough look at Israel and the Arabs at the time of the initiation of both plans would lead to the conclusion that neither side possessed the prerequisites for successful diplomacy that could lead to a just and long-lasting solution of the conflict. The Arabs lacked the strength factor, and their 'just solution' depended on an Israeli magnanimity which was not forthcoming. Israel did not have wide public support for peace talks with the Arabs. And as George Ball observed, 'By the time the Arabs offered Israel what she could have gladly accepted in 1949, Israel's expectations had expanded extravagantly.'[9] There was no synchronization in the psychology of peace between Israel and the Arab world, and for domestic political reasons, among others, the US remained impotent to bridge the gap.

Every move in the diplomatic chess game need not be spelled out in advance. But the objectives must be clear, and their relevance to national purposes understood.

In deference to Israel, the US was forcing the Arabs to spell out all their conditions for peace publicly and in advance. This broke the accepted rules of the game. It smacked of blatant bias, because the US failed to ask Israel to spell out, publicly and in advance, what were its envisaged borders, the limits of its envisaged withdrawal from occupied lands and its national objectives. The US was thus leaning on the weaker side – the Arabs – to squeeze as many concessions as possible before any negotiations started, in order to create the right atmosphere for Israel to step in.

In purely philosophical and legal terms, the right of self-determination cannot be denied. It is part of the American historical and political tradition.

In declaring that the right of the Palestinians to self-determination could be expressed only through Jordan, the US was allowing itself to maintain double standards, in deference to one party in the conflict. And as Professor Fuad Ajami observed: 'It is those same virtues of self-determination and equality that the US is denying the Arabs. And sometimes the convert tends to remember these virtues better than the teacher himself.'[10]

To persuade reluctant adversaries to meet, there must be at least some indication of what it might be possible to achieve. The Arabs were denied any such indication. Issues such as Jerusalem, the settlements and sovereignty were ultimately left for the negotiations. With the US siding with Israel, and in the absence of a balance of power between the contending parties, it was obvious who would have the upper hand in conducting such negotiations. As Mrs Sharaf, the then Jordanian Information Minister, put it:

For any negotiations to be fair, one side or the other should have an equal chance to get what it wants from the talks. The issue of the future status of Jerusalem is of the greatest importance to Jordan. Would any Israeli leader including Peres be ready to say that there is even a 50/50 chance of returning East Jerusalem to Arab sovereignty? The answer to that question is no. And there is the same preconditional block on other issues such as self-determination for the Palestinians, the removal of Jewish settlements from the occupied lands and PLO participation.[11]

After a long period in a state of war it is impossible to restore peace and normalize relations quickly. The US insistence on spelling out article 7 of the Fez Plan in advance, and committing the Arabs to a quick peace and normalization of relations with Israel even before the negotiations started, seemed incompatible with the rules of the diplomatic game and with historical experience. In the absence of trust, it seemed logical for the peace negotiations ultimately to be directed by the permanent members of the UN Security Council. As Jordan explained to the US,

It is wrong to insist only on a US role. The US must include in its calculations the possibility of failure or success. If the negotiations fail, then the US would not bear alone the consequences of failure as happened in Lebanon. Let the onus of the failure fall on an international conference.[12]

The American answer that 'We do not want the USSR to get the credit for success',[13] was indefensible as the main concern should have been who could achieve true peace which is ultimately in the best interest of all concerned. These are some of the basic rules of diplomacy which were seriously missing in 1982.

But one formidable reality was apprehended in the Arab world, namely that political institutions and agreements might be hastily established or destroyed, but the people and the cause would not recede without reasonable restitution. Hence the determination to meet the requirements. Any further moderation would have been seen as capitulation. And if this happened, it was feared that national forces within the Arab ranks and constituencies would be at work to overturn not only an unbalanced settlement, but also the Arab decision-makers who had made it possible. Such a settlement was seen as leading to a phoney peace, presenting a breathing space for future disturbances – a fertile ground for Israel to penetrate in a determined effort to redraw the political map of the Middle East. In other words, such a settlement would be counterproductive.

Fez was described as one of the most difficult summits in Arab history. The bargaining took a long time, but a consensus was eventually reached. Palestinian acquiescence was deeply appreciated by the moderate camp led by Jordan and Saudi Arabia. Hence, their determination for a positive demonstration – especially to the Arafat camp within the PLO – that moderation pays in the end. But an opposing psychological development had by then taken place in Israel which made it far more difficult to give up what had been acquired by military means. No outside power jumped in to close the gap. Hence the area fell into the grip of yet another stalemate despite the two freshly articulated peace plans.

Assessing the Fez and Reagan plans

The Arab Fez Plan did not deviate from the line adopted by the international community and expressed through a myriad of General Assembly and Security Council resolutions since 1947. Hence the widespread support it received, except from Israel and the US. The Plan envisaged two states, a Palestinian and a Jewish State – a principle which had been established in the UN Partition Plan, Resolution 181 of 1947. But the new territorial realities of the 1980s had also been grasped, a fact proven by the acceptance of a mini-state in the West Bank and Gaza alone, as opposed to the whole area allotted to the Palestinian State in 1947. The Fez Plan accepted the principles of Resolution 242 and Israel's right to exist within secure and recognized boundaries, without making explicit reference to them. It also recognized

Palestinian rights as mentioned in the same resolution. Thus, the Fez Plan went a long way to meeting President Reagan's Plan, but it was framed in an Arab mould, and in a way which made it more palatable to Arab constituencies and to the popular Arab perception of a just peace in the Middle East. A more detailed comparison between the major points in both plans indicates the disparities as well as the common denominators that could have been a starting point for peace-making.

Point one of the Fez Plan stressed that Israel must withdraw from all territories occupied in 1967, including Arab Jerusalem. The Reagan Plan stressed,

In the pre-1967 borders, Israel was barely 10 miles wide at its narrowest point. The bulk of the Israeli nation lived within artillery range of hostile Arab armies. I am not about to ask Israel to live that way again . . . When the border is negotiated between Jordan and Israel, our view on the extent to which Israel should be asked to give up territory will be heavily affected by the extent of true peace and normalization and the security arrangements offered in return . . . The withdrawal provision of Resolution 242 applies to all fronts including the West Bank and Gaza . . . Jerusalem must remain undivided, but its final status should be decided through negotiations.[14]

Leaving the Jerusalem issue aside for the moment, we can say that if Resolution 242 were to be applied on all fronts, if security arrangements were to be taken into account, including disarmament or at least reduction of forces on both sides, and if true peace were to be offered by each side, then the 1967 borders would become irrelevant as security for Israel. Complete peace in return for complete withdrawal, in the absence of security measures, would be irrelevant to Jordan. But if security were to be guaranteed for all parties, then Israel's return to the 1967 borders would indicate that the US was using its will and determination towards achieving true peace, based on the inadmissibility of the acquisition of territory by force, in accordance with the Fourth Geneva Convention and Resolution 242, on which the Reagan Plan was based.

Point two of the Fez Plan stressed the necessity of dismantling the Israeli settlements established in Arab territory since 1967. The Reagan Plan envisaged

The US will not support the use of any additional land for the purpose of settlements, during the transitional period . . . The immediate adoption of a settlement freeze by Israel, more than any other action, could create the confidence needed for wider participation in these talks . . . Further settlement activity is in no way necessary for the security of Israel and only diminishes the confidence of the Arabs that a final outcome can be freely and fairly negotiated.

In the talking points accompanying a letter sent by President Reagan to Menachem Begin and the Arab governments prior to his speech on 1

September 1982, it was stressed that 'the US will oppose dismantlement of the existing settlements' but their status 'must be determined in the course of the final status negotiations'. The US would not support their continuation as extra-territorial outposts.

Israel's defiance of President Reagan's approach by the construction of further settlements proved the truth of a statement made repeatedly by King Hussain: faced with a choice between peace and territory, Israel had chosen territory. Despite the plight of the Israeli economy, the settlements continued, the US continued to supply the finance required to build them, and President Reagan began to reinterpret international law by stating that the settlements were not necessarily illegal, and to defy the international consensus, as expressed in Security Council resolutions, through the use of the American veto. His argument that further settlements would diminish the confidence of the Arabs, and that a final outcome could still be freely and fairly negotiated, became irrelevant. With the announcement in December 1983 of a US strategic alliance with Israel, the abandonment of his role as an honest broker for peace became a permanent perception.

Point three of the Fez Plan stressed the guarantees to be offered for freedom of worship for all religions in the holy places and holy shrines. President Reagan ignored the significance of this point. It was not mentioned in his plan.

Point four of the Fez Plan reaffirmed the right of the Palestinian people to self-determination, Palestinian national rights under the PLO and the indemnification of all Palestinians who did not want to return to their homes. President Reagan envisaged

The next step in the Camp David process is: autonomy talks to pave the way for permitting the Palestinian people to exercise their legitimate security rights . . . The question now is how to reconcile Israel's legitimate security concerns with the legitimate rights of the Palestinians . . . Due consideration must be given to the principle of self-government by the inhabitants of the territories and to the legitimate security concerns of the parties involved . . . Palestinians feel strongly that their cause is more than a question of refugees. I agree. The Camp David Agreement recognized that fact, when it spoke of the legitimate rights of the Palestinian people and their just requirements.

After his announcement that the evacuation of the PLO from Beirut was complete, President Reagan stressed, in his talking points, 'we will maintain our commitment to the conditions we require for recognition of, and negotiations with, the PLO', a reference to the commitment given to Israel by Kissinger in 1975. As far as self-determination was concerned, the talking points stressed that 'in the Middle East context, self-determination has been identified exclusively with the formation of a Palestinian State. We will not support this definition of self-determination.'

Among many other issues, President Reagan completely ignored the question of the displaced Palestinians. Of the 5 million Palestinian people, only 1.3 million or so are in the West Bank and Gaza. They are the ones President Reagan wanted to accommodate. The rest, scattered throughout the world, would according to his plan be doomed to permanent exile. Reagan's 'solution' of the Palestinian problem, which precluded the exercise of the whole Palestinian population's right to self-determination without external interference, to national independence, sovereignty, to return to their homes and property and to select their own representatives, was thus simply not an option most of the Arabs could consider. But in admitting that the Palestinians had a case and that their case was more than just a refugee problem, President Reagan was indirectly admitting that the Palestinian case was a national one.

As the Arabs in general and the Palestinians in particular did not have the means to defend these national rights, there was no immediate danger from theorizing in Washington, or even from attempting to solve the problem in a way that met all apprehensions except those of the Arabs. Hence, President Reagan left the Arabs with only three options. First, to abandon their rights in despair, like many other just causes in history. On the basis of historical experience and of the Arab character this was not likely to happen. Second, to work endlessly at building up Arab strength through military means, technological know-how, and raising the standard of living and education for the Arab masses. This option was being pursued assiduously as a long-term goal. Third, a shorter-term goal, was to go the whole way with President Reagan by working on the amalgamation of the two plans and by removing obstacles – that is, Arab obstacles – from the path of the implementation of the Reagan/Fez plans, thus embarrassing President Reagan into action. If he did not act, the Arabs would lose no more than they already had done. They would also ultimately put the onus of any failure in peace-making on the US and Israel. It seems that the so-called moderates were set on this line of action, knowing that in the short term the status quo, which they could not change on their own and which was favourable to Israel, was almost certain to be maintained.

Point five of the Fez Plan stressed that there should be a transitional period for the West Bank and the Gaza Strip under the auspices of the UN, not exceeding a few months. President Reagan envisaged

There must be a period of time during which the Palestinian inhabitants of the West Bank and Gaza will have full autonomy over their own affairs . . . The purpose of the five-year period of transition, which would begin after free elections for a self-governing Palestinian authority, is to prove to the Palestinians that they run their affairs and that such Palestinian autonomy poses no threat to Israel's security . . . I want to make the American position well understood: the purpose of this transition period is the peaceful and orderly transfer of authority from Israel to the Palestinian inhabitants of the West Bank and Gaza. At the same time, such a transfer must not interfere with Israel's security requirements.

When it comes to true peace, a period of several months or even five years is not a major point of contention. But the Fez summit thought it prudent, for two reasons, to restrict the transitional period to a few months, just long enough for an orderly transfer of power under UN supervision. First, the Palestinians had been running their own affairs in the West Bank and Gaza despite Israeli harrassment, including the closure of Palestinian universities which required holding classes secretly in private homes and institutions. The dismissal and deportation of freely elected mayors, and attempts to assassinate them, had made things more difficult. Nevertheless they had been able not only to run their own affairs but also the affairs of many institutions and departments throughout the Arab world. As the most highly educated category of Arab communities, the Palestinians did not need to prove their capabilities to President Reagan or anybody else by going back to the outdated logic of the Palestinian Mandate half a century or so ago.

Secondly, the five-year period within which Palestinian autonomy was to be tested, in case it should become a threat to Israel's security, was thought to be unwarranted; for no serious observer could doubt Israel's ability to defend itself or think that a Palestinian entity, disarmed and sandwiched between Israel and Jordan, would be able to pose any real threat to Israel. Israel's security was already beyond question. Israel was one of the world's leading military powers; as the invasion of Lebanon had indicated, it was the only serious military power in the region. For all practical purposes, an Arab–Israeli war along the lines of the 1967 and 1973 conflicts was impossible in the foreseeable future. The conflict was no longer one to be solved by military means, and most Arab states had accepted Israel as a fact, as did the Fahd and Fez Plans. Therefore President Reagan's insistence on absolute security guarantees for Israel was regarded as meaningless. As Kissinger had observed, 'there is no such thing as absolute security'. Absolute security could be fulfilled only through peace, based on justice.

Point six of the Fez Plan stressed the establishment of an independent Palestinian State with Arab Jerusalem as its capital. President Reagan envisaged:

Peace cannot be achieved by the formation of an independent Palestinian State in those territories – West Bank and Gaza – nor is it achievable on the basis of Israel's sovereignty or permanent control over the West Bank and Gaza . . . The US will not support the establishment of an independent Palestinian State in the West Bank and Gaza, and we will not support annexation or permanent control by Israel . . . The final status of these lands must be reached through the give and take of negotiations . . . It is the firm view of the US that self-government by the Palestinians of the West Bank and Gaza in association with Jordan offers the best chance for a durable, just and lasting peace.

President Reagan deemed it necessary to prevent Israel from establishing permanent sovereignty or control over the West Bank and Gaza. It was believed that annexation would sooner or later produce an Arab majority which would destroy the essence of the Jewish State. And if Israel sought to escape this dilemma by expelling the Arabs, it would lose the moral support of even its best friends. Hence, Israel's abandonment of the heavily populated Arab territories appeared essential. The only question was: How much territory? Reagan left it to the 'give and take' of negotiations – an elastic concept which gave Israel ample room to manoeuvre, especially since it would be negotiating from strength. But for the Arabs it was academic to measure the amount of security and normalization of relations, including cultural and economic relations, to be offered by the Arabs in advance, but to express no matching concern for Arab security in general and Palestinian security in particular. As far as the Arabs were concerned the concept lacked a solid framework based on the principle of the inadmissibility of the acquisition of territory by force in accordance with the UN Charter and international law. Moreover, after a reassuring gesture, namely by stating that he understood the Palestinian yearning for their identity, President Reagan offered the Palestinians a palliative: to express their identity through another sovereign state, at the price of their own self-determination.

As far as Jerusalem was concerned, President Reagan's prescribed solution did not cause direct offence to the Arab world. By saying that the city must remain undivided, its status to be decided through negotiations and its Palestinian inhabitants to participate in the election of the West Bank and Gaza authority, he left ample room for acceptable interpretations. Although an undivided Jerusalem could meet Israel's position on the unity of the city, it could also meet Resolution 181 of 29 November 1948, which left a demilitarized Jerusalem as a *corpus separatum* under the aegis of a UN Trusteeship Council. Or, if the previous US position on East Jerusalem was maintained, it could mean returning East Jerusalem to the Arabs on the principle that 'The part of Jerusalem that came under the control of Israel in the June War of 1967, like other areas occupied by Israel, is occupied territory',[15] and hence returnable in accordance with Resolution 242. Or, according to the Rogers Plan, 'The final status is to be determined by Israel and Jordan taking into account the interests of the other countries in the area and the international community',[16] provided that Jerusalem remains a unified city, and that 'there should be roles for Israel and Jordan in the civic, economic and religious life of the city'. But although the Reagan initiative suggested that the eastern sector of Jerusalem was part of the occupied West Bank – in as much as it gave the inhabitants the right to vote in the election of the proposed West Bank and Gaza Authority – it left open to doubt the practical value of this right when their elected representatives could exercise no authority over an undivided Jerusalem or over its inhabitants who voted them to office.

Reagan's prescription was thus vague and valueless. While it promoted the concept of an undivided city – just as Israel had proclaimed it to be – it deferred the whole issue for negotiation, but detailed no substantive set of principles by which these negotiations should be conducted. Taking into consideration Israel's answer to the Reagan initiative, namely 'Jerusalem is one city, indivisible, the capital of the State of Israel: thus shall it remain for all generations to come', and the past record of US retreats whenever faced with a defiant Israel, then, to all intents and purposes, the Reagan recipe – despite Arab optimism – was likely to have sealed, as *The New York Times* of 3 September 1982 put it, 'a thinly disguised Israeli dominion over all of Jerusalem'.

In contrast, points seven and eight of the Fez Plan stressed that the Security Council should guarantee peace among all states of the region, including an independent Palestinian State. President Reagan ignored the Palestinian element – the core of the Middle East problem – in the negotiations. Apart from the inclusion of a few nominal Palestinian representatives, the future of the Palestinians would be decided by the Arab states and Israel. Only under US supervision would direct negotiations, based on Resolution 242, be undertaken. Only with Arab recognition of Israel, and of its right to security and peace, would an enduring solution be reached. Any formula for peace that eventually emerged would have to be sanctioned by all participants. In President Reagan's view, this would be the best guarantee for peace. Although his rationale cannot be contested, there were then three major US misconceptions of realities intrinsic to the Middle Eastern political arena.

First, the Arab states could not speak for the Palestinians, who have had an appointed representative since the Rabat Decision of 1974. Second, when he announced the details of his plan, President Reagan seemed obsessed with Israel's security at a time when the Arabs had already shown – in the Fahd and later in the Fez Plan – their willingness to guarantee the security of all states in the area, including Israel. Coming so soon after the Israeli invasion of Lebanon, and the US collaboration in it, the Arabs were crying out for just such a similar guarantee of their own security from Israel. The fact that Reagan did not urge Israel to end practices that feed Arab apprehensions about their own security awoke Arab suspicions as to whether he could act as a judicious arbiter of peace. Third, if Resolution 242 was the foundation of

Reagan's own plan for peace, then it would not have been unreasonable to invite the other members of the Security Council to join the peace negotiations and give a helping hand in implementing a resolution which they had drawn up with the US in November 1967, but which had lain dormant ever since.

A comprehensive analysis of and comparison between the Fez and Reagan plans leads inevitably to the conclusion that, as far as the so-called moderate Arab states, including Jordan, were concerned, both plans were complementary. The only major differences were over the description of the Palestinian state/entity, over who would represent the Palestinians, and over the right of the Palestinians to self-determination. Hence Jordan's determination to reconcile these differences by devising a Jordanian–Palestinian formula that would meet President Reagan's requirements without deviating from the landmarks of peace set out at Fez. At that particular juncture in history, the question became, even if such a formula were devised, could President Reagan be seriously relied on to take action?

Pessimism was not inappropriate, but the moderate Arabs could not afford to see President Reagan follow rather than dictate events in the Middle East. They were determined not to give up. 'For us, inactivity on peace initiatives is not an option, because time is not on the Arab side. Even if the chance is one in a million, that one chance must be put to the test', the Jordanian Information Minister of the day declared.[17]

Time was indeed not on the Arab side. Creeping annexation of the West Bank was working against Jordan's stability. But a stalemate was also working against Reagan's credibility and standing, hence Jordan's argument that the US also needed Jordan, if only to demonstrate that it still had a viable peace initiative. During the stalemate which followed, and while the US and Israel became involved in their 1984 election campaigns, Jordan steered through several lines of foreign policy undertakings both in the regional and in the international sphere, the main idea of which was to put its own house in order, and to prepare the international community for a major movement towards peace.

11 Jordan embarks on several lines of foreign policy

The planned year of action

According to conventional Arab wisdom, 1985 was to be the year of action in the American political cycle. Having assumed that the US could take no foreign-policy initiatives before its presidential elections were over, moderate Arab leaders had high hopes of the re-elected President Reagan acting decisively on the question of a comprehensive Middle East settlement.

The same conventional wisdom held that it was in the US national interest to bring Israel to accept a settlement of the Palestinian question based on the restitution of minimum, but essential, Arab rights, as advocated by America's Arab friends in the Middle East. In so doing, the US would not only refute the accusations of the radicals that the long-standing hopes vested in the Arabs' friendship with the US were only a mirage, but would also serve its own long-term interests by preventing the disintegration of the moderate Arab middle ground in the region. With Israel's growing economic dependence on the US, it was thought that the President, free from re-election pressures and, by extension, from the pressures of the Israeli lobby in Washington, could be persuaded to exert powerful leverage on Israel for the concessions necessary to establish peace. Even better, from the Arab point of view, was the landslide success President Reagan achieved without the help of the Jewish vote. He thus owed the Jewish lobby nothing in return.

These same Arab leaders were desperate to avoid stagnation setting in in the Middle East peace process. Past experience had shown that inaction led to erosion in political positions as well as on the ground, and that prolonged deadlock was more likely to explode into more crises, more stalemate and further stagnation, which presented a fertile ground for radicalism. If stagnation was allowed to continue, then the main threat would come from the likelihood of more Islamic revolutions on the Iranian model, carried out by people whose grievances had not been adequately dealt with. And, in such a situation, the Soviet Union would then have a better chance for further penetration into the region. The Arab world looked to Washington to break this vicious circle.

135

The problem with this line of thinking was the expectation that the US would depart from its own conventional wisdom, built up over the years, which insisted on dividing Middle Eastern countries, including Israel, into pro- and anti-Soviet. In this simplified scheme of things, the moderate Arab leaders and Israel were obstinately seen as belonging to the second category. US–Israeli co-operation was therefore regarded as being in the best interests of the moderate Arab states, since it tilted the balance of anti-Soviet power in their favour. What the US ignored was that through its close identification with Israel and its policies – as demonstrated in Lebanon – and its acquiescence in Israeli practices on the West Bank and Gaza, it was steering the Arab population towards identifying with and celebrating the Lebanese resistance movement in South Lebanon. Speaking at the formal opening session of the Arab Inter-parliamentary Union meeting in Amman on 11 March 1986, King Hussain saluted the Lebanese resistance movement as 'the flame that confronts Israeli occupation in South Lebanon'. Indeed, a new force of Arab nationalism, not comprehended by the glib phrase 'Islamic Fundamentalism', was in fact being created in the Middle East. The Israeli defeat in Lebanon, psychologically as well as politically and militarily, had shown what a guerrilla resistance – Shi'a or otherwise – could do to Israel's vaunted reputation of invincibility.

Representatives of this new force gathered in Derby in England, in March 1985, for a two-day conference to co-ordinate strategy. They were the leaders of an increasingly powerful Shi'a International, and were attending the second meeting of Islamic revolutionaries to be held in Britain in four months. The well-known Middle East political analyst, Patrick Seale, was there. He wrote in *The Observer* of 7 April 1985:

> The guerrilla war against Israel and the long-drawn-out Gulf conflict are throwing up new forces which could change the face of Arab politics . . . In addition to the Shi'a International, two other revolutionary groupings have come on stage in March 1985. Half a dozen Palestinian factions opposed to Arafat and his peace strategy have joined forces in a Syrian-sponsored Salvation Front . . . Libya too has been playing host to the so-called Pan-Arab Revolutionary Command, drawing membership from Nasserist, Marxist and fundamentalist factions. These three new forces . . . oppose the so-called moderate Arab axis and beyond it what they perceive as the moderates' ring master, the US.

In an effort to understand what was going on in the Middle East, a sub-committee of the US House Foreign Affairs Committee held a series of hearings on Islamic Fundamentalism and Radicalism in the Middle East on 15 July 1985. Two distinguished professors spoke.[1] Fuad Ajami presented the first testimony:

> Islamic Fundamentalism today represents the struggle between the old privileged classes and the traditionally underprivileged ones . . . The great traditions of the Arab

Middle East are coming apart . . . Much of the revolution is imposed from Iran but plenty of fervour is indigenous to the Arab world.

Augustus Norton, Associate Professor of Comparative Politics at the US Military Academy, added, 'There is one common denominator shared by many, if not all of the Islamic movements . . . and it is a deeply felt sense of disenfranchisement.' Yet the US, no doubt influenced by Israel, continued to claim that the problem was basically one of terrorism perpetrated by the PLO and some Moslem fanatics. Hence, as part of President Reagan's intensified policy of combating terrorism around the world, the US military and CIA personnel started to train anti-terrorist units for foreign governments, including Lebanon, according to government sources in Washington.[2]

Jordan's Foreign Minister had presaged this general despair in 1982.

The US does not want to understand that it is humiliation, frustration, instability and degradation which pushes the area towards radicalism, not only among the Islamic Fundamentalists but also among the Leftist movements, which are not necessarily Soviet movements although backed by the Soviet Union.[3]

Such a statement indicated the urgent need perceived in some Arab quarters for the US to move firmly, once and for all, to solve the problems involving Israel both in Lebanon and in the West Bank and Gaza, before the whole area was engulfed by radicalism and terrorism. It also indicated rejection of Washington's thesis about curbing terrorism. Without identifying and treating the causes of such terrorism, it was felt, this thesis was irrelevant in the Middle East context.

Prince Hassan of Jordan, the master of 'middle ground politics' in the region, summed things up as follows:

People who speak of Islamic Fundamentalism as if there are different kinds of regional Islam, Libyan Islam, Saudi Islam, Iranian Islam etc . . . have one point of wishful thinking in common: to degrade the centrality of the traditional political issues such as Palestinian self-determination and the Arab–Israeli conflict in order to create a more convenient new concept, namely, the ethno-religious mosaic relationship between the people of the Middle East, including Israel, whereby a minority among minorities could establish its hegemonial power over the rest of the Middle East. People who adopt a holistic approach as a substitute for the partial 1967 approach to the Arab-Israeli conflict, and conclude that the Palestinian question is over, or Arab nationalism is dead, are in fact accepting that the Israeli border is the River Jordan, a springboard for Israeli expansionists to central and south Jordan. By doing so, they are encouraging radicalism among Arabs, Palestinians and Israelis alike, thus torpedoing any hope of coexistence or any common ground between moderate Arabs and moderate Israelis.[4]

These diverse opinions about the political complexity of the Middle East reveal unanimity on one point: a deep sense of apprehension about the future of the region, and its urgent need of some sense of stability that could not be provided by the people of the region themselves. Help had to come from outside, and this was something Jordan was determined to explore.

Jordan's approach to the re-elected President Reagan was preceded by heated diplomacy, both in the regional and the international arena. The driving force was its belief that any movement to further the Arab–Israeli peace process had to be made during 1985–6, before the start of yet another round of election activity in the US and, more importantly, before the intransigent Likud took over the government in Israel – in October 1986 – in accordance with the 'government of national unity' agreement struck between Likud and Labour after the 1984 elections left the two major parties at near parity.

The fact that Jordan was taking the initiative at this point was because events in the West Bank were creating an urgent need for peace. In providing a haven for fleeing Palestinian refugees, as a result of the various Arab–Israeli wars, Jordan enfolded within its borders the tensions, frustrations and intellectual and ideological divisions of a large sector of the Palestinian population. The first mass exodus occurred in 1948, when some 300,000 people were pushed across the River Jordan into Jordan.[5] Another mass ejection of about 240,000 people took place during the 1967 war. In total, almost half a million Palestinians were uprooted and forced to leave the West Bank and Gaza between June and December 1967.[6]

The ceasefire line around Israel extended for 490 miles, 300 of which abut directly onto Jordan. Jordan feared the Israeli settlements were becoming an irreversible step to annexation. The speed of their construction seemed to destroy whatever chance once existed for a meaningful territorial compromise, by creating factors which could be difficult to dismantle in the event of peace.

Just over half of all the land on the occupied West Bank was under the control – direct or indirect – of the Israeli authorities. This was the principal finding of a research survey, completed in early 1985, by the West Bank Data Base Project, led by Dr Meron Benvinisti and funded by the Rockefeller and Ford Foundations.[7] While only 2.5 per cent of the West Bank's 1,400,000 acres were actually earmarked for Jewish settlements, much larger tracts had been declared state lands. These were previously registered in the name of the Jordanian government before their seizure by Israel in 1967. Additional areas had been designated as military training areas or requisitioned for other 'public purposes'.

The land set aside for Jewish settlements, moreover, could eventually absorb up to a million people, according to the survey, since most of the Jewish settlements were urban rather than agricultural. At the time the report was published, there were some 45,000 Jewish settlers in the West Bank, living among a population of more than 850,000 Palestinian Arabs. By April

1987 when a second updated report was published, the Jewish numbers had gone up to 65,000.[8] The survey found a geographical pattern in the land sequestrations: the eastern third of the West Bank and the areas contiguous to the pre-1967 border with Israel were almost entirely designated for Israeli use. But a planned road network designed to bypass Arab population centres and to fragment and dissect Arab-populated regions could involve the compulsory purchase and/or seizure of a further 25,000 acres throughout the West Bank.

While there was considerable sequestration under the Labour-led government between 1967 and 1977, the process accelerated sharply under the Likud, between 1977 and 1984. And the Peres-led government of national unity announced, on 10 January 1985, its approval of six more settlements to be located throughout the West Bank in areas traditionally excluded from Labour's settlement ideology. Labour Party thinking had hitherto called for settlements in key security zones like the Jordan Valley, and in areas with a low Arab presence. The new ones were to be sited close to Arab population centres with the function of housing Israelis who could commute to work in Israel. The decision was seen by some political observers not only as a victory for the Likud hardliners, but also as a message to King Hussain that the Peres-led government, too, could establish settlements throughout the area.[9] Dr Benvinisti commented, 'Land seizures are to be seen as rule by law rather than rule of law, since they ignore principles of natural justice.' He added that 'Land is valued as national patrimony, not a piece of commercial estate. Gain or loss of space is regarded as victory or defeat, just like a battleground.'[10] By mid-1987 there were 118 settlements in the West Bank compared with 109 in 1984; by the end of the 1980s the settler population was forecast to reach 100,000.

An alarmed Palestinian Mayor, Elias Freij of Bethlehem, echoed Jordan's apprehensions in an interview with Radio Israel:

The West Bank should be reserved for the Palestinians following a political resolution of the Arab–Israeli conflict. Unless there is a solution in a year or two, the situation will really become irreversible. What will be left for the people in the West Bank?[11]

The hardliners' answer may have been laid in Professor Yuval Ne'eman's statement to *The Times* of 20 July 1982: 'A situation must be created in which there would be no place to create a Palestinian State other than in Jordan where there is one already.' This was one of the main reasons why King Hussain was desperate to achieve a comprehensive peace in the region, with each state, including Israel, enjoying security within its own recognized borders.

Water, a scarce resource in Jordan and a key element in its economic development, was another important facet of the conflict. The announcement of Israel's plans to divert water from the Sea of Galilee and the Jordan River rallied Arab leaders to convene the first Arab summit in Cairo in 1964. Operations aimed at diverting water were one of the reasons contributing to the outbreak of the 1967 war. In addition to the draining of the Hula Basin and the construction of a canal from the Sea of Galilee to Bet Sh'an in Israel, a water supply grid had been constructed that permitted the pumping of up to 11,300 million cubic feet of the Jordan River, each year, to the centre and south of Israel. Israel had a long history of confrontation with Jordan over water. In 1967, it blew up the foundations for a Syrian–Jordanian dam at Mukheiba. In 1970, Israeli guns destroyed the upper end of the Mukheiba canal itself. And, over the past sixteen years or so, it had successfully mobilized political pressure to prevent the construction of the Maqarin Dam, which could have permitted year-round utilization of the river's waters by Jordan. Another chapter in the 'water war' was opened in early 1984 when Israel stymied Jordan's efforts to repair a blocked key inlet to the East Ghor Canal, serving 30,000 acres of Jordan's irrigated area. The spectre of withering crops was seen by Jordan at the time as one of the means used to force it into direct talks with Israel.

Most damaging to Jordan's economic infrastructure could be the completion of a canal planned to carry water from the Mediterranean to the Dead Sea. In fact, on 28 May 1981 Begin unveiled a plaque on Mount Ben Yair, South of Massada, to inaugurate work on what was named the Mediterranean-Dead Sea Canal Project.[12] In August 1980, the Israeli Cabinet had approved in principle the construction of a 100 km canal to syphon water from the Mediterranean to the Dead Sea, at an estimated cost of $720m. Jordan regarded the announcement as a unilateral decision to tamper with the Dead Sea, an international waterway. According to Jordan's calculations, which were backed by a UN study on the environmental, agricultural and financial impact of the project on Jordan, the Canal could deprive 660 hectares of irrigation, and make a much wider area useless; the damage to agriculture was put at more than $66 bn. Potassium and phosphate production depended largely on Dead Sea brine and on its density. Israel's project could dilute it at the surface, forcing a decrease in its production of up to 15 per cent, according to Jordanian estimates. By drawing water out of Lake Tabariya, the level of the River's waters could be drastically reduced. The project could also damage the prospective development of Jordan's tourist industry along the Dead Sea shore, which could be flooded, and existing and future archaeological developments in the Jordan Valley, particularly in Jericho.

A pilot tunnel to the Dead Sea was actually completed but, in early June 1985, the temporary suspension of further work was announced, as the project would have cost twice as much as originally estimated and was therefore no longer considered economically feasible until further notice.[13]

More than any other Arab state, Jordan felt the anguish of the West Bank, with which it was in daily contact through the controlled traffic across the bridges. Israel had different views on the open bridge policy. Since 1967, it had followed a selective policy of decapitating the Palestinian community by deporting its leaders as well as unwanted Palestinians for what were claimed as security reasons. A total of 1,156 people were expelled between 1967 and 1978, and several hundreds subsequently.[14] The bridges became the nearest and most convenient exit point. According to former President Carter, 'about 12,000 Palestinians a year were being induced or forced to leave their homes and move east, either into Jordan or to join the many wandering refugees in other countries'.[15] Fearing future deportations across the River, Jordan began to scrutinize this traffic. As a former Jordanian Information Minister put it, 'Jordan is not going to be the dumping ground for people whom Israel finds politically inconvenient.'[16] Elaborating on the consequences of such deportation, Prince Hassan stated: 'The influx of disgruntled and politically alienated people into Jordan would serve only one purpose: the radicalization of its politics and the destabilization of its society.'[17]

Besides deportations Israel's other practices in the occupied territories such as the extensive appropriation of Arab private property, the destruction of Arab public and private buildings for the sake of erecting Jewish settlements, the imposition of collective punishments, confiscation of religious property for public purposes, and the obstruction of foreign aid via Amman for educational, housing and agricultural projects had led to rising anxieties in both Jordan and the West Bank and Gaza.[18]

A leading Jordanian policy-maker explained:

It looks very much as if the Middle East may be in for a period of redrawing of political and perhaps physical maps. The worst thing we can do is remain silent. We have to be seen to be positive and to be courageous or we run the risk of being swept away by a tide of radicalism.[19]

Jordan therefore revived the call for an international conference. It may have sounded contradictory to hear the Arab world calling for an international conference and at the same time insisting that the US undertake peace efforts in the Middle East. Looking at it from the Middle East perspective, however, there did not seem to be any contradiction.

Moderate Arab states had seen the futility of dealing with the Palestinian question over the last thirty years or so without concentrating on the main Israeli source of support. Hence the US presence at the negotiating table became vital. Furthermore, in no way could the Arab world, whether radical or moderate, accept the rationale put forward by Kissinger to an Arab leader, 'We want to make the Palestinian problem a problem for the Arabs – not Israel – to solve.'[20] If the creation of Israel resulted in the exile of a great percentage of the Palestinians then not only Israel, but also the US, Europe and the Soviet Union could in no way be relieved from responsibility, not only for dealing with the repercussions of their decision to create Israel, but also for solving the problem, permanently and on a just basis. This was the basic rationale for an international conference.

The presence of the Soviet Union at such a conference was seen as vital not only because it had global interests – as did the US – including interests in the Middle East, that could not reasonably be ignored, but also because it would be able to put a brake on what the other participants view as US excesses. Hence the presence of both superpowers was seen as essential, if only to neutralize each other's attempts to work against true peace in the Middle East. In other words, it could ensure fair play.

On the basis of past experience, however, the co-chairmanship of the two superpowers alone did not guarantee movement towards peace. For example, at the first Geneva Conference of December 1973, the US – despite Kissinger's assurances – was not serious about implementing Resolution 242 on all fronts, including the Jordanian front (see Chapter 2). What could the USSR do? Only rearm the Arabs for another round of fighting which was incapable of changing the situation on the ground. But when the US did summon up the courage to announce its own peace plan, it soon lost the zeal for action in the face of Israeli objections. This was where Europe came in. The Arab world called upon Europe to use its good offices with the US, to make it stand by its word, instead of collapsing into the impasse: Here was our plan and this was yours. Yours couldn't be implemented and we couldn't stand by ours.

King Hussain summed up the situation in his address to the UN General Assembly in September 1985:

We are prepared to negotiate under appropriate auspices with the government of Israel promptly and directly under the basic tenets of Security Council Resolutions 242 and 338. These negotiations must result in the implementation of 242 and resolve all the aspects of the Palestinian problem. It is Jordan's position that the appropriate auspices are an international conference hosted by the Secretary General of the UN to which are invited the five permanent members of the Security Council and all the parties to the conflict, for the purpose of establishing a comprehensive, just and lasting peace in the Middle East. My country believes that the Palestinian issues and the Middle East crisis fall squarely within the responsibilities of the UN, as well as those countries with a special interest in the conflict. It thus regards any consultation on the Middle East situation between the US and the USSR as both necessary and positive.[21]

Former Prime Minister Badran shed further light on the Jordanian attitude:

We call for an international conference to avoid polarization of the conflict between the two superpowers. We need another auxiliary force. The permanent members of the Security Council could prevent the US from its blatant and outright bias toward Israel . . . When we speak about an international conference we mean the provision of an international umbrella for peace talks, to avoid Israel and the US ganging up against the weaker side – the Arabs – during which their peace conditions could be dictated to the Arabs. As an international conference under the co-chairmanship of the US and the USSR was tried in 1977 and did not work, and as the European attitude has become clearer and more judicious and fair, we are inviting them to help the cause of peace . . . In no way will we agree to America and Israel ganging up against an individual Arab state such as Jordan. It happened with Lebanon, and the 17 May Agreement provides vivid proof of the futility of US insistence on making peace on one's own. If we add to that the continuous US adoption of the Israeli point of view, an international conference with a stronger role than that offered by the US remains the only venue for peace-making in the Middle East.[22]

King Hussain's use of the words 'appropriate auspices' was significant. Resolution 338 used the same expression for negotiations between the parties concerned. The Arab World, including Jordan, however, understood it to mean an international conference in which all parties to the conflict could participate, including the PLO. The King explained in his address to the nation on 19 February 1986:

The international community affirmed that 'appropriate auspices' meant an international conference, by acting on the precedent of the Geneva Conference of 1973. The balance of negotiations between the conflicting parties was then in favour of Israel, the occupying power. This gave Israel an undue advantage, hence its ability to persist in its occupation. Therefore, a new framework is sought to rectify the existing inequality through an international conference, in which the five permanent members of the Security Council would participate, since it was from the Security Council that 242 and 338 emanated, enunciating the principles of an equitable settlement, and since the Security Council is the international body responsible for interpreting the various resolutions and guaranteeing their implementation.

As Abu Odeh, Minister of the Court, put it in 1985: 'An international conference will provide the terms of reference for arbitration. It will eventually ratify and implement what is agreed upon.'[23]

King Hussain's second bold political move was to recall the National Assembly. On 5 January 1984, a Royal Decree called for a full session of the Jordanian National Assembly, comprising the Upper and Lower Houses of Parliament, to consider amendments to the Constitution to enable the appointment of new representatives of the occupied West Bank, when elections next took place in Jordan. It was the first time since Israel's conquest of the West Bank in 1967 that King Hussain had called for a full session of the National Assembly which, when originally elected, comprised an equal number of deputies, 30, from each bank of the River Jordan. Only 46 were still alive. A quorum of two-thirds was needed under the Constitution to fulfil the task that it had been called on to do. Seven West Bank and seven East Bank seats in the Lower House were vacant.

The National Assembly had been formally dissolved in 1974, when the Rabat summit designated the PLO under Arafat as the sole legitimate representative of the Palestinian people, and it had last met in 1976 to authorize its own indefinite prorogation. Since then, a National Consultative Council appointed by the King had ruled the country. It too was formally dissolved on 5 January 1984.

The amendment of 9 January 1984 provided for representations of the West Bank by co-opted members, seven of whom were chosen by a majority vote in the Lower House, thus bringing the membership of the House up to 53. And the first by-elections in Jordan since 1967 filled seven seats from the East Bank on 12 March.

This major political move was the first step in Jordan's undertaking to put its own house in order.* Had the King left it much longer, natural causes might have rendered the Assembly permanently inquorate, and therefore unable to amend the rules under which its successor would be elected. And some amendments were necessary, given the *de facto* amputation of the West Bank from Jordan by Israel in 1967. King Hussain indicated at the formal reopening of the Assembly that dialogue, co-ordination and co-operation with the PLO had always been the most prominent feature of Jordan's foreign policy and that his government would act with determination to reach a practical formula for co-operation with the PLO. But he also made it clear that, although he regarded the PLO as a vital partner in reviving Middle East peace negotiations, it was the free and legitimate PLO, meaning the moderate Arafat and his loyalists, on whom he pinned his hopes. This was an indirect reference to the challenge to Arafat's leadership that had taken place a few months earlier, in the form of a Syrian-backed revolt in Lebanon against his leadership of the Palestinian National Liberation Movement (Fatah), the major guerrilla group within the PLO.

By recalling the National Assembly Jordan transmitted three significant politico-diplomatic waves. First, a signal to all concerned that it was determined to overcome any paralysis in the effort to revive peace negotiations within the framework of an international conference. Second, a signal to Arafat that he ought to come back for talks with Jordan on behalf of the Palestinians. Third, a signal to Israel that if it decided to annex the West Bank formally, Jordan would provoke intensive confrontation with it, on each and every platform, including legal and international forums, stressing in the process that despite the Rabat political decision – which was the basis of all

---

* This forum was extended in 1986 to include 71 seats for the East Bank and 71 for the Palestinians in the West Bank and in refugee camps in Jordan. After severing the legal relationship between the two banks on 31 July 1988, King Hussain allowed general elections in the East Bank in November 1989. Out of 80 seats the Islamists won the majority of 28. The rest was distributed unequally among other blocs.

the attempts at politico-diplomatic co-ordination with the PLO – the West Bank was still formally, and from the legal point of view, part of the Kingdom of Jordan.

Negotiations with the PLO resumed in March 1984, with the aim of devising a joint formula for action that could win Arab majority backing. But a change of course could take place only gradually, after permission was granted for the PNC's 17th session to be held in Amman in November 1984. King Hussain's diplomatic master-stroke, however, took place a few weeks earlier, when on 25 September 1984 he decided to break ranks with the majority of Arab states and restore diplomatic relations with Mubarak's Egypt.

It may be recalled that all Arab countries, apart from Oman, Sudan and Somalia, broke all diplomatic relations with Egypt as a gesture of protest at Sadat's decision unilaterally and directly to deal with the common enemy, by signing a peace treaty with Israel in 1979 (see Chapter 4). On 25 September 1984, after a full Cabinet meeting, a Jordanian Foreign Ministry statement announced the restoration of diplomatic relations. The statement was expanded on Jordanian television that same evening, as follows:

As a mark of appreciation for Egypt's solidarity with the struggle of the Arab people in Palestine, Iraq and Lebanon, and so as not to allow a temporary break in relations to become a permanent base for our enemy [Israel] to exploit us one by one, it was decided to restore political and diplomatic relations with the Arab Republic of Egypt as from today.[24]

Jordan's move merely placed an official stamp on what had already been long apparent. Egypt's importance in the Middle East transcended Arab rhetoric. Its history, geography, demographic weight, military power, cultural influence and diplomatic seniority have always given it the central place in Arab politics. All major movements of Arab policy towards Israel since 1948, whether in favour of war, armistice or peace, have been initiated by Egypt. The Camp David Accords could not change this status held among most of the Arab countries, at least at the popular level. Most Middle Eastern airlines continued to fly in and out of Cairo. Aside from Libya, Syria and South Yemen, who severed diplomatic relations completely, the rest of the Arab world did no more than withdraw their ambassadors, leaving their remaining embassy staff in Cairo intact. Private Arab investment continued to flow into Egypt. There was no evidence that Saudi Arabia and Kuwait had even withdrawn the $2 bn that they had on deposit in Egyptian banks at the time of the 1978 Baghdad Summit which initiated the punitive action against Sadat. Nor had there been any moves against the two million Egyptian expatriate workers in the Arab countries, including Jordan. Arab banks still operated in Cairo. Arab students continued to enrol in Egyptian universities.

Even Arab oil was still pumped through the Suez–Mediterranean pipeline. The Arabs, after all, whether on the popular or the official level, were not against the Egyptian people, but only against Sadat's policies.

Sadat did not live to see the conclusion of his treaty with Israel on 25 April 1982 – when Israel completed its withdrawal from Sinai – for he was assassinated on 6 October 1981 while celebrating the anniversary of the 1973 war. With his removal from the scene, official Egyptian relations with the rest of the Arab world started to warm up under the new president, Husni Mubarak who, while promising to abide by the peace treaty with Israel, initiated a new policy of halting the media war against the Arab leaders. King Hussain responded on 26 April 1982 by congratulating Egypt on recovering Sinai: 'Egypt's role will remain pioneering, firm and solid for the return of the rights of the people of Palestine, just as Egypt will remain at the forefront of every joint Arab action in defence of Arab honour and dignity.'[25] In a parallel move he told the press about his wish for the inclusion of Egypt in a new Arab union that would recover all the remaining Arab territories occupied by Israel: 'One of our dearest aspirations is to see the Arab nation, including Egypt, resume its march in unison so that the entire Arab territories, and first and foremost Jerusalem, will return to the Arabs.'[26] On 2 June he restated 'There is a big hope in the Arab world that things will return to how they used to be and that Egypt can play a major role for the best interests of the Arab nation.'[27]

Mubarak's support for the Arab cause, despite the Treaty with Israel, struck a chord, especially in Jordan. Among the Egyptian policies noted with appreciation were:[28] Mubarak's criticism of Israeli aggression against the Palestinian and Lebanese people (Egypt withdrew its ambassador from Tel Aviv in protest at the Israeli invasion of Lebanon); the cessation of all Egyptian propaganda against the other Arab states; Mubarak's refusal to meet the Israeli Prime Minister before Israel withdrew its forces from Lebanon, advanced towards an acceptable solution of the Palestinian problem and resolved the issue of Taba; Egypt's help for Iraq in the war with Iran; its call for all parties concerned with the Middle East issue, including the PLO, to participate in peace negotiations (Egypt urged Israel to recognize the Palestinian people's legitimate rights as a prelude to reaching an acceptable solution to the Arab–Israeli conflict); its backing for the PLO leader when he was besieged in Tripoli; its freeze on normalization of relations with Israel, in the cultural, economic, political and tourism fields; and its support for Arab rights in East Jerusalem, and its rejection of the Israeli version of Palestinian autonomy in the West Bank and Gaza. These were all seen as deliberate steps to advance the wider Arab, and particularly the Palestinian, cause. And Jordan was determined to arrest the deterioration in the Arab camp that had set in since Camp David by enlisting Egypt's leverage.

The first meeting between King Hussain and President Mubarak took place in New Delhi on 7 March 1983, at the Non-Aligned summit. While still technically on the Arab boycott list, Egypt signed a new protocol with Jordan in December 1983 which aimed at reviving economic ties between the two countries. It was the first of its type to be concluded since 1978.[29]

When King Hussain broke ranks with the majority of the Arab states by this unilateral move towards Egypt, he was widely accused in the Arab world, and especially by Syria, of breaking Arab summit resolutions. In return, the King accused Syria of being the first to violate summit resolutions by meddling in PLO affairs and siding with Iran against an Arab country, Iraq, thus violating the Arab League's joint defence pact. Jordan believed that restoring diplomatic relations with Egypt was a positive step. As King Hussain stated in December 1984:

Our decision is the result of a general conviction that since Egypt is a vital part of the Arab world, and with Egypt's unstinting contribution to Arab causes under its present leadership, the time has come to restore our relations and fullest co-operation in order adequately to face our common destiny. Egypt's reunification with its Arab family will reinforce the stability of the region and strengthen the responsible Arab constituency.[30]

Prince Hassan added:

The purpose of collaboration with Egypt is to put her experience to the service of all the peoples and states in the region in the exploration of fresh avenues in the search for a new instrument of peacemaking.[31]

Such statements indicated that Jordan was banking on Egypt's moral and diplomatic weight to break the stalemate in the peace process. The Camp David Accords had, in Jordan's view, fulfilled their purpose of enabling Egypt to regain its occupied territory. They were seen not as a defence pact or an alliance between Egypt and Israel, but as a political and military programme, the fulfilment of which marked the end of a chapter in Middle East politics. Their effect had been to plunge Arab politics into disarray, and it was increasingly clear that no breakthrough in either war or peace was likely if Cairo remained apathetic and inactive.

Egypt's return to the Arab fold via Jordan was more significant than the official explanations admitted. Three main factors must have had a part in the Jordanian decision. First, that it was wrong to keep Egypt under Mubarak isolated, and thus a fertile ground for outside domination, whether American or Israeli, simply because of what were regarded as earlier misguided policies. A move towards dialogue with the new president would, it was hoped, steer Egypt gradually back towards non-alignment by establishing a balanced relationship with the Arab world. Second, the keenly felt danger from the Gulf War required the mobilization of all available resources to face it. Iranian religious fanaticism, Jordan believed, would not stop at Sunni Iraq if the opportunity to spread further afield arose. Who else was better able to confront Shi'a Iran than a strong, resourceful and vast Sunni Egypt? And third, the community of interests between Syria and Iran against Iraq and in Lebanon must have worried Jordan deeply. Syria proclaimed that it had received a promise from Iran that it would withdraw from Iraq as soon as Saddam Hussain fell from power. But Jordan believed that such an Iranian victory would not stop there, but would swallow up Iraq and rebound on the rest of the Arab world, including Syria itself. Assad's hatred of Saddam Hussain could, it was felt, have dangerous repercussions. Only Egypt could balance Syria on the regional level.

The official Jordanian inlet back into the Arab mainstream allowed a grateful Mubarak to pay his first official visit to an Arab country within two weeks of Jordan's announcement of the restoration of diplomatic relations. His visit to Amman on 9 October was followed by King Hussain's visit to Cairo on 1 December. During these and other meetings including contacts at ministerial level, the foundations for firm bilateral relations were established within a programme of co-operation in transport, industry, tourism, fishing in the Red Sea, agriculture and investments. A development bank with branches in both capitals was opened to fund joint projects in the fields of energy, electricity and agro-industry. A new trade protocol was signed to cover expanding economic relations, and a joint shipping enterprise was started to transport goods between the Jordanian port of Aqaba and ports on the Suez Canal. A ferry service between Aqaba and the Egyptian Sinai terminal of Nweibe was under way by the end of April 1985 and many other co-operative ventures were to follow.

Political co-ordination began to take shape with Jordan's next major foreign policy undertaking: the 17th session of the Palestinian Parliament in exile, the PNC, held in Amman in November 1984. This was the most important session of the Palestinian Council since the inauguration of the PLO in 1964. The Council met after a ferocious battle for survival against Syria and the pro-Syrian radicals within the PLO. It was a very different affair from the 16th PNC, attended by the eight groups comprising the PLO, in Algiers in February 1983, although that too followed a battle for survival against Israel. The fratricidal conflict in the Bek'aa and around Tripoli had left self-inflicted wounds that were far worse than those inflicted by Israel. It was a different PLO that met in Amman, one dominated by Fatah, more compact, more coherent and more decisive. The session completed the process which Arafat himself set in motion in December 1983 when, after being rescued from the trap laid for him in Tripoli, he went straight to Egypt. He had shed the hardliners, dumped the consensus politics, consolidated his leadership of the moderate majority and emerged with greater freedom of manoeuvre than ever before. In the view of one Council member, 'The days of romantic radicalism were over.'[32] Allowing the PLO schism to be consecrated in Amman was a hard decision for Jordan to make. But, once taken, Amman converted the nightmares of both Syria and Israel into reality. While Jordan wanted to break the deadlock and move forward towards peace, Syria's fear was of isolation, of peace not on its own terms, although its stated objection was to peace arrived at via the Reagan Plan or Camp David II. Israel's nightmare was rather different – of Arab moderation. It knew how to deal with a violent and extremist PLO, but it had no answer to Arafat's moderation, which it was determined to destroy.

It became increasingly clear that Israel and Syria were 'status quo powers', formally opposed to each other in Lebanon but frequently forming a tacit alliance or agreement against attempts to break the impasse. Both used the same technique to deny Arafat a quorum in the PNC, but for different purposes. Both were united in their determination to prevent Arafat acquiring such a mandate: Syria by threatening to excommunicate any PLO faction which attended the PNC, and Israel by sticking to its policy of refusing to allow any PNC member from the occupied territories – who were mostly pro-Arafat – to attend on pain of being permanently exiled. Israel's efforts to deny the Palestinians the opportunity to state their conditions for peace gave rise to the charge that what Israel really feared was a PLO in pursuit of an internationally acceptable peace formula. At that point, the Americans could have given no greater boost to the peace process than by persuading Israel to allow the traditionally moderate West Bankers to cast their vote without fear of reprisal. Despite King Hussain's appeal to President Reagan to use his good offices with Israel, the President refused to budge. Faced with the prospect of a moderate Jordan acting in concert with a moderate PLO, inaction was the only thing Israel wanted. But faced with what was seen as an expansionist Israel, inaction was not an option for either Jordan or Arafat's PLO.

It was against this background that the 17th session of the PNC assumed such fateful proportions. King Hussain's address contained an indirect reference to Syria's attempt to dominate the PLO:

Your Council meets today with a legal quorum. You are meeting after you have defeated the attempts to impose tutelage on you. For their part your people have renewed their confidence in you after you have proved to the entire world your ability to preserve the independence of Palestinian decision-making, the competence of your institutions and the earnest policies of your organization, the PLO, the sole legitimate representative of the Palestinian Arab people.

Arafat for his part responded warmly:

This session affirms the fraternal bonds between the two peoples within the one family, both now and in the future, as well as affirming our common destiny in confronting the challenges, dangers and tribulations set against us . . . Despite the bitterness we have experienced, there are political axioms that cannot be changed or overlooked, namely that the bonds of kinship, fraternity, Arabism, common destiny and common cause uniting our Jordanian and Palestinian people will remain stronger than anything that might be imposed by temporary or transient circumstances.

In Amman, there was clearly a determination not to go for a separate peace, but to break the ground for movement towards a settlement. Both sides stressed the importance of eventual Syrian participation, wider Arab backing and a role for the USSR in any peacemaking process. Hence the platform adopted contained nothing to which Damascus could legitimately object on political grounds. Ironically, all the Arabs were ideologically united as never before on both the terms for peace, as outlined in the Fez Plan, and the vehicle for movement, an international conference. But the division between them was on how to move from A to B. The split was deeply entrenched, and it inhibited, indeed prohibited, movement towards a peaceful settlement.

To break the stalemate King Hussain, in his address to the PNC, revealed a plan of action involving a joint Palestinian–Jordanian initiative as the framework through which negotiations – based on Security Council Resolution 242 and the right of the Palestinian people to self-determination, in accordance with the principle of territory for peace – would be held in an international conference, under the supervision of the UN, with the participation of the permanent members of the Security Council and all parties to the dispute, including the PLO, which would have to attend on an equal basis with the other parties. As for the question of the Jordanian–Palestinian relationship after the land occupied by Israel had been restored, he affirmed that this was the primary responsibility of the two peoples of Jordan and Palestine to determine.

No one has the right to determine this relationship on their behalf, or to interfere in it, whether he be an enemy, brother or friend. This is because it would be a detraction from Jordan's sovereignty and open interference in the Palestinian people's right to determine their own destiny.

He once more reassured the PLO that he had no intention of speaking on its behalf nor of outbidding it: 'There is nothing to differ over so long as Palestine is the aim on which we meet.'

During the PNC session, a report calling for detailed discussions between the PLO and Jordan with the aim of working out a joint strategy was approved and referred to the PLO Executive Committee for further study. The PNC had already approved the principle of confederation between an independent Palestinian state and Jordan when it met in Algiers in February 1983. Whether an independent Palestinian state should be set up before confederation with Jordan, or after the recovery of occupied territory, was to be agreed upon during the coming negotiations.

Two developments during the PNC session indicated further lines of strategy. Saudi Arabian support for the convening of the PNC in Amman was affirmed, when a message to this effect from King Fahd was read out to the Council and warmly applauded on 24 November. And the head of the PLO's political department called for a joint Arab move to renew full links with Egypt. In what amounted to an important vote of confidence in Arafat's leadership, the Council exonerated him from any blame for his controversial visit to Egypt in December 1983. While condemning the Camp David Agreements in spirit and letter, the Council noted recent changes in Egyptian policy and called on the Executive Committee to adopt certain policies to delineate future relations with Cairo, in co-ordination with the other Arab countries. Arafat also stressed in his address the importance of Egypt's assumption of what he called 'its natural and vanguard role in our Arab nation away from the Camp David policy'. He added

Egypt's culture, its people and their human and military strength have not accepted the Camp David policy . . . Egypt has entrenched its struggle on several fronts to confirm that it is an indivisible part of this Arab nation and has its rights and duties . . . The Jordanian concept of Egypt and relations with its people is close to our Palestinian concept.

Thus, an axis for peace comprising Jordan, Egypt and the PLO – with the implicit blessing of Saudi Arabia – was beginning to take shape. It was crowned on 11 February 1985 with what became known as 'The Plan for Joint Jordanian–Palestinian Action'.

The PLO–Jordan Agreement of 11 February 1985[33]

Based on the Fez decisions agreed upon by the Arabs, and UN resolutions relating to the Palestinian question, in accordance with international legality, and based on reciprocal understanding to build a special relationship between the Jordanian and the Palestinian people, the Government of the Hashemite Kingdom of Jordan and the Palestinian Liberation Organization agree to co-ordinate their efforts in order to achieve a peaceful and just settlement to the Middle East issue and to end Israeli occupation of Arab lands including Jerusalem, according to the following bases and principles:

(1) Land for peace as set out in the UN and Security Council resolutions.
(2) The right of self-determination for the Palestinian people. The Palestinians will exercise their inalienable right of self-determination when the Jordanians and the Palestinians can do so in the context of an Arab confederation relationship, to be established between the two states of Jordan and Palestine.
(3) A resolution of the problems of Palestinian refugees in accordance with UN resolutions.
(4) A resolution of the Palestinian question in all its aspects.

(5) For this purpose, negotiations will take place under the auspices of an international conference, in which the five permanent members of the Security Council and all the parties to the conflict will participate, including the PLO, the sole legitimate representative of the Palestinian people, within a joint delegation (a Jordanian–Palestinian delegation).

Clauses 2 and 5 of the Agreement were clarified as follows:

Clause 2   Self-determination for the Palestinian people, in a Palestinian state confederated with the Hashemite Kingdom of Jordan.

Clause 5:   For this purpose, negotiations will take place within the framework of an international conference, in which the five permanent members of the Security Council and all the parties to the conflict will participate, including the PLO, the sole legitimate representative of the Palestinian people. Other Arab parties concerned will take part in the conference; among them will be a Jordanian–Palestinian delegation comprising equal representatives of the Jordanian government and the Palestinian Liberation Organization.

In his address to the UN General Assembly in September 1985 King Hussain stressed that:

The Arabs reaffirmed their collective desire for peace, through the adoption of an Arab peace plan – the Fez Plan – formulated with the participation of the PLO and accepted by it. Nevertheless, on the basis of a number of realistic considerations, it became evident that the peace efforts required an approach that would enable the participation of the PLO in the process, hence the Accord regulating joint political action by Jordan and the PLO. It was to serve as a mechanism for the Arab peace plan and part of the Arab joint efforts forming one of its links.

Prince Hassan shed further light on this.[34]

The Fez Plan provided only a general framework for peace but lacked a definitive programme for action, as laid down by UN resolutions 242 and 338. On the other hand, while Fez accorded the PLO, as the sole legitimate representative of the Palestinian people, a central role in any future peace negotiations, the UN Resolution 242 did not and could not do so. Naturally Jordan's or Syria's participation was not an issue . . . The question that remains to be tackled is the ways and means by which the PLO can take its rightful place at the negotiating table. This is the missing element which is needed to transform the Fez Plan into a practical plan. Jordan has taken on the responsibility of evolving such a transformation. The intention is to facilitate the PLO's participation in deliberations about the future status of the territories under Israel's occupation. Hence, the Accord of 11 February between the PLO and Jordan.

The PLO Executive Committee also referred to the Accord as a plan for action,[35] and as a pad to launch the Fez resolutions towards an eventual international conference. Both parties regarded the Accord as the beginning of a collective Arab action, to be followed by the mobilization of the international community, and as one of the links in the chain of collective Arab efforts providing a mechanism for implementing the Fez Plan while paving the way for the PLO to engage in the international effort aimed at establishing a just, permanent and comprehensive peace.[36]

The Arab front

King Hussain and Yasser Arafat explained the dimensions, foundations and objectives of the Accord at the Arab summit held in Casablanca between 7 and 9 August 1985 and attended by heads and representatives of 17 Arab states and the PLO, but without Syria, Libya, South Yemen and Algeria. Referring to the danger from Israel, King Hussain emphasized that 'According to the Israeli Labour Party, between the Mediterranean Sea and the Jordan River there is no room for more than one entity. The Likud defined it as: the land is ours and the people are yours, i.e., Jordan's.' And he warned, 'Let us remember that the two parties are members of the same government.' On the attitude of the outside world, Hussain said

The international community sees solutions not through a court of law, but through a concept of international relations which are governed by the give and take of common interests, mutual benefits, pressures, settlements and adjustment of positions.

He therefore appealed to the Arabs to agree on the priorities of each stage, to sift the constants from the variables, the possible from the impossible, and delusions from reality. He then went on to define the elements of the Jordanian–Palestinian relationship as a distinctive bond between the two peoples, forged through kinship and common interests, geographical and economic, contiguity between Jordan and the West Bank, and historical and demographic linkages. He said there was a confluence of destiny between them for good or ill, and that the paramount danger threatening them was an occupied Palestine and an uprooted Palestinian people, on the one hand, and a threatened Jordan in its role as an Arab barricade against Zionist expansion, on the other. He also cited Jordan's constant policy of not pursuing a separate course and of not attempting to replace the PLO, the sole legitimate representative of the Palestinian people. Jordan and the PLO, he said, shared all these considerations. He concluded:

It was only natural that Jordan be expected to extend the hand of co-operation and co-ordination to the PLO, not with the intent of excluding any other party or deviating from the course of a comprehensive settlement but as a prelude to such a settlement . . . I am confident that given your national and historic responsibilities, you are fully aware of the importance attached to your support and backing of this joint action.

Bearing in mind that not all Arab states attended, and not all the key figures such as King Fahd of Saudi Arabia and Saddam Hussain of Iraq (and Husni Mubarak of Egypt who was not invited), the summit deliberately left the door open for the hardline Arab states – most prominently Syria – yet without blocking the joint Jordanian–Palestinian initiative. The cautious phrasing of the final communiqué gave qualified support to joint Palestinian–Jordanian moves to find a negotiated settlement for the Palestinian question – as long as Jordan and the PLO did not steer away from the essence or principles of the Fez Plan – and thus seemed to please both the supporters and the opponents of the 11 February Accord. The supporters found in it the necessary Arab blessing and support, especially in view of the fact that both King Hussain and Yasser Arafat had stressed its compatibility with the Fez Plan. On the other hand, the opponents were able to block full Arab endorsement of the Accord. Perhaps most ironic of all was the fact that the absence of the hardliners was instrumental in this outcome.

The Saudi delegation led by Crown Prince Abdullah made it clear from the outset that it would not allow any resolutions to be adopted if these led to a total break with Syria and the other absentees. King Hassan of Morocco – as the conference host – had similar worries. He was keen for the summit not to collapse but at the same time not to become a divisive turning point in Arab history. He therefore played a conciliatory role in bridging the different points of view and in reconciling those attending with those who were absent. The outcome was a situation in which it was impossible to come up with a strong new Arab position in the absence of key Arab leaders. In the end the 11 February Agreement was mentioned in the final communiqué, but not fully endorsed. In an attempt to please everyone, King Hassan commented on 10 August 1985:

The Arab Summit approved co-operation between Jordan and the PLO in efforts to solve the Palestinian problem but not necessarily the proposals contained in the 11 February Agreement. In our deliberations and discussions they – Jordan and the PLO – found only our blessings for this plan . . . No peace plan should steer away from the 'legal iron path' of the 1982 Fez Plan.[37]

Casablanca was enough for Jordan. 'Most Arab leaders privately gave clear and decisive support to joint Palestinian–Jordanian Middle East moves', Jordan's Foreign Minister, Taher Al Masri, announced on 12 August.[38] 'The summit was successful and satisfactory. This will give us good momentum and a strong hand in pursuing the peace process with the US.' Masri was depending on the attitudes of individual leaders, which almost without exception were positive, something which was not exactly reflected in the communiqué. Best of all perhaps was the appointment by the summit of special committees to clear the inter-Arab atmosphere. Prince Abdullah of Saudi Arabia was assigned, along with a Tunisian high official, the task of resolving disputes between Syria and Jordan and Iraq and Syria. Morocco, the UAE and Mauritania were asked to reconcile Iraq and Libya, and end the rift between Libya and the PLO. The biggest success was the restoration of relations between Syria and Jordan.

The international front

Intensive contacts between Jordan, the PLO and the international community were rewarded by an encouraging reception for the 11 February Agreement from the UN Secretary General, all the EEC countries and three of the permanent members of the Security Council, France, Britain and China. The Soviet Union, however, disagreed with Jordan on two points. First, the description of the international conference. As defined in Geneva in 1973 and as it would have been again in Geneva in 1977, the Soviet Union envisaged the participation of the two superpowers and the exclusion of the other permanent members of the Security Council. But leaving it to the superpowers alone to solve the Middle East conflict, in a way that was not at the expense of the peoples of the Middle East, was out of the question not only for Jordan but for the rest of the Arab world too, as clauses 7 and 8 of the Fez Plan indicated. Nor was it seen to be in the interests of Western Europe, whose need for a stable Middle East was far more urgent, if only because of the economic interdependence between the two regions. The Soviet Union also objected to the form of Palestinian representation proposed in the Jordanian–Palestinian Accord. It even refused to meet a joint Jordanian–Palestinian delegation. The basis of this Soviet attitude was deep resentment of any solution achieved via Washington.

Eventually, the Soviet Union agreed to settling the Middle Eastern problem by collective efforts at a special international conference under UN auspices attended by the permanent members of the Security Council and all sides involved in the conflict, including the PLO as the sole legitimate representative of the Palestinian people. As Mikhail Gorbachev stressed to King Hussain on 22 December 1987 during his visit to the Kremlin, 'The international conference must not be a cover for separate arrangements . . . And this means that all sides, including the PLO, should participate collectively in working out a fair comprehensive settlement in the Middle East, including the Palestinian problem. This should be done both on a multilateral and bilateral basis.'[39]

The US front

In theory, the 11 February Accord went a long way towards meeting the US conditions for peace negotiations. By accepting all the UN resolutions connected with the Palestinian problem it meant in effect PLO acceptance of Resolutions 242 and 338, as demanded by the US. As far as the PLO was concerned, 242's negative aspects would be outweighed by the insistence on the right to self-determination, and neutralized by the call for an international conference, making the whole initiative a palatable package deal which it could accept as the basis for negotiations. Resolution 242 rejects the acquisition of territory by force, but it refers to the Palestinians only as a refugee problem. In his peace plan President Reagan had accepted that the Palestinian question was more than this; 242 therefore, in conjunction with all other UN resolutions, could in theory have met the requirements of both President Reagan and the PLO, and stayed in line with world opinion. Furthermore, 242 incorporates the concept of 'Land for Peace' which was prominent in the Accord, and in the Fez and Reagan Plans.

Other conditions specified by the US were the PLO's renunciation of terrorism as a tactic for regaining territory, its recognition of Israel's right to exist within secure and recognized boundaries and its acceptance of autonomous Palestinian rule in conjunction with Jordan. Joining ranks with moderate Jordan in a confederal relationship, and approving the Fez political programme, which recognized the right of every state in the area to live in peace within secure and recognised boundaries, were seen as fulfilling these American conditions. And, by specifying an international conference, the Accord was in line with both Resolutions 242 and 338 which all members of the UN Security Council, including the US, had approved (242 called for outside help in resolving the conflict, 338 suggested a procedure for negotiations).

What the US must have disliked about the Amman Accord was the need to respect all UN resolutions concerning the Palestinian question. Some UN resolutions concern the Palestinian right to self-determination, the right of return and the PLO's status as the sole legitimate representative of the Palestinian people; these are unacceptable to Israel, and thus by extension to the US. Instead the US demanded an unequivocal declaration by the PLO of its acceptance of 242 on its own, before negotiations even took place, despite the resolution's lack of reference to the Palestinians.

Jordan knew of US misgivings about an international conference, which would legitimize the Soviet role in the search for peace. Because of what was seen as staunch US support for Israel, meaningful Israeli concessions as a result of US persuasion may not have been expected either. Jordan's strategy must have had an element of posturing in it, if only to put the other side in the wrong on the international plane. Crown Prince Hassan explained:

The US, as a superpower, cannot turn a blind eye. American interest in the Arab world was not induced by the energy crisis and should not be confined to oil and its availability on the world market, important though these are to the well-being of the

West . . . Concern with the region is a function of the strategic balance between the superpowers and a consequence of world power politics.[40]

King Hussain complemented this view in his address to the UN General Assembly:

Following the conclusion of the Accord, Jordan and the PLO proceeded to make contact with a number of great power capitals for the purpose of intensifying the peace process. Because of the special relationship between the US and Israel – the party that has so far blocked the road to peace – Jordan made intensive representations to Washington in the hope that the US would shoulder its responsibilities as a superpower with a stake in world peace, a record of upholding human rights and a history of faith in freedom and in the right of peoples to self-determination. It was hoped that the US would join hands with the many other countries who supported this initiative, and bring its influence, coupled with theirs, to bear on rallying the will of the international community in order to achieve stability, peace and prosperity that would serve the interests of all the nations of the region and beyond.

Behind King Hussain's hopes in the US was a deep anxiety, which he had expressed at Casablanca:

In this joint action lies the last possible chance to rescue the land, people and holy places. If it succeeds, well and good. If not, God help Palestine, its people and all of us in the region to face the consequences.

Taking on the role of a messenger between the US and the PLO, Jordan embarked on a marathon bout of diplomatic activity as will be related in the following chapter. It took a whole year – from February 1985 to February 1986.

12 US and Jordan: more wheeling and dealing

Phase one: selling the idea to Washington

King Fahd of Saudi Arabia was reported to have received a telephone call from King Hussain on 11 February 1985, informing him of the details of the Jordanian–PLO Accord, while he was on a state visit to Washington. It was also reported that he already had a copy of the document in his possession. This was the first direct contact between an Arab leader and the second Reagan Administration, and it took place in the wake of two developments which the Arabs regarded as hostile. First, the proposed increase in US military aid to Israel from $1.4 bn in 1985 to $1.8 bn for the following year. Second, the parallel decision to halt arms sales to the Arabs for the foreseeable future.

The latter decision, which was made public on 30 January 1985, was clearly an attempt to pre-empt the King, who had a multi-billion dollar request pending. The White House statement was toned down, however, and accompanied by an assurance that it reflected nothing significant, but rather heralded a breathing space for a reassessment of US policy. Since Prime Minister Peres had just received assurances of a huge increase in US military aid, which, it had already been made clear, would not be affected by this latest decision, the arms embargo against the Arabs, however temporary, appeared to be a deliberate snub to the very man the Reagan Administration was supposedly trying to court, if only because of his country's special relationship with the US and its huge petrodollar reserves in US banks.

Jordan expected King Fahd to promote the 'Accord' in Washington. The rationale behind this expectation was explained by the Speaker of the Jordanian Upper House of Parliament:

The duty of all the Arabs, leaders and institutions, is to concentrate on the American arena because of the US special relationship with Israel, in spite of its many-sided interests in the Arab world. We have to defend our cause in the US by indicating to the American decision-makers and to the American public, the extent of damage caused by their one-sidedness and support for Israeli aggression and expansion.[1]

King Fahd, however, never mentioned the 'Accord' to US officials. The question he left unanswered in Washington was: did he refrain from doing so in deference to Syria who rejected Amman's course of action or because he really opposed it?

Washington did not express outright rejection of the Accord and even described it as a positive beginning, but it did not endorse all its principles. The immediate response was no to an international conference, no to the PLO without a loud, clear and unequivocal acceptance of Resolution 242 on its own, and no to direct US involvement, on the grounds that talks should be held directly with Israel.

Peres, on the other hand, shortly before, had already indicated what kind of talks Israel envisaged. In a speech to the Knesset on 3 December 1984, just after the PNC meeting in Amman, he invited King Hussain for talks – without the PLO – provided that 242 would be a basis and not a precondition for negotiations. Resolution 242 was thus demoted to an item on the agenda, something merely to be discussed, and not a framework for discussions. Apart from its affirmation that the withdrawal of Israel's armed forces from occupied territories should be applied on all fronts, there were other conditions laid down in 242 that were most unwelcome to the Israeli government: first, the reassertion of the principle of the inadmissibility of acquisition of territory by war and, second, a just settlement of the refugee problem. Although the latter has given great offence to the Palestinians and occasioned their rejection of 242, it would, in Israel's view, utterly overwhelm the Zionist State. For these reasons Israel has sought to weaken the centrality and the determinant character of Resolution 242. But King Hussain continued to emphasize that the principle of territory in exchange for peace, as embodied in 242, was the framework within which negotiations would have to be held, and was therefore not negotiable. He thus almost immediately denounced Peres's offer of talks as a deceptive manoeuvre since he saw the test of Israel's seriousness about talks as first and foremost its commitment to Resolutions 242 and 338 in all their aspects.

In such an atmosphere, it might have been an uphill task for King Fahd to mention the 'Accord', let alone push it forward. He might have thought that by showing real patience while in Washington much more could be achieved, at a more appropriate time, through a discreet form of persuasion. King Fahd laid the ground for future Arab contacts with the US mainly via President Mubarak of Egypt.

March 1985: Mubarak sponsors the Accord

Mubarak's backing of Jordan's approach to the PLO was the first signal of his displeasure with the Camp David stipulations which foresaw no role for the PLO, made no mention of Palestinian self-determination and were engineered solely under US auspices. It implied his unease with the concept of Palestinian autonomy envisaged by Carter, Sadat and Begin in the Camp

David Agreements, and the gradual emergence of Egyptian scepticism about the US as the sole supervisor of peace talks. At the same time, Mubarak could not accept the US posture of passivity or benign neglect, because it seemed to him hypocritical for the US to remain aloof and to feign neutrality and, at the same time, hand Israel ever increasing amounts of economic and military aid. Therefore, when President Reagan described the Jordanian–Palestinian Accord as only a positive beginning and insisted that it was up to the Arabs and the Israelis to negotiate directly without active US participation, Mubarak must have feared that the momentum for peace created by the Amman Accord would soon be dissipated.

What followed is still open to conflicting interpretations. But in what certainly appeared to be an impetuous move, Mubarak launched new ideas of his own, just a few days before his intended visit to the US. Professor Vatikiotis of London University has suggested, for example, that Mubarak's plan indicated close co-ordination between the Egyptian government and the Peres wing of the Israeli government. But there is no need to go to such lengths to explain what Mubarak was trying to do. It could easily be understood as a genuine attempt to help King Hussain, by jolting the US into action on a basis to which Washington itself could have no objection. Mubarak's move did not stem directly from the Amman Accord, nor were there any signs of consultation with Jordan or the PLO before he made his views public in a *New York Times* interview published on 1 March 1985. In the light of President Reagan's rejection of an international conference and the participation of the PLO in any peace negotiations, Mubarak suggested that a joint Palestinian–Jordanian delegation should meet the President for a preliminary dialogue aimed at preparing the way for future negotiations. The joint delegation did not have to include PLO members. Arafat could collaborate with King Hussain in the selection of moderate Palestinian members of the delegation, on the assumption that every Palestinian was a PLO supporter anyway, and that through such figures he would have no problem in putting across the PLO's point of view to President Reagan. Mubarak did not even press the US to recognize the PLO prior to any future negotiations; a precedent already existed, as he saw it, in the US negotiations with the Vietcong to end the US entanglement in Vietnam. As regards an international conference, Mubarak saw no problem in convening one at the very end of the process, in order to sanction the already agreed terms of a settlement. In other words, a first-stage dialogue between President Reagan and a Jordanian–Palestinian delegation would lead, in his opinion, to discussions with Israel and the US and eventually to an international conference.

The PLO was swift to condemn the Egyptian proposals and to dissociate them from the Jordanian–Palestinian agreement. The Jordanian government, apparently embarrassed, remained silent for a while. However, editorials in Jordan's daily press strongly criticized the proposals. On the eve of King Hussain's scheduled meeting with Mubarak a few days later – on 6 March 1985, in Ghardaqa on the Red Sea – Mubarak changed his tune by restating his commitment to the Palestinian right to self-determination and to recognition of the PLO as the sole legitimate representative of the Palestinian people. King Hussain must have seen no harm in going along with Egypt in the idea of conducting a preliminary dialogue between the US and a Jordanian–Palestinian delegation, although he insisted that PLO representatives would have to be included in the joint delegation, and that Jordan was no substitute for the Palestinians and their legitimate representatives. In other words, even though Jordan ought to be involved in the dialogue, in the final analysis it could not speak for the Palestinians. Egypt, for its part, accepted the Jordanian position, according to the final communiqué issued at the end of Mubarak's visit.

Mubarak's formal initiative was not innovative in substance. What was innovative was the suggested procedure. And what was significant was its timing. It came hard on the heels of the Amman Accord. But to make the Accord more palatable to Israel and the US, Mubarak repackaged it in an effort to narrow the gap between the different parties. He saw his initiative as a natural extension of the Accord, although Jordan and the PLO did not read it this way. The PLO's outright rejection contrasted with an eventual cautious welcome from King Hussain, on the basis that there was no harm in this tactical deviation as long as the ultimate aim was still an international conference. Since the US was maintaining that for any progress to be made, the impetus had to come from the Arabs, both Hussain and Mubarak saw the Amman Accord as constituting a clear Arab statement of seriousness of intent.

Syria and Israel both regarded Mubarak's initiative as an extension of the Camp David process. The Syrian cabinet declared that it would make the foiling of the Amman Accord its official policy.[2] In fact Syria took the view that it need do no more than sit back and wait for the initiative's ultimate failure, simply because the US would not give its Arab allies the help they needed. On the other hand, conflicting views in the Israeli coalition government led to a lukewarm response that fell half-way between cautious welcome and outright rejection. The question seemed to be, if the Mubarak approach were to be adopted and carried through, what price would Israel ultimately have to pay in exchange for peace? And before that happened what price would it pay in accepting Palestinian representation in the negotiations?

The basic policy of both Labour and Likud remains to prevent the emergence of a Palestinian leadership that enjoys unchallenged international recognition, simply because that is seen as the first step towards the establishment of a Palestinian State. Successive Israeli governments have persistently withheld recognition from any body which could be seen as a representative Palestinian leadership, even if this appeared in conjunction with Jordan. Mubarak's initiative sparked off a disagreement over the make-up of the Palestinian delegation, or more precisely over the degree of its dissociation from the PLO leadership. Ezer Weizman, Minister without Portfolio, expressed one strand of Labour thinking when he said that Israel should not pry into the political biography of every member of the proposed Palestinian delegation. But the Likud view, as expressed by David Levy, the Housing Minister, recalled the same American three 'nos' upon which the coalition rested: no negotiations in any form with the PLO, no Palestinian state and no consent to an international conference. Should Labour depart from these principles, he warned, Likud would withdraw from the coalition and bring it down. He further insisted on a thorough scrutiny of the Palestinian delegation to ensure that it was not under PLO domination or influence. Peres, indicating his willingness to attend the meeting envisaged by Mubarak, provided that the Palestinian element did not include PLO representatives, was trying both to avoid appearing intransigent and to avoid the collapse of his coalition government – except in a way which would be electorally favourable to him – while all along hoping that the Arabs would eventually help him out of a difficult position.

In the event, that was just what the PLO and Syria did, by rejecting the Mubarak initiative outright. The US helped Peres too. During talks at the White House with President Mubarak on 12 March 1985, President Reagan showed little interest in Mubarak's suggestion. Undeterred, the Egyptian President took his cause to the American public. Speaking at the National Press Club in Washington at the end of his visit, his central message was that the US could not afford to stay on the sidelines. A dialogue would not only clarify the different positions but would reinforce the momentum for peace. The role of a great power like the US was not simply to endorse what was agreed upon, but to help the parties reach agreement. He stressed that it was a myth that the fall-out from the escalation of tension and radicalization in the Middle East would not reach the US. The US seemed to agree with this last point when, following its veto in the UN Security Council on 12 March of a resolution condemning Israeli army activities in Southern Lebanon, it went in fear of anti-American reprisals such as followed a similar US veto in 1983. The US aircraft carrier, *Eisenhower*, was stationed off the Lebanese coast for the possible evacuation of US citizens, and security was tightened at US diplomatic missions in the region.

Putting on a brave face, President Mubarak departed from Washington saying that he had left his idea for President Reagan to think about, and that he did not expect an immediate response. The then Jordanian Foreign Minister, Taher Al Masri, followed hard on his heels to further cajole the US into action, but without any visible success.

US policy options

The flurry of Middle Eastern diplomatic activity during 1984 and the early part of 1985 met with no immediate commensurate American response. This seemed like uncharacteristic caution on the part of an administration with a history of more robust diplomatic and military moves in the region. There was no evidence of a lack of confidence in the positive peace moves and willingness to compromise emanating from the Arab world. Rather, America's reticence seemed to reflect a lack of confidence in itself. Weary and wounded from the Lebanese experience, it preferred to remain on the sidelines. Thus a new view took shape in Washington, namely that the Middle East, designated over the years a strategic area vital to US interests, did not matter much after all. There was no immediate oil crisis, no danger of a new war and no immediate threat from the Soviet Union, which was preoccupied elsewhere. As William Quandt, one of Washington's foremost Middle East experts put it, 'The Middle East was indeed fading away in the US, in much the same way as South East Asia did before it.'[3]

In the short run, maintaining the status quo in the Middle East was convenient in the face of other priorities. Washington showed little sign that it even understood the need for action. 'If the Arabs expect President Reagan to create a new balance in the Middle East, they are probably mistaken. The step will have to be taken on their own home ground', said a senior State Department official.[4]

Instead, the US turned what attention it was prepared to give the Middle East onto King Hussain who it believed had to be persuaded to go ahead with direct negotiations with Israel, without the PLO and, moreover, without substantial US help. For his part, the King declared that there was no way he could go any further until the US agreed to meet a Jordanian–Palestinian delegation. He also ruled out any eventual peace talks which did not include the PLO. 'I have done my utmost to move towards peace. We must not miss this opportunity. This is the last chance', he solemnly declared on 18 March 1985.[5]

Less than a week later, Washington transmitted its implied response via a decision by the Congressional Committee to continue imposing restrictions on the sale of advanced weapons to Jordan. The message was clear: Jordan was not doing enough, and unless and until it committed itself to recognizing Israel and entering into direct negotiations with Israel without the PLO, it would not be eligible for the sale of any American weapons. As Kim Hoagland of *The Washington Post* observed:

By undermining King Hussain's credibility at what was a delicate stage in the peace process, President Reagan should have been embarrassed by this impinging upon his presidential authority by the Congress . . . [But] the sub-committee step must have been a reflection of Mr Reagan's failure to pick up the signal that King Hussain sent through his speech to the PNC 17 and also his failure to praise more specifically the Arafat-Hussain Agreement signed on 11 February 1985 in which Arafat accepted even [UN] resolutions. Instead of picking up the ball that Hussain has been trying to hand him, President Reagan and his administration looked passively in the opposite direction.[6]

Another form of pressure on Jordan came in what seemed to be a co-ordinated effort between Secretary of State Shultz and his assistant, Richard Murphy. On 11 April 1985, Shultz told a meeting of AIPAC, the American–Israeli Public Affairs Committee, that US support for Israel would never weaken and that there would be no peace in the Middle East until there were no longer any delusions in the Arab world that it would ever diminish.[7] He went on to express solid support for the Israeli preference to hold direct talks as the way to peace, rather than an international conference. Shultz also urged the Arabs to let King Hussain move to the negotiating table, stressing that 'We know these Arab nations that are moving towards peace are taking risks. They should know that the US will help them defend themselves.' Such an assurance was of doubtful credibility. The strength of the US commitment to defend its friends was not impressive. US abandonment of the Shah of Iran, Amin Gemayel of Lebanon, and of its undertaking to defend the Palestinian civilians in Lebanon following the PLO's expulsion were only some of the recent obvious examples.

At the same time as Shultz was delivering his speech, Richard Murphy arrived in Damascus, on his tour of Middle East capitals, to promote the idea of direct negotiations with Israel without the PLO. In Damascus he presented the American conditions as: either the PLO must announce its unequivocal recognition of Israel and Resolutions 242 and 338, as the price for US acceptance of the idea of PLO participation in the Jordanian–Palestinian delegation; or it must acquiesce in the participation of Palestinians on the understanding that neither the PLO nor the Palestinian representatives would publicize their relationship. In other words, choose your representatives, but do not publicly acknowledge it.

Encouraged by the solidarity with the PLO expressed by the 42 Palestinian leaders Murphy met during his visit to Israel, Arafat proclaimed his outright rejection of the two US conditions as a choice between signing the PLO's death warrant and capitulation by abandoning whatever diplomatic cards the PLO had, in advance of any negotiations. One elaboration of this rejection came ironically from Israel itself. Expressing a current of opinion which was tentatively taking root after Israel's self-inflicted disaster in Lebanon, Meir Merhav asked in *The Jerusalem Post* of 10 March 1985:

Would it make sense to talk to Palestinians who, if they were offered anything, could not accept it until they had asked permission of the PLO, and who, for fear of being labelled quislings or defeatists, would have to be even less accommodating than the PLO itself? If Israelis want peace, with whom should they make it except with their enemies the PLO, especially since, by denying the Palestinians in the occupied territories all freedom of political expression, they had made sure that the PLO would have a monopoly in expressing the political will of the Palestinians.

In the meantime, the US continued to play on Jordan's myriad fears, hoping that this policy would eventually bear fruit. Jordan feared that the issue of Israel's withdrawal from Lebanon, a side-issue compared with the Palestinian problem, would dominate whatever time the second Reagan administration was willing to give to the Middle East, and would represent the pinnacle of US Middle East diplomatic efforts for another three years to come. It also feared the Syrian–Iranian axis, which was generating coalition-building among some Arab moderates against both Syria and Iran. But its fear of Israeli expansion was producing a growing sentiment in favour of compromise, and the pressure on it to move to the negotiating table on US and Israeli terms continued to be applied. Only if the manoeuvring between King Hussain and Yasser Arafat, among the Palestinian factions themselves, and among the Arab states in general reached the point where direct negotiations on US and Israeli terms appeared possible, would the US add its weight to the momentum. In other words, the US was prepared to re-engage only when the Arabs had agreed on a common approach. As the Arabs found it difficult to agree even on holding an Arab summit to sort out their differences, this was an impossible task. President Mubarak of Egypt commented:

President Reagan was urging all along Jordanian-Palestinian co-ordination. When this co-ordination took place, he retreated by reverting to talks about who would represent the Palestinians, and instead of putting pressure on Israel, he started putting pressure on the Arabs for further concessions.[8]

The Americans may have believed that the movement gathering momentum in the Arab world following the Amman Accord had come too soon, and that Mubarak's proposal for a dialogue between the US and a Jordanian–Palestinian delegation was premature. To put pressure on Peres at that particular time, it may have been thought, could place his coalition government in jeopardy. The national unity government took office with a Labour–Likud consensus on only two issues – rescuing the economy and getting out of Lebanon. Any move to give up occupied land in return for peace, it was thought, would lead to a major political crisis and new elections in Israel. The hope was that Peres, by pushing ahead with the Lebanese withdrawal and economic reforms, could use his 25 months as Prime Minister to change the shape of Israeli politics so that the Labour Party would become the dominant force in the coalition and the country, even after the scheduled handover to Shamir, the right-wing Likud leader.

Washington may have believed that the right moment for a peace initiative, which would inevitably split the government over the issue of the West Bank, would be when Peres's popularity was at its peak so that he could hold new elections in which peace would be the main issue. The problem with this line of thinking was that Washington could not control the timing, nor could it foresee with any certainty the movement of Israeli public opinion. In any event Peres could not call a general election whenever he felt like it, as this needed the backing of the majority of the Knesset. Moreover, the US could not guarantee that the momentum for peace created by the Arabs could be kept alive, still less that the content of Arab peace moves, or the opposition of Arab hardliners, would not wreck the chances in the event of a stalemate. But peace is not a self-sustaining process. Waiting until Israel became a willing partner in negotiations, while continuing to pressurize the Arabs, particularly Jordan, for more concessions even before real negotiations started, was a course that threatened to destroy any chance of peace, if only through sheer discouragement or neglect of any initiative.

The outspoken wreckers of peace moves were Assad of Syria and Shamir of Israel. Dismissing contemptuously Israel's attitude to peace, Syria argued that despite Camp David the Israelis were still in dispute with the Egyptians over a few acres of coastal Taba. How, therefore, could one expect them to get out of East Jerusalem? And even if Reagan put pressure on Israel – a most unlikely scenario – who in Israel's coalition would allow a Palestinian flag to fly over East Jerusalem?

Jordan agreed to a large extent with Syria's analysis. But where the two parted company was over US behaviour towards the dispute. Jordan argued that the US ought to behave like a superpower by playing an honest impartial role, since US interests were not confined to Israel, which was only a very small part of the whole region. Syria dismissed Jordan's expectations as wishful thinking, and it may have been right. Jordan's insistence on coaxing the US into positive action arose from its despair at the prospect of any Israeli concessions without US persuasion, which was not forthcoming.

Back in Israel, Deputy Prime Minister and Foreign Minister Shamir was due to replace Peres in October 1986, under the terms of the coalition agreed on 1 September 1984. He claimed that, 'Lebanon was not an ideological problem, whereas Judea and Samaria are.'[9] He further warned, 'Between Labour and Likud, that could threaten the coalition.' To stress the point further, Minister of Housing Levy stated, 'Likud would never accept that we embark on a search for territorial compromise with Hussain.'[10] And Moshe Arens, Minister without Portfolio, declared, 'Even if King Hussain would really accept actual territorial compromise, a rupture in the coalition will still take place.'[11]

Israel in the last stages of its military involvement in Lebanon was disillusioned with its own ability, military or otherwise, to transform its relationship with its neighbours. In despair, Moshe Arens stated, 'Israel is a strong country, but a small country. Israel can win wars but it is far more difficult to obtain political aims by war since we cannot impose total defeat on larger Arab countries.'[12] This disillusion was translated into a declining interest in a serious exploration of the prospects for an agreement of any sort with the Arab countries that involved new exchanges of territory for peace. The frustration with the Camp David Accords, which had secured only a cold peace with Egypt, appeared to have extended to Peres's Labour Party. This frustration appeared to be producing a new attitude in favour of a political arrangement with Jordan that excluded giving up territory altogether. 'It could be that we have to come to an understanding on sharing jurisdiction on the West Bank and Gaza',[13] said Ezer Weizman of the Labour Party, a Minister without Portfolio in the coalition government. 'Today you have to say that the autonomy plan designed by Begin in 1979 was a good beginning. The final result may be something in between autonomy and a territorial concept.' The new Labour attitude was not so far away from that of the Likud, as explained by David Levy:[14] 'We have to talk about political sharing, about the autonomy of the people who live there but not about territory.'

If then Israel was unable to obtain political aims by military means, unable to part with occupied territory for the sake of the much desired peace, and unable to respond decisively to Arab readiness for compromise, the odds against stability in the foreseeable future appeared heavy indeed, unless the US chose to act.

At this particular juncture, two requirements for the solution of the Arab–Israeli conflict stood out in Arab eyes as unwise to ignore. First, extending the principle of self-determination to the Palestinians. The subjection of peoples to alien subjugation and domination constituted a violation and denial of fundamental human rights and was contrary to the UN Charter. Second, the inevitability of recognizing the PLO and its minimum requirements for peace, namely a confederated relationship between the West Bank, Gaza and Jordan. This very much scaled-down Palestinian goal was in line with Reagan's original framework for peace announced on 1 September 1982. But the US saw no urgent need for quick action.

Phase two: back to the peace process

Amid all the peace appeals bombarding Washington, the US could not stay aloof for long without appearing obstructionist. It decided on a low-profile return to the peace process steered by Jordan. The outstanding issue between the two sides was the US insistence on direct negotiations between Israel and its neighbours and Jordan's insistence on negotiations in an international conference.

On 4 April 1985, King Hussain appointed Zeid Rifai as his new Prime Minister. He had had the experience of heading the Jordanian delegation to the 1973 Geneva Conference, dealing with Kissinger during his shuttle diplomacy, heading the Jordanian delegation to the Rabat summit of 1974 and engineering the rapprochement with Syria in 1975. Between April and September 1985, intensive US–Jordan discussions concentrated on the PLO representation of the Palestinians within the concept of a Jordanian–Palestinian partnership. Jordan and the PLO submitted a programme for action to Washington comprising four stages. First, dialogue between a Palestinian delegation and the US. Second, following the dialogue, the PLO would declare its acceptance of UN resolutions 242 and 338. Third, the US would then recognize the PLO and a meeting would be held in Washington between US officials and PLO members to discuss a peace settlement and normalization of relations. Fourth, Arab efforts would then be channelled, in conjunction with the US and other countries, to convening an international conference.

The US reaction was to send Richard Murphy to assess the seriousness of the approach. Having received a positive report, Washington accepted the idea of meeting a Palestinian delegation in preparation for the next two stages provided that the Palestinian delegates were not leading members of the PLO or of any guerrilla organization. Secretary of State Shultz then ventured back to the Middle East on 9 May for a four-day visit to Israel, Jordan and Egypt – his first to the area since the abortive 17 May 1983 agreement which he had engineered between Israel and Lebanon. According to one American source who attended the meeting in Jordan, much of the strategy of the trip was a reflection of the fundamental difference between the US and Jordanian approaches: 'the US constantly tried to find the answer to how any single event short of bilateral negotiations leads to bilateral negotiations between whatever group of Arabs and Israelis, that would justify US participation'.[15] But, judging from Shultz's public statements during his trip, it seemed that the US, despite its continued reluctance to engage more vigorously in the quest for a solution of the Palestinian question, now believed that peace negotiations had to take place before the end of 1985, that the negotiations could be the last chance for a Middle Eastern settlement, and that the

Palestinians would have to be represented in any direct negotiations on the future of the West Bank and Gaza. Shultz insisted, however, on getting a promise in advance that the process would lead to direct negotiations with Israel.

There was no sign of a breakthrough on how the peace talks might take place, nor on who would represent the Palestinians. However, Shultz declared, somewhat ambiguously, after his meeting with King Hussain in the Jordanian coastal resort of Aqaba, that a Palestinian delegation had to be devised within which different people would be needed for different purposes.[16] What Shultz did not explain publicly was ultimately spelled out by King Hussain in his major speech to the nation on 19 February 1986. While the US Secretary did not rule out, at least in front of the Jordanians, the possibility of PNC members being included in the Palestinian delegation, his major concern was how the US could guarantee that, after the first meeting took place in accordance with stage one, the PLO would then follow the envisaged programme by announcing its acceptance of Resolutions 242 and 338. If the PLO did not do this, his argument ran, then it would have scored a major political goal by securing *de facto* American recognition, exposing the administration to criticism and domestic and political difficulties. One of the American team put it this way when interviewed in Washington:

Much of the discussions I recall reflected that basic difference; a willingness on Jordan's part to take one step at a time with a greater confidence that one step would lead to the final step – bilateral negotiations – compared to our approach of searching for a sure route, not so much minding the various steps on the way but looking for some kind of assurances that the bilateral talks would take place in the end . . . the King's four-point approach tended to take discreet steps.[17]

Although many political observers doubted if Shultz at that time even wanted the PLO to accept resolutions 242 and 338, there was nevertheless an attempt to assuage these American fears when Prime Minister Rifai agreed with Yasser Arafat the text of a press statement that King Hussain would deliver during his visit to Washington from 28 to 31 May 1985, after the conclusion of his talks with President Reagan. And so, from the White House rose garden, King Hussain declared on 29 May: 'As a result of my recent talks with the PLO and in view of our genuine desire for peace, we are willing to negotiate within the context of an international conference a peaceful settlement on the basis of the pertinent UN resolutions, including 242 and 338.'[18] To prepare the ground for this announcement Arafat gave a comprehensive interview to *The Washington Post* two weeks before, in which he declared his readiness to accept 242 and 338 provided that the US explicitly endorsed the right of the Palestinians to self-determination.

On 2 June, Peres received a message from Shultz to the effect that King Hussain's declaration went far beyond any public pronouncement made by Arab leaders in the past, and that, more importantly, the King's position had the approval of the PLO's leader and the Executive Committee. Shultz also reaffirmed Washington's unequivocal rejection of an international conference that invited the Russians back into the peace process, but its willingness to talk with selected PNC members. It had been explained in Washington that the US saw a difference between the PNC and the PLO. While Israel maintained that there was an organic relationship between the two, the US did not regard membership of the PNC as an automatic disqualification under the terms of its assurances to Israel. President Reagan went further when he agreed publicly that conditions had 'never been more right than they are now to pursue this peace'. And he added, 'Who knows whether these conditions will ever come as close together again.' Echoing King Hussain, he concluded 'Perhaps, it is the last chance.'[19]

The US approached Jordan for four Palestinian names, to be chosen in co-ordination with the PLO, two from the occupied territories and two from outside. On 12 July, seven names were submitted to Washington from which four were to be chosen. They were immediately transmitted to Israel. But as one of the American team put it:

In terms of formal response, we never accepted or rejected any of the names. The question we were asking was: regardless of the names, if there is a meeting, what happens next. We were not focusing on the identity of the participants, but the process itself. But I can assure you that the names were dealt with internally very seriously. At this stage, what Jordan could see was a US which could not, or would not move without Israel's consent. Israel objected to the whole process. Hence the names were only a pretext for further foot-dragging.[20]

It was only when the world press began speculating about the identity of the chosen Palestinians that the Zionist lobby in Washington decided it was time to voice publicly its objections to the intended meeting and apply such pressure on the administration that the latter began, as King Hussain put it in his address to the nation on 19 February, 1986, 'to justify, then defend and finally retreat' from its intentions as stated to Jordan.[21] The US also reiterated its doubts about the PLO's commitment to accept 242 and 338 after the completion of the first stage of the programme, despite repeated assurances from both Jordan and the PLO. To further reassure the Americans, a meeting took place between Rifai and Arafat, on 15 August 1985, during which Arafat reaffirmed his commitment to the four-stage procedure. This was relayed to Washington, which continued to insist on a prior promise that the process would lead to direct negotiations with Israel.

King Hussain's answer was dramatically presented to the world community in his address to the UN General Assembly on the occasion of the UN's

Fortieth Anniversary on 27 September. 'We are prepared to negotiate under appropriate auspices with the government of Israel "promptly and directly" under the basic tenets of Security Council Resolutions 242 and 338.' The choice of 'promptly and directly' was meant to address those Americans who had used the same term in the Smith Amendment when Congress refused to supply Jordan with military assistance unless the President certified that it would negotiate 'promptly and directly' with Israel under the basic tenets of UN Resolutions 242 and 338 (see Chapter 7).

Jordan knew it was heading towards a dead end as early as 7 September when it received a message to that effect from the US. But keen observers pinpointed August as the real turning point particularly when Richard Murphy flew to the Middle East for a possible meeting with a joint Jordanian–Palestinian delegation. 'If Murphy had had his way', one American source commented, 'the meeting would probably have taken place. But en route, one of the proposed Palestinian names was rejected, so the meeting never took place. This gave the impression that the Americans were not serious.'[22] Ambassador Neumann commented: 'Murphy is a travelling salesman. He does what he is asked to do. He does not argue. He does not put his job at risk.'[23] One of Murphy's companions denied this incident ever taking place, but put the blame squarely on Jordan. 'It was the Jordanians who changed course', he said. 'There was no decision made saying let us stop talking about names. But I think we understood perhaps it had played its course.'[24] Nevertheless another highly placed American official pondered:

Perhaps in 1985, the US missed an opportunity . . . The US made a tactical mistake because a lot of time passed. Instead of going back to the King on the names Shultz insisted that if the King would commit himself to direct negotiations right away . . . perhaps we could do this . . . we mishandled it.[25]

The US did not in fact miss an opportunity. The opportunity was never there. The US did not want an international conference with the Soviet Union there on equal terms. It wanted direct negotiations between the parties under its auspices just as in Camp David.

Other political currents were at work in the Arab world in August with the Arab summit conference in Casablanca. Syria did not attend, which was understood as a snub to Jordan and the PLO for their joint action in co-ordination with the US. The summit, however, appointed Prince Abdullah of Saudi Arabia and the Head of the Arab League to a mission to improve relations between Jordan and Syria. Within a few weeks relations between the two countries were restored. A few months later King Hussain acknowledged the blame for the deterioration in the relationship in a letter addressed to Prime Minister Rifai on 10 November which was broadcast from Amman and carried by all Jordanian newspapers the following day. After speaking of the era of the second half of the 1970s which witnessed 'joint determination to build a solid basis of co-operation and co-ordination and to weave a closely-knit fabric among the institutions in the two countries' (Syria and Jordan), he referred to the Moslem Brotherhood which was discovered to be working against Syria from Jordan. This indirect message to Syria was enough for keen political observers to foresee future Jordanian action: less concentration on the PLO; more concentration on Syria and steadier calls for an international conference. Prime Minister Rifai was the right man for the job.

Jordan's alternative concentration on an international conference became evident just as King Hussain was planning his visit to address the UN General Assembly and then to Washington for further talks with President Reagan. As noted earlier, the idea of an international conference was first revived in May 1985, when it was flatly rejected by the US. Jordan's concentration started to focus instead on what it regarded as the key issue leading to an international conference, namely, to get the US talking to a Palestinian delegation, to get the PLO to accept Resolutions 242 and 338, and to get the US to accept self-determination for the Palestinians. When this did not work, Jordanian and American officials began their preparatory meetings in Washington just before the King's arrival. Following his address to the UN on 27 September, King Hussain conducted extensive discussions in Washington during which the US suggested that the Soviet Union should participate only after it had restored diplomatic relations with Israel – an Israeli condition adopted by Washington. Jordan argued that an international conference without the Soviet Union would be fatally flawed. If it was to be excluded on the grounds that it had no diplomatic relations with Israel – one of the parties to the conflict – then the US was in the corresponding position of not recognizing the PLO – another party to the conflict. Furthermore, it was futile to plan seriously for such a conference if any one party had the right to set conditions on who else could attend. That applied as much to the five permanent members of the Security Council as to the parties to the conflict. Hence it was necessary to extend unconditional invitations to Syria, the PLO and the Soviet Union.

As explained by one American participant in the talks, the US public posture towards the idea of a conference was totally negative primarily for reasons transcending the Middle East region. But at the same time the US undertook vigorous diplomatic activity up to late January 1986 trying to see if there was any kind of 'convergence' on what a conference might look like. To set the course of future action the US accepted, on the third day of King Hussain's discussions in Washington, several points presented by Jordan: that the UN Secretary General would issue invitations to an international conference under UN auspices to the five permanent members of the Security Council and the parties to the conflict; that Resolutions 242 and 338 would be the basis for the conference; and that the PLO would have to accept both resolutions before it could attend. As far as the last point was concerned, King Hussain explained in his speech on 19 February 1986 that the Americans held to their position of requiring acceptance by the PLO of Resolutions 242 and 338 since these formed the basis for the convening of the conference. 'We agreed to this understanding on the basis that Mr Arafat had himself agreed to this, last August.' But there remained one major point of disagreement: while Jordan stressed that the international conference must have a clear mandate, the US insisted on its ceremonial definition. Despite prolonged discussions between the two sides, the gap remained wide.

While King Hussain was still in Washington, an intensive cycle of terrorism and counter-terrorism began in the Middle East, with the Larnaca affair, the *Achille Lauro*, and the Israeli raid on the PLO headquarters in Tunis. This inevitably hardened attitudes. On his return to Amman King Hussain informed the PLO about the talks in Washington and required them to meet three conditions; to accept Resolutions 242 and 338 in order to be invited to the international conference; to accept the principle of participation in negotiations with the government of Israel as a part of a joint Jordanian–Palestinian delegation within the context of the international conference; and to renounce terrorism.

On 7 November 1985, Arafat denounced terrorism in all its forms, irrespective of its source, in the presence of President Mubarak, in what became known as the Cairo Declaration. But when the PLO Executive Council met soon afterwards in Baghdad to discuss the other American conditions, particularly the acceptance of Resolution 242, it decided unanimously to refuse to do so.

In January 1986, King Hussain went to London on a private visit during which two rounds of talks were held with Richard Murphy, on 18 and 20 January. Murphy expressed no American objection to the right of all parties to the conflict to submit their disputes to the conference. But he reiterated the American position that the PLO must first accept Resolution 242 in order to establish a dialogue with the US, and he in no way committed the US to agreeing to the invitation of the PLO to the conference. King Hussain then asked for a clear statement of the American position, which arrived only four days after his return to Amman in the form of a written statement delivered on 25 January 1986, as follows:

When it is on public record that the PLO has accepted 242 and 338, is prepared to negotiate peace with Israel, and has renounced terrorism, the US will then start contact with the Soviet Union with the purpose of participating, together with the other four permanent members of the Security Council, in the international conference which would be convened by the Secretary General of the UN.

The disagreement over the powers of the conference to settle disputes among the negotiating parties remained unresolved.

Jordan expected Arafat to accept the American conditions because it discerned in them a significant change in the US position in the PLO's favour. When the US and Jordan had started their dialogue at the end of March 1985, the US was saying it would enter into talks with the PLO when it accepted Resolution 242; now it had gone one step further by accepting that the PLO should be invited to the international conference. But the PLO still refused to accept 242 within this context. Instead, it added what Jordan regarded as a new condition, namely, an amendment to make 242 acceptable through the addition of a statement from the US recognizing the rights of the Palestinians, including their right to self-determination within the context of a confederation with Jordan, in accordance with the 11 February 1985 agreement. Jordan's argument then was identical to that of King Hussain's opening address to the 17th session of the PNC in November 1984: that the subject of self-determination, within the context of a confederation, was a matter for the Jordanians and the Palestinians alone; that no other party had anything to do with it; and involving the US or others in this matter meant that Jordan was voluntarily opening the door to others to interfere in its common concerns and those of a people who had a sovereign right to their land and their own decision-making – unless they [the PLO] were dealing with Jordan on a basis of lack of confidence.

Jordan nevertheless relayed the PLO position to Washington on 27 January 1986. The US reiterated King Hussain's position, namely, that: the 11 February Agreement was a Jordanian–Palestinian accord that did not involve the US; the US supported the legitimate rights of the Palestinians, as stated in the Reagan Plan; and the PLO, like any other party, had the right to propose anything it wished, including the right of self-determination, at the international conference.

On 28 January this American response was passed to Arafat, who insisted that Jordan try again, but the US answer remained the same. The following day the Americans suggested to Jordan that the peace conference could still go ahead with only the participation of Palestinians from the occupied territories, leaving the door open for PLO participation when it accepted Resolution 242. It was Jordan who rejected this idea, on the grounds that it involved not only the PLO but also Jordan, and Jordan's position was that there should be no separate settlement. To the annoyance of King Hussain, President Reagan then informed Jordan, on 31 January, that the US was unable to supply it with any more military equipment, despite the repeated plea to Washington that there should be no linkage between the American–Jordanian arms deal – a bilateral issue – and the peace process, which had international dimensions.

In what appeared to be a calculated carrot-and-stick policy, the US then presented Jordan, on 5 February, with a new text containing Washington's approval of the convening of an international conference on the basis of 242 and 338 and recognition of the 'legitimate rights' of the Palestinian people, which in fact meant a return to the position Reagan had adopted in his plan of September 1982. A meeting was held the same night between Arafat and King Hussain during which Arafat reaffirmed the same PLO position. The next day during a meeting with Prime Minister Rifai, Arafat gave his final answer: despite the positive development of the US returning to its previous attitude of 1982, recognition of 'legitimate-rights' did not necessarily encompass the right of self-determination. The US, he thought, ought to give this concept its explicit prior approval. The US refused to do so. As one highly placed American official put it when interviewed in Washington: 'I have never been convinced that the use of this issue would at any particular point of time produce a different substance to the outcome.' When the comment was made that since self-determination is an international norm, no one ought to have the right to tailor self-determination for the Palestinians but the Palestinians themselves, he responded only by saying that in the context of the Middle East and the reality of the existence of Israel that was not possible. Although he praised King Hussain and Yasser Arafat for their courage he put the blame for the breakdown of the talks on 'decision-making bodies or governments or individuals who at certain points of time shy away'. He pointed to the PLO Executive Committee meeting in Kuwait in April 1983 and in Baghdad in November 1985. He refused to accept any share of the blame.[26]

King Hussain announces the deadlock

It was an angry King who, on 19 February 1986, announced the end of a chapter in his search for peace. 'We have gone through a gruelling year of intensive effort and faced a host of obstacles in many instances exceeding the limits of our endurance.' Indeed, it was on the rock of Resolution 242 that the King's patience finally broke and Jordan's initiative foundered.

King Hussain informed the nation on 19 February of the advantages of accepting 242:

Hinging on this agreement was an immediate opening of an American–Palestinian dialogue on the basis of which we would have continued our efforts for convening an international peace conference to which the PLO would be invited to participate as the representative of the Palestinian people ... The PLO will attend at the invitation of the UN Secretary General to represent its people and speak on its behalf with their adversary under the eyes of the world, side by side with the other parties concerned and the five permanent members of the Security Council.

Hussain also explained that Jordan would be able to carry the Fez resolutions to a point just short of the international peace conference for which it called.

But buoyed up on the one hand by the progress achieved in providing a real opportunity for peace, and pained on the other by the impediments that had arisen when Jordan was so close to the finishing line, he announced that he felt it imperative to give a full public account of the situation and turn the matter over to the Palestinian fora in the occupied territories and the diaspora, as well as Arab capitals and organizations. In announcing the end of co-ordination with the PLO, he declared:

I and the government of the Hashemite Kingdom of Jordan hereby announce that we are unable to continue to co-ordinate politically with the PLO leadership until such time as their word becomes their bond, characterized by commitment, credibility and consistency.

Prime Minister Rifai explained in an interview at a later date that Arafat was committed to working with Jordan and the US and had never mentioned to Jordan his insistence on prior US recognition of Palestinian self-determination except in the very last stages. It was surprising to hear this statement from Mr Rifai because, as far as the Western media were concerned, Arafat's insistence on Palestinian self-determination had always been clear from the very beginning.

King Hussain had ended one phase of political action with the PLO leadership, but he made it absolutely clear that 'the principles and tenets of the Jordanian–Palestinian Accord will continue to embody the foundations governing relations between the Jordanian and the Palestinian people'.

The PLO explains

Following intensive discussions within the PLO, a low-key statement was issued in reply to King Hussain's address of 19 February 1986. Many developments have taken place since then (see Chapter 13), but in order to put these developments in perspective, the following is a resumé of the statement as broadcast from Radio Amman in March 1986.[27]

The course of Jordanian–Palestinian relations, which started to evolve after the signing of the Camp David Accords between Egypt and Israel, was directed by three major factors. First, the special relationship between the two Arab peoples of Jordan and Palestine. Second, the danger emanating from Israel's call for an alternative Palestinian homeland in Jordan. And third, the danger from a parallel Israeli attempt to solve the Palestinian problem by devising a form of administrative self-rule for the portion of the Palestinian population still living in the West Bank and Gaza. These last two dangers necessitated a co-ordination of effort between the Jordanians and the PLO within the framework of a balanced relationship that could create an effective nucleus for collective Arab action. All three factors combined assumed even more importance after the Israeli invasion of Lebanon in the summer of 1982, and led at Fez to the establishment of a solid Arab (including the Palestinians) perception of peacemaking. The PLO saw the Fez Plan as an important political step which was crowned by the 11 February 1985 Agreement between Jordan and the PLO.

But the US continued to refuse to recognize the PLO. It continued to refuse to recognize the national rights of five million Palestinians, including their right to self-determination. It insisted on Palestinian recognition of Resolutions 242 and 338, which underlined the refugee status of the Palestinians. And it continued to insist on Palestinian recognition of Israel's right to exist within secure and recognized boundaries yet to be defined, even in the absence of Israeli and US recognition of Palestinian national rights. It also continued to insist on putting an end to armed struggle against an Israel which deprived the Palestinians of their right of return or of establishing their homeland on the West Bank and Gaza, and to equate terrorism with national liberation and the right of peoples to resist occupation. The Palestinians were instead required to acquiesce in what they regarded as a sheer capitulation, for the sake of US approval of the PLO's participation in an international conference within a joint Palestinian–Jordanian delegation, while Israel was to be left free to reject any dealings with the PLO even if all the concessions insisted upon by the US in advance were made.

Resolution 242 on its own, unaccompanied by the other pertinent UN resolutions on the Palestinians and the Palestinian problem, was rejected because it ignored the essence of the Palestinian cause, the land, the people, their rights and their representation. Accepting 242 on its own, without linking it to the Palestinian right of self-determination, as the basis of an international conference for a Middle East settlement would have meant accepting the removal of the Palestinian cause from the agenda of the conference – despite US assurances to the contrary – which would then have been transformed into a discussion of the border issues dealt with by the resolution. Resolution 242 tackled the Palestinian question from no other aspect than as a refugee question since it was designed to resolve the 1967 conflict between the Arab states and Israel.

As far as self-determination is concerned, the Palestinians realize that they cannot be denied the inalienable right of all peoples upheld by the UN Charter, UN resolutions, Arab summits, Non-aligned summits, the Venice summit of the EEC, the top Christian religious bodies and the European Parliament to name but a few. Hence it was the PLO's view that the Palestinian right of self-determination was not merely an internal or bilateral matter between Jordan and the PLO, as both Jordan and the US saw it, but a natural, firm and sacred right that necessitates not only US acceptance in principle, but also US and Israeli acceptance of its exercise on the land liberated from occupation. Furthermore, the PLO does not see Jordan as preventing the Palestinians from exercising this right, but Israel and the US. The actual Palestinian choice after the liberation of the West Bank and Gaza of a Palestinian state confederated with Jordan, or with any Arab country they may choose, is seen as the true exercise of this right. The PLO also sees the right of self-determination as one of the essential principles upon which the convening of the international conference depends. It cannot therefore be ignored, eliminated or compromised. It is the sole guarantor of a comprehensive and just settlement for the Palestinian people, whether in exile or under occupation.

The PLO, as well as Jordan, continued to reject the US understanding of the mandate to be granted to the international conference. But where the PLO and Jordan parted company was over the continued PLO belief that the US had attempted to delude the Palestinian people into thinking there was a real chance for peace, if US demands for radical concessions were met. The real bone of contention was thus ultimately not with Jordan but with the US. 'It is because of the lack of US credibility and its adoption of Israel and its cause that even Jordan, which has accepted 242 since 1967, the Rogers Plan, the Reagan Plan and the Geneva Conference, has not been able to achieve its foreign policy goals to date', the PLO maintained.

The US retreated from the promise it had made to Jordan by refusing to meet a Palestinian delegation which included two Palestinians it had already approved. 'As the PLO never accepted 242 without its association with all UN resolutions on Palestine or the right of self-determination the onus of the failure of the latest peace moves falls squarely on US obduracy, intransigence and lack of credibility', according to the PLO. Moreover, the PLO declared that its foremost aim was to realize Palestinian national rights. Regaining the land was not just a tactical choice, but a national aspiration, responsibility for which fell on the PLO, the Palestinian people and the whole Arab nation.

The PLO believes that the predicament of the Palestinian people has to be considered in depth, in its totality, as a predicament that involves all Palestinians both inside and outside the occupied territories. Those under occupation suffer oppression, repression, alien settlements, confiscation of their land, and deprivation of their national identity. Those outside, who form the bulk of the Palestinian nation, suffer the pains of exile, pursuit and siege. But the PLO rejects the divisibility of Palestinian people or the fragmentation of their cause. The only way for a solution to the Palestinian problem, the PLO maintains, is through the recognition of the inalienable national rights of all the Palestinian people scattered throughout the world, including the right of self-determination, with all that that entails.

An evaluation of the situation

Jordan

Because of its historical and geographical links with Palestine, the Palestinians and the Palestinian cause, because of proximity to developments in the occupied territories, and because of its understanding of Zionist thinking – how it takes advantage of Arab disarray, weakness and paralysis – and of Israel's military superiority, Jordan is deeply aware of the danger inherent in the state of no war/no peace in the Middle East, not only for the Palestinian inhabitants of the West Bank and Gaza, but also for its own national security.[28] The threat from Israel, whether in the form of Labour's call for implementation of 'the Jordanian option' or of the Likud's call for a resolution of the Palestinian problem on Jordanian territory at the expense of sovereign Jordan, has heightened Jordan's apprehensions more than those of any other Arab country adjacent to Israel.

At the same time, Jordan considers that the Palestinians are a displaced community, hence their cause has become – as King Hussain put it in his 19 February address – 'inseparable from that of their return to the Palestinian land, which, today, is accepted as the West Bank and Gaza'. It believes that the Palestinians without the PLO, the symbol of their nationalism, are weak, that both are weaker without Jordan, and that all three are weaker still without the backing of the Arab nation as a whole. Within this intricate political web, Jordan has to guard its own national interests and further its own security needs.

In accepting Resolution 242, Jordan gave the first indication of its priority in policy options, namely, the restoration of the occupied territories and the establishment of a just, comprehensive and permanent peace that would put an end to any future Israeli threats of designs against it. At the same time, it was determined to do all it could, not only to support the Palestinian cause, but also to relieve the lot of the people under occupation in the West Bank who carry Jordanian passports.

By the same token, in rejecting 242, the PLO gave the first indication of its priority in policy options, namely, realization of the national rights of the Palestinian people – both in the diaspora and in the occupied territories – in Palestine. Foreseeing the complications that might arise, Jordan at one time suggested the separation of the two objectives – liberation of occupied territories and realization of national rights – in the international arena. In other words, if the Arab states concentrated on regaining the occupied territories through Resolution 242, then the PLO could carry on the struggle after the liberation of the land was completed to establish the principle of national rights. Jordan's suggestion was rebuffed by the PLO; the reason, according to Jordan, was mistrust, the fear that if the Palestinian-occupied lands were to return to Jordan, there was no guarantee that they would then be handed over to the PLO. As a guarantee of national rights, Jordan then suggested – in 1972 – the formation of a United Arab Kingdom, which was rejected not only by the PLO but also by the rest of the Arab world, including Egypt's Sadat who for a while severed diplomatic relations with Jordan as a gesture of protest. At Rabat, in 1974, the Arab heads of state backed the PLO, which was recognized as the sole legitimate representative of the Palestinian people. Eight years later, this was re-emphasized at Fez.

According to King Hussain, the linkage of the two issues in this way enabled Israel to construct a case against the PLO, to the point where Arab energy became consumed in defending the PLO, and this defence gradually replaced the basic issue.

Things got to the point where the PLO, legitimate rights, and territory became one, or came to be regarded as synonymous with the Palestinian issue. Hence, there was confusion about priorities. The land no longer enjoyed the highest priority as the key to the restoration of national rights.

In 1973, Jordan accepted Resolution 338 because, as well as reaffirming Resolution 242 – which established the principle of withdrawal in return for peace – it suggested negotiations for a settlement under appropriate auspices. But the PLO also rejected 338 not because it shunned the principle of negotiations with Israel, which is implied in the concept of an international conference, but because 338 set the seal on 242 without allowing for any alterations or additions to meet the Palestinian question directly. Added to this was the PLO's persistent refusal to differentiate between the role of the Arab states in attempting to regain occupied territory and its own role of representing the struggle of the Palestinian people to restore their national rights. There was further discord between Jordan and the PLO in 1982, when Jordan initially accepted the Reagan Plan and the PLO rejected it on the grounds that – among other things – it ignored Palestinian national rights.

At Fez in 1982, both sides compromised. Their collaborative venture was consecrated in the 11 February 1985 Accord, on the basis that they would eventually lose both Palestine and Jordan if they did not take positive action together in the quest for peace. But the basic difference in their approaches remained and both continued to have their own different sets of problems, and their own different constituencies to answer to. Any major advance towards the achievement of peace was bound to depend on each side's perception of where its own interests in the peace process lay.

By February 1986, King Hussain genuinely believed that he had extracted vital concessions from the US which had brought an international conference significantly closer. Only a few months earlier, the US would consider talking to the PLO only after it had accepted Resolutions 242 and 338, and Washington had been totally opposed to an international conference which would bring the Russians back into the peace process. Even Peres in his speech to the UN General Assembly on 21 October 1985, accepted the principle of an 'international forum' before the US did. Jordan saw US acceptance of the principle of an international conference – even without the mandatory powers urged by Jordan – as signifying that it had made concessions, not only on the issue of Soviet participation, but also on PLO participation, provided that the PLO would state its willingness to accept Resolutions 242 and 338. The US had in fact gone even further, by reaffirming the stand it had taken in 1982, that is, that it was prepared to discuss the legitimate rights of the Palestinians as well as the implementation of Resolution 242 without prior PLO declaration of its acceptance of Israel's right to exist, on the grounds that this was already contained in 242 and 338.

When the PLO leadership refused to give an unconditional acceptance of the two resolutions, unless the US first subscribed to the universally accepted norm of self-determination or to the other UN resolutions directly connected with the Palestinian question, the differences between the Jordanian and PLO approaches that had for a while lain dormant erupted once more. On 19 February 1986, King Hussain decided to end political co-operation with the PLO leadership, thus signalling the end of a chapter in peacemaking which had consumed a whole year – a year of activity without action and motion without movement. Throwing the ball back into the Arab – and in particular the Palestinian – court, he urged Palestinians everywhere to decide whether they accepted the course taken by the PLO leadership; and if not, what political options they should now pursue. To make his position absolutely clear, King Hussain granted an interview to the *New York Times* in which he challenged Arafat's leadership by calling on Palestinians everywhere to decide who should now lead them.

The Palestinians must now make a decision. Are they happy with creeping annexation of their land by Israel and their possible expulsion from Palestine? If they are unhappy, what do they want us to do about it?[29]

King Hussain did not actually suggest what alternatives the Palestinians should explore: 'Once they define what direction they want, they can create an apparatus to express themselves.' But he added, 'if it is the PLO, we will respect this'.[30] To reaffirm his relationship with the PLO as such, despite his differences with its leadership, King Hussain again said in his address to the formal opening session of the Arab Parliamentarian Union in Amman – 11/13 March 1986 – that Jordan would never be a substitute for the PLO in the search for peace in the Middle East, because the PLO was the sole legitimate representative of the Palestinian people. But in dropping the current PLO leadership as a negotiating partner, closing the Fatah offices in Amman and expelling one of the PLO leaders – Abu Jihad – he had in no way abandoned the inhabitants of the West Bank. He and Jordan would maintain their support for them, so long as this support did not clash with Jordan's national security. By thus reaffirming his commitment to the Rabat decision and Jordan's refusal to stand in for the Palestinians or the PLO in any peace negotiations, by pledging his support for the Palestinians under occupation, and by offering to co-operate with a new Palestinian leadership that would relieve the people under occupation by making the liberation of the land the first priority, it appeared that King Hussain expected to win the support of what was regarded as the Palestinian silent majority inside the occupied territories.

The reactions of the Palestinians in the West Bank and Gaza must therefore have come as a disappointment. Shortly afterwards, at the funeral of the assassinated Mayor of Nablus – Zafer Al Masri, a newly appointed moderate – the Palestinians were seen on television in human waves carrying banners expressing support for the PLO and attacking the governments of Israel, Syria and Jordan. As many political commentators in the West pointed out,[31] Jordan's excommunication of Arafat had certainly not generated instant enthusiasm in the occupied territories. However flawed, the PLO remained the only symbol of Palestinian identity and the only means of self-expression, and that held true for Israel and the Arab states alike.

The Jordanian–PLO rift touched a raw nerve in Palestinian politics, and put the Palestinians under occupation in a very tight position indeed. West Bankers carried Jordanian passports. And most, while declaring their support for the PLO, had been careful not to burn their bridges with Amman, as careful, indeed, as Yasser Arafat, who responded to the King in a softly worded statement that trod a delicate line between maintaining strongly held principles and extending the hand of friendship. Some Palestinians from inside the occupied territories have shown a reserved solidarity with the King, but no one has declared a willingness to withdraw their confidence in the PLO as the sole legitimate representative of the Palestinian people, or to suggest a new Palestinian partner for the King. Instead, the majority have called for a reconciliation.[32] This attitude led some Western political observers to suggest that, however bad Jordan's relations with Arafat, and however muddled and fractious the PLO might be, abandoning Arafat for good was just not credible.[33] 'If King Hussain can find another figure of stature to lead the PLO, well and good', *The Guardian* commented. But it added: 'So far he hasn't'.

The rift must have pleased Syria and the Soviet Union who were against a Jordanian–PLO rapprochement because of their suspicion of another version of Camp David under US auspices. It must also have pleased Israel, if only to kick the PLO out of the equation. But it did not seem to have a lot to do with serious personal differences between King Hussain and Yasser Arafat. As Tariq Aziz, the then Iraqi Foreign Minister, put it, 'The whole matter amounts to differences in analysis, evaluation and inference of the current political movement.' And as Arafat explained 'What took place is a sort of a dialogue. Sometimes, the tone of the dialogue becomes sharp, but it quietens down. Hence the dialogue continues.' He added

There is no serious difference between King Hussain and the PLO leadership. Our difference is with the US. We appreciate all that Jordan did for us. We trust Jordan but we do not trust the US or its promises, especially after our experience with the US in 1982 in Lebanon.[34]

King Hussain continues to believe in a comprehensive peace 'that will satisfy future generations and have the blessing of the Arab world'. He continues to maintain that 'any other agreement constitutes a time bomb as illustrated by many examples from the situation in Europe after World War Two'.[35] A consummate tactician, but operating in a domestic and regional arena which leaves him little room for manoeuvre, King Hussain must have taken into consideration the fragility of Israel's coalition government, the sluggishness of the US peace efforts, Europe's helplessness, and the shaky nature of Arab support. He must have concluded that he was too exposed to take more than his fair share of the risks for peace. Thus the peace process lay, yet again, frozen in immobility.

The PLO

The PLO's perception of the basis of a lasting peace in the Middle East was outlined and underlined yet again in a statement issued on 26 November 1985, after the Baghdad meetings of the PLO Executive Committee, of its Central Council of 70 members, of the Secretariat of the PNC and of the Central Committee of Fatah. The statement stressed that 'Our peace initiative must be based on international legitimacy as expressed by all UN General Assembly and Security Council resolutions.'[36] This accorded with the categoric personal statements to foreign correspondents of Arafat and his aides, before and after the Baghdad meetings which proposed the acceptance of Resolutions 242 and 338 in full, but within the context of other pertinent UN resolutions or of a recognition of the Palestinian right to self-determination. Among these pertinent resolutions are the original UN Partition Plan – Resolution 181 of 1947 – which established universal acceptance of the principle of a Palestinian state, and Resolution 194 of 1948, paragraph 11 of which called for the repatriation or compensation of the Palestinian refugees. At no time was there any sign that the PLO might compromise on this point, and it thus seems surprising that Jordan and the US could hope at that time for a real change of mind.

The PLO maintained that its last bargaining counter was too high a price to pay simply for participation in an international conference whose mandatory powers had not even been agreed. To take such a step in advance, it felt, without any reciprocal gesture from Israel or the US, would be to commit political suicide. As an editorial in *The Guardian* of 21 February 1986 put it, 'If they concede now, what will they have to bargain with when the ceremonials of Geneva are over and substantial bargaining takes place?' The PLO also maintained that its own participation or some other form of Palestinian participation which it had approved was an undisputed right, if only because discussions on Palestine without the Palestinians would be absurd. And without evidence of US credibility, it felt that talks, in any event, would be unlikely to achieve anything concrete.[37]

The PLO's argument was lent some credence, following a statement by the Israeli coalition government in January 1986 that Israel's permanent sovereignty over Jerusalem and the Haram Al Sharif (Temple Mount) could not be questioned, in other words, the future of Jerusalem – which was of such crucial importance to Jordan, and the entire Moslem and Arab worlds – would be excluded from the agenda of peace talks; this alone seemed to guarantee the conference's failure. Furthermore, as soon as Israel knew the details of the Jordanian–American dialogue spelt out by King Hussain on 19 February 1986 it protested that Washington had given undertakings without prior consultation with Tel Aviv. An apologetic US administration made it clear that the PLO's invitation to an international conference, even after its acceptance of Resolutions 242 and 338, had to be agreed by Israel; in other words, Israel was left with a veto over the PLO's presence even if the PLO decided to offer a major political concession and enter negotiations with its hands tied. As Arafat put it:

The goal is not to attend an international conference just for the pleasure of attending. It is to ensure through the conference the establishment and the implementation of the legitimate rights of the Palestinians in accordance with international legality as laid down by the UN. International legality is not only one or two resolutions as the US chooses to see it.[38]

Another point of contention between the US and the PLO was the demand that the PLO end all acts of 'terrorism' against Israel, including military operations in the occupied territories against the occupier, before the negotiations began and before Palestinian rights were acknowledged. Arafat argued that the Algerians had maintained their struggle against France during the first and second Evian negotiations, that the same thing had happened during the negotiations on Zimbabwe and Vietnam, and that there was nothing strange in continuing to resist the occupier until the right of five million Palestinians to self-determination was established. 'When we accepted self-determination with a confederation with Jordan, it was a gesture of flexibility that was not appreciated by President Reagan', he commented.[39] But when he renounced terrorism in the Cairo Declaration, and restricted military operations to the occupied territories, he was differentiating between the legitimate resistance of a national liberation movement against occupation, and terrorism as such. Nevertheless just as the PLO has its own wings, comparable to the differences between Likud and Labour, Arafat's announcement in Cairo, aimed at meeting a US condition for peace, invoked the wrath of other PLO factions – stationed in Syria – not because of the contents of the declaration, but because of the political purpose for which it was employed. 'The declaration was made on an American request and Arafat should not have accepted, particularly since confining operations to the Israeli occupied territories has always been the established policy of the PLO', Nayef Hawatmeh of the DFLP declared.[40]

It could be argued that the PLO was obstinate, and that its obstinacy was harmful not only to itself but also to the whole peace process. As *The Daily Telegraph* of 4 March 1986 put it, 'If self-determination were to be the ultimate aim, there might be stages in arriving at it. It may be left in the substance of negotiations.' Or, as Jordan put it and the US agreed, Palestinian self-determination was a matter strictly between Jordan and the PLO, especially since it had been agreed by both sides that it would be exercised within a Jordanian–Palestinian confederation, and thus that it should not be given priority over ensuring Israel's withdrawal from the West Bank and Gaza. But the PLO consistently stressed that self-determination could mean an independent Palestinian state and confederation could be seen as the outcome of the natural right of self-determination. If it had been agreed in principle to put the cart before the horse, it was merely to remove obstacles and assure the US Administration, which had itself proposed a similar formula in September 1982, that such a confederal relationship had already been decided upon, and that all that was needed was American will and determination to move positively towards peace after acknowledging that five million Palestinians could exercise a right already recognized by the vast majority of the world.

The PLO via Jordan suggested three formulae for such an American move:

When it is decided to send an invitation to the PLO to attend an international conference with effective mandatory powers to solve the Palestinian problem and put an end to the Middle East conflict with the attendance of the five permanent members of the Security Council, and all parties concerned, the PLO will agree to participate within a Jordanian–Palestinian delegation with the aim of implementing UN and Security Council resolutions related to the Palestinian question, along with 242 and 338, within the framework of negotiations on a geographical basis to guarantee the legitimate rights of the Palestinian people including their right to self-determination within a confederation with Jordan as stressed by the 11 February 1985 Agreement with Jordan. The PLO will repeat its stand on terrorism as outlined in the Cairo

Declaration. Upon the receipt of a written commitment from the US to Palestinian self-determination, the PLO will declare its acceptance of 242 and 338 simultaneously with the US declaration of such a commitment.[41]

When the Americans rejected this and warnings came from within his own ranks, as well as from the factions in Syria, that 'if he accepts 242 on its own he will deal himself, the PLO and the whole Palestinian question out of the equation, especially given the American and Israeli determination to finish off the PLO as a political force',[42] Arafat spelt out an unequivocal 'No' to any compromise on the question of representation, or of self-determination, leading everyone to blame him for the collapse of the peace process.

Arafat's room for manoeuvre was thus considerably reduced. But the official Arab silence that greeted King Hussain's condemnation of Arafat, the renewed support for the PLO from the bulk of the population under occupation, and the US reiteration that 'even if a package had been agreed it would not be imposed on anybody',[43] meaning Israel, gave the PLO leader's morale a boost, and cause for satisfaction that he had refused to make a major political decision which would have left him excommunicated by Syria, shunned by the USSR and pilloried by a majority of the PLO and the Palestinian people.

Israel

The intense peace diplomacy originating in the Arab world led Prime Minister Shimon Peres to unveil his own peace plan – presumably in answer to the 11 February 1985 Accord between Jordan and the PLO – in Jerusalem on 10 June 1985. It entailed five steps: preparatory talks between the US, Israel, Jordan, Egypt and Palestinian representatives who were not PLO members; the establishment of a small Jordanian–Palestinian–Israeli team which would prepare an agenda for a Jordanian–Palestinian–Israeli conference, with the participation of the US; enlistment of the support of the permanent members of the Security Council for direct negotiations between Jordan, a Palestinian delegation and Israel without their committing themselves to supporting either side; the appointment of authentic Palestinians from the occupied territories acceptable to all sides to represent the inhabitants; and the convening of a ceremonial opening session of a conference within three months at a place to be agreed on.[44]

The initiative was doomed to failure. For Peres the vague term 'conference' was more a formality than anything else. For Jordan the key word was 'international'. Talks would not be only direct bilateral ones as demanded by Israel. They would also be multilateral, i.e. including representatives from the main conference, so that any agreement would be within both a regional and an international framework. In short – no repetition of Camp David, no bilateral and separate solutions.

On 21 October 1985, Peres unveiled another initiative at the UN General Assembly in New York. This conceded a role in the peace process to a vaguely defined international 'forum', in contrast to King Hussain's earlier reference to 'UN auspices'.

The 'forum', which admitted a UN role, was supposed to help launch and sustain the peace process. But Peres made clear that although the negotiations might be initiated with the help of an international forum, they would soon be reduced to talks between Israel and Jordan, to be conducted between an Israeli delegation on the one hand, and a Jordanian or a Jordanian–Palestinian one on the other, provided that the unnamed Palestinian representatives partnering Jordan 'represent peace not terror'.[45] The next day, Peres confirmed to the press that his formulation was intended to exclude the PLO. But to meet Jordan's desire for an international conference he had presented the framework of an international forum only to underwrite the direct talks between Israel and Jordan, and excluded a Soviet role altogether until the USSR re-established diplomatic relations with Israel.

The irony of Peres's initiative was that, while most of the Arabs dismissed it as nothing new, his partners in the Israeli coalition, the Likud, condemned it as a violation of agreed policy. And while Peres was putting forward his proposal in New York, Jordanian and Syrian negotiators were agreeing in Riyadh to adopt a joint political stand rejecting partial and separate peace talks with Israel. Nonetheless in the short run, Peres's plan improved his standing in Washington.

In January 1986, Peres conducted a European tour in which he donned the mantle of the patient and peaceable statesman. He ended up speaking earnestly at the Royal Institute of International Affairs in London about 'Israel's willingness to take risks in the pursuit of peace'. 'By choice', he said, 'we oppose any form of violence or terrorism or war or annexation.' Quoting the Jewish saying, 'The hero of heroes is he who make his enemy his friend', he maintained that his government's policy was designed 'to facilitate peaceful coexistence between Arab and Jew in mutual respect and dignity'. But as the London-based magazine, *Middle East International*, commented in an editorial on 7 March 1986:

In the light of Israel's role in Lebanon, of its annexation of Arab Jerusalem and then the Golan Heights and its relentless colonization of the West Bank and Gaza, all in contemptuous defiance of international law and of the UN, the emptiness of his rhetoric should be plain to all. And in relation to the Palestinians, it reveals itself at its most hypocritical.

Peres offered a recipe for peaceful co-existence between Arab and Jew 'in mutual respect and dignity' through 'Palestinian self-expression, Palestinian self-existence and self-respect'. 'Just stale old autonomy', Patrick Seale commented in the *Observer* of 26 January 1986.

Peres also offered the mechanism for implementing this vision: a regional conference without any specification of who might attend. But by stressing that 'it was impractical to try to involve Assad of Syria in political negotiations',[46] and by underlining the fact that the Soviet Union would not be welcome because it did not have diplomatic relations with Israel – although Israel attended the Geneva conference in 1973 co-chaired by the two superpowers without Soviet–Israeli diplomatic relations – Peres implied that he would definitely like to start (and perhaps finish) with direct face-to-face negotiations with Jordan without the PLO, Syria or the Soviet Union.[47]

In an effort to appear as the last person to put obstacles in the way of peace, Peres used the undefined concept of an international forum as a fig-leaf for concluding a separate deal with Jordan – much as Israel had done with Egypt and had tried to do with Lebanon – which would accommodate an arrangement for the inhabitants of the West Bank and Gaza without the PLO. Thus, Peres was exploiting the enormous gulf between the image held in the West and political reality as it exists in the Middle East to bury under platitudes and pious euphemisms about Palestinian self-expression the real issue at stake: the incontestable right of the Palestinian people to self-determination. Peres also ignored the PLO factor necessary for any comprehensive peace in the Middle East. As President Mubarak put it,

You in America cannot understand what we mean. We mean comprehensive peace. Genuine peace, not just any kind of solution where we can say we reached a solution, but terrorism can continue. That is why I am telling you the PLO is the sole legitimate representative of the Palestinian people whether we like it or not.[48]

The eclipse of the PLO's fortunes following the breakdown of co-operation between King Hussain and the PLO leadership caused euphoria among Israel's politicians. 'It is an historic opportunity for advancing peace in the Middle East', the Israeli Minister of Defence proclaimed. 'It had been Israel's policy that Hussain could and should not have the PLO as a negotiating partner with Israel, and that Hussain should cut ties with the PLO and enter into negotiations directly with Israel and with other non-PLO Palestinians', he added. And he called on the Palestinians of the West Bank and Gaza to come forward and join with King Hussain.[49]

Peres, for his part, began to devise other schemes. For example, devolution proposals that would allow Palestinians more say in administering their own local affairs, and a 'Marshal Plan' to save his adversaries from economic collapse. In other words, he was retreating from the idea of autonomy envisaged at Camp David and trying instead to solve the Palestinian problem, not by directly addressing its underlying causes, but by drawing attention to a possible economic relationship between Israel – which, it was taken for granted, would have a substantial share of the economic aid – Jordan, the Palestinian entity and perhaps the rest of the Middle East as well, on the lines of a Benelux type of relationship. But Israel would not spell out how much it was offering in terms of occupied territory – the only currency the Arab world was interested in – nor halt its intervention in Lebanon, nor stop fuelling the Iran–Iraq War through covert assistance to Iran, nor remove Jordan's fear of being attacked. Thus, it left unanswered the problem of how the Middle East's economic hardship, which pre-dated the collapse in oil prices, and arose from military spending to provide a defence against Israel, could be alleviated before a just, comprehensive and long-lasting peace was established.

Having said that Israel recognized the rights of the Palestinian people, Peres was forced to explain at the Labour Party conference held on 17 April 1986 that 'Israel should adopt the principle that while it does not recognize an independent Palestinian State, it is prepared to reach an agreement giving the Palestinians some structure via Jordan. We are willing to conclude interim agreements.'[50] After interviewing Peres, the Israeli newspaper *Ma-ariv* said on 10 April that there was a paragraph in the Camp David Agreements, in which Israel had clearly recognized that the Palestinians had legitimate rights and just demands, but that this fact had not been publicized because Begin had persuaded Carter to have the English term 'Palestinian people' translated into the Hebrew term 'the Arabs of Eretz Israel' (the Arabs of the Land of Israel). Defence Minister Rabin opened the political debate on 17 April by saying that Israel wanted to achieve peace by solving the Palestinian problem in a Jordanian context and thus preserve Israel's Jewish character: 'We prefer the preservation of Israel's Jewish character and contents to biblical borders.' It is thus obvious that Israel under Peres's premiership was firmly convinced that the only way to peace was some sort of a development of the 'Jordanian option'.

Peres's vision of how to achieve his goals became clear when he hammered out a document of understanding with King Hussain on 11 April 1987 which became known as 'The London Document' (see Appendix E). Although it dealt with the procedures, formalities, decisions and nature of an international conference, it left the substance of issues to the eventual negotiations between the parties concerned. The 'London Document' was presented to the US government but never had the chance of being approved and signed by the governments of Jordan and Israel.

What made Jordan strike a deal with Peres was the absence of effective US mediation. Prince Hassan elaborated:

Whilst in theory the US proclaimed a reluctance to play any role affecting domestic Israeli politics, US practice was different. Shultz favoured Peres; but when Shamir visited Washington in 1988 he was promised 75 F-16s, thus strengthening his stance against the latter.[51]

But why the agreement to hold bilateral talks on a geographical rather than a functional basis, a point which Jordan and Syria had insisted on during the preparatory talks preceding the intended Geneva conference in 1977 during the Carter era? 'The situation is now different. Egypt has regained Sinai', he remarked.

We are talking in 1988 about transitional arrangements and final status. As far as Syria is concerned, the understanding is that she will engage in talks about the final status from the start, simply skipping the transitional arrangements. Jordan is apprehensive of talks on transitional arrangements lest they end up as a partial settlement. But if there is an agreement or a common understanding on what the final status is, then effectively whether it is functional or geographic is one and the same thing.

The problem with the 'London Document' was its conclusion with Peres who did not speak for a united Israeli government. Shamir held that his partner's political activity lay outside the guidelines of the national unity government and that he had no mandate to agree on an international conference. In the end Peres threatened to force an early general election if the Cabinet did not give him a mandate to pursue his peace efforts. He failed to secure that mandate and to muster a majority within the Knesset to dissolve the national unity government and hold elections. The Accord remained in abeyance until further notice.

13 Postscript: evaluation and conclusion

We are witnessing the birth of a nation. It is beautiful . . . it is glorious . . . it is heroic.

Ambassador Robert Neumann[1] June 1988, Washington

The Intifada and beyond

The Western media date the beginning of the Palestinian *Intifada* (uprising) from 9 December 1987 when serious disturbances were sparked off in the occupied territories following a road accident in Gaza involving an Israeli vehicle and resulting in the deaths of four Arabs. But, during a long interview with the present writer on 15 November 1988 at the end of the PNC meeting in Algiers, Yasser Arafat pinpointed the Sabra and Shatila massacres of September 1982, during the Israeli invasion of Lebanon, as the landmark, for it was then that he appealed to his people under occupation to move in defiance. According to him, incidents started building up from that time, sometimes unreported, sometimes with ferocity but always with momentum. Arafat listed these with amazing precision. His claim seemed credible judging by the increased awareness on the part of the Palestinians under occupation of each subject debated and each step taken during the November 1988 PNC meeting, even before any reporting in the press took place; the reading of the 'Palestinian Document of Independence' in Al Aqsa Mosque in Jerusalem at the same time as Arafat was reading it in the PNC meeting (see below); and the simultaneous celebrations afterwards, both in Algeria and the occupied territories. These all signified remarkable co-ordination. A West Bank Palestinian lawyer explained:

The United Command for the escalation of the uprising is faceless, nameless, address unknown. The relationship with the PLO is organic rather than hierarchical. In a sense it is all PLO.[2]

The combination of despair, the political immobility that has existed for twenty years or so, the growing economic integration with Israel and the absence of any semblance of a peace process have grappled the occupied Palestinians in a new spirit of unity against the occupier. So the young have thrown the stones but the old gave the logistical support and sustained the

191

effort. The *Intifada* has become part of the Palestinian way of life. And it succeeded for a while in arousing international concern at a time when the world had all but forgotten about their plight or found it more convenient to forget.

The provisions of the Geneva Convention (Articles 49/33/27 for instance) could hardly be reconciled with the policy of force enunciated by Defence Minister Rabin in January 1988 in answer to the *Intifada*. But the measures adopted since, the drafting of thousands of troops into the occupied territories, the institution of beatings, the use of rubber bullets, the imposition of curfews, the breaking of bones witnessed on TV screens all over the world, the mass arrests and detentions, the administrative measures such as deportation and internment, have infused a moral and spiritual strength into a close-knit society, hence an organized pattern of struggle has been woven into the fabric of daily life to the extent that many political observers have come to believe that as long as there is an occupation there will be an *Intifada*. The price paid from 9 December 1987 to 30 September 1990 according to PLO sources was 1,223 dead, 94,214 wounded, 88,301 jailed, 101 expelled, 1,887 houses demolished, 1,190 houses sealed with always between 17,000 and 28,000 in prison.

President Reagan, seemingly disengaged from serious Middle East diplomacy, was of the opinion that 'the demonstrations, the violence, the deportations and the general strikes clearly showed that a new threshold had been crossed in the West Bank and Gaza, and the only way to break out of the status quo was to give the Palestinians a reason for hope, not despair'. Hence, as he put it, 'action was needed urgently'. His views were conveyed to King Hussain.

Action emerged soon after. What became known as the 'Shultz initiative' was announced on 4 March 1988. Secretary of State Shultz suggested a ceremonial international conference leading directly to bilateral peace negotiations based on Resolution 242 between Israel and a Jordanian–Palestinian delegation, Israel and Syria and Israel and Lebanon. The conference would not be able to veto or impose any decision taken bilaterally; it could only follow reports about the progress of the bilateral negotiations. Moreover, all participating parties had to renounce violence and terrorism. As far as negotiations between Israel and the Jordanian–Palestinian delegation were concerned, Shultz suggested a mechanism: a six-month negotiating period for a transitional arrangement starting on 1 May 1988 leading to its implementation nine months afterwards. In the seventh month – i.e. December 1988 – negotiations on the final status could begin, to be concluded within a year, i.e. by December 1989. No mention of the PLO was made officially in the letters sent by Shultz to both Jordan and Israel, thus giving the impression that its representation would be left to Jordan and the rest of the Arab world to sort out.

Seasoned political observers discerned different interpretations of the Shultz initiative on the part of the individual Arab countries and Israel. For instance, Jordan understood the whole process to involve an indivisible package which would include agreement on principles, a time-framework and the method of direct negotiations, provided that there were no negotiations except in the conference, not even preliminary talks. The statement of principles was to include only the modalities for the conference, the transitional arrangements and the final status on the basis of UN Resolution 242. As far as talks on final status were concerned, they would begin on the agreed date irrespective of progress in the transitional arrangement talks. Reports from Israel indicated that they saw the proposal as an international conference simply to launch direct bilateral negotiations. Shamir envisaged no withdrawal and opposed a fixed date for starting final status talks. In other words, he favoured only a transitional arrangement agreed through bilateral negotiations with Jordan and certain Palestinians under its wing, hoping in the meanwhile that that would become the final status. Final status was understood by most Arabs to be, as Prince Hassan put it, 'peace on the basis of the present situation on the ground – peace in place – the exchange of peace for peace, not territory for peace.'

With the usual lack of mutual trust, the following questions inevitably arose in this context: What was to prevent foot-dragging on talks concerning the transitional arrangement and final status? What would the whole procedure look like if agreement was reached and implemented on the transitional arrangement only to discover a deadlock on final status? Where would the logical venue be for solving misunderstandings or implementing agreements, with a restricted international conference with no role but to start the bilateral talks and then read about their progress? Would the Soviet Union agree to sit on the sidelines with the other three permanent members of the Security Council, while the US, which had a credibility problem in the first place, was left to do all the running, thus steering events to its own, and probably Israel's, benefit? When would talks on the vital issues of land and resources be launched? Would the Palestinian inhabitants of East Jerusalem be included in discussions on the future of the West Bank and Gaza? Would legitimate rights mean civil rights or political rights or both, and would political rights include national rights? What about the future of the Palestinians in the diaspora? Who would supervise the West Bank and Gaza during the transitional period?

Jordan is reported to have sent such a set of questions to the US for consideration. It is doubtful whether it ever received any written reply, the reason given in Washington being determination never to repeat what happened in similar circumstances during Camp David. Prince Hassan listed the areas of difference between the US and Jordan as follows: the nature of the international conference, the nature of self-determination for the Palestinians, PLO participation, the timing of and linkage between the transitional arrangement and final status, and US reluctance to spell out more clearly its previous commitment and understanding of UN Resolution 242 because of domestic politics and the fear of its being turned into an election issue. He then compared the different US approach towards a similar case. In terms of the Geneva Accord with regard to Afghanistan of February 1988, the US had three priorities: withdrawal of Soviet troops, self-determination and the return of refugees. In other words, there was agreement on a monitored peace process with defined ground rules and terms of reference. This was not the case with the Palestinian question.

The Shultz initiative was doomed to failure. As Robert Neumann put it: 'A negotiator waits until the moment is right. A statesman ripens the moment. Shultz was not a statesman.'[4] What he meant was explained by Harold Saunders:

Shultz was worried about how you unlock the door to the negotiating room: but the blockages to negotiations lay not in finding the right formulation for unlocking the door to the negotiating room. The blockages lay in the political arena . . . You have to put into the interim step enough real hope and guarantee of the final . . . [but] the Israeli body politic has not commited itself to negotiate at all definitively about getting out of the West Bank and Gaza . . . [Moreover] Shultz did not like dealing with the PLO, first, because of the Israeli reaction and that of the Jewish community in the US and second because a personality like Shultz was instinctively uncomfortable with a group like the PLO or a man like Arafat. Shultz was a man who liked to deal in an orderly way with known parties within a structured situation.[5]

On 8 April 1988 Prime Minister Rifai declared at a press conference that Jordan had handed to Shultz during talks in Amman a paper containing the basic principles which Jordan adhered to in any process to settle the Arab–Israeli conflict and the Palestinian question. These principles were broadcast from Radio Amman the same day as follows:

(i)   The inadmissibility of the acquisition of territory by war. Israeli withdrawal from the occupied territories is the basis for the settlement of the Arab–Israeli conflict, and the establishment of a just and durable peace.

(ii) The settlement of the Arab–Israeli conflict requires the settlement of the Palestinian problem in all its aspects, including the right of the Palestinian people to self-determination.

(iii) The settlement of the Arab–Israeli conflict and the Palestinian problem must be a comprehensive settlement. Negotiations to arrive at a comprehensive settlement can only take place within an international conference.

(iv) The international conference will not be merely a ceremonial international gathering structured for the sole purpose of launching direct negotiations. It should reflect the moral and constant weight of the five permanent members of the Security Council in assisting all the parties to the conflict to arrive at a comprehensive, just and lasting peace.

(v) The principles of Security Council Resolution 242 apply to all the occupied Arab territories and are the basis for negotiations in the bilateral committees.

(vi) In exercising its sovereign right, Jordan is prepared to attend the international conference with the other involved parties. Jordan will not represent the Palestinian people at the conference, nor will it negotiate the settlement of the Palestinian problem on behalf of the PLO. Jordan is also prepared to attend the conference in a joint Jordanian–Palestinian delegation if the parties concerned accept this arrangement.[6]

The position of the rest of the Arab world became clear at the emergency summit held in Algiers from 7 to 9 June 1988 to discuss ways and means to sustain the *Intifada*. Seventeen Arab heads of state, including King Hussain and Yasser Arafat, attended. The final communiqué reiterated conditions for peace precisely as set out at Fez in September 1982. The Shultz initiative took an indirect knock when the conference noted 'US perseverance in a policy favouring Israel and hostile to the national rights of the Palestinian people'. It condemned this policy which 'encourages Israel to continue its hostilities and violations of Human Rights, hinders efforts to establish peace, and contradicts US responsibilities, in its capacity as a permanent Security Council member, to maintain international peace and security'.[7] The Arab leaders stood for one minute's silence in honour of the *Intifada* and its victims, and promised it financial support through the PLO, 'the sole legitimate representative of the Palestinian people', as well as available international channels.

The moment was ripe for King Hussain to take the next logical step – to sever legal and administrative links with the West Bank. He announced his decision to that effect on 31 July 1988.

A Jordanian position statement[8] explained that the decision was made

in response to the wishes of the PLO; in conformity with the decision of the Arab states to seek an independent state in the occupied territories; to allow the PLO to shoulder its responsibilities; to enhance the Palestinian national struggle and highlight the Palestinian identity by focussing on the territorial dimension of their struggle; to emphasize that Jordan has no territorial designs and ambitions in the occupied territories; and to remove any lingering doubt that the association was tantamount to a Jordanian occupation of Palestinian territory.

In case Peres felt let down after signing the London Document of April 1987 with King Hussain the Jordanian statement made it clear that 'in the final analysis Jordan found little difference between the two partners in the national coalition government of Israel. Israel has been unable to produce an official consensus on which it could proceed to meaningful negotiations. Despite the effort of Mr Peres . . . he was unable to force the issue as indeed was the case when he was Prime Minister.' And, as far as the US was concerned, the statement emphasized that 'the essence of the problem is not whether Jordan participates in peace negotiations and the procedural problems this may entail; it is the Israeli occupation of Palestinian-inhabited territory as the uprising has graphically indicated daily since December 1987 . . . The disengagement has placed the peace process . . . in its proper perspective.'

Yasser Arafat was quick to react. On 13 September he addressed the European Parliament in Strasburg. He endorsed the Cairo Declaration against terrorism, and Resolutions 242 and 338 as the basis for an international conference, along with all other UN resolutions relevant to the Palestinian question or the legitimate rights of the Palestinian people, foremost among them their right to self-determination. And he announced the Palestinian intention to set up an independent Palestinian state, with a republican, democratic multi-party system, on the land to be freed from Israeli occupation.[9]

On 13–15 November the Palestinian National Council was convened in Algiers. With the final decisions resting, not with Arafat, but with the PNC itself, Resolutions 242 and 338 were officially endorsed by 253 votes in favour with 46 against and 10 abstentions. The convening of an international conference was urged on the basis of 242 and 338 and the guaranteeing of the 'legitimate national rights of the Palestinian people, foremost being the rights of self-determination in accordance with the principles and provisions of the UN charter'.[10] In the early hours of 15 November Arafat read out the 'Palestinian Document of Independence',[11] the major paragraph of which stated:

The Palestinian National Council declares in the name of God and on behalf of the Palestinian Arab people, the establishment of the State of Palestine with its capital as Jerusalem . . . The State of Palestine shall be for Palestinians, wherever they may be . . . their religious and political beliefs and human dignity shall therein be safeguarded under a democratic parliamentary system based on freedom of opinion and the freedom to form parties, on the need of the majority for minority rights and the respect of minorities for majority decisions, on social justice and equality, and on non-discrimination in civil rights on grounds of race, religion or colour or as between men and women, under a Constitution ensuring the rule of law and an independent judiciary and on the basis of true fidelity to the age-old spiritual and cultural heritage of Palestine with respect to mutual tolerance, co-existence and magnanimity among religions.

Of the then 160 UN member countries 93 recognized the State of Palestine including all Arab countries, except Syria, 36 African, 18 East European, 14 Asian and 3 West European countries.

The Algiers resolutions effectively authorized Arafat to make the Stockholm Declaration on 7 December following a meeting with a group of American Jewish members of the Tel Aviv Centre for Israeli–Palestinian Peace under the auspices of the Swedish Foreign Ministry. Articles 2 and 3 of the Declaration underlined that 'the PNC . . . established the independent Palestinian state of Palestine and accepted the existence of Israel as a state in the region'. The Declaration also announced its rejection and condemnation of terrorism in all its forms including state terrorism.[12] On 13 December Arafat addressed the UN General Assembly at a session specially convened in Geneva because of the American refusal to allow him a visa to enter the US. On terrorism he declared: 'I, as Chairman of the PLO, hereby once more declare that I condemn terrorism in all its forms and at the same time salute those sitting before me in this hall who, in the days when they fought to liberate their countries from the yoke of colonialism, were accused of terrorism.'[13] Arafat reiterated the PNC recognition of the State of Israel and its right to exist in security and re-affirmed the acceptance of Resolution 242 but, like the PNC, he linked it with other related UN resolutions.

This the Americans found objectionable. Within two hours Israel described the speech as a 'monumental act of deception'. Soon after, the US declared it ambiguous on the key issues. Attempts to quibble over the wording of Arafat's declarations became increasingly desperate and absurd. So again Arafat appeared at a crowded press conference on 14 December where he reiterated in strong terms that 'the survival of the Palestinian people does not imply the destruction of Israel. Our desire for peace is a strategy not an interim tactic.'[14] After yet again renouncing terrorism in all its forms he declared, this time without conditions, Resolutions 242 and 338 as the basis for negotiations of a peace settlement.

In an extraordinary turn of events, the US announced the same evening that Arafat had finally met its conditions for direct talks between the US and the PLO. Shultz's statement was as follows:

The Palestinian Liberation Organization today issued a statement in which it accepts the United Nations Security Council resolutions 242 and 338, recognizes Israel's right to exist in peace and security and renounces terrorism. As a result the United States is prepared for a substantive dialogue with PLO representatives. I am designating our ambassador to Tunisia as the only authorized channel . . . Nothing here may be taken to imply an acceptance or recognition by the United States of an independent Palestinian state. The position of the US is that the status of the West Bank and Gaza cannot be determined by unilateral action on either side, but only through a process of negotiation. The United States does not recognize the declaration of an independent Palestinian state. It is also important to recognize that the United States' commitment to the security of Israel remains unflinching.[15]

With only two weeks left before the end of the Reagan era, Shultz did no more than make a crack in the wall erected by Kissinger in 1975. He left the scene with the goal of peace in the Middle East still elusive, the Palestinian problem crying out for a solution, and the outlook anything but bright.

The peace process under George Bush

The first official contact between the US and the PLO for more than thirteen years began in Tunis on 15 December 1988. Sporadic meetings between the two sides continued until the end of May 1990 without any tangible results being reported. Hence, there was no regret at PLO headquarters when the US suspended the dialogue as a protest against an abortive raid on the Israeli coast on May 31 by the Palestinian Liberation Front for which the PLO refused to take the blame.

It was not, however, until 6 April 1989 that the Middle East peace process started to gain momentum through what became known as Shamir's four-point plan, unveiled as Israel's answer to the *Intifada* in time to coincide with Shamir's visit to Washington.[16] Its main thrust was for elections to be held in the West Bank and Gaza Strip to facilitate the formation of a non-PLO delegation to negotiate a 5-year 'interim settlement' during which a 'self-governing administration' could be established. The interim period of five years could be followed by a negotiated 'final settlement' of the Palestinian problem. Shamir also proposed that Israel, Egypt and the US should re-confirm their commitment to the 1979 Camp David agreements, that the US should steer an effort to solve the 'humanitarian' aspect of 'Arab refugees' in the West Bank and Gaza, and that the US and Egypt should call on all Arabs to 'desist from hostility towards Israel and to replace belligerency and boycott with negotiation and cooperation'.

The Palestinians of the West Bank and Gaza only (excluding East Jerusalem and the diaspora) would select negotiators to talk to the Israelis about yet further talks to decide the future shape of autonomy, after which, presumably, 'there would be a round of municipalities to give the Palestinians real control over street lighting and refuse collection', was the cynical comment of Professor Yazid Sayegh of Oxford University.[17] According to George Bush, however, the proposals were 'a contribution to a political process of dialogue and negotiations'.[18] King Hussain, on the other hand, predicted that, without prior Israeli agreement to exchanging land for peace, the proposals would lead to deadlock; it would be 'to engage in a process of considerable apparent motion without substantial progress'.[19] While rejecting the Shamir plan as it stood out of hand, the PLO, for its part, kept the door conditionally open to the election idea, provided it was one element of a comprehensive plan; in other words, the elections were to be part of a comprehensive settlement of the Arab–Israeli conflict achieved through an international conference, with the Palestinian case presented by the Palestinians themselves through a delegation yet to be formed. But there were legitimate questions and concerns in the Arab world which were eventually expressed in an Egyptian ten-point plan presented to Israel on 16 September 1989.

President Mubarak's[20] plan endorsed the idea of elections by stressing the right of every person in the West Bank (including East Jerusalem) and the Gaza Strip to stand as a candidate, campaign and vote in the elections to be held under international supervision with a prior commitment on the part of the Israeli government to accept the results. The Israeli government was also to agree that the elections would lead not only to an 'interim' phase of 'Palestinian self-government' but also to a final settlement based on UN Security Council resolutions 242 and 338 and on the principle of an exchange of land for peace; withdrawal of the Israeli army from the voting areas prior to elections; a ban on Israelis entering the territories on election day (except for those who worked or lived there); preparation of the elections by a joint Israeli–Palestinian committee over a period not exceeding two months; and a US guarantee of all the above provisions plus the imposition of a freeze on further Israeli settlements.

Seven of these points dealt with the modalities of the elections but three dealt with the principle of land for peace which was unacceptable to the Israeli government. Egypt, however, proposed a first-stage meeting of Egyptian, Israeli and UN officials to discuss the second stage of an Israel–Palestinian meeting which it was suggested should take place in Cairo.

Referring to the discussions as 'talks of surrender', Shamir refused to proceed with the initial meeting without first receiving, in advance, certain US 'guarantees' concerning what he regarded as the 'danger of Israel being led into negotiations with the PLO and towards a Palestinian state'.[21] On 20 September Secretary of State James Baker clarified the situation by stating his view of the Egyptian plan as representing not an alternative but acceptance of the Israeli plan which, he said, enjoyed US support. Shamir procrastinated, though within his Cabinet he could have found Labour not only accepting most of the Egyptian plan, but also regarding it as a catalyst. Indeed, Mubarak's ten points highlighted the ambiguities of Shamir's position, exposing not only the underlying differences between Labour and Likud, but also stimulating new ones within the parties themselves.

The composition of the Palestinian delegation to Cairo lay at the heart of intensive Israeli discussions with Secretary Baker who insisted that the delegation should include at least one Palestinian with links with East Jerusalem. Israel refused to budge. In no way was the PLO to be allowed to sneak in by the back door or via the delegation to steer the peace process from its headquarters in Tunis. In the end Israel rejected the Egyptian proposals on 6 October 1989.

In an effort to resuscitate the process James Baker stepped in within days with his five-point framework for elections in the occupied territories: agreement on an Israeli–Palestinian dialogue in Cairo; acceptance that Egypt could be no substitute for the Palestinians; US acceptance that Israel would attend only when a satisfactory list of Palestinians had been drawn up; agreement that Israel would discuss its peace initiative while the Palestinians would be free to bring up other issues and that a meeting of US, Israeli and Egyptian foreign ministers should take place at a later date.[22]

A heavily conditional Israeli acceptance of the American initiative came on 5 November: the agreement could take place only on the assumption that the PLO would have no role either in the selection of the Palestinian delegation or in determining the shape of the talks. In no way would Israel accept Baker's leniency towards allowing Palestinian representatives to raise issues relating to their own opinions on how to make the elections and the negotiating process work, nor his implicit acceptance that the agenda of the Cairo talks could be broader than that favoured by Israel. In other words acceptance was forthcoming, but only with American assurances that PLO representatives would take no part in the negotiations, and that the agenda would be confined to discussions of the logistics of Israel's own election proposals.

For its part, the PLO rejected[23] Baker's proposals on the basis that it was the only party with the right to form and announce the delegation; that the agenda should be open and without prior conditions; that the Palestinian side adhered to the peace initiative announced at the PNC meeting of November 1988 and to the right to discuss it; that the meeting must be regarded as a preliminary dialogue between the two sides and a step on the way to holding an international peace conference as a framework for final negotiation on a comprehensive settlement; and that the proposed meeting must be attended, among others, by the five permanent members of the Security Council. The PLO was adamant that Palestinians from East Jerusalem and the diaspora should take part in the Cairo talks.

Egypt – which exchanged ideas with the PLO on its position – accepted in principle the US proposals on 6 December 1989. This flurry of diplomatic activity coincided with the festering violence in the occupied territories where the *Intifada* was marking its second anniversary on 9 December. There was an obvious frustration among Palestinians in general at what was regarded as an attempt by both the US and Egypt to pressure the PLO into accepting an almost invisible role at that stage. On the other hand, Egypt's acceptance of the Baker plan – after exchanging ideas with the PLO – could be seen as the first indication that the PLO leadership may have accepted such an initial role. Hence Cairo's move made the Egyptian government an unacceptable interlocutor for Tel Aviv. The late Abu Iyad (Salah Khalaf) – then number two in the PLO leadership explained that the PLO was willing to show a cautious conditional flexibility on the US proposals but would not accept being excluded from the initial process altogether. 'We are being asked to forgo our right to select the Palestinian representatives . . . Mr. Shamir wants to have a dialogue with himself in the mirror', he was reported as saying.[24] The PLO was concerned about the legal precedent that might be established if it gave up its right to nominate Palestinian representatives. 'After all', he said, 'what was our battle with Syria all about which tried for all these years to form a parallel PLO?'

The Egyptians, while insisting that they did not speak for the Palestinians, appeared ready to fudge the principle of PLO selection of the Palestinian delegation in order to ensure a PLO indirect participation, and to circumvent the ideological issues by choosing the delegates with the approval of the PLO without saying so publicly so as not to give Shamir the excuse to refuse. And Arafat seemed to be giving tacit support to the Egyptian strategy; he had not publicly opposed Egypt's diplomatic initiatives. Bassam Abu Sharif – one of his personal advisers – explained at a later date that Israel was using Palestinian representation as an excuse for not dealing with the substantive issue, i.e. putting an end to the occupation.[25] He confirmed that during the short-lived dialogue between the US and the PLO and following the presentation of the Baker plan there was in fact a preliminary understanding between the two sides about the nature of the Palestinian delegation from inside and outside the occupied territories.

But Israel was piling on more conditions. Forced by right wingers in Likud, Shamir modified his own plan almost to the point of extinction. Added to his list of prohibitions were no negotiations before the end of the uprising and no halt in the settlement building. Peres, on the other hand, emerged from a meeting with President Mubarak on 24 January 1990 conceding that there were differences over the central issues of the composition of the Palestinian delegation and the agenda for talks, but that two Palestinians deported by Israel might be added to the main figures from within the occupied territories, and that the delegation was free to consult with other Arabs. The words were hardly out of his mouth before they were being rejected back in Jerusalem. Peres's aide, Yosi Beilin, commented at a later date: 'Everybody understood that behind that delegation there was the PLO. Personally, I would like to talk with the PLO under certain conditions . . . I don't believe there is a more moderate organization than the PLO or at least the leadership of Fatah.'[26]

By March 1990, Israel's coalition government had collapsed over Shamir's refusal to move ahead, and by April the whole process had ground to a halt. Secretary of State Baker was obviously angry. Washing his hands of the whole affair he told the new Shamir government in June that his number was in the book if it wanted to resume talks. It never did.

The Middle East peace process lay in abeyance until the eruption of the Gulf crisis following Saddam Hussain's occupation of Kuwait on 2 August 1990. The war that ensued revived the issue of Israeli occupation of the West Bank and Gaza through what was referred to as 'linkage'. Abu Iyad explained the significance of the term to the Arab world only a few days before his assassination in December 1990:

We do not mean by linkage that the Iraqis should stay put in Kuwait until Israel withdraws from the occupied lands. What we mean by linkage is the implementation of UN resolutions and invoking the instrument of international legality which is being used forcefully and impressively in the Gulf crisis to solve the question of Palestine. International legality must not have two standards. It should not be allowed to do so.[27]

Throughout the Gulf crisis the five permanent members of the Security Council adamantly rejected any attempts to link Iraqi withdrawal from Kuwait with a settlement of the Arab–Israeli conflict. Most Americans, and most analysts, however, understood that in the real world there was such a linkage. The question became, in the words of William Quandt, 'how to structure an American diplomatic initiative to deal with that reality and the Bush Administration has chosen to try to minimize the degree of explicit diplomatic language'.[28] At the same time, by going to war to defend the principle of non-acquisition of territory by war, President Bush had already established in practical terms in the minds of the international community the existence of a link.

If the idea of refusing Saddam Hussain credit for the push towards Palestine was deeply ingrained in the minds of Western decision-makers, the idea of sequential rather than simultaneous attempts to deal with the two occupations came from the Arab world, particularly from King Hussain and Yasser Arafat. George Bush got the message. In his State of the Union address on 6 March 1991 he declared: 'Our commitment to peace in the Middle East does not end with the liberation of Kuwait . . . The time has come to put an end to the Arab–Israeli conflict.'[29] He then went on to outline what the peace process should consist of – a comprehensive settlement grounded on Resolutions 242 and 338 and the principle of territory for peace, provided that Israel's security and 'legitimate Palestinian political rights' were taken care of. This was one step forward from Ronald Reagan who, in his September 1982 plan, underlined Palestinian 'legitimate' rights. It was the first time that the US had spoken publicly, at this level, of the political nature of Palestinian aspirations.[30]

After issuing a joint communiqué with his Soviet counterpart, Alexander Bessmertnekh – promising joint US–Soviet efforts to promote 'Arab–Israeli peace and stability' – James Baker departed for the Middle East. He landed in Israel on 11 March, a day marked by the death of six Arab infiltrators in a border clash, the shooting of several Palestinians in and around Jerusalem and a general strike in East Jerusalem aimed to show him that the *Intifada* was still breathing defiance to occupation. Having recently given Israel $650m. to offset the cost of the Gulf War, Baker may have expected a more receptive Israel. But despite cordial diplomatic exchanges, the underlying spirit was expressed by Yuval Ne'eman, Science Minister and Leader of the Tehiya Party, at a cabinet meeting when he referred to Baker as 'a sorcerer's apprentice ignorantly dabbling in the region's politics'.[31] The American attempt soon turned into a hard struggle faced with Shamir's implacable opposition to the principle of giving up occupied land for peace, to the applicability of both UN Resolutions 242 and 338 on the Palestinian and Syrian fronts, and to the freezing of settlement building on occupied lands.

One element of agreement existed from the start between the US and Israel, namely, to remove altogether the PLO from any calculations on future peacemaking in the Middle East. The PLO's support for Iraq during the Gulf War had greatly damaged its standing, not only in Washington but also in the Gulf area and within government circles in countries which sided with the West against Iraq – in particular Egypt and Syria. A pre-determined and highly political campaign was launched in the Western media calling on Yasser Arafat, whom they held to be an unsuitable leader for the PLO, to step down. The campaign, however, did not succeed. As Nabil Sha'ath, one of Arafat's aides and advisers, put it: 'It is only the Palestinians who can choose their own representatives. It is only they who can remove them through democratic means in our parliament [the Palestinian National Council].'[32] James Baker must have recognized the truth of this in Israel when he met a group of Palestinian representatives on the same day the PLO issued a statement in Tunis (11 March 1991) sanctioning the talks. The group presented him with a document approved by the PLO which stressed that the Palestinians would only enter a process that culminated in nationhood, and ruled out open-ended arrangements. It also indicated that any transitional steps would have to be structured within a comprehensive and coherent plan with a specific time-frame for its implementaion. And, as if to answer Baker's earlier comment that Arafat could no longer be seen by the US as the spokesman for the Palestinians, the group firmly announced that only the PLO could represent them in their quest for an independent state alongside Israel and only the PLO could remain the sole legitimate representative of the Palestinian people. Secretary Baker was well aware that the meeting could not have taken place without the green light from the PLO and that the PLO had nominated each and every Palestinian participant. But his whole approach depended on coaxing Israel into making a move, any move, and then building on it. What became important was to trigger a process which, he believed, would eventually put pressure on Israel and the others to reach a compromise.

It took James Baker five trips to the Middle East between March and July 1991 to persuade the parties concerned to attend a peace conference. After much wheeling and dealing, a date was eventually announced by the Bush–Gorbachev Moscow Summit of 30 July 1991. It was 30 October 1991. The venue was Madrid.

The parties concerned could not have agreed to participation in the conference without a carefully worded letter of invitation and assurances concerning US understandings and intentions about the conference and the ensuing negotiations. The hitherto unpublished invitation (see Appendix H) outlined the plan of action: 'The United States and the Soviet Union are prepared to assist the parties to achieve a just, lasting and comprehensive peace settlement, through direct negotiations along two tracks, between Israel and the Arab states, and between Israel and the Palestinians . . . The objective of this process is real peace.'

Presidents Bush and Gorbachev extended the invitation to the governments of Israel, Egypt, Syria, Lebanon and Jordan and to the Palestinians. The European Community, represented by its President, was also invited as a participant alongside the United States and the Soviet Union. The Gulf Co-operation Council was invited to send its Secretary General as an observer and, in deference to Israel, the United Nations was asked to send only an observer representing the Secretary General. As Israel also insisted, the invitations specified that 'the conference will have no power to impose solutions . . . or veto agreements . . . It will have no authority to make decisions . . . no ability to vote on issues or results.' And 'it can re-convene only with the consent of all the parties'. Only the Palestinians from the West Bank and Gaza were asked to attend within the context of a joint Jordanian–Palestinian delegation. Negotiations were to be conducted in phases, beginning with talks on 'interim self-government arrangements', and were to last for five years. Beginning with the third year, however, negotiations on the final settlement were to start. The invitation also specified that these 'permanent status negotiations' and the negotiations between Israel and the Arab states would take place only on the basis of Resolutions 242 and 338.

The hitherto unpublished letter of assurances to the Palestinians referred to the Israeli presence in the West Bank and Gaza, including East Jerusalem, as 'occupation'. '. . . Palestinians should gain control over political, economic and other decisions that affect their lives and fate', it stated. And it repeated the objections outlined by President Bush's State of the Union address to Congress of 6 March. 'Only Palestinians can choose their delegation members who are not subject to veto from anyone.' But it also envisaged a joint Palestinian–Jordanian delegation as the only 'pathway' for achieving the 'legal political rights' of the Palestinians. In anticipation of objections from some Palestinian quarters, the Americans also promised that the Palestinian delegation would be able to raise 'any issue of importance to them' during the negotiations (see Appendix I). And, as if to meet apprehensions concerning who would represent the Palestinians, the letter specified that 'in this phase the process will not affect their claim to East Jerusalem or be prejudicial or precedential to the outcome of the negotiations'. Moreover, Palestinians from East Jerusalem and the diaspora who recognized UN Resolution 242, renounced terror, and accepted the existence of Israel in peace 'should be able to participate in the negotiations on the final status'.

With the insistence of both the letters of invitation and the assurances on Resolutions 242 and 338 – which deal with relations between states as the basis for negotiations – the US Administration deemed it necessary to allow the Palestinians to participate in any bilateral or multilateral negotiations on refugees. They were also allowed to participate in all multilateral negotiations dealing with other subjects concerning the future of the Middle East (for the role of the UN and East Jerusalem see Appendix I). Thus, Jordan bounced back to the centre of the peace process as the official umbrella under which the Palestinians would be allowed to enter the process. And, as if to outline the envisaged future role of Jordan, the letter of assurance re-affirmed that 'confederation is not excluded as a possible outcome of negotiations on the final status'.

Evaluation

Again there was nothing innovative in the latest US approach to peacemaking in the Middle East. Successive US endeavours had eventually culminated in Madrid. The Madrid conference was, no doubt, a considerable political achievement, a launch for many other bilateral and multilateral negotiations yet to come. Nevertheless, Madrid could not have been possible without the changing balance of power in the Middle East following the second Gulf War and the resultant Arab disarray, and in the world at large with the gradual erosion of Communism leading ultimately to the break-up of the Soviet Union. The uni-power status of the United States and its enhanced prestige in whipping together a vast international coalition of support had led to the conference table, albeit without sufficient time for consultations and preparatory groundwork among the Arab parties concerned. 'We were in this ironic situation as Arabs attending a conference and dealing with the Israelis without even a modicum of shared Arab position', Prince Hassan elaborated when interviewed a few months after the conference.[33] He added: 'The Arabs were left on their own to battle it out with the Israelis, disillusioned and unaided.'

The Americans must have learnt a lesson from the shortcomings of Camp David about the absence of the Palestinian–Jordanian component from deliberations concerning their future. But amendments on this score were overshadowed by a 'process of erosion'. After all, what they were talking about was a self-government arrangement, not autonomy as at Camp David. Another stark reality hit the Arabs: 'When you have today preferential American relations with Israel and still a hot–cold love-hate relationship with the Jordanian–Palestinian dimension, it is very difficult to speak of ourselves as full partners in a peace process. This is what I find worrying', Prince Hassan commented.[34] The Arab world must have shared the Prince's anxieties. As William Quandt had predicted: 'What would determine the results would be the actual balance of power inside the conference, which is in favour of Israel, and American dynamism, the quality of which cannot be known in advance.'[35]

Outside the conference, the PLO's options in terms of inter–Arab diplomacy were dramatically whittled down following the Gulf War. The area also saw a mass exodus from the Gulf of half a million or so Palestinian–Jordanian workers accused of supporting Saddam Hussain against Kuwait. It also saw the undercutting of financial support to Jordan and the Palestinians inside and outside the occupied territories. Moreover, the Palestinians had in one way or another lost full Arab political sponsorship. 'The people recognize the politics and economics of despair that this installs on the ground', Prince Hassan lamented.[36] His worry was about the spread of extremism, radicalism and fundamentalism – all obstacles to the middle-ground option. And he was correct. Rightists and fundamentalists were gradually gaining the upper hand in Middle Eastern societies.

Setting aside all previous apprehensions and inhibitions, the divided and disillusioned Arab leaders chose to jump on the Bush–Baker peace band-wagon as the only way out. After all, not since Camp David had a US Administration sounded so serious or the Middle East been at the top of the US foreign–policy agenda, albeit not at the presidential level as at Camp David. The Arabs now had a ticket for the Middle East peace bandwagon, but without knowing the destination. They had no other option. Under the new Pax Americana in the post-Cold War world, the only choice was whether the peace process would proceed with the Arabs or without them. The bandwagon, in any case, was moving under the American flag. Anyone who hesitated to jump on to it would have lost the chance of a lifetime to be seen and heard while his future was being moulded in Washington.

A totally new Middle East was indeed emerging. Its chief novelty was the special US relationship with the Gulf area. Pure material self-interest was the motto on both sides and particularly in some Arab calculations. When the Secretary General of the Gulf Co-operation Council was asked if he and his colleagues did not feel embarrassed at putting all their eggs in the American basket, he replied: 'Not at all. We have our own self-interest to look after'.[37] But in other Arab quarters[38] the hope was to create a new Helsinki-type process for regional unity and co-operation by means of multilateral negotiations to be launched and adopted by the Americans as a result of the Madrid peace conference. There was only one reassuring element as far as the Jordanians and the Palestinians were concerned. The American constants remained the same: East Jerusalem was still regarded as occupied, and so were the West Bank, the Gaza Strip and the Golan Heights. Moreover, Resolutions 242 and 338, which disallowed the acquisition of territory by force, were the basis for movement. Yet, there was awareness that 'the political tenets of the peace process in the 1970s were different from what they were in the 1980s and the 1990s. Hence the determination to take stock and interact pragmatically with what was on offer, exploring all along the final American understanding of these tenets.'[39]

The result was a perilous situation for the Palestinians under occupation. They were obliged to enter a process which was called comprehensive but which was basically an open-ended step-by-step diplomacy unsupported by an Arab or any other position, and to conduct discussions on an agenda that was not yet clear but which was heavily inspired by the occupiers. But there was also hope of moving from bilateral to multilateral agendas, enhanced by greater participation in issues such as Jerusalem with its inter-religious dimension supported by legal, administrative and political discussions on the future status of the city. Other concerns were the Palestinian diaspora and the issues of water resources, disarmament and security, all issues with transnational implications involving all countries in the region but awaiting discussion on a world-wide basis.

James Baker was a tough, dispassionate and objective Secretary of State, but to the people of the Middle East he seemed lacking in the kind of sensitivity to regional concerns that was essential for long-term success. With blueprints from Washington, accompanied by American dynamism and pressure if need be, Baker expected success. Jordan and the Palestinians also hoped for success. Behind the Palestinian team stood the PLO in Tunis, guiding and instructing each and every step. Behind the Jordanian team were Jordan's six principles of 8 April 1988. Their insistence on an international conference was met in part by the presence of Europeans alongside the co-sponsors of the peace process, and the subsequent launching of multilateral negotiations guaranteed the international framework.

Jordan had always insisted on not representing the Palestinians and not negotiating on their behalf. If doubt remained about its constitutional position since it severed administrative and legal links with the West Bank – on 31 July 1988 – Prince Hassan indicated:

Jordan for political reasons disengaged to give greater prominence to the struggle of the Palestinians and indeed we see the *Intifada* as a symbol of that struggle . . . But we would not go so far as to dismiss the geopolitical importance of Jordan, and there I would be more specific and say that a sovereign state only cedes sovereignty to another sovereign state. [Moreover] Jordan was not an occupier from 1948 to 1967. The legality of its position continues to the present day.

By virtue of Resolutions 242 and 338 Jordan's role in the peace process remains essential. By virtue of its geopolitical and demographic dimensions it remains important. And by virtue of its unamended Constitution Jordan remains an indivisible sovereign state. Moreover, as resolved by both Houses of Parliament in April 1950 (see Chapter 1), it had always been understood, as clause 2 specified, that 'Jordan intends to preserve all Arab rights in Palestine, to defend these rights by all lawful means in the exercise of its national rights but without prejudicing the final settlement of Palestine's just cause within the sphere of national aspirations, inter-Arab co-operation and international justice.' This particular clause has never been amended.

Confederation has been agreed by the leaders of both Jordan and the PLO, and has been backed by the Palestinian National Council. Democratic processes in both Jordan and the Palestinian quarters require referenda at the appropriate time. But confederation is a contractual agreement between states. The Americans do not rule it out as the outcome of negotiations on the final status of the West Bank and Gaza. But the resolution of this jigsaw puzzle depends mainly on decision-makers in the United States who have plenty of leverage to exercise on both sides of the Arab–Israeli divide.

Conclusion

In 1956, several years after the unimplemented UN Partition Plan established the principle of two states in Palestine, John Foster Dulles was asked,[41] 'What about the Palestinians?' He replied: 'Well . . . they are unlucky because they fell under the feet of elephants. The old generation will die and the young will forget.' Many years later the PLO chairman was asked to comment on this. 'We are still here. The old generation died but the zealous young have changed the whole atmosphere in the area.' But the 'zealous young' are not satisfied. Prohibited from establishing their own state on any part of the land of Palestine, the PLO has become the symbol of their nationalism. And no Palestinian is willing to concede either of two basic rights: to self-determination and to the free choice of their own representatives. Despite the attempts in many quarters to delegitimize the PLO, Palestinian nationalism and the chairman's ability to survive remain. Both Israel and Syria, in pursuit of different national goals, have tried to sink him. King Hussain has abandoned co-operation with him at least for a time. Other groups inside the PLO contest his moderate leadership. The US has steadfastly refused to allow him an independent role in any peace negotiations. In Israel, both Labour and Likud have sworn not to deal with him or his organization. In 1982, all Israel's might was used against him and his organization in Lebanon. And, in 1991, the anti-Iraq coalition ostracized, marginalized, ignored and completely excluded the organization and its leader from the peace process. Yet Arafat has remained irrepressible. Why? Because in his own words: 'I represent the will of a people to survive.' And survival to the Palestinians means mainly self-determination, for to them it is 'as much a basic human need, if not more so, than calorie intake'.[42]

Viewed from Tel Aviv as leading to a zero sum game, Palestinian self-determination is challenged and opposed by all means. Viewed from the Middle East, the US appears to be 'omnipotent'; but faced with Prime Minister Shamir, and before him Menachim Begin, it also appears 'impotent'.[43]

While the Israelis have it within their power to frustrate Palestinian political rights and ambitions, the Palestinians have it within their power to keep Israel in an indefinite state of siege. As Feisal Husseini of the West Bank put it: 'We are too weak to impose a solution. But we have the power to frustrate any move that does not take our interests into consideration.'[44] This apparent self-confidence comes with the realization that, despite the optimistic tone set by Ambassador Robert Neumann in June 1988 as the inscription to this chapter, West Bank and Gaza Strip leaders know that, after more than five years of *Intifada*, practical re-assessment of tactics and strategy is urgently needed. As Husseini put it in 1991:

What we've done up to now is to weaken the authority of occupation in many parts of our area. But at the same time occupation has prevented us from establishing our own authority in those same areas. Thus an inevitable vacuum has occurred which is eventually being filled by some youngsters taking the law into their own hands. But the *Intifada* is not dead; it has lots of energy and stamina. Therefore it will continue until Palestinian aspirations are met.[45]

In the meanwhile, extremism is being witnessed on both sides of the Arab–Israeli divide. As a result, moderate regimes may crumble and Arafat may eventually vanish; but the Palestinian problem, which pre-dates the PLO, will not fade away. If today's opportunities are allowed to slip away without achieving solid, long-lasting results for the Palestinians, tomorrow's international order may look back with nostalgia to the good old days of the PLO under the moderate Arafat.

George Antonius wrote as long ago as 1938,[46] 'the passion aroused by Palestine has done so much to obscure the truth that the facts have become enveloped in a mist of sentiment, legend and propaganda which acts as a smoke-screen of almost impenetrable density.' This statement is still valid today. It is within the power of the US – reinforced spectacularly during and after the Gulf War – to penetrate this obscurity and to reorganize, with the international community, the political jigsaw of the Middle East. The American President is indeed in a unique position to do so.

Israel came into being as a result of action by the international community. And sooner or later it will take the international community to clear up the mess created and to bring the region, to everyone's long-term benefit, into an era of peace and construction rather than war and destruction. In F.W. Maitland's famous words: 'We study the days before yesterday in order that yesterday may not paralyse today and today may not paralyse tomorrow.' It is in the light of this dictum that the present book offers its contribution to the better understanding of peace-making in the Middle East.

Appendix A Comparison of Middle East peace proposals

UN resolution 242, 22 November 1967

The Security Council,

Expressing its continuing concern with the grave situation in the Middle East,

Emphasizing the inadmissibility of the acquisition of territory by war and the need to work for a just and lasting peace in which every State in the area can live in security,

Emphasizing further that all Member States in their acceptance of the Charter of the United Nations have undertaken a commitment to act in accordance with Article 2 of the Charter,

1. *Affirms* that the fulfilment of Charter principles requires the establishment of a just and lasting peace in the Middle East which should include the application of both the following principles:
   (i) Withdrawal of Israeli armed forces from territories occupied in the recent conflict;
   (ii) Termination of all claims or stages of belligerency and respect for and acknowledgement of the sovereignty, territorial integrity and political independence of every State in the area and their right to live in peace within secure and recognized boundaries free from threats or acts of force;
2. *Affirms further* the necessity:
   (a) For guaranteeing freedom of navigation through international waterways in the area;
   (b) For achieving a just settlement of the refugee problem;
   (c) For guaranteeing the territorial inviolability and political independence of every State in the area, through measures including the establishment of demilitarized zones;
3. *Requests* the Secretary-General to designate a Special Representative to proceed to the Middle East to establish and maintain contacts with the States concerned in order to promote agreement and assist efforts to achieve a peaceful and accepted settlement in accordance with the provisions and principles of this resolution;
4. *Requests* the Secretary-General to report to the Security Council on the progress of the efforts of the Special Representative as soon as possible.

UN resolution 338, 22 October 1973

The Security Council

1. *Calls upon* all parties to the present fighting to cease all firing and terminate all military activity immediately, no later than 12 hours after the moment of the adoption of this decision, in the positions they now occupy;

2. *Calls upon* the parties concerned to start immediately after the cease-fire the implementation of Security Council Resolution 242 (1967) in all of its parts;

3. *Decides that*, immediately and concurrently with the cease-fire, negotiations shall start between the parties concerned under appropriate auspices aimed at establishing a just and durable peace in the Middle East.

A *September 1978–September 1982*

	Camp David Accords September 1978	EC Venice Declaration 13 June 1980	Reagan Plan 1 September 1982	Fez Arab Plan 9 September 1982
Acceptance of UN SCR 242	'The agreed basis for a peaceful settlement of the conflict between Israel and its neighbours is UN SCR 242 in all its parts.'	Declaration based on SCRs 242 and 338.	'UN Resolution 242 remains wholly valid as the foundation stone of America's Middle East peace effort.'	Not mentioned.
Territory	Negotiations should be based on provisions of SCRs 242 and 338 in all their parts.	Israeli territorial occupation since 1967 should be ended.	SCR 242 remains wholly valid and applied to all fronts including West Bank and Gaza. Extent of Israeli withdrawal will be heavily affected by extent of peace offered in return.	Israel must withdraw from all Arab territories occupied in 1967.
Palestinian rights	Solution from negotiations must recognize the legitimate rights of the Palestinian people and their just requirements.	Justice for all the peoples in the region which implies recognition of the legitimate rights of the Palestinian people. Palestinian people are not simply refugees and must be able to exercise fully their right to self-determination.	Legitimate rights and just requirements; Palestinians more than refugees. 'Due consideration must be given to the principle of self-government by the inhabitants of the territories.'	Right to self-determination and compensation for those who choose not to return.
Palestinian state	Negotiations between Egypt, Israel, Jordan and elected representatives of West Bank and Gaza, during transitional period to determine final status of West Bank and Gaza.	Palestinians' right to self-determination.*	Self-government by the Palestinians of the West Bank and Gaza – in association with Jordan. US would not support independent Palestinian State; or annexation or permanent control by Israel.	Creation of an independent Palestinian State; transitional UN trusteeship.

September 1978–September 1982 cont.

	Camp David Accords September 1978	EC Venice Declaration 13 June 1980	Reagan Plan 1 September 1982	Fez Arab Plan 9 September 1982
PLO/Palestinian representation	Palestinian people should participate in negotiations on Palestinian problems.	PLO should be associated with negotiations.	Future of the West Bank and Gaza to be decided by territories' inhabitants in conjunction with Israel and Jordan.	PLO is the sole legitimate representative of the Palestinian people.
Secure borders & recognition of Israel's right to security	Sovereignty, territorial integrity and right to live in peace within secure boundaries of all States in the area to be recognized.	The right to existence and the security of all States in the region, including Israel, should be recognized and implemented. The use of force should be renounced.	Israel's right to a secure future recognized. Borders to be subject to negotiation.	UN Security Council to guarantee peace among "all States of the region including the independent Palestinian State".
Settlements in West Bank and Gaza	Not mentioned.	Constitute a serious obstacle to the peace process and are illegal under international law.	Immediate freeze on settlements. "The US will not support the use of any additional land for the purpose of settlements."	Settlements set up by Israel since 1967 must be removed.
Transition mechanism	Transition period, not exceeding five years, after free elections for a self-governing authority in the West Bank and Gaza. Not later than third year of transition period, negotiations would begin to determine final status of West Bank and Gaza.	Not mentioned.	Five-year transition period to begin after free elections for a self-governing Palestinian authority, and during which Palestinian inhabitants of West Bank and Gaza would have full autonomy over their own affairs.	West Bank and Gaza to be placed under UN supervision for a transitional period not to exceed a few months.

Jerusalem	Not mentioned: Egypt and Israel agreed to set out their respective positions in side letters which were not part of the agreement.	No unilateral initiative designed to change the status of Jerusalem is acceptable, and any agreement on the city's status should guarantee freedom of access to holy places.	Jerusalem must remain undivided – final status negotiable.	Israel must withdraw from Arab Jerusalem. Jerusalem to be the capital of an independent Palestinian State. Freedom of worship to be guaranteed for all religions.
Guarantees	'The UN Security Council shall be requested to endorse the peace treaties, and ensure that their provisions shall not be violated. The permanent members of the Security Council shall be requested to underwrite the peace treaties and ensure respect for their provisions.'	'The necessary guarantees for a peace settlement should be provided by the United Nations by a decision of the Security Council and, if necessary, on the basis of other mutually agreed procedures.'	Not mentioned.	Security Council to draw up guarantees for peace for all States in the region and to provide guarantees for the implementation of all Fez principles.
International conference	Not mentioned.	Not mentioned.	Not mentioned.	Not mentioned.

*Later reformulation, eg. as at Brussels, 27 March 1984: settlement to entail "acceptance of the right of the Palestinian people to self-determination, with all that this implies".

B *July 1984–October 1985*

	Jordan/PLO Agreement 11 February 1985	Peres Plan for talks with Jordan 21 October 1984
Acceptance of UN SCR 242	Land to be exchanged for peace 'as established in UN and Security Council Resolutions'.	Negotiations to be based on SCRs 242 and 338.
Territory	Termination of Israeli occupation of the occupied Arab territories, including Jerusalem.	Negotiations to deal with the demarcation of boundaries.
Palestinian rights	Palestinian people's right to self-determination.	Not mentioned.
Palestinian state	The Palestinians to exercise their inalienable right to self-determination "when Jordanians and Palestinians are able to do so within the context of the formation of the proposed confederated Arab States of Jordan and Palestine'.	Negotiations to deal with demarcation of boundaries as well as the resolution of the Palestinian problem.
PLO/Palestinian representation	PLO, the Palestinian people's sole representative, to attend negotiations, within a joint Jordanian/Palestinian delegation.	Negotiations to be conducted between an Israeli delegation and a Jordanian, or a Jordanian/Palestinian, delegation 'both comprising delegates that represent peace not terror'.
Secure borders & recognition of Israel's right to security	No specific mention but principle of land in exchange for peace stated.	Not mentioned.

Settlements in West Bank and Gaza	Not mentioned.	Not mentioned.
Transition mechanism	Not mentioned	Not mentioned.
Jerusalem	Settlement to involve termination of Israeli occupation of Arab territories, including Jerusalem.	Not mentioned.
Guarantees	Not mentioned.	Not mentioned.
International conference	Peace negotiations to be held within framework of an international conference. Participants: five permanent members of UN Security Council, plus all parties to conflict including the PLO within Jordanian/Palestinian delegation.	Negotiations may be initiated with the support of an international forum. Permanent members of Security Council may be invited to support initiation of negotiations (but not those with diplomatic relations with only one side of the conflict). The forum not a substitute for direct negotiations between Israel and Jordan or a Jordanian/Palestinian delegation.

C 1988

	Mubarak Plan January 1988	Shultz Proposals March 1988	Peres/Rabin pre-election plan 17 October 1988
Acceptance of UN SCR 242	Not mentioned.	Participants in a conference must accept SCRs 242 and 338, and renounce violence and terrorism.	Negotiations to be based on SCRs 242 and 338.
Territory	Not mentioned.	All negotiations will be based on SCRs 242 and 338, in all their parts.	Israel would not return to the boundaries of 1967.
Palestinian rights	Respect for the political rights and basic freedoms of the Palestinian people under occupation.	Objective is a comprehensive peace providing for security of all the States in the region and for the legitimate rights of the Palestinian people.	Not mentioned.
Palestinian state	Not mentioned.	Palestinian issue to be addressed in negotiations between the Jordanian/Palestinian and Israeli delegations.	Negotiations to deal with demarcation of boundaries of any Palestinian entity as well as the resolution of the Palestinian problem "within a Jordanian/Palestinian framework".
PLO/Palestinian representation	Not mentioned.	Palestinian representation to be within the Jordanian/Palestinian delegation.	Palestinians to be allowed to elect leaders to negotiate an interim agreement on condition that there is first a three to six months' period of calm in occupied territories. Elected leaders must be authentic local residents; "their past records would not be inspected".
Secure borders & recognition of Israel's right to security	Not mentioned.	Not mentioned.	Not mentioned.

Settlements in West Bank and Gaza	A halt to all settlement in the West Bank and Gaza.	Not mentioned.	Not mentioned.
Transition mechanism	A halt to all forms of violence and repression in the occupied territories for six months.	Negotiations to begin on arrangement for a transitional period, with objective of completing them within six months. The transitional period to begin three months after agreement and to last for three years. Seven months after transitional negotiations begin, final status negotiations to begin, and be completed within one year. The latter to be based on all the provisions and principles of SCR 242. Final status talks to start before the transitional period begins.	Although negotiations for a comprehensive peace must include Jordan and the Palestinians, an interim agreement could be negotiated with the Palestinians alone.
Jerusalem	Not mentioned.	Not mentioned.	Jerusalem and its suburbs to remain a part of Israel.
Guarantees	A guarantee of the safety and protection of the Palestinian people under occupation through the proper international mechanisms.	Not mentioned.	Not mentioned.
International conference	Movement towards the summoning of international peace conference with the aim of reaching a comprehensive peaceful settlement, including recognition of the right of all States in the region to live in peace, and the enabling of the Palestinian people to exercise their right of self-determination.	Two weeks before the opening of negotiations, an international conference to be attended by the parties involved in the Arab–Israeli conflict and the five permanent members of the UN Security Council. The conference will not be able to impose solutions or veto agreements reached.	Negotiations on a final settlement to be opened by an international conference with no coercive authority.

	PNC Declaration November 1988
Acceptance of UN SCR 242	Stressed the need to convene an international conference . . . on the basis of SCRs 242 and 338 and other relevant UN resolutions.
Territory	Israel to withdraw from all the Palestinian and Arab territories it has occupied since 1967.
Palestinian rights	International conference to guarantee legitimate national rights of the Palestinian people, foremost being the right to self-determination.
Palestinian State	PNC meeting declared an independent Palestinian State in the occupied territories along the lines of SCR 181 of 1947.
Representation	UNSC permanent members and all parties to the conflict in the region, including the PLO, the Palestinian people's sole and legitimate representative, on an equal footing.
Secure borders & recognitiuon of Israel's right to security	UN Security Council to implement and guarantee security and peace arrangements among all the countries in the region, including the Palestinian State.
Settlements in West Bank and Gaza	Settlements set up by Israel on Palestinian and Arab territories occupied since 1967 to be removed.

Transition mechanism	Occupied territories to be placed under UN supervision for a specific period of time.
Jerusalem	In each case mention of occupied territories includes Arab Jerusalem.
Guarantees	UNSC to implement and guarantee security and peace arrangements among all the countries in the region, including the Palestinian State.
International conference	International conference to be convened under UN supervision, with participation of UNSC permanent members and all parties to the conflict in the region, including the PLO.

Source: Foreign and Commonwealth Office, London.

Appendix B Jordan–US exchange of questions and answers on the Camp David Accords, September 1978

Question One

Does the US intend to be a full partner in the negotiations on the West Bank, Gaza Strip and the Palestinian question in general? At what stage of the negotiations would the US participate and what role would it play?

Answer

Yes. The US would be a full partner in all stages of the Arab–Israeli peace negotiations, leading to a just, durable and comprehensive peace in the Middle East. The US would use its full influence for a successful conclusion. President Carter would play a personal active role in the negotiations.

Question Two

What does Paragraph (A) of the Framework for Peace – referring to representatives of the Palestinian people – mean?

Answer

There was no attempt to give a comprehensive explanation. The people of the West Bank and Gaza are specified in some cases. On one occasion, the paragraph referring to 'other Palestinians as would be agreed' clearly means representatives from outside the West Bank and Gaza, not necessarily Egyptian or Jordanian representatives. Of course Palestinians who are Egyptian or Jordanian citizens may become members of the negotiating delegations representing Jordan or Egypt. In other cases the Self-governing Authority is mentioned.

The US explains the term 'Representatives of the Palestinian People' not on the basis of any authority or a single organization representing the Palestinian people, but as including those elected or chosen to participate in the negotiations. It is expected that they will accept the goal of the negotiations as set out in Security Council Resolution 242, and in the framework of a settlement will be prepared to live in peace and good neighbourly relations with Israel.

Question Three

Why was a five-year transitional period for the West Bank and Gaza specified?

Answer

The five-year transitional period, as far as the West Bank and Gaza were concerned, was an American suggestion put forward to the parties concerned, for the first time, in the summer of 1977. The basic point was the idea of a transitional period, and not the specific five-year period. But when the five-year period was suggested it was approved.

We believe that during the transitional period of a few years, the Israeli military government and its civilian administration should withdraw. During the transitional period, a Self-governing Authority for the populations of the West Bank and Gaza should be established. Satisfactory solutions for actual problems resulting from the transition to the peace stage should be found. We regard the transitional period as necessary to build up confidence and to promote advancement and changes in attitudes, leading to a conclusion of the final settlement that would guarantee the security of Israel as well as the security of the other parties.

Question Four

(A) According to the US, what is the geographic definition of the West Bank and Gaza? Does the definition of the West Bank include Arab Jerusalem and its environs which were occupied by Israel during the 1967 War?

Answer

We believe that the West Bank and Gaza Strip are: All the areas west of the River Jordan which were under Jordan's administration before the 1967 War and all the areas situated east of the western borders of the British Mandate in Palestine – known as the Gaza Strip – which was until the 1967 War under Egyptian administration.

We believe that there should be a differentiation between Jerusalem and the rest of the West Bank because of the city's special circumstances. We believe that a solution to Jerusalem has to be found through negotiations. Its final status and the nature of the solution should be different in some aspects from the nature of the solution for the rest of the West Bank. No measure concerning Jerusalem undertaken by one party since the 1967 War should be allowed to prejudice the final status of the city. The US attitude towards the city remains the same as stated by Ambassador Goldberg in his UN speech of 14 July 1969.

(B) At the end of the five-year transitional period, under whose sovereignty would the West Bank and Gaza fall?

Answer

The final status of the West Bank and Gaza, including the sovereignty issue, must be decided during negotiations between Egypt, Israel, Jordan and the elected representatives of the people of the West Bank and Gaza, provided that the negotiations are based on Security Council Resolution 242 in all its aspects. Negotiations must start no later than the third year after the beginning of the transitional period. According to the script of the Framework of Agreement, the outcome of the negotiations, including the sovereignty issue, must be submitted to the elected representatives of the West Bank and Gaza for approval.

As the negotiations for a peace treaty between Jordan and Israel and the negotiations for the final status of the West Bank and Gaza are related to each other, the Framework specifies that the representatives of the West Bank and Gaza must participate in all these negotiations. The Palestinians will have to be part of all the negotiations dealing with the final status of the West Bank and Gaza.

(C)   What is the US attitude towards all these issues?

Answer

The US expressed its opinion concerning the geographical definition of the West Bank and Gaza areas in paragraph 4(A) above. Also, the US explained its opinion concerning sovereignty over the West Bank and Gaza in paragraph 4(B) above.

(D)   Would any Israeli forces remain in any part of the West Bank and Gaza after the five-year transitional period? If the answer is yes, what right or what pretext would they have to stay?

Answer

Security arrangements in the West Bank and Gaza after the five-year transitional period, including the possibility of leaving behind some Israeli security forces and determining the period of their stay, must be dealt with in negotiations about the final status of the West Bank and Gaza. These negotiations must start no later than the third year after the beginning of the transitional period.

(E)   What is the US attitude towards this issue?

Answer

The US thinks that agreement on the final status of the West Bank and Gaza must satisfy both the legitimate aspirations of the Palestinian people and Israel's security needs. Provided that all parties agree, the US would not object to the stationing of a limited number of Israeli security forces in specific areas to provide for the security needs of Israel.

Question Five

During the transitional period, under whose authority would the self-governing Palestinians ultimately fall? Under the UN's authority or that of a similar neutral international body? Who would supply the finance for the autonomy administration? And what would be the limitations imposed on its authority?

Answer

The Framework for Peace indicates that the parties concerned, Egypt, Israel, Jordan and the Palestinians in the Egyptian and the Jordanian delegations, would negotiate an agreement specifying the authority and responsibilities of the self-governing authority in the West Bank and Gaza.

The self-governing authority would be established during the transitional period as agreed by the three parties, and the agreement would specify the scope of its authority. It must specify full autonomy of the people.

Provided that the parties agree, there is nothing in the Framework for Peace which would deny the choice of having, or not having, a supervisory role for the UN or any other similar neutral institution.

During the transitional period, representatives from Egypt, Jordan, Israel and the Palestinian authority would form a continuing committee whose duty would be to deal with issues of reciprocal concerns.

The finance for the Self-governing Authority has not been discussed at Camp David. It is subject to agreement between the parties concerned.

Question Six

(A) According to the Framework for Peace, would East Jerusalem and its environs – land and people – which were occupied in the 1967 War, fall under the jurisdiction of the Self-governing Authority?

Answer

As specified above, the Jerusalem issue was not discussed at Camp David. It must be discussed at subsequent negotiations. As far as relations between the population of East Jerusalem and the Self-governing Authority are concerned, they must be agreed upon during negotiations for the transitional period.

(B) What is the US attitude towards the Jerusalem issue?

Answer

During negotiations for Jerusalem, the US would support the idea of allowing the population of East Jerusalem, who are not Israeli citizens, to participate in elections for the Self-governing Authority and in its work. It may not be realistic to expect East Jerusalem to fall under the jurisdiction of the Self-governing Authority during the transitional period. No arrangement, however, should prejudice the final status of Jerusalem. It must be decided during negotiations starting no later than the third year of the transitional period.

Question Seven

(A)   At the end of the five-year transitional period, what would be the status
of occupied Arab Jerusalem?

Answer

The future of the West Bank and the Gaza Strip, the relationship of these two areas
with their neighbours, and the question of peace between Israel and Jordan must be
decided during the negotiations referred to in paragraph A.1(C) of the Framework for
Peace. The US believes that the status of East Jerusalem, occupied by Israel in the
1967 War, must be decided upon during these negotiations.*

The Framework for Peace envisages these negotiations as taking place between
Israel, Jordan, Egypt and the Palestinian representatives of the West Bank and Gaza.

(B)   What is the US opinion on this issue?

Answer

The US indicated its attitude towards the Jerusalem issue in paragraph 4(A) above.
No procedures undertaken by one party in Jerusalem since the 1967 War must
prejudice the final status of Jerusalem.

Whatever solution is agreed upon, Jerusalem must remain one undivided entity.
There must be freedom of access to all holy places, whether Christian, Moslem or
Jewish, and freedom of worship. The basic rights of all the population must be
guaranteed. Holy places must fall under the authority of the representatives of the
religions concerned.

Question Eight

(A)   What would be the ultimate future of the Israeli settlements during and
after the transitional period? What would happen to the properties acquired
and constructions made there and what would their status be?

Answers

The Framework for Peace does not deal with the status of the Israeli settlements in the
occupied territories nor does it deal with properties acquired or construction made
there.

The scope of responsibility shouldered by the Self-governing Authority in the West
Bank and Gaza during the transitional period will be specified in an agreement secured
during negotiations between Egypt, Israel, Jordan and the Palestinians from the West
Bank and Gaza – as the Framework for Peace specifies – or other Palestinians as agreed

---

*   All provisions regarding Jerusalem could be included in the agreements that emerge from
either or both of these negotiations.

upon, from among the two delegations of Egypt and Jordan. During these negotiations, undertaken during the transitional period, the future of the Israeli settlements and their relationship with the Self-governing Authority must be decided.

The Framework for Peace specifies the establishment of a continuing committee representing Egypt, Jordan, Israel and the Palestinian Authority to discuss issues of mutual concern during the transitional period.

As far as the Israeli settlements and their future status after the transitional period are concerned, this must be decided during the negotiations about the final status of the West Bank and Gaza referred to in paragraph A.1(C).

(B)   As far as settlement policies are concerned, what would Israel's commitments be throughout the transitional period?

Answer

The US believes that Israel should not build new settlements in West Bank during the period of negotiations on the establishment of the Self-governing Authority. These negotiations must consider the question of the existing settlements, and any activity related to the establishment of new settlements during the transitional period.

(C)   What is the US attitude towards the two issues mentioned above?

Answer

The US regards any Israeli settlement established during the Israeli occupation as a violation of the Fourth Geneva Convention relating to the protection of individuals in time of war. But under a peaceful relationship, the parties to peace should define the mutual rights of inhabitants to do business, to work, to live, and to carry on other transactions in each other's territory.

Question Nine

(A)   Will the Israeli citizens who reside at present in the settlements be eligible for participation in the establishment of the Self-governing Authority and its subsequent activities?

Answer

The Israeli citizens living in the settlements established in the West Bank and Gaza may participate in the deliberations concerning the establishment of the Self-governing Authority, as individual members of the Israeli negotiating team. There is no specific reference to their participation as an independent delegation. The negotiations during the transitional period would specify whether or not they should take part in the Self-governing Authority.

(B)   What would be the status of the Israeli settlers living in the West Bank and Gaza during the transitional period? Would they be citizens of both areas? If so, what would be their citizenship at the end of the transitional period?

Answer

The negotiations referred to in paragraph, A.1.(b) which would specify the responsibilities of the Self-governing Authority, would deal with the status of the Israeli settlements and settlers in the West Bank and Gaza. How many would stay, and their status after the transitional period, would also become clear during the negotiations leading to the final status of the West Bank and Gaza, referred to in paragraph A.1.(c).

Question Ten

(A)   At the end of the five-year transitional period, would the people of the West Bank and Gaza be able to practise their right of self-determination and decide their own political future in complete freedom?

Answer

The Framework for Peace allows for the representatives of the West Bank and Gaza to participate actively and thoroughly in the negotiations that decide the final status of the West Bank and Gaza, and to sanction or reject the agreement concluded in these negotiations. The Framework specifies that the agreement concluded should recognize the legitimate rights of the Palestinian people and their just requirements. Wide acceptance of the agreement is believed to be to the advantage of all parties concerned. During the agreement's implementation in an atmosphere of complete freedom, there would be a strong local police force under the jurisdiction of the Self-governing Authority, that would observe the implementation of these rights without any political interference.

(B)   What is the US opinion concerning this issue?

Answer

The US supports the rights of the Palestinians to participate in the determination of their own future. The US believes that the Framework for Peace allows for the participation of the Palestinians in all steps taken for the determination of the political future of the West Bank and Gaza.

The US believes that paragraph A.1.(C)(2) does not exclude the people of the West Bank and Gaza from holding elections, following the conclusion of an agreement about the final status of the West Bank and Gaza, to choose their own representatives, who would in turn give the agreement concluded a vote of confidence.

Question Eleven

(A)   What solution does the Framework envisage for the problem of the Palestinian refugees living outside the occupied territories? What does the Framework envisage for the restoration of their rights?

Answer

Paragraph A.4 of the Framework indicates that Egypt, Israel and the other parties concerned should agree on a solution to the refugee problem, and that the agreed procedure must be just, prompt and permanent.

Paragraph A.3 of the Framework envisages that the continuing committee must make arrangements for those who left the West Bank and Gaza since 1967 to be allowed to return. Moreover, by the time the political institutions of the Self-governing Authority take shape, as a result of negotiations between the parties, the relationship between those political institutions and the Palestinians who are resident outside the area should be discussed between them.

(B)   What does the US regard as a basis for the solution of this problem, and how could these rights be specified?

Answer

The United States believes that a resolution of the refugee problem should reflect applicable United Nations Resolutions. Any programme for implementation must provide those refugees living outside the West Bank and Gaza with a choice and opportunity of settling themselves permanently in the context of present-day realities and circumstances.

Question Twelve

What future does the Framework envisage for the rest of the occupied Arab territories? What is the US attitude towards this issue?

Answer

The Framework specifies that the agreement is a model for peace between Israel and the neighbouring Arab countries. It specifies that peace must be just, durable and comprehensive, and all negotiations must lead to the implementation of all the paragraphs and principles of Resolutions 242 and 338.

Paragraph C.1. specifies particularly that the principles of the Framework must be adopted by all treaties between Israel, Jordan, Syria, Lebanon and Egypt. As far as the West Bank is concerned, paragraph A.1(C) points out that negotiations should be conducted on the basis of all the paragraphs and principles of Resolution 242, in order to find a solution for the issue of borders among other issues concerned.

The US still supports a comprehensive peace between Israel and all its Arab neighbours. As far as a peaceful settlement between Syria and Israel is concerned, the US supports all the principles and paragraphs contained in Resolution 242 for the implementation of such a settlement.

Question Thirteen

As far as security requirements are concerned, does the US support reciprocal arrangements, or does it see that these requirements should be implemented by one side only?

Answer

The US strongly supports reciprocal arrangements according to security needs within the Framework for Peace negotiations in the Middle East.

The preamble of the Framework refers specifically to reciprocity as the basis for security arrangements. The Framework also refers to the need of all parties for security. It refers to the security of Israel as well as to the security of its neighbours.

Question Fourteen

As Resolution 242 is the basis for negotiations leading to the settlement of the West Bank and Gaza issue and other issues connected with the conflict, what would the United States do if contradictory interpretations appear between the negotiating teams, particularly in view of the United States Government's previous interpretations of Security Council Resolution 242 and commitments based thereon which were the basis of acceptance by Jordan of Resolution 242?

Answer

The US will hold to its interpretation of 242, especially to that paragraph which specifies that withdrawal should take place on all fronts. If contradictory interpretations arise, the US will try – as it did in the intensive negotiations at Camp David – to reach a consensus among the parties and it will explain its own interpretation accordingly for a solution to the conflict. US interpretations of 242 remain the same since 1967.

Signed
Jimmy Carter

Source: Ministry of Foreign Affairs, Amman, translated from the Arabic.

Appendix C US Assistance to Jordan 1975–1989

US Economic assistance to Jordan 1975–1984 (US$m)

	1975	1976	1976*	1977	1978	1979	1980	1981	1982	1983	1984
I. Regular program											
1. Budget Support	67.5	37.0	66.0	45.0	40.0	30.0	20.0	n/a	n/a	n/a	n/a
2. Technical Assistance Grants	1.8	2.4	1.1	4.5	5.0	5.0	19.0	10.0	5.0	10.0	13.0
3. Development loans	18.6	7.0	15.5	20.5	48.0	58.0	30.0	n/a	10.0	10.0	7.0
II. Pl. 480											
1. Title I (loan)	6.4	11.2	n/a	9.2	6.3	5.4	n/a	n/a	n/a	n/a	n/a
2. Title II (Grant)	2.4	1.7	0.2	1.7	2.0	2.0	0.8	0.7	0.6	0.15	n/a
Total	96.7	59.3	82.8	80.9	101.3	100.4	69.8	10.7	15.6	20.15	20.0

US Fiscal Year July 1–June 30 for the years 1975–6 and from October 1–September 30 for the years 1977–84.
* Represents transition quarter: July/September.

US assistance to Jordan 1984–1989 (US$m) as of 5 July 1989

	US fiscal year ($000)					
	1984	1985	1986	1987	1988	1989
I. Economic (USAID)						
A. ESF						
Regular program (projects)						
1. Grants	10	15	9.5	6.6	11	15
2. Loans	7	5				
B. FY 1985 Supplemental Act – grants						
1. Projects		30	30	30		
2. Commodity Imports Program		50	50	60		
3. Jordan West Bank/Gaza Program			5.5			
C. Assistance to Jordan West Bank/Gaza Program – Grants		(25)*		14	7	(7.2)*
D. Housing Guarantee Program (East Bank) – Authorization				(10)*	(17.8)*	20**
30-year commercial loans – Borrowing		–	–	15	–	27
E. Food assistance (Section 416) – Grant				3.7	6.2	5
F. Centrally Funded Programs – Grants						
Sub-total USAID	17	100	95	129.4	24.2	67
II. Agricultural commodities (CCC Credit)						
GSM – 102 (3-year credit)		22.7	12.4	2.5	3	13
GSM – 103 (7-year credit)		–	–	17	10	65
EEP – Wheat subsidy						4
III. Military assistance (MAP)						
A. Credits	115	90	81.3	39.9	26.5	10
B. IMET (grants)	1.7	1.9	1.8	1.7	1.7	1.7
Total	133.7	214.6	190.5	190.5	65.4	160.7

* Non-add
** This amount will be borrowed in July 1989 and interest will be capitalized over 3 years for a total authorization of $27m.
Source: Ministry of Finance, Amman, Jordan.

Appendix D Arab assistance to Jordan paid in accordance with the 1978 Baghdad Summit Conference and 1980 Amman Arab Summits

Disbursement in US$m

Country	Scheduled annual amount	1979	1980	1981	1982	1983	1984	1985	1986	1987	1988	1989	Total
Saudi Arabia	357,143	357,143	357,143	357,143	357,143	357,143	357,143	357,143	357,143	357,143	297,620	59,524	3,571,431
Libya	196,428	n/a	n/a	n/a	n/a	n/a	n/a	n/a	n/a	n/a	n/a	n/a	n/a
Kuwait	196,429	196,429	196,429	196,429	196,429	196,429	117,857	25,000	25,000	41,178	59,034	65,176	1,315,390
Iraq	185,714	185,713	185,713	185,713	123,808	n/a	n/a	n/a	n/a	n/a	55,405	41,782	7,781,340
UAE	142,857	142,500	142,500	142,500	142,500	10,000	15,000	65,000	65,000	65,000	50,000	n/a	840,000
Algeria	89,286	89,290	n/a	n/a	n/a	n/a	n/a	n/a	n/a	n/a	n/a	n/a	89,290
Qatar	82,143	82,143	82,143	82,143	54,762	n/a	27,381	14,000	n/a	n/a	n/a	n/a	342,572
Total	1,250,000	1,053,218	963,928	963,928	874,642	563,572	517,381	461,143	447,143	463,321	462,059	166,482	6,936,817

Arab assistance to Jordan in accordance with the 1980 Amman Summit Conference. Disbursements in US$m

Country		Scheduled annually	1979	1980	1981	1982	1983	1984	1985	1986	1987	1988	Scheduled total	Paid total
Saudi Arabia	Libya	72,748	72,748	72,748	n/a	n/a	n/a	n/a	n/a	n/a	n/a	n/a	727,480	145,496
	Algeria	33,200	n/a	n/a	n/a	n/a	n/a	n/a	n/a	n/a	n/a	n/a	298,800	n/a
		105,948	72,748	n/a	n/a	n/a	n/a	n/a	n/a	n/a	n/a	n/a	n/a	n/a
Kuwait	Libya	39,988	39,988	n/a	n/a	n/a	n/a	n/a	n/a	n/a	n/a	n/a	399,800	39,988
	Algeria	18,192	n/a	n/a	n/a	n/a	n/a	n/a	n/a	n/a	n/a	n/a	163,728	n/a
		58,180	39,988	n/a	n/a	n/a	n/a	n/a	n/a	n/a	n/a	n/a	563,608	39,988
Iraq	Libya	37,800	37,800	37,800	37,800	n/a	n/a	n/a	n/a	n/a	n/a	n/a	378,000	113,400
	Algeria	17,196	n/a	17,257	17,225	n/a	n/a	n/a	n/a	n/a	n/a	n/a	154,764	34,482
		54,966	37,800	55,057	55,025	n/a	n/a	n/a	n/a	n/a	n/a	n/a	532,764	147,882
UAE	Libya	29,192	29,100	n/a	n/a	n/a	n/a	n/a	n/a	n/a	n/a	n/a	291,290	29,100
	Algeria	13,198	n/a	n/a	n/a	n/a	n/a	n/a	n/a	n/a	n/a	n/a	n/a	n/a
		42,390	29,100	n/a	n/a	n/a	n/a	n/a	n/a	n/a	n/a	n/a	410,702	29,100
Qatar	Libya	16,700	16,700	16,700	n/a	n/a	n/a	n/a	n/a	n/a	n/a	n/a	167,000	33,400
	Algeria	7,500	n/a	7,600	n/a	n/a	n/a	n/a	n/a	n/a	n/a	n/a	67,500	7,600
		24,200	16,700	24,300	n/a	n/a	n/a	n/a	n/a	n/a	n/a	n/a	234,500	41,000
Total		285,714	196,336	152,105	55,025	n/a	n/a	n/a	n/a	n/a	n/a	n/a	2,767,854	403,466

Notes: (1) Total amount paid for Libya was $361,384,000 from the scheduled due total of $1,964,280,000.
(2) Total amount paid for Algeria was $42,082,000 from the scheduled due total of $892,860,000.
(3) Oman granted Jordan Jordanian Dinars 49,000,000 in 1985; Jordanian Dinars 39,000,000 in 1986 and Jordanian Dinars in 1987 totalling Jordanian Dinars 98,760,000.

Source: Ministry of Finance, Amman.

Appendix E Peres–Hussain Agreement (the London document), 11 April 1987*

(Accord between the Government of Jordan, which has confirmed it to the Government of the United States, and the Foreign Minister of Israel, pending the approval of the Government of Israel. Parts 'A' and 'B', which will be made public upon agreement of the parties, will be treated as proposals of the United States to which Jordan and Israel have agreed. Part 'C' is to be treated with great confidentiality, as commitments to the United States from the Government of Jordan to be transmitted to the Government of Israel.)

A three-part understanding between Jordan and Israel

A. Invitation by the UN secretary general: The UN secretary general will send invitations to the five permanent members of the Security Council and to the parties involved in the Israeli–Arab conflict to negotiate an agreement by peaceful means based on UN Resolutions 242 and 338 with the purpose of attaining comprehensive peace in the region and security for the countries in the area, and granting the Palestinian people their legitimate rights.

B. Decisions of the international conference: The participants in the conference agree that the purpose of the negotiations is to attain by peaceful means an agreement about all the aspects of the Palestinian problem. The conference invites the sides to set up regional bilateral committees to negotiate bilateral issues.

C. Nature of the agreement between Jordan and Israel: Israel and Jordan agree that: (1) the international conference will not impose a solution, will not veto any agreement reached by the sides; (2) the negotiations will be conducted in bilateral committees in a direct manner; (3) the Palestinian issue will be discussed in a meeting of the Jordanian, Palestinian, and Israeli delegations; (4) the representatives of the Palestinians will be included in the Jordanian–Palestinian delegation; (5) participation in the conference will be based on acceptance of UN Resolutions 242 and 338 by the sides and the renunciation of violence and terror; (6) each committee will conduct negotiations independently; (7) other issues will be resolved through mutual agreement between Jordan and Israel.

This document of understanding is pending approval of the incumbent governments of Israel and Jordan. The content of this document will be presented and proposed to the United States.

---

* The London document was agreed to by Peres and Hussain in their meeting in London in April 1987. See *Ma'ariv*, 1 January, 1988, in Foreign Broadcast Information Service, *Daily Report: Near East and South Asia*, 4 January, 1988, pp.30–1.

Appendix F   Shamir's four-point plan, April 1989

Text of the official Foreign Ministry formulation of the Prime Minister's proposals

The four-point plan

(1) The Camp David partners – reconfirmation of the commitment to peace
Ten years ago, the peace treaty between Israel and Egypt was concluded on the basis of the Camp David accords. When the accords were signed, it was expected that more Arab countries would shortly join the circle of peace. This expectation was not realized. The strength of Israeli–Egyptian relations and the co-operation between the three partners to the accords have a decisive influence on the chances for Middle East peace, and the Israeli–Egyptian treaty is the cornerstone to the building of peace in the region.

Therefore, the Prime Minister has called on the three countries whose leaders affixed their signatures to the Camp David accords, the USA, Egypt and Israel, to renew, 10 years later, their commitment to the agreements and to peace.

(2) The Arab countries – from a state of war to a process of peace
The Prime Minister urged the USA and Egypt to call on the other Arab countries to desist from hostility towards Israel and to replace belligerency and boycott with negotiation and co-operation. Of all the Arab countries, only Egypt has recognized Israel and its right to exist. Many of these states actively participated in wars against Israel by direct involvement or indirect assistance. To this day, the Arab countries are partners in an economic boycott against Israel, refuse to recognize it and refuse to establish diplomatic relations with it.

The solution to the Arab–Israeli conflict and the building of confidence leading to a permanent settlement require a change in the attitude of the Arab countries towards Israel. Israel, therefore, calls on these states to put an end to this historic anomaly and to join direct bilateral negotiations aimed at normalization and peace.

(3) A solution to the refugee problem – an international effort
The Prime Minister has called for an international effort, led by the USA, and with the significant participation of Israel, to solve the problem of the Arab refugees. The refugee problem has been perpetuated by the leaders of the Arab countries, while Israel with its meagre resources is absorbing hundreds of thousands of Jewish refugees from Arab countries. Settling the refugees must not wait for a political process or come in its stead.

236

The matter must be viewed as a humanitarian problem and action must be taken to ease the human distress of the refugees and to ensure for their families appropriate living quarters and self-respect.

Some 300,000 people live in refugee camps in Judaea, Samaria and the Gaza district. In the 1970s, Israel unilaterally undertook the rehabilitation of residents of refugee camps in Gaza and erected 10 neighbourhoods in which 11,000 families reside. This operation was carried out in partnership with the residents despite PLO objections.

The time has now come to ensure appropriate infrastructure, living quarters and services for the rest of the residents of the camps who, at the same time, are victims of the conflict, hostages to it, and an element which perpetuates its continued existence. Goodwill and an international effort to allocate the necessary resources will ensure a satisfactory solution to this humanitarian effort and will help improve the political climate in the region.

(4) Free elections in Judaea, Samaria and Gaza on the road to negotiations
In order to bring about a process of political negotiations and in order to locate legitimate representatives of the Palestinian population, the Prime Minister proposes that free elections be held among the Arabs of Judaea, Samaria and Gaza – elections that will be free of the intimidation and terror of the PLO.

These elections will permit the development of an authentic representation that is not self-appointed from the outside. This representation will be comprised of people who will be chosen by the population in free elections and who will express, in advance, their willingness to take part in the following diplomatic process:

The aim of the elections is to bring about the establishment of a delegation that will participate in negotiations on an interim settlement, in which a self-governing administration will be set up. The interim period will serve as an essential test of co-operation and co-existence. It will be followed by negotiations on the final settlement, in which Israel will be prepared to discuss any option which will be presented.

Source: The Jerusalem Post, 14 April 1989 and BBC Monitoring Report, 15 April 1989.

Appendix G   Baker's five-point plan

Statement Issued by the Department of State, December 6, 1989

(1) The United States understands that because Egypt and Israel have been working hard on the peace process, there is agreement that an Israeli delegation should conduct a dialog with a Palestinian delegation in Cairo.

(2) The United States understands that Egypt cannot substitute itself for the Palestinians and Egypt will consult with Palestinians on all aspects of that dialog. Egypt will also consult with Israel and the United States.

(3) The United States understands that Israel will attend the dialog only after a satisfactory list of Palestinians has been worked out.

(4) The United States understands that the Government of Israel will come to the dialog on the basis of the Israeli Government's May 14 initiative. The United States further understands that Palestinians will come to the dialog prepared to discuss elections and the negotiating process in accordance with Israel's initiative. The United States understands, therefore, that Palestinians would be free to raise issues that relate to their opinions on how to make elections and the negotiating process succeed.

(5) In order to facilitate this process, the United States proposes that the Foreign Ministers of Israel, Egypt, and the United States meet in Washington within 2 weeks.

Source: US Embassy, London

Appendix H   Invitation to Madrid Peace Conference, 18 October 1991

After extensive consultations with Palestinians, Arab states and Israel, the United States and the Soviet Union believe that an historic opportunity exists to advance the prospects for genuine peace throughout the region. The United States and the Soviet Union are prepared to assist the parties to achieve a just, lasting and comprehensive peace settlement, through direct negotiations along two tracks, between Israel and the Arab states, and between Israel and the Palestinians, based on United Nations Security Council Resolutions 242 and 338. The objective of this process is real peace.

Toward that end, the President of the United States and the President of the USSR invite you to a peace conference, which their countries will co-sponsor, followed immediately by direct negotiations. The conference will be convened in Madrid on October 30, 1991. President Bush and President Gorbachev request your acceptance of this invitation no later than 6:00 p.m. Washington time, October 23, 1991, in order to ensure proper organization and preparation of the conference.

Direct bilateral negotiations will begin four days after the opening of the conference. Those parties who wish to attend multilateral negotiations will convene two weeks after the opening of the conference to organize those negotiations. The co-sponsors believe that those negotiations should focus on region-wide issues such as arms control and regional security, water, refugee issues, environment, economic development, and other subjects of mutual interest.

The co-sponsors will chair the conference which will be held at ministerial level. Governments to be invited include Israel, Syria, Lebanon, and Jordan. Palestinians will be invited and attend as part of a joint Jordanian–Palestinian delegation. Egypt will be invited to the conference as a participant. The European Community will be a participant in the conference alongside the United States and the Soviet Union and will be represented by its Presidency. The Gulf Cooperation Council will be invited to send its Secretary General to the conference as an observer, and GCC member states will be invited to participate in organizing the negotiations on multilateral issues. The United Nations will be invited to send an observer, representing the Secretary General.

The conference will have no power to impose solutions on the parties or veto agreements reached by them. It will have no authority to make decisions for the parties and no ability to vote on issues or results. The conference can reconvene only with the consent of all the parties.

With respect to negotiations between Israel and Palestinians who are part of the joint Jordanian–Palestinian delegation, negotiations will be conducted in phases, beginning with talks on interim self-government arrangements. These talks will be conducted with the objective of reaching agreement within one year. Once agreed, the interim self-government arrangements will last for a period of five years. Beginning the third year of the period of interim self-government arrangements, negotiations will take place on permanent status. These permanent status negotiations, and the negotiations between Israel and the Arab states, will take place on the basis of Resolutions 242 and 338.

It is understood that the co-sponsors are committed to making this process succeed. It is their intention to convene the conference and negotiations with those parties who agree to attend.

The co-sponsors believe that this process offers the promise of ending decades of confrontation and conflict and the hope of a lasting peace. Thus, the co-sponsors hope that the parties will approach these negotiations in a spirit of good will and mutual respect. In this way, the peace process can begin to break down the mutual suspicions and mistrust that perpetuate the conflict and allow the parties to begin to resolve their differences. Indeed, only through such a process can real peace and reconciliation among the Arab states, Israel, and the Palestinians be achieved. And only through this process can the peoples of the Middle East attain the peace and security they richly deserve.

Source: Madrid Peace Conference, 30 October 1991.

Appendix I Letter of Assurances to the Palestinians 18 October 1991

The Palestinian decision to attend a peace conference to launch direct negotiations with Israel represents an important step in the search for a comprehensive, just and lasting peace in the region. The United States has long believed that Palestinian participation is critical to the success of our efforts.

In the context of the process on which we are embarking, we want to respond to your request for certain assurances related to this process. These assurances constitute US understandings and intentions concerning the conference and ensuing negotiations.

These assurances are consistent with United States policy and do not undermine or contradict United Nations Security Council Resolutions 242 and 338. Moreover, there will be no assurances provided to one party that are not known to all the others. By this we can foster a sense of confidence and minimize chances for misunderstandings.

As President Bush stated in his March 6, 1991 address to Congress, the United States continues to believe firmly that a comprehensive peace must be grounded in United Nations Security Council Resolutions 242 and 338 and the principle of territory for peace. Such an outcome must also provide for security and recognition for all states in the region, including Israel, and for legitimate political rights of the Palestinian people. Anything else, the President noted, would fail the twin tests of fairness and security.

The process we are trying to create offers Palestinians a way to achieve these objectives. The United States believes that there should be an end to the Israeli occupation which can occur only through genuine and meaningful negotiations. The United States also believes that this process should create a new relationship of mutuality where Palestinians and Israelis can respect one another's security, identity, and political rights. We believe Palestinians should gain control over political, economic and other decisions that affect their lives and fate.

Direct bilateral negotiations will begin four days after the opening of the conference; those parties who wish to attend multilateral negotiations will convene two weeks after the opening of the conference to organize those negotiations. In this regard, the United States will support Palestinian involvement in any bilateral or multilateral negotiations on refugees and in all multilateral negotiations. The conference and the negotiations that follow will be based on UN Security Council Resolutions 242 and 338.

The process will proceed along two tracks through direct negotiations between Israel and Arab states and Israel and Palestinians. The United States is determined to achieve a comprehensive settlement of the Arab–Israeli conflict and will do its utmost to ensure that the process moves forward along both tracks toward this end.

In pursuit of a comprehensive settlement, all the negotiations should proceed as quickly as possible toward agreement. For its part, the United States will work for serious negotiations and will also seek to avoid prolongation and stalling by any party.

The conference will be co-sponsored by the United States and the Soviet Union. The European Community will be a participant in the conference alongside the United States and the Soviet Union and be represented by its Presidency. The conference can reconvene only with the consent of all the parties.

With regard to the role of the United Nations, the UN Secretary General will send a representative to the conference as an observer. The co-sponsors will keep the Secretary General apprised of the progress of the negotiation. Agreements reached between the parties will be registered with the UN Secretariat and reported to the Security Council, and the parties will seek the Council's endorsement of such agreements. Since it is in the interest of all parties for this process to succeed, while this process is actively ongoing the United States will not support a competing or parallel process in the United Nations Security Council.

The United States does not seek to determine who speaks for Palestinians in this process. We are seeking to launch a political negotiating process that directly involves Palestinians and offers a pathway for achieving the legitimate political rights of the Palestinian people and for participation in the determination of their future. We believe that a joint Jordanian–Palestinian delegation offers the most promising pathway toward this end.

Only Palestinians can choose their delegation members, who are not subject to veto from anyone. The United States understands that members of the delegation will be Palestinians from the territories who agree to negotiations on two tracks, in phases, and who are willing to live in peace with Israel. No party can be forced to sit with anyone it does not want to sit with.

Palestinians will be free to announce their component of the joint delegation and to make a statement during the opening of the conference. They may also raise any issue pertaining to the substance of the negotiations during the negotiations.

The United States understands how much importance Palestinians attach to the question of East Jerusalem. Thus, we want to assure you that nothing Palestinians do in choosing their delegation members in this phase of the process will affect their claim to East Jerusalem, or be prejudicial or precedential to the outcome of negotiations. It remains the firm position of the United States that Jerusalem must never again be a divided city and that its final status should be decided by negotiations. Thus, we do not recognize Israel's annexation of East Jerusalem or the extension of its municipal boundaries, and we encourage all sides to avoid unilateral acts that would exacerbate local tensions or make negotiations more difficult or preempt their final outcome. It is also the United States' position that a Palestinian resident in Jordan with ties to a prominent Jerusalem family would be eligible to join the Jordanian side of the delegation.

Furthermore, it is also the United States' position that Palestinians of East Jerusalem should be able to participate by voting in the elections for an interim self-governing authority. The United States further believes that Palestinians from East Jerusalem and Palestinians outside the occupied territories who meet the three criteria should be able to participate in the negotiations on final status. And the United States supports the right of Palestinians to bring any issue, including East Jerusalem, to the table.

Because the issues at stake are so complex and the emotions so deep the United States has long maintained that a transitional period is required to break down the walls of suspicion and mistrust and lay the basis for sustainable negotiations on the final status of the occupied territories. The purpose of negotiations on transitional arrangements is to effect the peaceful and orderly transfer of authority from Israel to Palestinians. Palestinians need to achieve rapid control over political, economic, and other decisions that affect their lives and to adjust to a new situation in which Palestinians exercise authority in the West Bank and Gaza. For its part, the United States will strive from the outset and encourage all parties to adopt steps that can create an environment of confidence and mutual trust, including respect for human rights.

As you are aware with respect to negotiations between Israel and Palestinians, negotiations will be conducted in phases, beginning with talks on interim self-government arrangements. These talks will be conducted with the objective of reaching agreement within one year. Once agreed, the interim self-government arrangements will last for a period of five years. Beginning the third year of the period of interim self-government arrangements, negotiations will take place on permanent status. It is the aim of the United States that permanent status negotiations will be concluded by the end of the transitional period.

It has long been our position that only direct negotiations based on UN Security Council Resolutions 242 and 338 can produce a real peace. No one can dictate the outcome in advance. The United States understands that Palestinians must be free, in opening statements at the conference and in the negotiations that follow, to raise any issue of importance to them. Thus, Palestinians are free to argue for whatever outcome they believe best meets their requirements. The United States will accept any outcome agreed by the parties. In this regard and consistent with longstanding US policies, confederation is not excluded as a possible outcome of negotiations on final status.

The United States has long believed that no party should take unilateral actions that seek to predetermine issues that can only be resolved through negotiations. In this regard the United States has opposed and will continue to oppose settlement activity in the territories occupied in 1967, which remains an obstacle to peace.

The United States will act as an honest broker in trying to resolve the Arab–Israeli conflict. It is our intention, together with the Soviet Union, to play the role of a driving force in this process to help the parties move forward toward a comprehensive peace. Any party will have access to the co-sponsors at any time. The United States is prepared to participate in all stages of the negotiations, with the consent of the parties to each negotiation.

These are the assurances that the United States is providing concerning the implementation of the initiative we have discussed. We are persuaded that we have a real opportunity to accomplish something very important in the peace process. And we are prepared to work hard together with you in the period ahead to build on the progress we have made. There will be difficult challenges for all parties. But with Palestinians' continued commitment and creativity, we have a real chance of moving to a peace conference and to negotiations and then on toward the broader peace that we all seek.

Source: Madrid Peace Conference, 30 October 1991.

Notes

Prologue

1. Michael Brecher, *The Foreign Policy System of Israel* (Oxford University Press, London and New York, 1972), p. 137.
2. Bahgat Korany and Ali E. Hillal Dessouki, *The Foreign Policies of Arab States* (Westview Press: Boulder, Co. and London, and the American University in Cairo Press, Egypt, 1984), p. 35.
3. Mohamed E. Salim, 'The Survival of a Nonstate Actor: The Foreign Policy of the Palestinian Liberation Organization', in Korany and Dessouki, ibid., p. 35.
4. John Amos II, *Palestinian Resistance, Organization of a National Movement* (Pergamon Press, New York, 1980), p. 150.
5. Salim, 'The Survival of a Nonstate Actor', p. 198. For a detailed analysis see Ernest Hass, *Beyond the National State, Functionalism and International Organizations* (Stanford University Press, Stanford, CA., 1964), pp. 469–75. See also Judy Bartelson, *The Palestinian Arabs: A Non-State National System Analysis* (Sage, Beverly Hills, CA., 1976), pp. 11–12.
6. Salim, 'Survival of a Nonstate Actor', p. 198.
7. Yehoshafat Harkabi, *Washington Post Outlook*, 7 August 1988.
8. Ibid.
9. Robert Neumann, interview, August 1988, Washington.

1 Introduction

1. Walter Laqueur and Barry Rubin (eds.), *The Arab–Israeli Reader, A Documentary History of the Middle East Conflict* (Penguin Books, Harmondsworth, 1984), p. 900.
2. Ibid. and Benjamin Shwadran, *Jordan, a State of Tension* (New York, Council for Middle Eastern Affairs Press, 1959), p. 138; quoted from 'Parliamentary Papers, Mandate for Palestine' together with a note by the Secretary-General relating to its application to the territory known as Trans-Jordan (md. 785, 1922).
3. Laqueur and Rubin, *Arab–Israeli Reader*, p. 900.
4. Ibid., pp. 141–2.
5. Hassan Ben Talal, Crown Prince of Jordan, *Palestinian Self-Determination: A Study of the West Bank and Gaza Strip* (Quartet Books, London, 1981) p. 64. See also Hassan Ben Talal, *A Study on Jerusalem* (London and New York, Longman in association with the publishing committee, Amman, 1979), p. 23.

6. Shwadran, *Jordan*, p. 296.
7. Hassan Ben Talal, *Palestinian Self-Determination*, p. 41.
8. Shwadran, *Jordan*, p. 298.
9. Korany and Dessouki, *Foreign Policies of Arab States*, p. 3.
10. Address to the Royal United Services Institute (RUSI), London, 6 December 1984.
11. Michael C. Hudson, 'The Integration Puzzle in Arab Regional Politics' in Hudson, Michael C. (ed.) *The Arab Future: Critical Issues* (Centre for Contemporary Arab Studies, Georgetown University, 1979), pp. 81–5.
12. Hassan Ben Talal, *Search for Peace* (Macmillan, London, 1984), p. 55.
13. Brecher, *Foreign Policy System of Israel*, pp. 1–7.
14. Susan Strange, 'What About International Relations!' in Strange, Susan (ed.), *Paths to International Political Economy* (George Allen and Unwin, London, 1984), p. 184.
15. Jordan shares these dilemmas with other Arab countries. See Korany and Dessouki, *Foreign Policies of Arab States*, p. 8.
16. Address to the RUSI, 6 December 1984.

2 Kissinger's legacy and imprint on the Middle East

1. See David H. Ott, *Palestine in Perspective: Politics, Human Rights and the West Bank* (Quartet Books, London, 1980), p. 1.
2. *Keesing's Contemporary Archives* (Vol. XX, 1974), pp. 26317–18.
3. Interview, July 1987, Amman. The story that followed was narrated by former Prime Minister Rifai as heard from President Assad. Kissinger's version appeared in the US edition of Henry Kissinger, *Years of Upheaval* (Little, Brown and Company, Boston, Toronto, 1982), pp. 782, 783.
4. *Keesing's Contemporary Archives*, (Vol. XX., 1974), pp. 26317–18.
5. Zeid Rifai, interview, July 1987, Amman. Peter Rodman, however, was interviewed as the Deputy Adviser to the President for National Security Affairs in June 1988. Although he denied using the word 'ceiling' to Rifai, he admitted saying that a prior understanding took place between the US, Egypt, Syria and Israel and excluding Jordan about the subject matter of the next phase of negotiations. 'It was not a question of deception. It was a question that Jordan was going to be a harder case and it was going to wait until after the Syrian negotiations. Jordan was not tricked at the conference, but it was let down. The negotiations fell through in 1974.' But he added: 'Jordan was right to worry that the longer it was left out, the longer it took the risk of being left out for good.'
   Rodman regretted saying all this to Jordan's Prime Minister. He explained that he wanted to make a point. 'My point was that we should try to duplicate the same conditions for Jordan and for the Palestinians and have as much prior understanding as we can have on the subject matter and the approach.'
6. Zeif Rifai, interview, July 1987, Amman.
7. Henry Kissinger, *Years of Upheaval* (Weidenfeld and Nicolson, London, 1982) pp. 450–656.
8. Ibid., p. 515.

9. Ibid., pp. 619 and 753.

10. Ibid., pp. 747–92 for details.

11. Nadav Safran, *Israel, the Embattled Ally* (Belknap Press, Cambridge, MA. and London, 1987), p. 642.

12. Bernard Reich, *Quest for Peace, United States–Israel Relations and the Arab–Israel Conflict* (Transaction Books, New Brunswick, NJ., 1977), p. 293.

13. Ibid., p. 359, for more details.

14. Peter Rodman, interview, June 1988, Washington.

15. Zeid Rifai, interview, July 1987, Amman. Rodman denied hearing anyone say that the Jericho offer was a final peace treaty. He understood the offer to imply a first step that the Israelis could 'sell to their body politic' in order to get them used to the idea. He was convinced by Israel's explanation that any bigger step would cause a government collapse and the coming of Menachem Begin to power. Harold Saunders, who accompanied Kissinger during his shuttle diplomacy, stressed the same point, but added that Kissinger often stated a cardinal principle in his step-by-step approach: 'The interim step will only be viable if we do not address issues of a final settlement. You have to match an interim move on territory with an interim move on peace.' Interview, July 1988, Washington. Another associate, former Assistant Secretary of State Atherton, stated, however, that Kissinger had many private meetings without his staff. Interview, July 1988, Washington.

16. See Arab League, *Taswiyat Al Niza Fi Al Shark Al Awsat, Masharee' Wa Mubadarat* (*The Settlement of the Conflict in the Middle East, Plans and Initiatives*), The General Secretariat, 15 June, 1985, p. 286.

17. Adnan Abu Odeh, former Minister of Royal Court and former Information Minister in Jordan, interview, August 1985, Amman.

18. Kissinger, *Years of Upheaval*, p. 199.

19. Zeid Rifai, interview, July 1987, Amman. This statement reminded the writer of an event related by the US Ambassador to Rabat in 1974. Ambassador Neumann said that Kissinger was the driving force behind sending an American citizen on a Saudi military plane as an emissary from King Feisal with a message to the head of the Saudi delegation to the Rabat summit. 'It was an unusual thing to do', Mr Neumann said. But he also complained that Kissinger told him the minimum about what was going on. This annoyed him and he protested directly to Kissinger. Interview, July 1988, Washington.

Ambassador Veliotes, who served in Israel in 1974, also complained of being kept in the dark. 'Kissinger was not allowing anyone to communicate anything to the Embassy', he said. Interview, July 1988, Washington.

20. Mudar Badran, interview, August 1985, Amman.

21. Zeid Rifai, interview, July 1987.

22. Adnan Abu Odeh, interview, August 1985, Amman.

23. Ministry of Foreign Affairs Archives, Amman.

24. Mudar Badran, interview, August 1985, Amman. William Quandt suggested that the key moment in the conference came when King Hussain was asked what he had been able to get from the Americans. When he said that the Americans had offered 'nothing', the other Arab leaders all turned to the PLO. The logic was that

since Jordan could not deliver any Israeli concession via the US, why not turn to the PLO? Interview, June 1988, Washington.

The same point was made by Robert Oakley of the National Security Council, interview, July 1988, Washington.

25. Zeid Rifai, interview, August 1985, Amman.

26. According to Saunders Kissinger did not understand Sadat's lack of influence in the Arab world. Thus, he must have miscalculated Sadat's ability to control the situation at Rabat. Ambassador Veliotes stressed the same point. Ambassador Atherton, on the other hand, concluded that Rifai must have over-estimated Kissinger's 'manipulative capabilities'. Interviews, July 1988, Washington.

27. Adnan Abu Odeh, interview, August 1985, Amman.

28. Address to the 17th Session of the Palestinian National Council, Amman, November 1984.

29. Philip Windsor, interview, London School of Economics, 5 January 1986, London.

30. Stephen J. Artner, 'The Middle East: A Change for Europe?' *International Affairs* (Vol.LVI, No.3, Summer 1980), p. 422. Ambassador Neumann also emphasized this point at a later date. 'The role of the PLO was emphasized in order to keep them in hand and to pull them away from too extremist tendencies.' The Arab leaders may have wanted to 'make sure by controlling them that they would not become a menace to the respective Arab countries', he said. Assad's role in doing so was cited as an example. Interview, July 1988, Washington.

31. In an interview with Mario Soares, 30 January 1983, Ministry of Foreign Affairs Archives, Amman.

32. Ministry of Foreign Affairs Archives, Amman, translated from Arabic.

33. Harold Saunders, interview, July 1988, Washington.

34. Robert Oakley, interview, July 1988, Washington.

35. Also the conclusion of William Quandt. See William Quandt, *Decade of Decisions* (University of California Press, Berkeley and London, 1979), p. 211.

36. Quoted by Alfred M. Lilienthal, *The Zionist Connection* (Dodd, Mead and Company, New York, 1979), p. 751.

37. William Quandt commented: 'The problem is that the stability of the status quo is likely to be illusory, and maintaining the military balance in Israel's favour is not necessarily a deterrent to war and to the use of oil as a political weapon.' See Quandt, *Decade of Decisions*, p. 289.

38. The Brookings Institution, *Towards Peace in the Middle East, Report of a Study Group*, 1975. See also Quandt, *Decade of Decisions* pp. 290, 292.

39. Following the outbreak of the Palestinian uprising (*Intifada*) in the West Bank and Gaza he suggested a way out for Israel on the following lines: cede a demilitarized Gaza and demilitarized parts of the West Bank not essential to Israel's security to Arab sovereignty; retain security posts in those ceded areas to verify demilitarization; grant the people of these ceded areas self-government except in the Israeli security zones and let Jordan alone, or Jordan with Egypt and Saudi Arabia, act as a custodian under UN auspices until a final peace settlement is reached. Kissinger suggested a 5-year interim peace settlement to test practical coexistence between Israel and the self-governing Arab entity. He also expressed a desire to see the

Allon Plan serve as a starting point for discussion. In such an approach, he would see ideas implicit in Camp David being applied. Kissinger urged Israel to implement major portions of such a plan unilaterally, though it would then have to retain a larger role in the security field. For more details see Kissinger's article in the *Washington Post Outlook*, 15 May 1988.

40. Quoted by Quandt, *Decade of Decisions*, p. 278. Two of Kissinger's associates gave an illuminating account of their understanding of a step-by-step diplomacy: 'Atherton argued that "it was politically too much for Israel and the US to discuss the two issues of final borders and sovereignty at one time. If it happened it was bound to overburden peace negotiations. But although there was no termination date given, the disengagement agreements indicated that they were only a step towards a final peace."' Interview, July 1988, Washington.

    Harold Saunders was not as sympathetic towards what was achieved. 'Step-by-step is only valid if it is done with commitment to stay on the road and to reach the final destination. The value of the process lies, in part, in leaving something open-ended. The steps have to be designed to create new political opportunities. It is not open-ended in terms of the equation of the final settlement.' Clarifying further he added: 'I favour step-by-step only if the steps are creatively designed to make it more politically possible to move towards the final destination. The only way with a "body politic" which is deeply divided is to get interim agreements that are politically "eligible", in order to make an "eligible" peace, provided that there is a commitment to the end-purpose.' Interview, July 1988, Washington.

41. Mudar Badran, interview, August 1985, Amman.

42. Kissinger, *Years of Upheaval*, p. 612.

43. As quoted by Reich, *Quest for Peace*, p. 405.

44. Quoted by Noam Chomsky, *The Fateful Triangle: The United States, Israel and the Palestinians* (South End Press, Boston, 1983), p. 351. See also Henry Kissinger, *White House Years* (Weidenfeld and Nicholson and Michael Joseph, London, 1979), p. 556.

45. *Davar*, 13 November 1981. Column by David Bloch, quoted by Chomsky, *The Fateful Triangle*, p. 464.

46. Marwan Al Qassem, in talks with the Prime Minister of Holland, 13 September 1982, Ministry of Foreign Affairs Archives, Amman.

47. Ibid., talks with Hans-Dietrich Genscher, Foreign Minister of West Germany, 12 July 1982. Ambassador Neumann echoed what Qassem was saying when he complained: 'Every American Administration falls into the trap. The Israelis feel insecure . . . that is true. But when you feel that insecure, nothing that you do will ever make them feel secure.' He added: 'Each concession is taken as a given and it leads to the next. There is no limit to Israel's arrogance. They simply accept what we give as a demonstration of their power. Grateful? No. The word does not exist in their cultural pattern.' Interview, July 1988, Washington.

3 Carter picks up the threads

1. Zbigniew Brzezinski, *Power and Principle: Memoirs of the National Security Advisor, 1977–1981* (Weidenfeld and Nicolson, London, 1983), pp. 81 and 83.

2. Laqueur and Rubin, *Arab–Israeli Reader*, p. 608.
3. Ministry of Foreign Affairs Archives, Amman. For the published items see also Moshe Dayan, *Breakthrough, A Personal Account of the Egypt–Israel Peace Negotiations* (Alfred A. Knopf, New York 1981) pp. 70–1.
4. Ministry of Foreign Affairs Archives, Amman.
5. Ibid. These points were translated from the Arabic as read in the Archives.
6. For details see William Quandt, *Camp David, Peacemaking and Politics* (The Brookings Institution, Washington, DC, 1986) pp. 77–81.
7. Ministry of Foreign Affairs Archives, Amman.
8. Ibid.
9. For further details see Quandt, *Camp David*, pp. 85 and 100.
10. Ministry of Foreign Affairs Archives, Amman. For a comprehensive review of Israel's attitude towards Geneva see Moshe Dayan, *Breakthrough* (Weidenfeld and Nicolson, London, 1981), pp. 1–74.
11. Ibid. Dayan, however, showed some flexibility during his talks with President Carter on 19 September and 4 October 1977. On 19 September Carter specifically asked him to accept a unified Arab delegation, including Palestinians who would not be well-known PLO members, for the opening session of Geneva; thereafter, negotiations could be held bilaterally, except on the Palestinian question. Dayan did not object provided that the committee to discuss the Palestinian question discussed the refugee problem and not territory. The Palestinians would have to be part of a Jordanian delegation. Dayan then introduced the idea of West Bank Mayors joining with King Hussain, even if they were with the PLO, provided they had not carried out military operations against Israel.

He showed more flexibility on 4 October. He told Carter that Israel would accept Palestinians in the opening session of the Conference within a unified Arab delegation and not as members of the Jordanian delegation. They could also include PLO sympathizers and even PLO members from the West Bank and Gaza, provided Israel was communicating with them. He even went so far as to concede that the future of the West Bank and Gaza could be discussed in a multilateral setting including Israel, Jordan, Egypt and the Palestinians. Dayan told Vance the same day – after an American assurance that Israel would be informed in advance who the Palestinians would be for 'reasonable Israeli screening' – that Palestinians within a unified Arab delegation could have the same status as the other Arab participants. Even the future of the West Bank and Gaza could be discussed with the Palestinians, and not just with Jordan and Egypt. It was understood in Washington that, in the last resort, it was the more militant Israeli Prime Minister – Menachim Begin – not his foreign minister who influenced the Israeli Cabinet. For further details see Quandt, *Camp David*, pp. 113, 114, 127, 128.
12. This consistent Israeli attitude forced Carter to change tactics. While he had previously thought that Geneva would make sense only if there was careful preparation, by the end of July he began to regard Geneva as no more than a forum in which negotiations would take place. And the reason for this, according to William Quandt, was Begin. Begin would not budge on substance in the

pre-Geneva period, thus undercutting the idea of a 'well-prepared conference'. See Quandt, *Camp David*, p. 87.

13. Stanley Hoffman, 'A New Policy for Israel', in John N. J. Moore (ed.) *The Arab Israeli Conflict, Readings and Documents* (The American Society of International Law, Princeton, NJ, 1977), p. 834.
14. BBC News, 2 October 1985.
15. Ministry of Foreign Affairs Archives, Amman. William Quandt's account, though, indicated that Sadat counted on American pressure on Israel. His insistence that the US should work out all the details before any negotiations began and that Geneva would essentially consist of a signing ceremony, clashed with Carter's change of tactics – by the end of July 1977 – in deference to Israel. Carter's new emphasis on Geneva as a venue for real negotiations alarmed Sadat lest Syria gain a veto over his moves. See Quandt, *Camp David*, p. 97.
16. Ministry of Foreign Affairs, Amman.
17. Ibid.
18. Mudar Badran, interview, August 1985, Amman.
19. Ministry of Foreign Affairs Archives, Amman. Most of Assad's analysis seemed correct. According to Quandt, Sadat, who was genuinely popular with the American public, was in Carter's view worth a fight with Begin. But the Palestinians had no US constituency. Moreover, while Carter reassured Assad that nothing could keep the Arab parties from co-ordinating their positions at Geneva if they chose to do so, and that the various working groups could periodically report back to the plenary session, no mention was made in the Dayan–Carter working paper of 4 October 1977 of a role for the plenary other than to convene the conference. Reference to the PLO was dropped, and most galling to the Syrians, they were the only party left out of the discussions on the future of the West Bank and Gaza. See Quandt, *Camp David*, pp. 316 and 135–6.
20. One of Washington's experienced politicians, Ambassador Veliotes, commented: 'The sad thing is that we were caught in our own rhetoric. The initial agreement with Israel in September 1975 did not preclude contact with the PLO; it precluded negotiations with the PLO . . . recognition of the PLO as the negotiating partner. It was cleverly put to leave a loop-hole. Vance closed that loop-hole without talking to anyone because he thought it was dishonourable.' Veliotes suggested that talking might not have led to a mutually agreed settlement, but it was a step in the right direction. Interview, July 1988, Washington.

Former Assistant Secretary of State Atherton maintained that Kissinger's promise to Israel had been either misinterpreted or given a very strict interpretation by subsequent American administrations. It was also taken out of context. The promise was made in the context of reconvening Geneva. Interview, July 1988, Washington.

21. Quandt, *Camp David*, pp. 118–19.
22. *Al Ahram*, Cairo, 10 November 1977.
23. *Al Ba'th*, Damascus, 18 November 1977.
24. *L'Orient-Le Jour*, Beirut, 18 November 1877.
25. *Ha-Olam Hazah*, Israel, 23 November 1977.

26. *Al Ahram*, Cairo, 22 January 1978.
27. Events between December 1977 and September 1978 have been vividly narrated and analyzed by William Quandt. See Quandt, *Camp David*, pp. 158–219.

4 The Camp David accords and Jordan

1. For further details see Quandt, *Camp David*, pp. 177, 218 and 219.
2. Seth P. Tillman, *The United States in the Middle East, Interests and Obstacles* (Indiana University Press, Bloomington, IN, 1982) p. 99. See also Brzezinski, *Power and Principle*, p. 97.
3. Jimmy Carter, *Keeping Faith, Memoirs of A President* (Collins, London, 1982). pp. 277, 292, 281.
4. Ibid., p. 409.
5. Ibid., pp. 300, 302, 354, 396, 395.
6. Mudar Badran, interview, August 1985, Amman.
7. Brzezinski, *Power and Principle*, p. 283.
8. *Al Ahram*, Cairo, 10 July 1980, quoted by *Documents and Statements on Middle East Peace, 1979–1982* (A report presented for the Subcommittee on Europe and the Middle East of the Committee on Foreign Affairs, US House of Representatives, by Foreign Affairs and National Defence Division, Congressional Research Service, Library of Congress, June 1982, printed for the use of the Committee on Foreign Affairs, US Government Printing Office, Washington, 1982).
9. Ministry of Foreign Affairs Archives, Amman.
10. Ibid.
11. Mudar Badran, interview, August 1985, Amman.
12. *The Washington Post*, 26 May 1980.
13. Paul C. Bradley, *The Camp David Peace Process* (Tompson and Rutter, Grantham, NH., 1981), p. 40. See also the official documentation of USAID, US Foreign Assistance Programs to Egypt and Israel, 1974–88.
14. These points were emphasized during talks between the Foreign Minister of Jordan, Marwan Al Qassem, and the Belgian Foreign Minister on 13 September 1982, Ministry of Foreign Affairs Archives, Amman.
15. Ministry of Foreign Affairs Archives, Amman.
16. When interviewed in 1988, however, Prince Hassan presented Jordan's view: 'When we speak of the occupied territories obviously we include Arab Jerusalem. But please distinguish between the importance of the region from Ramallah to Bethlehem which is a part of the Jerusalem region, and Jerusalem – the corpus separatum – that is to say, the ecumenical problem within the old city walls. Within the ecumenical problem, obviously there is the outstanding problem of the protection of the holy places and of the people against fanatics who defile Moslem holy places.'
    Prince Hassan's solution to the question of Jerusalem outlined the following points. First, the unity of the City must be maintained with no physical barriers dividing East and West Jerusalem. Second, political sovereignty applies as much to the Palestinians as to the Israelis. Third, there must be an arrangement concerning the ecumenical question. The greatest single contribution to sanity in

the region is to separate church and state. Fourth, there must be an overall borough solution.

17. Details of the Begin Autonomy Plan can be found in Ott, *Palestine in Perspective* p. 4. But for a thorough understanding of Israel's thinking at Camp David see Dayan, *Breakthrough*, pp. 98–279.

18. Tillman, *The United States in the Middle East*, pp. 208–9.

19. Mudar Badran, interview, August 1985, Amman. The name of the Sheikh has not been disclosed.

20. Hanna Odeh, former Minister of Finance, interview, August 1985, Amman.

21. Mudar Badran, interview, August 1985, Amman.

22. *The New York Times*, 20 March 1979.

23. Ibid., 25 April 1980.

24. Interview with King Hussain in NBC, 'Meet the Press', 22 June 1980, quoted in *International Documents on Palestine* (Institute of Palestinian Studies, Beirut, 1980), p. 197.

25. *The New York Times*, 20 March 1979.

26. Kissinger, *White House Years*, pp. 345 and 374.

27. Interview with King Hussain on CNN (US Cable News Network), broadcast from Amman Home Service, 18 August 1984. A detailed account can also be obtained from the BBC, Summary of World Broadcasts, 20 August 1984.

28. At the National Democratic Conference in Louisville, KY., November 23, 1975. See Jimmy Carter, *The Presidential Campaigns*, Vol.I, (United States Government Printing Office, Washington, 1978), p. 82.

29. Tillman, *United States in the Middle East*, p. 223, quoted from 'Memorandum of Agreement between the Governments of Israel and the US: The Geneva Peace Conference', 1 September 1975 in 'Early Warning System in Sinai', Hearings before the Committee on Foreign Relations, US Senate, p. 941.

30. A lot of this information is derived from a report sent by the Arab League Office at the United Nations to all Arab governments, File 2, No.326, 23 September 1980, translated from Arabic.

31. Ministry of Finance, Amman. For details see Appendix D.

5 An evaluation of the development of American strategy for the 1980s

1. Brzezinski, *Power and Principle*, p. 81.

2. Ibid., pp. 261 and 262.

3. Tillman, *The US in the Middle East*, p. 99. Also reported widely in the American Press, 6 March 1978. Ambassador Robert Neumann commented that in face of Begin's tough stand, Carter determined to rescue a portion of what he regarded as a singular political achievement at Camp David, so he de-emphasized the Palestinian question and settled for Egyptian–Israeli peace. This was not only a 'political judgment', but also a judgement tied to Carter's personality. It was too difficult for Carter to pursue a single determined course. Interview, July 1988, Washington.

4. Tillman, *The US in the Middle East*, p. 24. See also *The New York Times*, 3 July 1978 and *The Washington Post*, 15 August 1978.

5. Brzezinski, *Power and Principle*, p. 235.
6. See Carter, *Keeping Faith*, p. 269 for his reaction upon receiving the news of Sadat's assassination.
7. Quoted by Arthur Schlesinger Jr., 'Foreign Policy and the American Character', *Foreign Affairs* (Vol.LXII, No.1, Fall 1983), pp. 1–16.
8. Brzezinski used this expression in a speech delivered at Georgetown University on 23 April 1981, repeated in *Power and Principle*, p. 530.
9. Press interview in mid-January 1980, documented in *International Documents on Palestine 1980*, p. 10.
10. *Al Nahar Al Arabi Wa Dawli*, Paris, No. 186, 24–30 November 1980.
11. Jimmy Carter, *The Blood of Abraham* (Sidgwick & Jackson, London, 1985), p. 200.

6 The evolution of Reagan's strategy

1. Interview with King Hussain on CNN (US Cable News Network) broadcast from Amman Home Service, 18 August 1984. A detailed account is also given in BBC Summary of World Broadcasts (SWB), 20 August 1984.
2. *The Washington Post*, 15 August 1979.
3. *Christian Science Monitor*, 2 February 1981.
4. *Mideast Observer*, 15 February 1981. Ambassador Neumann commented that President Reagan did not usually have deep understanding of anything. He had certain ideological concepts but with complex issues he floundered. He came to office with no understanding of why the Middle East was important, what was the Palestinian question, nor even the Israeli issue. 'Both Reagan and Carter are the products of peculiar unusual circumstances in American history; Carter as a reaction to Vietnam and Reagan as a reaction to Carter.' Interview, July 1988, Washington.
5. Ambassador Veliotes, who served in both Israel and the Arab world, commented that there were a lot of people who came to the Reagan Administration with the belief that there was no Palestinian problem, and that the real concern of the Arabs was not the Palestinians but Moscow. Hence two agendas were developed: an overt agenda, i.e., militarization of the problems of the Middle East which was part and parcel of the way the administration was looking at most of the world, and a hidden agenda, i.e., if you stop worrying about the Palestinians you had no real danger point of controversy with Israel. The second part of the scenario was that Israel's dependence on the US became very uncomfortable to it and its supporters in the US unless it could be perceived as offering something tangible in return; hence the strategic co-operation. Interview, July 1988, Washington.
6. The information in this paragraph came from an Uncensored Draft Report by the US General Accounting Office (GAO) in the Ministry of Foreign Affairs Archives, Amman, a censored version of which appeared on 24 June 1983, Amman.
7. Ministry of Foreign Affairs Archives, Amman.
8. Yitzhak Shamir, 'Israel's Role in a Changing Middle East', *Foreign Affairs* (Vol.LX, No.4, Spring 1982), pp. 789–801.

9. Kenneth Dam, Assistant Secretary of State: Address to Council of American Law, 16 May 1985, Ministry of Foreign Affairs Archives, Amman.
10. Walid Khalidi, 'Regio Politics: Toward a US Policy on the Palestinian Problem', *Foreign Affairs* (Vol.LIX, No.5, Summer 1981), pp. 1050–63.
11. J. E. Peterson, 'American Policy in the Gulf and the Sultanate of Oman', *American Arab Affairs* (no.8, Spring 1984), p. 119.
12. George Shultz, Statement before the Committee on Foreign Affairs, US House of Representatives, 19 February 1985, Ministry of Foreign Affairs Archives, Amman.

7 The US, Israel and Jordan: collaboration and discord

1. *Issue Brief*, Order Code IB85066, Israel: US Foreign Assistance Facts, Clyde K. Mark, Foreign Affairs and National Defense Division, Congressional Research Service, 15 January 1988, pp. 12, 13.
2. *The International Herald Tribune*, 3 November 1981, and *The Times*, London, 4 November 1981.
3. Prince Hassan of Jordan, interview, 4 September 1985, Amman.
4. Ministry of Foreign Affairs Archives, Amman.
5. Quoted in Michael Collins Dunn, 'Looking Over Jordan, The Politics of a US Arms Sale', *Defence and Foreign Affairs*, December 1985, p. 35. Dunn argued that the story of arms supply to Jordan has more to do with US domestic politics, power and other considerations. See ibid., pp. 22, 23, 28, 29, 30, 35, 38.
6. *The International Herald Tribune*, 21 June 1980.
7. Hassan Ben Talal, *Search for Peace*, p. 140.
8. Most of the information below was checked and confirmed by General Tayseer Za'rour, General Command Headquarters, Amman, August 1985.
9. *The International Herald Tribune*, 21 June 1981.
10. *The Guardian*, 28 June 1984.
11. Sharif Zeid Ben Shaker, interview, August 1985, Amman.
12. *The Observer*, 28 February 1982, Patrick Seale's interview with King Hussain. See also, *The Guardian*, 30 January 1984.
13. Prince Hassan of Jordan, interview, 4 September 1985, Amman.
14. Interview with *L'Espresso*, 2 February 1981, documented in *Documents and Statements on Middle East Peace, 1979–1982*, p. 92.
15. Ministry of Foreign Affairs Archives, Amman.
16. *Al Mustaqbal*, Paris, 5 September 1981.
17. *Time Magazine*, 14 April 1980.
18. This point was also stressed by Jordan's Foreign Minister, Marwan Al Qassem, during talks held in Amman with the Foreign Minister of the Netherlands, on 9 February 1983. Qassem elaborated that 'Israel's excuse that the Arab world is vast therefore it can absorb the Palestinians is erroneous. The problem is not "their distribution", it is the fact that they have been kicked out of their own country. They refuse to be distributed because they fear that their cause will be cancelled by default.' Ministry of Foreign Affairs Archives, Amman.
19. BBC, SWB Monitoring Report, 24 November 1984.

20. This point was stressed during talks between Foreign Minister Qassem and the Foreign Minister of Belgium, held in Amman in September 1982. Ministry of Foreign Affairs Archives, Amman.

21. This point was stressed during talks between Foreign Minister Qassem and the West German Foreign Minister, held in Amman in July 1982. Ministry of Foreign Affairs Archives, Amman.

22. This point was stressed during talks between Foreign Minister Qassem and the Foreign Minister of Belgium, held in Amman in September 1982.

23. This point was stressed by Foreign Minister Qassem, during talks with the West German Foreign Minister in July 1982, Belgian Foreign Minister on 13 September 1982 and the Dutch Foreign Minister on 9 February 1983. Ministry of Foreign Affairs Archives, Amman.

8 Two cases of collaboration and discord

1. *The Times*, London, 5 August 1982.
2. *Monday Morning*, Lebanon, 6–12 September 1982.
3. Ministry of Foreign Affairs Archives, Amman.
4. *Israel in Lebanon*, Report of the International Commission to inquire into reported violations of international law during the invasion of Lebanon, 28 August 1982–29 November 1982 (Ithaca Press, London, 1983), p. 18.
5. As in the 'Caroline Case'; See D. J. Harris, *Cases and Materials on International Law* (Sweet & Maxwell, London, 1979), pp. 678–81.
6. This point has been stressed by the Report of the International Commission, *Israel in Lebanon*, p. 17.
7. Alexander Haig, *Caveat* (Weidenfeld and Nicolson, London, 1984), p. 327.
8. *The Washington Post*, 15 June 1982.
9. For details, see *Keesing's Contemporary Archives* (vol.XXIX, 1983), p. 31916.
10. George W. Ball, *Error and Betrayal in Lebanon* (Foundation for Middle East Peace, Washington DC, 1984), p. 45. See also Zeev Schiff and Ehud Ya'ari, *Israel's Lebanon War* (George Allen and Unwin, London, 1985) p. 221. Sharon lost his patience to the extent that during one meeting with the late Philip Habib he virtually ranted at him, upsetting the diplomat to the point where he required medical attention.
11. Ball, *Error and Betrayal*, pp. 45 and 46 based on 'Facts on File', 1982, p. 6832 f. (13 August). Michael Deaver's account was rather different. He did not recall Begin's reaction, but he recalled Begin telephoning back after twenty minutes to say the bombing had ceased. Reagan looked up and said seriously: 'I didn't know I had that kind of power'. Michael Deaver commented: 'For a time, all too brief, there was a recess in the madness of Lebanon.' See Michael K. Deaver with Mickey Herskowitz, *Behind the Scenes* (William Morrow and Company, Inc., New York, 1987), pp. 165, 166.
12. *The Washington Post*, 19 December 1982. See also Helena Cobban, *The Palestinian Liberation Organization, People, Power and Politics* (Cambridge University Press, Cambridge, 1984) p. 124.

13. As explained to Jordan by Habib. Ministry of Foreign Affairs Archives, Amman.
14. Ministry of Foreign Affairs Archives, Amman.
15. According to Mudar Badran, interview, August 1985, Amman.
16. Shultz's unsuccessful experience in the Middle East may have been related to his own personality and inability to understand complex political problems in a civilization not his own. Before venturing in the Middle East his own experience in negotiating was limited to situations that had a common conceptual framework. Lebanon proved to be more than he could handle. As Ambassador Neumann put it: 'Behind that passive appearance there is a passionate man, very proud and arrogant. He did not listen to his advisers. I told him many times that in no way could the Syrians possibly accept the Agreement. He did not listen . . . what Shultz does not want to believe, he resists. But however limited, he is not a fool.' Interview, July 1988, Washington.
17. Ball, *Error and Betrayal*, p. 150, based on 'Facts on File', 1983, pp. 609, 813–14, 26 October 1983.
18. *The Washington Post*, 27 November 1983.
19. Ministry of Foreign Affairs Archives, Amman.
20. *The Guardian*, 25 February 1985.
21. Ibid., 11 April 1985.
22. Findings by a first-hand observer, David Hirst, as reported by him to *The Guardian*, 11 April 1985.
23. Lebanese Embassy, London.
24. In talks with the Foreign Minister of West Germany, 12 July 1982, Ministry of Foreign Affairs Archives, Amman.
25. As stated in an interview in July 1988 in his office in Washington. He wished to remain anonymous.
26. The interviewer was Patrick Seale and the interview was published in *The Observer*, 24 March 1985.
27. *The Times*, London, 12 April 1984. It has been suggested in Washington that this unprecedented level of co-operation with Israel had strengthened the Likud. It may have had an impact on the Israeli elections of 1984. Ambassador Veliotes, interview, July 1988, Washington.
28. *The New Statesman*, 24 August 1984.
29. *The Spectator*, 4 February 1984.
30. For more details on the two letters see *The Wall Street Journal*, 14 and 15 April 1983.
31. Interview in Washington, 13 July 1988.
32. Ministry of Foreign Affairs Archives, Amman.
33. BBC News programmes, 11 February 1985. See also *The International Herald Tribune*, 9 February 1985.
34. Ministry of Foreign Affairs Archives, Amman.
35. King Hassan of Morocco, heading the Fez summit Committee of Seven, in private talks with President Reagan, 22 October 1982, Ministry of Foreign Affairs Archives, Amman.
36. Abdul Halim Khaddam, with the Committee of Seven headed by King Hassan of Morocco, in private talks with President Reagan in Washington, 22 October 1982,

and in private talks with Mrs Thatcher in London, 18 March 1983 with the Committee of Seven headed by King Hussain of Jordan.

37. Cobban, *The Palestinian Liberation Organisation*, pp. 134–5, quoted from FBIS, 23 February 1983, p. A 16. The PLO was also against the Reagan Plan for two main reasons: 'First it denied Palestinians the right to return. If Western countries, including the US and Britain, supported the right of the Soviet Jews to return to a country they have never seen or lived in, they ought to support the Palestinians' right to return to their homeland and the land of their ancestors. Second, it denied the Palestinians their right of sovereignty, which was vital for the Palestinian identity, sense of belonging and equality.' These points were put to Mrs Thatcher on 18 March by Professor Walid Khalidi, the appointed PLO spokesman acceptable to the British government, who met the British team as a member of the Fez Summit Committee of Seven. The Committee toured the capitals of the five permanent members of the Security Council. King Hussain headed the committee to all the capitals concerned except Washington, when King Hassan of Morocco headed the committee. Details are in the Ministry of Foreign Affairs Archives, Amman and *Al Sira'a Al Arabi Al Israeli, Muhadathat Al Lajna Al Subaiyyah* of the Arab League.

38. Laqueur and Rubin, *The Arab–Israeli Reader*, p. 690.

39. *The Guardian*, 14 April 1983.

40. Ibid., 12 April 1983.

41. Ibid., 20 April 1983.

42. *The International Herald Tribune*, 25 April 1983.

43. Hassan Ben Talal, *Search for Peace*, p. 127. The American Ambassador in Jordan at the time, Ambassador Viets, backed this conclusion. He said that he found King Hussain appalled at how quickly the US jumped back when Begin first attacked the Plan. 'We backed away from our proposal, the single greatest foreign-policy undertaking the Reagan Administration has taken, as fast as we could', he said. King Hussain became deeply concerned that even if he got an agreement with Arafat, the US would not be able or willing to put pressure on Israel to undertake meaningful negotiations. He concluded: 'In support of Jordan's effort and the King I must say that to the very end King Hussain was carrying the burden of keeping the Plan alive right up until Arafat promised to come back within 24 hours and never showed up. That was the final nail.' Interview, July 1988, Washington.

44. *The Washington Post*, 4 March 1984.

45. *The International Herald Tribune*, 21 February 1984.

46. *The New Statesman*, 30 March 1984.

47. Ambassador Viets described the circumstances surrounding the Reagan Plan and Israel as follows: 'It was like a boxing match. It took a series of very hard blows in the first round and that was it. The Administration never recovered. It was at that point that the friends of Israel in this country moved in very fast and began to lay the groundwork for what has developed into a huge change in the bilateral relations between the US and Israel, when Israel became the dominant party and the relation is totally out of control.' Interview, 5 July 1988, Washington.

But Peter Rodman of the National Security Council viewed the developing strategic co-operation between Israel and the US from a different angle. 'The strategic relationship gives Israel some basis for trust in us. It gives us some margin to use our influence with them [Israel]. The strategic co-operation does not promote peace negotiations, but neither does it harm it. On the other hand, we are not going to let our ally be vulnerable to Soviet military equipment [in Syria]. The Soviet presence in Syria is part of the issue we are dealing with.' Interview, 6 July 1988, Washington.

9 The US and Jordan: how 'much' became 'too much'

1. Hassan Ben Talal, *Search for Peace* p. 129–30.
2. Sally V. Mallison, 'Juridical Analysis of the Israeli Settlements in the Occupied Territories', Georgetown University, Washington DC, a paper prepared for a seminar on 'The Inalienable Right of the Palestinian People', 25–29 August 1980, at the Vienna International Centre, Vienna, organized by the Committee on the Exercise of the Inalienable Rights of the Palestinian People, as authorized by General Assembly Resolution 34/65 of 12 December 1979. Ministry of Foreign Affairs Archives, Amman.
3. *Documents and Statements on Middle East Peace*, p. 61.
4. Mallison, 'Juridical Analysis'.
5. *Documents and Statements*, pp. 61–2.
6. *The New York Times*, 3 February 1981. Ambassador Robert Neumann spoke of a personal experience connected with an official meeting concerning the 'settlements'. 'I looked up and there were all these people looking at me with the utmost suspicion and hostility. And I said to myself, let's be practical. If I say: take this [they are not illegal] out they'll put it right back in and I will have no further influence. What can I do that is possible? After all, politics is the art of the possible. To leave the door a little bit open I put in two words: 'not necessarily' illegal. And it passed.' Interview, July, 1988, Washington.
7. Hassan Ben Talal, *Search for Peace*, p. 140.
8. Reported in *Time Magazine*, 26 March 1984.
9. The writer's interview with King Hussain, 18 March 1984, broadcast by the BBC Arabic Service in World at One and World at Six, 18 March 1984.
10. *The International Herald Tribune*, 16 March 1984.
11. *The Guardian*, 20 April 1984.
12. Interview with King Hussain, 18 March 1984.
13. *Time Magazine*, 26 March 1984.
14. *The Times*, 15 March 1984 and *The International Herald Tribune*, 14 March 1984.
15. General Command Headquarters, Amman, August 1985.
16. Ibid.
17. *The Daily Telegraph*, 20 September 1985 and *The Financial Times*, 14 August 1985.
18. The announcement was broadcast by the BBC News, 6 January 1985.
19. *The Guardian*, 14 June 1985.
20. BBC news programmes, 4 February 1986.

10 The Arab framework for peace

1. Hassan Ben Talal, 'Jordan's Quest for Peace', *Foreign Affairs* (Vol.LX, No.4, Spring 1982), pp. 802–3.
2. Ministry of Foreign Affairs Archives, Amman.
3. Mudar Badran, interview, August 1985, Amman.
4. *Documents and Statements*, p. 55.
5. Ibid., p. 53. See also R. H. Curtiss, *A Changing Image: American Perceptions of the Arab–Israeli Dispute* (American Educational Trust, Washington DC, 1982) p. 131.
6. The following details of the meeting have been narrated by one of the participants who wishes to remain anonymous.
7. Details of the talks can be found in the Ministry of Foreign Affairs Archives, Amman, and in an Arab League publication: *Al Sira'a Al Arabi Al Israeli, Muhadathat Al Lajna Al Subaiyyah (The Arab Israeli Conflict, Discussions of the Committee of Seven)*. The General Secretariat, Secretary General's Office, 1985.
8. Philip Habib delivering the Fifth Samuel D. Berger Memorial Lecture, 'Diplomacy and the Search for Peace in the Middle East' (Institute for the Study of Diplomacy, Georgetown University, School of Foreign Service, 30 April 1985), Ministry of Foreign Affairs Archives, Amman.
9. Ball, *Error and Betrayal*, p. 91.
10. Fuad Ajami addressing a Sub-Committee of the House Foreign Affairs Committee holding a series of hearings on Islamic Fundamentalism and Radicalism in the Middle East, 15 July 1985, Ministry of Foreign Affairs Archives, Amman.
11. *Middle East International*, London, 9 November 1984.
12. Mudar Badran, interview, August 1985, Amman. Badran mentioned specifically that King Hussain advised this.
13. Ibid. Ambassador Veliotes gave three reasons for the insistence on an American role: first, American national ego; second, the belief that an international conference would increase the influence of the Russians in the Middle East; and third, the belief that an international conference would end up pitting everyone present against the US and Israel. Interview, 13 July 1988, Washington. But Ambassador Viets gave a fourth reason: disagreement might arise between the permanent members of the Security Council. The French, for instance, might float their own plan. Russia and China might disagree with the US. If that happened, the parties directly concerned with the peace process would stop negotiating, sit tight and watch. Interview, 13 July 1982, Washington.
14. Ministry of Foreign Affairs Archives, Amman and Arab League, *Taswiyat Al Niza'Fi Al Shark Al Awsat, Masharee'Wa Mubadarat*, pp. 21–45.
15. Ambassador Yost's speech before the UN Security Council, 1 July 1969, Ministry of Foreign Affairs Archives, Amman.
16. Secretary of State Rogers, 'A Lasting Peace in the Middle East: An American View'. Address before the 1969 Galaxy Conference on Adult Education, Washington DC, 9 December 1969, press release No.371, ibid.
17. BBC World Service, 24 Hours, 11 January 1985.

11 Jordan embarks on several lines of foreign policy

1. Ministry of Foreign Affairs Archives, Amman.
2. *The Guardian*, 4 April 1985.
3. Marwan Al Qassem in talks with the Belgian Foreign Minister, 13 September 1982. Ministry of Foreign Affairs Archives, Amman.
4. Prince Hassan, interview, September 1985, Amman.
5. Hassan Ben Talal, *Search for Peace*, p. 112.
6. Amman's Royal Scientific Society Publication, *The Significance of Some West Bank Resources to Israel* (Economic Department, compiled by Dr Bassam Saket, Muhammad A. Samadi and Muhammad S. Amerah, April 1979).
7. A comprehensive coverage of the Benvinisti Report was broadcast by the BBC in its news programmes on 11 February 1985.
8. See Meron Benvinisti, *The West Bank Data Project, 1987 report* in *The Jerusalem Post*, Israel, 1987, p. 52.
9. *Middle East International*, London, 25 January 1986.
10. BBC news programmes, 11 February 1985. Also reported widely in the British press.
11. *The Guardian*, 1 April 1985.
12. Ministry of Foreign Affairs Archives, Amman.
13. *The Times*, 14 June 1985.
14. *Middle East International*, 9 November 1984.
15. Carter, *The Blood of Abraham*, p. 143.
16. Mrs Leila Sharaf, *Middle East International*, 9 November 1984.
17. Quoted by Carter, *The Blood of Abraham*, p. 145.
18. For more details see Amman's Royal Scientific Society Publication, *The Significance of Some West Bank Resources to Israel*.
19. *The Times*, 26 March 1984. Name was not mentioned.
20. As told by Abdul Halim Khaddam, the then Syrian Foreign Minister, during talks in London between the Arab Committee of Seven and Mrs Thatcher and her team, 18 March 1983, Ministry of Foreign Affairs Archives, Amman.
21. On the occasion of the UN Foundation Fortieth Anniversary, 27 September 1985.
22. Mudar Badran, interview, August 1985, Amman.
23. Adnan Abu Odeh, interview, August 1985, Amman.
24. Ministry of Foreign Affairs Archives, Amman.
25. *Documents and Statements*, p. 328.
26. *The Guardian*, 28 April 1982.
27. *Al Shark Al Awsat*, London, 2 June 1982.
28. These eight points were stressed by the political paper presented to the first conference for Jordanian expatriates held in Amman, 20–24 August 1985, Ministry of Labour, Amman.
29. *The Times*, 27 December 1983.
30. Address to the Royal United Services Institute for Defence, London, 6 December 1984.
31. Hassan Ben Talal, *Search for Peace*, p. 142.

32. Expressed to Gerald Butt of the BBC and broadcast on BBC news programmes, 30 November 1984.

33. Translated literally from the Arabic version, Ministry of Foreign Affairs Archives, Amman.

34. Prince Hassan, interview, September 1985, Amman.

35. PLO statement in answer to King Hussain's address to the nation on 19 February 1986, PLO Office, London.

36. From King Hussain's address to the nation, 19 February 1986.

37. *Jordan Times*, 11 August 1985.

38. Interview with Reuters appearing in all Jordanian newspapers, 13 August 1985.

39. For more details see 'News and Views from the USSR', press release, Soviet Embassy, Information Department, Washington, 24 December 1987.

40. Hassan Ben Talal, *Search for Peace* p. 132.

12 US and Jordan: more wheeling and dealing

1. Ahmad Lawsi to *Al Shark Al Awsat*, London, 7 March 1985.

2. *The International Herald Tribune*, 26 February 1985 quoting Syrian official press agency.

3. *The Financial Times*, 12 March 1985.

4. Reported by the BBC, 15 March 1985.

5. *The International Herald Tribune*, 18 March 1985.

6. Interview with 24 Hours, BBC, 21 March 1985.

7. BBC World Service, 12 April 1985.

8. *Al Majalla Magazine*, London, 2 April 1985.

9. *The International Herald Tribune*, 20 March 1985.

10. Ibid.

11. Ibid.

12. Ibid.

13. Ibid.

14. Ibid.

15. This source preferred to remain anonymous. Interview, July 1988, Washington.

16. One name had been suggested and discussed during this particular trip: Shaikh Abdul Hamid Al Sayeh, Head of the PNC. But no American could certify how authoritative he was. Ibid.

17. Ibid.

18. As reported by King Hussain in his address to the nation, 19 February 1986. A highly placed American official also wishing to remain anonymous expressed an American dislike of the term 'pertinent UN resolutions'. 'We always held to the need for a very clear acceptance of 242 and 338 without the complications of the other resolutions involved.' When he was reminded that 242 does not refer to the Palestinians except as refugees he said: '242 has universal acceptance. Its equation of territory for peace is an important principle to maintain. Although there is no mention of the Palestinian problem being a political problem we had affirmed and reaffirmed time and again that the Palestinian problem is a political problem.' Interview, July 1988, Washington.

19. *The Daily Telegraph*, 30 May 1985.
20. Interview, July 1988, Washington. The press was circulating the following names: Fayez Abu Rahmeh (Gaza), Hanna Saniora (West Bank), Nabil Sha'ath (PLO) Khalid Al Hassan (PLO), Hatem Hussaini (PLO), Salah Ta'amri (PLO). Only the first two were acceptable to both the US and Israel. The US on its own had problems with the last three. The US and Israel disagreed over Nabil Sha'ath. But as it had been officially put in Washington: 'There were names on the list beside Fayez Abu Rahmeh and Hanna Saniora whom we would have been willing to meet as we tried to get answers to what happens after the meeting.'
21. 'We felt unable to go beyond Fayez Abu Rahmeh and Hanna Saniora, unless there were rapid movement to Arab–Israeli discussions. Jordan and the Palestinians were unable to agree to a meeting with just the two.' Ibid.
22. An American source who wishes to remain anonymous, interview, July 1988, Washington.
23. Interview, July 1988, Washington.
24. This interviewee was still holding office when interviewed in July 1988, Washington. But he promised to write his memoirs once out of office.
25. Another interviewee in the same situation, June 1988, Washington.
26. This interviewee prefers to remain anonymous. Interview, July 1988, Washington.
27. PLO Office, London.
28. King Hussain's address to the nation, 19 February 1986.
29. *The New York Times*, 23 February 1986.
30. *The Guardian*, 24 February 1986.
31. See, for example, David Hirst, *The Guardian*, 21 February 1986.
32. *Middle East International*, 7 March 1986.
33. See *The Daily Telegraph*, 4 March 1986, *The Guardian*, 21 March 1986 and *The Guardian*, Editorial, 19 February 1986.
34. *Al Shark Al Awsat*, London, 3 and 31 March, and 3 and 22 April 1986.
35. *Middle East International*, 7 March 1986.
36. Ibid., 24 January 1986.
37. Ibid., 2 January 1986, Jansen in an interview with Arafat.
38. *Al Anba'*, Kuwait, 23 February 1986.
39. Ibid.
40. *Middle East International*, 10 January 1986.
41. *Al Shark Al Awsat*, London, 21 February 1986.
42. Voiced by Hawatmeh of the DFLP in *The Middle East International*, 10 January 1986.
43. Ibid., 7 March 1986 and *Al Shark Al Awsat*, London, 27 February 1986 quoting Bernard Kalb.
44. Presented in *The Guardian*, 12 June 1985.
45. *The Washington Post*, 27 October 1985.
46. *The International Herald Tribune*, 23 January 1986.
47. The same conclusion was reached by Patrick Seale of *The Observer*, 26 January 1986.
48. *International Herald Tribune*, 24 December 1985.

49. BBC, 24 Hours, 20 February 1986.
50. *Middle East International,* 18 April 1986.
51. Prince Hassan, interview, 31 May 1988.

13 Postscript

1. Neumann, interview, June 1988, Washington.
2. Jonathan Kuttab, *The Daily Telegraph,* 3 February 1988.
3. Prince Hassan, interview, 31 May 1988.
4. Neumann, interview, June 1988, Washington.
5. Saunders, interview, June 1988, The Brookings Institution, Washington.
6. Embassy of the Hashemite Kingdom of Jordan, Washington. See also *Monitoring Report,* BBC, 11 April 1988.
7. *FBIS–NES–88–112,* 10 June 1988, pp. 11–14.
8. From Prince Hassan's offices, Amman, Jordan.
9. *Digest of the Arab Press,* Vol.III, Issue 18, 30 September 1988, pp. 5–8.
10. See BBC Summary of World Broadcasts, BBC, 17 November 1988.
11. *American Arab Affairs,* No.26, Fall 1988, pp. 182–5, documented from the PLO, and the United Nations.
12. PLO Office, London. See also *The Times,* 8 December 1988, *International Herald Tribune,* 8 December 1988.
13. PLO Office, London.
14. *The Times,* 15 December 1988.
15. *The Independent,* 15 December 1988.
16. For details see *Keesing's Record of World Events,* News Digest for April, 1989, Nol.36599. For full text see Appendix F.
17. *MEI,* 22 March, 1991.
18. *Keesing's Record of World Events,* News Digest for April, 1989, No.36599.
19. As quoted by the *Financial Times,* 21 July, 1991.
20. For more details see *Keesing's Record of World Events,* News Digest for September, 1989, No.36904, and *The Guardian,* 26 September 1989.
21. *International Herald Tribune,* 2 October 1989.
22. See *The Times,* 7 December 1989 for plan and reactions. For full text see Appendix G.
23. BBC, SWB Monitoring Report, 14 October 1989.
24. *Financial Times,* 8 November 1989.
25. BBC Arabic Service, World at One, 1 May 1991.
26. Interview, *Panorama,* The Palestinian Problem and the Gulf Crisis, BBC Arabic Service, 16 December 1990.
27. Ibid.
    Arabic Service, 16 December 1990.
28. Ibid.
29. Quoted in *Panorama,* The Middle East Peace Process, BBC Arabic Service, 26 June 1991 and 3 July 1991.
30. Richard Murphy told the writer that it is on record that George Shultz used the

same expression in his dealings with Arab leaders while in office, interview for BBC *Panorama*, ibid.

31. Quoted by the *Daily Telegraph*, 8 April 1991.
32. Interview for *The Other Opinion*, BBC Arabic Service, 8 March 1991.
33. Interview, 11 March 1992, Amman.
34. Ibid.
35. Interview, *Panorama*, The Middle East Peace Process, BBC Arabic Service, 26 June 1991 and 3 July 1991.
36. Interview, 11 March 1992, Amman.
37. Interview, *Panorama*, The Palestinian Problem and the Gulf Crisis, BBC Arabic Service, 16 December 1990.
38. Expressed by Prince Hassan, interview, 11 March 1992, Amman.
39. Ibid.
40. Ibid.
41. The following dialogue with Arafat appeared in *The Observer*, 29 April 1984.
42. As stressed by Hassan Ben Talal, *Search for Peace*, p. 102.
43. Jimmy Carter mentioned this. See Carter, *The Blood of Abraham*, p. 202.
44. Feisal Husseini, Interview, *Panorama*, The Middle East Peace Process, BBC Arabic Service, 26 June 1991 and 3 July 1991.
45. Ibid.
46. George Antonius, *The Arab Awakening* (Hamish Hamilton, London, 1938), p. 386.

Select bibliography

Amos II, John, *Palestinian Resistance, Organization of a National Movement* (Pergamon Press, New York, 1980).

Antonius, George, *The Arab Awakening* (Hamish Hamilton, London, 1938).

Arab League, *Taswiyat Al Niza'a Fi Al Shark Al Awsat, Masharee' Wa Mubadarat* (*The Settlement of Conflict in the Middle East, Plans and Initiatives*) The General Secretariat, Tunis, 15 June 1985).

Arab League, *Al Sira' Al Arabi Al Israeli, Muhadathat Al Lajna Al Subaiyyan* (*The Arab–Israeli Conflict, Discussions of the Committee of Seven*) (The General Secretariat, Secretary General's Office, Tunis).

Ball, W. George, *Error and Betrayal in Lebanon* (Foundation for Middle East Peace, Washington DC, 1984).

Bartelson, Judy, *The Palestinian Arabs: A Non-State Nation System Analysis* (Sage, Beverly Hills, CA., 1976).

Begin, Menahim, *The Revolt* (W.H. Allen and Howard & Wyndham Company, London, 1983).

Ben Talal, Hassan, Crown Prince of Jordan, *Palestinian Self Determination: A Study of the West Bank and Gaza Strip* (Quartet Books, London, 1980).

Search for Peace (Macmillan, London, 1984).

A Study of Jerusalem (Longman, London and New York, in association with the Publishing Committee, Amman, Jordan, 1979).

Benvinisti, Meron, *The West Bank Data Project: A Survey of Israel's Policies* (American Enterprise Institute for Public Policy, Washington DC, 1984).

Bradley, C. Paul, *The Camp David Peace Process* (Tompson & Rutter, Grantham, NH. 1981).

Brecher, Michael, *The Foreign Policy System of Israel* (Oxford University Press, London and New York, 1972).

Brzezinski, Zbigniew, *Power and Principle; Memoirs of the National Security Advisor, 1977–81* (Weidenfeld and Nicolson, London, 1983).

The Brookings Institution, *Towards Peace in the Middle East* (Report of a Study Group, 1975).

Bryson, Thomas A., *American Diplomatic Relations with the Middle East, 1784–1975,* A Survey (The Scarecrow Press, Metuchan, NJ., 1977).

Carter, Jimmy, *Keeping Faith, Memoirs of a President* (Collins, London, 1982).

The Blood of Abraham (Sidgwick and Jackson, London, 1985).

Cattan, Henry, *Jerusalem* (Croom Helm, London, 1981).

Chomsky, Noam, *The Fateful Triangle: The United States, Israel and The Palestinians* (South End Press, Boston MA., 1983).

Cobban, Helena, *The Palestinian Liberation Organization, People, Power and Politics* (Cambridge University Press, Cambridge, 1984).

Cordesman, Anthony H., *The Gulf and the Search for Strategic Stability* (Westview Press, Boulder CO., 1984).

Jordanian Arms and the Middle East Balance (The Middle East Institute, Washington DC, 1983).

Curtiss, Richard H., *A Changing Image: American Perceptions of the Arab Israeli Conflict* (American Educational Trust, Washington DC, 1982).

Dayan, Moshe, *Breakthrough* (Weidenfeld and Nicholson, London, 1981).

Elazar, Daniel J., *The Camp David Framework for Peace, A Shift Toward Shared Rule* (American Enterprise Institute for Public Policy Research, Washington DC, 1979).

Eveland, Wilbur Crane, *Ropes of Sand, America's Failure in the Middle East* (W.W. Norton and Company, London, New York, 1980).

Foreign Affairs and National Division, Congressional Research Service, *Documents and Statements on Middle East Peace, 1979–1982* (US Government Printing Office, Washington DC, 1982).

Franji, Abdallah, *The PLO and Palestine* (Zed Books, London, 1982).

Frischwasser, H.F. Ra'anan, *The Frontiers of A Nation* (Batchworth Press, London, 1955).

Green, Stephen, *Taking Sides* (Faber and Faber, London, 1984).

Gubser, Peter, *Jordan, Crossroads of Middle East Events* (Westview Press, Boulder, CO., and Croom Helm, London, 1983).

Haas, Ernest, *Beyond the Nation State, Functionalism and International Organizations* (Stanford University Press, Stanford, CA., 1964).

Haig, Alexander, *Caveat* (Weidenfeld and Nicolson, London, 1984).

Harris, D.J., *Cases and Materials on International Law* (Sweet and Maxwell, London, 1979).

Herzl, Theodore, *The Diaries of Theodore Herzl*, edited and translated by Lowenthal, Marvin (Victor Gollanz Ltd, London, 1958).

Hirst, David, *The Gun and the Olive Branch* (Faber and Faber, London, 1977).

Holsti, K.J., *International Politics* (Prentice-Hall, Englewood Cliffs, NJ., 1977).

Hudson, Michael C. (ed.), *The Arab Future: Critical Issues* (Centre for Contemporary Arab Studies, Georgetown University, 1979).

Institute for Palestine Studies, *International Documents on Palestine* (Beirut, 1980).

Al Muahada Al Misriva Al Israeliya (The Egyptian Israeli Treaty) (Serial Number 53, Beirut, 1979).

Israel Fi Al Istratigiyya Al Americiyya Fi Al Thamaninat (Israel in the American Strategy for the 1980s) (Serial Number 13, Kamil Mansour, Beirut, 1980).

Al Siyassa Al Americayya Fi Al Shark Al Awsat: Nixon, Ford, Carter, Reagan (American Policy in the Middle East: Nixon, Ford, Carter, Reagan) (Serial Number 67, Leila Baroudy and Marwan Bashiri, Independent Publication Services, Nicosia, 1984).

Bibliography

Keesing's Contemporary Archives (Vol.XX, 1974), Keesing's Publications, Longdon Group Limited.

Keesing's Contemporary Archives (Vol.XXIX, 1983).

Kissinger, Henry, *White House Years* (Weidenfeld and Nicolson and Michael Joseph, London, 1979).

Years of Upheaval (Weidenfeld and Nicolson and Michael Joseph, London, 1982).

Korany, Bahjat, and Dessouki, Ali E. Hillal, *The Foreign Policies of Arab States* (Westview Press, Boulder CO and London, and The American University in Cairo Press, Cairo, 1984).

Laqueur, Walter, and Rubin, Barry (eds.), *The Arab–Israeli Reader: A Documentary History of the Middle East Conflict* (Penguin Books, Middlesex, 1984).

Lester, Sobel A., and Kosut, Hal, *Peace Making in the Middle East* (Facts on File, New York, 1980).

Lilienthal, Alfred M., *The Zionist Connection* (Dodd, Mead and Company, New York, 1979).

MacBride, Sean, *Israel in Lebanon* (Ithaca Press, London, 1983).

Mangold, Peter, *Super Power Intervention in the Middle East* (Croom Helm, London, 1979).

Monroe, Elizabeth, *Britain's Moment in the Middle East, 1914–1971* (Chatto and Windus, London 1981).

Moore, John N.J. (ed.), *The Arab–Israeli Conflict, Readings and Documents* (Sponsored by the American Society of International Law, Princeton, NJ., 1977).

Novik, Nimrod and Starr, Joyce, *Challenges in the Middle East, Regional Dynamics and Western Security* (Praeger, New York, 1981).

Nye, Joseph S. and Deese, David A. (eds.), *Energy and Security* (Ballenger, Cambridge, MA., 1981).

Ott, David H., *Palestine in Perspective: Politics, Human Rights and the West Bank* (Quartet Books, London, 1980).

Perlmutter, Amos, Handel, Michael and Bar-Joseph, Uri, *Two Minutes Over Baghdad* (Corgi Books, London, 1982).

Quandt, William, *Decade of Decisions* (University of California Press, Berkeley/Los Angeles/London, 1982).

Camp David: Peace Making and Politics (Brookings Institution, Washington DC, 1986).

Reich, Bernard, *Quest for Peace, United States–Israel Relations and the Arab Israeli Conflict* (Transaction Books, New Brunswick, NJ., 1977).

Ramazani, R.K., *The Arab–Israeli Conflict: New Direction for United Policy in the Middle East* (Foreign Policy Report, Institute for Foreign Policy Analysis, Cambridge, MA., September 1977).

Safran, Naedav, *Israel, The Embattled Ally* (Belknapp Press of Harvard University, Cambridge, MA., and London, 1978).

Saket, Bassam, Samadi, Mohammad A., and Amerah Mohamma S., *The Significance of Some West Bank Resources to Israel* (Royal Scientific Society, Economic Department, Amman, April 1979).

Saunders, Harold, *Conversations with Harold Saunders, US Policy for the Middle East in the 1980s* (American Enterprise Institute for Public Policy Research, Washington, 1982).

Schiff, Ze'ev and Ya'ari, Ehud, *Israel's Lebanon War* (George Allen and Unwin, London, 1985).

Shakid, Haim and Rabinovich, Itamar, *The Middle East and the United States: Perceptions and Policies* (Transaction Books, New Brunswick, NJ., and London, 1980).

Shwadran, Benjamin, *Jordan, A State of Tension* (Council For Middle Eastern Affairs Press, New York, 1959).

Strange, Susan (ed.), *Paths to International Political Economy* (George Allen and Unwin, London, 1984).

Sub-Committee on Europe and the Middle East of the Committee on Foreign Affairs and National Division, *The Search for Peace in the Middle East, Documents and Statements, 1969–1979* (Congressional Research Services Library of Congress, US Government Printing Office, Washington, 1982).

Tillman, Seth P., *The United States in the Middle East, Interests and Obstacles* (Indiana University Press, Bloomington, IN., 1982).

Vance, Cyrus, *Hard Choices* (Simon and Schuster, New York, 1983).

Primary sources

Ministry of Foreign Affairs Archives, Amman, Jordan.
Ministry of Finance, Amman, Jordan.
Ministry of Labour, Amman, Jordan.
General Command Headquarters, Amman, Jordan.
Jordanian Embassy, London.
Jordanian Embassy, Washington.
Jordan Information Bureau, Washington.
PLO Office, London,
US Embassy, London.
Soviet Embassy, Washington.
The Brookings Institution, Washington.
Foreign and Commonwealth Office, London.
Interview with King Hussain of Jordan, Amman.
Interview with Yasser Arafat, Algiers.
Interviews with Crown Prince Hassan Ben Talal, Amman and London.
Interview with Field Marshal Sharif Zeid Ben Shaker, Prime Minister and former Commander-in-Chief of the Jordanian Armed Forces, Amman.
Interview with Mudar Badran, former Prime Minister of Jordan.
Interview with Zeid Rifai, former Prime Minister of Jordan.
Interview with Taher Al Masri, former Prime Minister of Jordan.
Interview with Adnan Abu Odeh, former Information Minister and Minister of Court, Amman.
Interview with Marwan al Qassem, former Foreign Minister and former Chief of the Royal Courts, Amman.

Interview with Hanna Odeh, former Minister of Finance, Amman.
Interview with General Tayseer Za'rour, General Command Headquarters, Amman.
Interview with General Tayseer Zarour, General Command Headquarters, Amman.
Interview with Mrs Leila Sharaf, former Information Minister, Amman.
William Quandt, former National Security Council (NSC) Staff Member, a Senior Fellow, The Brookings Institution, Washington.
Harold Saunders, former Assistant Secretary of State for Near Eastern Affairs and former NSC Staff Member, a Visiting Fellow, The Brookings Institution, Washington.
Alfred Atherton, former Ambassador to Egypt and former Assistant Secretary of State for Near Eastern Affairs, Washington.
Zbigniew Brzezinski, former National Security Affairs Advisor, Washington.
Les Janka, former Deputy Assistant Secretary of State, International Security Affairs, Department of Defence, Washington.
William Kirby, Deputy Assistant Secretary of State, Washington.
Robert Neumann, former Ambassador to Afghanistan, Morocco, Saudi Arabia and Advisor to Vice President Bush, Washington.
Jack O'Connell, Head of public relations firm representing Jordan.
Robert Oakley, NSC Staff – Middle East Affairs, former Ambassador to Somalia and Zaire, Ambassador to Pakistan, Washington.
Peter Rodman, Deputy Advisor to the President for National Security Affairs, former staff aid to Henry Kissinger, Washington.
Nicholas Veliotes, former Ambassador to Jordan and Egypt, former Assistant Secretary of State for Near Eastern Affairs, Washington.
Richard Viets, former Ambassador to Jordan, Washington.

European/American periodicals, magazines and newspapers

American Arab Affairs
Christian Science Monitor
Commentary
The Daily Telegraph
The Economist
The Financial Times
Foreign Affairs
Foreign Policy
The Guardian
International Affairs
The International Herald Tribune
Journal of International Affairs
L'Espresso
MERIP Reports
Middle East International
Mideast Observer
The New Statesman
The New York Times

Newsweek
The Observer
ORBIS
The Spectator
Time Magazine
The Times
The Wall Street Journal
The Washington Post

Arab newspapers and magazines

Al Ahram (Cairo)
Al Anba'a (Kuwait).
Al Ba'th (Damascus)
Al Majalla Magazine (London)
Al Mustagbal (Paris)
Al Nahar Al Arabi Wa Dawli (Paris)
Al Shark Al Awsat (London)
Journal of Palestine Studies
The Journal of the Arab British Chamber of Commerce (London)
Jordan Times
L'Orient-Le Jour (Beirut)
Monday Morning (Beirut)

Israeli Newspapers

Davar
Ha'aretz
Ha'Olam Hazeh
The Jerusalem Post
The Jerusalem Post Weekly
Ma'ariv

Index

Index

Cambridge Middle East Library